Kaizen

"改善"

Demystified

*A Practical and Systematic Method of Evaluating
Circumstances to Use the Most Efficient and Effective Type of
Kaizen to Improve Processes*

Jayant Trewn
Todd Sperl
Rob Ptacek
Deborah Salimi

ISBN 978-0-9898030-4-5

MCS Media, Inc. (The Lean Store)
888 Ridge Road
Chelsea, MI 48118
United States of America
Telephone 734-475-4301
E-mail: info@theleanstore.com

Cover concept and art direction: Jonathan Robison and Andrea Sperl
Page design: Janice McKinley
Content edit: Mary Woods-Gleenson, Master Black Belt and Patrick K. Eisle, Lean Sensei

Library of Congress Cataloging-in-Publication Data

This publication is designed to provide the most up-to-date, accurate and authoritative information for the improvement of administrative processes and practices. It is sold with the understanding that neither the authors, editors, nor the publisher are engaged in providing legal, accounting, or other professional service. If legal advice or other expert assistance is required, the services of a competent professional consultant should be sought.

All MCS Media, Inc. books are available at special quantity discounts to use as sales promotions, corporate training programs, and/or any other avenue conveying information on continuous improvement.

Table of Contents

Kaizen (改善), Japanese for "improvement" or "change for the better," refers to the philosophy or practices that focus upon continuous improvement of processes in manufacturing, engineering, game development, and business management.

Source: Wikipedia

Chapter 1. Introduction

Read First

The reader of this book should have a basic understanding of Lean and Six Sigma. However, we have provided a brief overview of Lean and Six Sigma in this Introduction chapter, as well as brief tool descriptions in the Lean Six Sigma Tools chapter. For a detailed description of all the Lean and Six Sigma tools consider *The New Lean Pocket Guide, The New Lean Office Pocket Guide, Lean Office Demystified II, The Lean Six Sigma Pocket Guide XL, The Practical Lean Six Sigma Pocket Guide, Practical Lean Six Sigma for Healthcare,* or *The A3 Pocket Handbook for Kaizen Events* books available at your favorite bookstore.

Many project management activities, forms/worksheets, guidelines, etc. are similar across the four main team-based Kaizen Event types as defined in this publication. ***Due to this similarity, and to ensure everyone understands the basic (or Standard as we are defining in this book) Kaizen Event, it is highly recommended the Standard 5 Day Kaizen Event section be read first in its entirety.*** This will ensure everyone is on the same page in reference to all the various activities comprising a Kaizen Event. This will lead to a practical understanding of how and why the other types have evolved from the Standard 5 Day Kaizen Event.

The type of Kaizen Event as defined in this publication will be primarily based on:

1. The team leader, process owner, etc. experience with Lean/Six Sigma projects (i.e., Kaizen Events).
2. Access to and user experience with emerging technology communication platforms.
3. The depth of knowledge of Lean and Six Sigma of the employees.
4. The physical location of the employees.
5. The current improvement methodology being used (D-M-A-I-C, PDCA, etc.).
6. The availability of the employee's time.
7. The availability of a Black Belt, Lean Sensei, Continuous Improvement Specialist, etc. for leading and/or facilitating projects.

These factors, along with organizational needs and requirements, and the information contained in this book, will provide a comprehensive understanding on how to select and run the most effective Kaizen Event.

Kaizen Demystified has the following five chapters:

Chapter 1. Introduction - Provides a general understanding on why this book was written as well as a fairly comprehensive overview of Lean and Six Sigma, and how they complement one another. Additional topics include Waste, Engaging Today's Workforce, Managing Change, Leadership and Coaching, and the A3 Report – all critical components to a successful Kaizen Event.

Chapter 2. Kaizen Event Types - Describes each of the five types of Kaizen Events as well as the suggested activities for conducting each type. Each team-based Kaizen Event type is segmented into the Planning Phase, PDCA (Plan-Do-Check-Act) Implementation Phase, and the Follow-up Phase. Each Kaizen Event type will also include at least one case study. The Standard 5 Day Kaizen Event type will be highly detailed, with the other types to a lesser degree.

Chapter 3. Lean Six Sigma Tools - Provides a brief description of the Lean and Six Sigma tools.

Chapter 4. Worksheets - Provides a full-size page view of the specific checklists, worksheets, and key matrixes referenced in each of the Kaizen Event types. The checklists and worksheets can be purchased as an Excel worksheet under any industry segment - ETools at www.TheLeanStore.com.

Chapter 5. Kaizen Event Leadership - Provides a listing of common issues facing the leader of a Kaizen Event as well as suggested how-to leadership skills to address those issues. Even though this chapter is last in this book, it should be considered one of the most important.

We have referenced Lean, Six Sigma, and Lean Sigma as improvement methodologies that most organizations are currently using to some extent. Each of these, as separate or combined programs, have proven successful in nearly every industry segment. Organizational improvement leaders must learn new business improvement methods and approaches, adopt which ones work best for their organization, and then implement a structured approach in its deployment while respectfully engaging the employees with effective leadership skills. It is in this 'structured approach in its deployment' and 'respectfully engaging the employees with effective leadership skills' that *Kaizen Demystified* was developed.

Note: Right-side book tabs are available for quick reference to the five chapters, including each of the five Kaizen Event types.

Publisher's Message

We are pleased to present *Kaizen Demystified*, perfectly timed for today's ever-changing and ever-demanding business environment requiring improved processes. Whether your industry is manufacturing, healthcare, financial, education, armed forces, services, government, or the construction industry, or, you are a manager, supervisor, team leader, or a front-line worker, this book will provide new insights and ideas for managing and facilitating continuous improvement and problem solving projects (i.e., Kaizen Events). *Kaizen Demystified* provides a "simple and practical" approach detailing five distinct methods on how Lean (and Six Sigma) tools and concepts can quickly and efficiently be applied and managed to solve business problems and improve processes. The five types of Kaizen Events detailed in this book are the: (1) Standard 5 Day Kaizen Event, also referred to as a Kaizen Blitz or Rapid Improvement Event, (2) Rolling Kaizen Event, (3) Web Based Kaizen Event, (4) Today's Kaizen Event, and (5) Wiki (or Quick) Kaizen Event. These are our terms as there is no industry standard. Each type will be thoroughly explained to "demystify" what it may mean for you. *Kaizen Demystified* will certainly support, supplement, and/or enhance your current "Kaizen" or "Lean" thinking and, most importantly, the doing and sustaining. In the end, there will be no mystery!

There have been numerous books and articles written, as well as blogs posted, on how Kaizen philosophically is a "way of life," as well as it being a pragmatic problem solving and continuous improvement methodology to apply Lean tools and concepts to an area or process. *Kaizen Demystified* primarily focuses on the pragmatic problem solving and continuous improvement method with detailed step-by-step instructions, along with the forms, worksheets, reports, checklists, example case studies, etc. for you to lead, facilitate, and/or initiate one of the five types of Kaizen Events as defined in this book. We acknowledge the importance of Kaizen as a philosophical concept (i.e., a holistic approach to life, both at work and at home that strives to balance the physical, mental, and spiritual needs of a person within their environment). While we will not specifically be addressing the entire holistic approach, we will be addressing part of it by providing the leadership and coaching skills to more effectively work with others. This will help the person leading the team, as well as, most importantly, the team members, as their stress will be reduced. Everyone will have a more positive approach to the issue or problem (i.e., improvement opportunity or project). These leadership and coaching skills will better engage all workers in soliciting their ideas and support in the improvement project. Regardless of the Kaizen Event type, a fundamental principle that must be present when working with employees at any and all levels of the organization is demonstrating a respect for the individual. Without this, project (or Kaizen Event) success will not happen!

We have customized or "harmonized" Kaizen from its original Toyota automotive beginnings for the various industries and business environments of the 21st century. We specifically used the word "harmonized" because an organization has to unify their organizational culture, systems and processes, type of workforce, and emerging technologies to effectively use Kaizen. The original concept and tool of Kaizen remains the same. *Kaizen Demystified* integrates all these for an integrated approach to problem solving and continuous improvement.

At the end of the day, and your subsequent interpretation and adaptation of Kaizen, you should come to the conclusion that "at the heart of Lean is Kaizen, and at the heart of Kaizen is the sincere engagement of people." It really gets no simpler than that! If this book enables you to positively impact employees to become more engaged in continuous improvement efforts within your organization, then *Kaizen Demystified* did its job.

We wish to thank the Black Belts, Lean Senseis, managers, supervisors from a wide range of industries, and especially the problem solving and continuous improvement team members for sharing their experiences with the authors throughout the years of writing this book.

Don Tapping
Publisher

Note: Continue to visit www.TheLeanStrore.com for *Kaizen Demystified for Healthcare* with specific case studies and examples of Kaizen Events for hospitals, clinics, and physician group practices.

Author's Bios

Learn from these authors who have conducted over 1000 Kaizen Events!

Jayant Trewn, PhD

Jayant Trewn is an Industrial Engineer specializing in Quality Systems design, development, implementation, and management. Jayant has accumulated over a decade of experience working in healthcare organizations such as Spectrum Health Medical Group, Beaumont Hospitals, and Lason Systems where he built healthcare delivery process improvement programs based on Lean, Six Sigma, and PDCA concepts. Jayant has authored the book *Multivariate Statistical Methods in Quality Engineering* and he has been published in international journals. He holds a Doctorate degree in Industrial Engineering from the College of Engineering, Wayne State University, Detroit, MI, USA. He earned his MBA in Information Systems at Wayne State University and his Bachelor of Engineering degree from Madras University, India.

Jayant can be contacted at jtrewn@leanfoxsolutions.com.

Todd Sperl

Todd Sperl is an enthusiastic, creative speaker and process improvement expert who looks beyond today's problems to find tomorrow's solutions. As Owner and Managing Partner of Lean Fox Solutions, Todd's vision is to improve the patient care experience from one healthcare touch point to the next. As a Master Black Belt and Lean Sensei, Todd's exceptional track record of process improvement has been based on his philosophy of total enterprise engagement in change. Todd received his BS in Psychology from the University of Wisconsin-River Falls and an MS in Industrial-Organizational Psychology from St. Mary's University in San Antonio, Texas.

Todd can be contacted at tsperl@leanfoxsolutions.com or visit www.leanfoxsolutions.com.

Rob Ptacek

Rob Ptacek is a Partner in the Global Lean Institute and President and CEO of Competitive Edge Training and Consulting, a firm specializing in leader and organizational development, and Lean Enterprise transformations. Rob holds a BS in Metallurgical Engineering from Michigan Technological University and a Masters of Management from Aquinas College. Rob has held leadership positions in Quality, Sales, and Operations Management, and has over 25 years of practical experience implementing continuous improvements in a variety of industries.

Rob can be contacted at ptacek@i2k.com.

Deborah Salimi, Project Management Professional (PMP), PhD

Deborah brings a practical approach to Lean, based on applied learning. Her experience spans three continents in manufacturing, project management, logistics, not for profit health care and higher education. She co-founded and is a key leader at the Lean Gulf Institute, spreading Lean awareness, professional development and empowerment through process improvement activities. She holds an Engineering degree from Boston University, an MBA and PhD.

Deborah can be contacted at deb@leangulf.org or visit www.leangulf.org.

The Purpose of *Kaizen Demystified*

Kaizen Demystified provides five proven approaches to applying the principles and practices of the Toyota Production System (i.e., Lean) and Six Sigma in a systematic methodology to improve work processes. The Toyota Production System or Lean is known for its world-class practices of having efficient processes due to well-adhered standards which are continually improved upon while empowering employees through the term known as Kaizen.

In this book you will learn how to:

❖ Accelerate improvements activities by selecting the right type of Kaizen Event
❖ Apply the "right" Kaizen Event methodology to specific projects within your organization
❖ Educate employees on the fundamentals activities required for a successful Kaizen Event
❖ Determine where wastes exist in processes and facilitate how to eliminate the wastes through Total Employee Involvement (TEI)
❖ Use current and future state value stream or process maps and PDCA (Plan – Do – Check – Act) to change/improve a process
❖ Improve processes while respecting people
❖ Effectively lead and coach others through applying basic leadership practices
❖ Confidently lead, facilitate, and/or initiate each of the five types of Kaizen Events
❖ Maximize resources for improvement projects
❖ Better engage employees in soliciting their ideas
❖ More effectively handle difficult issues that can impede a Kaizen Event when dealing with employees

Kaizen Demystified provides the step-by-step methodologies for planning, implementing, and sustaining improvement initiatives for five types of Kaizen Events. It is management's responsibility to commit the necessary resources (i.e., training, materials, time allocation, etc.). Management must also be actively involved to ensure a successful Kaizen Event for the organization.

Serious effort by everyone is required!

How to Get the Most Out of *Kaizen Demystified*

When attempting to learn new ideas from a book, it is recommended to not start with the first word and read it straight through until the end. The steps listed in this section will allow your reading to be easier, more fun, and much more effective.

There are a few things you can do to make it easier to absorb the content contained in this book. Spend as much time as you need to gain familiarity with all the material. To get a "Big Picture" view of the book:

1. Scan the Table of Contents to get a feel for the topics that are in bold as well as the similarities of the sub-headings.

2. Using the right-side book tabs, scan through each section to get a feel for its style, format, layout, design, and readability. Notice the illustrations (i.e., headings, worksheets, case studies, etc. that accompany each section). Note the "standard" forms and "look and feel" for each section.

3. Read the Introduction section pages 1 - 11.

After you have seen the "Big Picture" it is time to prepare yourself to learn the content of a single chapter. Follow these steps to get the most out of the readings:

1. Read the Standard 5 Day Kaizen Event section to understand the basic structure and activities that comprise all types of the team-based Kaizen Events.

2. Read the How to Select Your Kaizen Event Type section. This will direct you to the specific chapter with the step-by-step directions to run one of the five types of Kaizen Events.

3. Flip through the specific chapter, noticing the way it is arranged, specifically the bold headings and any illustrations that may be contained in the chapter. Note that the worksheets and forms are at a reduced size to help with the flow of reading. The full size worksheets and forms are included in Chapter 4. Worksheets that is easily accessed by using the right side book tab.

4. Read the specific Kaizen Event type as determined by your selection criteria from (2). Your organization will most likely have programs, systems, documents, etc. already in place for improvement and problem solving projects, and since no one size fits all, this chapter will provide additional guidance to enhance your current improvement project initiatives or provide new avenues to consider for projects. Use this as an overall guide on what will work (and make sense) for your organization as well as what may not work. For example, there is no point re-creating a Team Charter if your organization already has one that meets the Team Charter criteria.

5. Read and study the "Case Study" at end of the chapter to reinforce what you have learned through the actual application of that type of Kaizen Event. Note how the "overall" approach was used in the case study as well as how the various Lean Six Sigma tools or concepts were used. If there is something in the case study that you do not understand, go back to that particular section of the chapter and review it. The case studies highlight the main Kaizen phase activities to provide an overall understanding on how that type of Kaizen Event was conducted.

6. Review, through reading or browsing, the other types of Kaizen Event chapters to determine if some of those activities may be of value in the type of Kaizen you have selected. For example, if the Standard 5 Day Kaizen Event best fits your immediate need, and for some reason a team member that is critical to the project cannot be present at certain times, then there may be activities from the Web Based Kaizen Event that may be of value to use. Or, you may learn from the case study in the Web Based Kaizen Event chapter on how Google Drive was used for brainstorming and creating a Fishbone Diagram – which may be something that could be incorporated into a Rolling Kaizen Event to expedite one of the meetings. Or, as additional improvement ideas are explored in a Web Based Kaizen Event that are beyond the scope of the project, then possibly the Wiki Kaizen Event may be proposed and made available to team members. There are numerous ways the specific Kaizen activities (or characteristics) can be used in any type of Kaizen Event. Even though a "standard" approach is recommended for each Kaizen Event type, as with any process, there should be an avenue to adapt and improve! This book is not the final word on Kaizen. Kaizen also changes and improves.

7. Review Chapter 3. Lean Six Sigma Tools as needed for an brief description of the more common Lean Six Sigma tool set.

8. Use Chapter 4. Worksheets to review all the worksheets and modify as necessary.

9. Read Chapter 5. Kaizen Event Leadership to adequately prepare for leading a Kaizen Event. A Kaizen Event is not just following the technical aspects of the Kaizen Event phases, it is equally important to effectively engage the employees. There will always be people or "soft" issues (i.e., constraints, conflicts, resistance, etc.) during a Kaizen Event. The better prepared the leader is, the better the outcome of the Kaizen Event will be. Applying the appropriate tool(s) from this chapter will be critical to a successful Kaizen Event.

These steps will provide you with an efficient and effective method to read and apply the content contained in this book.

Those Who Would Benefit from *Kaizen Demystified*

The following are the various organizational level positions that would benefit from reading this book:

Top management (President, Owner, CEO, V.P., Directors, etc.) must have a general understanding of Lean and Six Sigma as well as support the methodology on how those tools can be implemented throughout the organization. *Kaizen Demystified* will provide this group with an overview of Lean and Six Sigma as well as the details required to establish a standard approach to continuous improvement. This group is responsible, as well as others, for creating the long-range strategic direction for the organization. Individuals in this group will typically become the Team Champions or Executive Sponsors (i.e., the person(s) who have the authority to commit organizational resources) for the improvement initiatives. This group must provide the following:

- ❖ The allocation of time for the various managers, supervisors, and process owners to direct and lead projects
- ❖ The necessary road map (i.e., methodologies) for departmental heads to follow when implementing an improvement project to ensure a standard approach is used
- ❖ Enthusiasm to the various departmental managers, supervisors, and process owners by visiting the project area and commenting positively, reviewing progress reports and providing feedback, requesting mini-presentations at certain milestones of the project, etc.
- ❖ The long term vision while supporting short-term strategies to attain the vision
- ❖ Measurements or targets (i.e., derived from the Balanced Scorecard or appropriate high level measurement system) for each department and/or project
- ❖ Communication channels to allow departments to share successes

These actions will allow project teams to be confident that top management is in full support of their efforts for improvement.

The most appropriate pages to read for this group would be 12-16, 20, 55-58, 59-64, and a few of the case studies on pages 143-165, 187-201, 228-246, 261-267, and 280-292.

Departmental heads (managers, supervisors, team leaders, Six Sigma Belts, Lean Senseis, Continuous Improvement Specialists, etc.) must have a thorough and practical working knowledge of Lean (and Six Sigma). *Kaizen Demystified* will provide this group with the details necessary to lead and actively support a continuous improvement or problem solving project. The individuals within this group will likely be the work team leader, process owner, or continuous improvement specialist for an improvement project. This group must provide the following:

- ❖ Appropriate training on the Lean and Six Sigma tools and concepts either by themselves or coordinating additional resources to provide the training (i.e., Black Belt, Lean Sensei, Continuous Improvement Specialist, etc.)
- ❖ A belief, along with demonstrated actions, that continuous improvement is important to the organization

❖ Relevant communication on the importance why improvements are necessary and how they are linked to the strategic direction of the organization and their daily work activities
❖ Negotiations with colleagues to referee cross-departmental resource priorities
❖ Effective leadership skills
❖ Ability to manage change
❖ Commitment to create a foundation of trust and honest dialogue among colleagues without coercion and/or retribution

Kaizen Demystified supports each of these actions. It provides the detailed framework for exactly what needs to be done and by who, as well as suggested time frames for all the various parts of the Kaizen Event.

The most appropriate pages to read for this group would be EVERYTHING! This is the operational group that must not only lead the change but fully understand Lean Sigma tools while embracing the Kaizen concept.

Employees (team members and employees working the processes) must have an understanding of Lean. *Kaizen Demystified* will provide this group with guidance on how continuous improvement projects are run as well as alternative methods to contribute their ideas. This group must provide the process "knowledge" required to effectively understand the current processes being analyzed and help solve problems and implement improvements. Without this group's "buy-in," improvements or changes will not be sustained, regardless of how impressive the improvements initially appear on paper. This group must provide the following:

❖ A desire to improve their process or work area
❖ An open mind that process change will be for the better
❖ Reliable knowledge on how their current processes run
❖ Ideas on how the process can be improved

Kaizen Demystified will provide numerous case studies to further assist this group's overall understanding of how Lean (and Six Sigma) can be applied through any one of the five Kaizen Event types. The most appropriate pages to read for this group would be 12-16, 23-34, 37-43, 57-70 and the case studies on pages 143-165, 187-201, 228-246, 261-267, and 280-306.

Lean Six Sigma - The Most Prolific Improvement Process in the History of the World

What is Lean?

Lean is a never-ending, systematic approach for identifying and eliminating waste and improving flow of a process while engaging employees. Lean is a way of thinking that can easily be applied to every type of organization. The entire focus of Lean is customer-driven; it is the customer who determines the value and the amount they are willing to pay for the product or service. The teachings of Edwards Deming and Philip Crosby throughout Japan (and Toyota) in the 1950s developed what is now known as Lean production. Toyota doubled productivity with car production while substantially improving quality during and after the 1950s. Toyota is recognized today as being the largest and most efficient automotive company in the world. Toyota's philosophy is based on continually meeting customer requirements efficiently and effectively with little or no waste while engaging employees in the improvement processes.

Lean is a compilation of world-class practices adapted from the United States, Japan, and Germany. Today, the Japanese refer to Just-In-Time as JIT - an American acronym. Similarly, takt, a German word, refers to "beat" or "rhythm." The important point to understand is that Lean has had a global birth; practitioners do not need to get caught up in whether a particular word or phrase is English, German, or Japanese but must understand the usefulness of what Lean comprises.

Lean is an umbrella for Total Quality Management (TQM), continuous improvement, zero defects, Total Employee Involvement (TEI), etc. that describes how to do things at the right time, in the correct amount, and without errors. It is a revolutionary philosophical process. Lean is the optimization of the entire value stream, not just one person or department. A value stream is defined as all the actions, both value-added (VA) and non value-added (NVA) that are necessary to deliver a product or service to a customer. Lean, when used appropriately, can provide a valuable component to Six Sigma projects (next section).

The Greek word arete (uh-REE-tay) means "habitual excellence" and is also synonymous with Lean. Lean is the process of applying common sense approaches to solving problems while striving for process excellence. It is the continued focus on the elimination of all process waste and should be a daily, hourly, or minute-by-minute review by all employees within an organization. This is not something that occurs overnight or in one year; it is a long-term commitment for positive change within an organization.

At the heart of Lean is the elimination of waste from the customer's perspective. The entire focus of Lean is customer-driven and it is the customer who determines the value and the amount they are willing to pay for the product or service. This is first accomplished through understanding what is of value or what the customer is willing to pay for. A value stream may include a single process comprised of many activities or a linked series of processes.

A stream is the flow of water from a spring that meanders down through various land formations to the ocean or sea. For the organization, a stream is a flow of work from an upstream process (request from customer or supplier or "spring") to the downstream process (product or service delivered to the customer or "ocean"). However, very seldom does this "flow" occur without some disruptions or hindrances. Examples of some hindrances that you may be facing in completing your daily work are:

- ❖ Lack of integration between production, materials, and planning
- ❖ Dependency on obtaining information from others that typically causes a delay in getting your work done
- ❖ Inefficient use of technology to improve flow
- ❖ Updates or modifications of reports due to inaccurate data
- ❖ Employees not trained to standards
- ❖ Out-dated systems, non-standard processes, etc. causing mistakes and contributing to inefficiencies
- ❖ Lack of communication and co-ordination of information
- ❖ Reports being generated in all different types of formats
- ❖ Lack of physical and/or electronic file/folder standards

Once these hindrances (i.e., wastes among some of them) are removed, then the work or service to be provided can flow smoothly.

A very effective tool to help identify waste is a value stream map. *A **value stream map** is a visual repre-sentation of the material, work, and information flow, as well as the queue times (and inventory levels, if appropriate) between processes for a specific customer demand.* Additionally a current state value stream map is created noting the current processes attributes such as cycle times, defects, number of operators, etc. The following is an example of a current state value stream map.

Current State Map for Classic Inc.

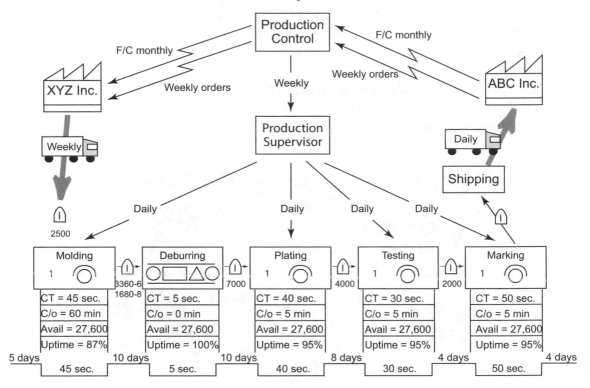

Once the current state value stream (or process) map is created, wastes are identified through brainstorming or conducting a Waste Walk. *A **Waste Walk** is an activity for project team members to visit the process area being considered for improvement, ask questions, and identify the wastes and other process attributes.* These are listed or displayed on the current state value stream or process map. Lean tools are then applied to eliminate those wastes which are typically represented by the Kaizen symbol on a future state value stream map. The following is an example of a future state value stream map.

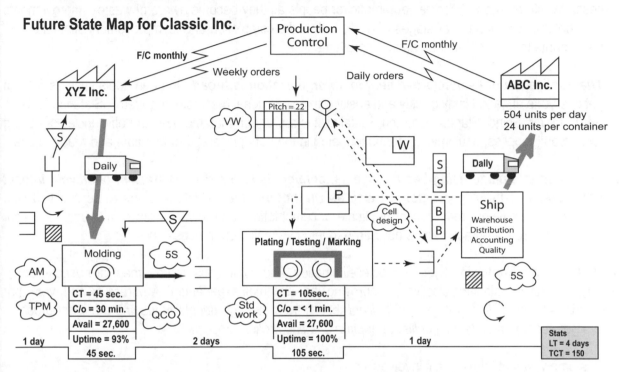

Future State Map for Classic Inc.

Subsequent implementation of the Lean tools to reduce or eliminate the waste identified would be accomplished by conducting a type of Kaizen. In the above future state value stream map, a Kaizen Event is identified by the star burst symbols (i.e., Quick Changeover, 5S, Standard Work, etc.). These would be scheduled as a type of Kaizen Event.

Lean is a way of thinking that can fairly easily be applied to every type of organization.

Note: There are numerous books on the value stream map tool. Also, process maps are another tool to visually display the process if there are multiple decisions being made throughout the process being examined or detailed steps of the process are required. There is an app called iBrainstorm that can assist in creating a basic value stream or process map at no cost.

There are three reasons why Lean can be used with confidence.

1. ***The training requirements and implementation time for Lean are minimal.*** Basic concepts of Lean can be taught very quickly and improvements can be implemented the same day. For example, when an individual understands that some of their daily activities are non value-added or waste (activities such as excess time spent walking, waiting, and moving), immediate changes can be made to improve the process. Waste reduction becomes automatic for people as they become aware of waste. Improvements are continuously made at all stages of work. Often, the completion of one improvement stimulates the participants to think of other areas for improvement.

2. ***The application of Lean improvement in an organization is broad.*** In Lean, tools such as 5S can get everyone engaged fairly quickly and easily with no additional resources required. 5S stands for Sort, Set-In-Order, Shine, Standardize, and Sustain. It is a program that improves the efficiencies of having resources (supplies, equipment, information, etc.) in the right place at the right time and ready to use.

3. ***Improvements made using Lean concepts, commonly referred to as Kaizen, positively impact other areas of the organization as well as the bottom-line.*** Customers are more satisfied with decreased wait times, reduction of duplicate documentation, and fewer errors or mix-ups. In Lean, employees are encouraged and empowered to improve their work processes.

Lean, the Toyota Production System, waste elimination, and continuous improvement are used synonymously, all with the similar objective of improving the customer experience. A phrase from Toyota that summarizes Lean is *"At Toyota we get brilliant results from average people managing a brilliant process. Others get average results from brilliant people managing broken processes."*

Lean is a new way of thinking that involves:

1. Being Creative – engaging the workforce to better solve problems through their "process" eyes
2. Using New Knowledge – allowing emerging technologies and the workforce to improve product and work flow, improve efficiencies, and reduce stress
3. Questioning Everything – ensuring that the status quo respectfully is analyzed and improved upon
4. Looking Beyond - creating current and future states to achieve a long-term improvement vision
5. Creating Real-Time Metrics – ensuring measurements are up-to-date and are part of a visual management system

Lean is a way of thinking and doing involving everyone. The understanding and implementation of Lean is done in a variety of ways. *Kaizen Demystified* was written to provide you with those ways.

What is Six Sigma?

Six Sigma is a statistical term. Six Sigma measures how much of the normal process variation (operational width) falls within the process requirements (specification width). Sigma (σ) measures the variation or "spread" of a process. *Six Sigma, as a business tool or project methodology, is a structured, quantitative, five phase approach to continuous improvement and problem solving.* The five phases are: Define - Measure - Analyze - Improve - Control and are commonly referred to as the D-M-A-I-C process (or phases).

Define Phase - the initial determination of purpose of the improvement, resources required, and a plan.

Measure Phase - a full and thorough documentation of the customer needs or market demand for the process being improved as a continuation of the Define Phase.

Analyze Phase - the detailed examination of the processes with corresponding ideas on how to improve the processes.

Improve Phase - the implementation of the tools and techniques as defined in the Analyze Phase using the Plan-Do-Check-Act (PDCA) model (or other similar model).

Control Phase - the use of visual management and control charts to ensure the process changes are maintained over time.

A graphical representation of the process or steps of these phases is represented in the following flow diagram:

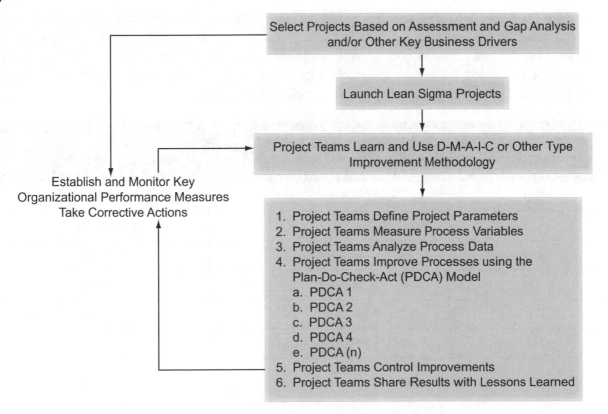

The term Six is the number of sigmas (standard deviations) as a measure from the mean in a bell-shaped normal distribution curve, as shown below:

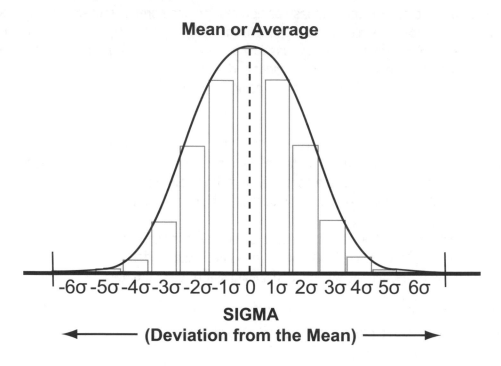

Mean or Average

-6σ -5σ -4σ -3σ -2σ -1σ 0 1σ 2σ 3σ 4σ 5σ 6σ

SIGMA
← (Deviation from the Mean) →

The goal of Six Sigma is to eliminate defects and minimize variability. In statistical terms, if an organization, department, or process achieves a Six Sigma level of performance, 99.99966% of its process outputs are defect-free and meet expectations. In other words, that organization, department, or process will have no more than 3.4 defects per million opportunities (of errors). The table below summarizes the sigma or variation level and error (or defect) rate per million opportunities (DPMO):

Process Capability or Sigma Level	Defects (or Errors) Per Million Opportunities (DPMO)	Percent Acceptable
6 σ	3.4	99.99966%
5 σ	233	99.9767%
4 σ	6,210	99.379%
3 σ	66,807	93.32%
2 σ	308,538	69.15%
1 σ	691,462	30.9%

Six Sigma forces organizations to pursue perfection by asking if 99% acceptability is good enough. If 99% acceptable is good enough, consider the following (based on an average number of such services performed every day in the United States):

99% Good (3.8 Sigma)	99.99966% Good (6 Sigma)
20,000 lost articles of mail per hour (based on 2,000,000/hr)	Seven lost articles per hour
Unsafe drinking water for almost 15 minutes each day	One unsafe minute every seven months
5,000 incorrect surgical operations per week	1.7 incorrect operations per week
Two short or long landings daily at an airport with 200 flights/day	One short or long landing every five years
2,000,000 wrong drug prescriptions each year	680 wrong prescriptions per year
No electricity for seven hours each month	One hour without electricity every 34 years

The following Sigma Level Versus Defects chart highlights the sigma levels for three broad categories of organizations:

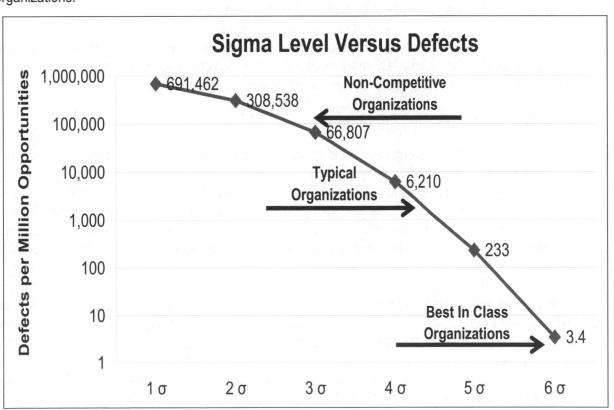

What is Lean Six Sigma?

Lean Six Sigma is the combination of customer-focused and waste elimination efforts of Lean with the quantitative analysis and structured D-M-A-I-C methodology of Six Sigma. Lean Sigma can be, and is for many organizations, a very powerful business improvement tool. It systematically blends the better of the two approaches to eliminate all waste (i.e., non value-added activities) and variation from a process which subsequently lowers the cost and improves the quality of the process. Lean Sigma allows organizations that aggressively adopt these practices to remain competitive, develop a cross-trained workforce, establish a safe workplace free of errors and process variation, and provide products and services in a cost-effective manner.

Lean Sigma tools are used to:

❖ Improve customer and employee satisfaction
❖ Identify and eliminate waste quickly and efficiently
❖ Increase communication and speed of services and information at all levels of the organization
❖ Reduce costs, improve quality, and provide world class service in a safe environment
❖ Initiate improvement activities and empower employees to make improvements themselves
❖ Track and monitor to control improvements to ensure sustainability
❖ Implement and manage change with a systematic mind set

Lean Sigma is truly a compilation of world-class practices. What you will begin to see when you understand and work with these tools is a renewed management philosophy that continues to embrace those values of improved quality, lower costs, faster delivery, and an energized workforce.

Lean Six Sigma Philosophies and Principles

A solid foundation stems from understanding and practicing Lean Sigma Philosophies and Principles. The philosophies of a continuous (relentless) elimination of waste and non value-added activities in everything we do and the conservation of all resources at every level of operation are keys to a successful Lean Sigma transformation. Additionally, Lean Sigma philosophy calls for the simplification of all tasks and efforts to eliminate process variation and improve flow. Absolute perfection is the goal. Very few organizations embrace Lean Sigma at this level. Lean management principles have been used effectively in manufacturing companies for decades, particularly in Japan.

Creating this foundation of Philosophies and Principles will ensure the required support is available as additional efforts in Lean Concepts and Six Sigma Concepts are applied through the use of Lean Sigma Tools. These building blocks are illustrated in the diagram on the next page. Starting with a strong foundation of Lean Sigma Philosophies and Lean Sigma Principles, these building blocks are used to support the Lean and Six Sigma Concept pillars. This will provide the Best Quality, Lowest Cost, Fastest Delivery, and Innovation for Delighted Customers and Profitable Growth.

Delighted Customers and Profitable Growth

Best Quality, Lowest Costs, Fastest Delivery, and Innovation

Lean Concepts

Lean Sigma Tools*

5S
A3 Reports
Continuous Flow
Data Collection and Presentation
Employee Balance Chart
Just-In-Time (JIT)
Layout
Leveling (Heijunka)
Mistake (or Error) Proofing
Performance Dashboards
Plan-Do-Check-Act
Problem Solving
Pull Systems and Kanbans
Quick Changeovers
Standard Work
Statistical Process Control
Takt Time and Demand Analysis Plots
Teamwork
Total Productive Maintenance (TPM)
Value Stream Mapping
Visual Controls
Voice of the Customer (VOC)

Six Sigma Concepts

Lean Concepts pillar: Plan-Do-Check-Act · Flow · Waste Elimination · Customer Focus · Performance Measures · Value and Waste · Quality First · Speak with Data and Facts · Total Employee Involvement · Seek Perfection

Six Sigma Concepts pillar: D-M-A-I-C · Quantitative Analysis · Look for Hidden Wastes · Voice of the Customer · Zero Defects · Scientific Method · Statistical Methods · Focus on Variation · Proven Methodology · Common Goal of Six Sigma

Lean Sigma Principles
Continuous Improvement in Processes and Results
Focus on Customers and Value Streams
Total Employee Involvement

Lean Sigma Philosophies
Conservation of Resources (Sustainability or Becoming Green)
Relentless Pursuit of Waste Elimination

* Not all inclusive of Lean Sigma tools

Lean Sigma Philosophies

The Lean Sigma Philosophies must exist as the solid foundation to build a Lean Sigma transformation. The two main Lean Sigma Philosophies are:

1. Conservation of Resources (Sustainability or Becoming Green)
2. Relentless Pursuit of Waste Elimination

Understanding these Lean Sigma Philosophies and applying the Lean Sigma Principles will help drive a Lean Sigma transformation. It is essential that employees at all levels of the organization be made aware of these Lean Sigma Philosophies.

Lean Sigma Principles

Lean Sigma Principles must also be present for transformations. They provide the unchanging, solid foundation to build and improve upon. The three key Lean Sigma Principles, supported by Lean Sigma Philosophies, are:

1. Continuous Improvement in Processes and Results – Do not focus only on the results or bottom-line. Instead, focus on processes that deliver consistent, waste-free results.
2. Focus on Customers and Value Streams – Focus on the entire process, from the customer pull or demand to demand fulfillment and customer satisfaction. Focus on how materials, information, or service requests flow through a process.
3. Total Employee Involvement – Organization leaders must ensure a safe work environment and provide an avenue for people to engage in improvement activities.

Creating this foundation of Philosophies and Principles will require that management support this endeavor by making employee training robust, being sincerely involved in improvement initiatives, and letting those closest to the process be involved in any change.

Six Sigma Concepts and Lean Concepts

The Six Sigma Concepts are:

- ❖ Scientific Method
- ❖ D-M-A-I-C
- ❖ Statistical Methods
- ❖ Quantitative Analysis
- ❖ Focus on Variation

- ❖ Voice of the Customer
- ❖ Proven Methodology
- ❖ Zero Defects
- ❖ Look for Hidden Wastes
- ❖ Common Goal of Six Sigma

The Lean Concepts are:

- ❖ Value and Waste
- ❖ Plan-Do-Check-Act (PDCA)
- ❖ Quality First
- ❖ Flow
- ❖ Speak with Data and Facts

- ❖ Waste Elimination
- ❖ Customer Focus
- ❖ Performance Measures
- ❖ Total Employee Involvement

Building the foundation of "Relentless Pursuit of Waste Elimination" from the previous Toyota House illustration requires a keen understanding of the various wastes as well as a method (i.e., Waste Walk) to help identify those wastes in a process or area.

Wastes

The overall goal of a Lean Sigma transformation is to understand, identify, and then eliminate (or reduce) waste. *Waste is any activity that does not add value to the product or service.* The following are the 12 wastes and are also referred to as The Dirty Dozen:

1. Overproduction
2. Waiting (or Delay)
3. Motion
4. Transport
5. Overprocessing
6. Inventory
7. Defects or Errors
8. People's Skills and Knowledge
9. Unevenness
10. Overburden
11. Environmental Resources
12. Social Responsibility

The following is a Pie Chart representing the twelve wastes and their relationship to value-added activities:

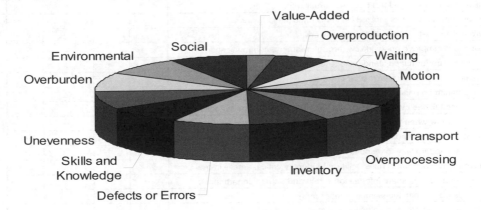

The following Waste Audit can be a starting point for an individual or a work group to further understand how wastes are manifested within current processes:

Kaizen Event	Waste Audit

Your Name (optional): [   ]   Event Dates: [   ]

Black Belt or Lean Sensei: [   ]   Department or Value Stream: [   ]

Instructions: Please ✔ the appropriate response to each statement.

Use the follwoing five level Likert item scale for scoring:
1 = Strongly Disagree
2 = Disagree
3 = Neither Agree nor Disagree
4 = Agree
5 = Strongly Agree

Statements	1 Strongly Disagree	2 Disagree	3 Neither Agree nor Disagree	4 Agree	5 Strongly Agree
1. We have no problems with mistakes or errors.					
2. We always have the right information when work needs to be done.					
3. We never struggle with getting the right data from our system.					
4. We only handle paperwork or an electronic document once, with no rework.					
5. We use the standard shortcuts and keystrokes to get to the data.					
6. We have a standard file naming convention.					
7. We have all our emails organized in appropriate folders for easy access.					
8. We never have to search for a tool, part, email, etc.					
9. We have our areas well organized using 5S principles.					
10. We are well cross-trained in each other's work.					
11. We continually improve our workflow through real-time communications.					
12. We know our performance standard for the day.					
13. We never have to recheck or reenter data.					
14. We have minimum paper copies around.					
15. We have established cycle times for our processes and they are monitored.					
16. We always know when work or information needs to be processed.					
17. We know the capability of our processes.					
18. We have a standard way to respond to emails.					
19. We have established email rules or filters to identify critical emails in real-time.					
20. We have a process to share information within and across departments.					
21. We have a robust continuous improvement program.					
22. We have all our employees trained in waste identification.					
23. We have a robust recycling program in place.					
24. We use visual management principles for processes and measurements.					
25. We have a process to share best practices with other organizations.					

Scoring Guidelines   Total: [   ]

A score of 90+ – Doing Very Well
A score of 80 - 89 – Good Foundation
A score of 70 - 79 – Some Good Things Happening, but More Needs to be Done
A score of 60 - 69 – Not Much Happening to Keep Pace with Competition

After your score is totaled, use the following Scoring Guidelines to provide the overall direction in eliminating the waste(s) identified. The total score could be a maximum of 125. For example, if an individual or work group scored an average of 4.0 on the 5.0 scale (80%) they would fit in the Good Foundation Scoring Guideline category.

Scoring Guidelines

A score of 90+ – Doing Very Well – Should be sharing best practices via conference speaking, blogs, white papers, etc. Keep the momentum going through reward and recognition. Consider larger, system level IT solutions.

A score of 80 - 89 – Good Foundation – Must have a good continuous improvement program, along with employee engagement already in place to score at this level. Keep the drive going by focusing on performance measurements/standards and visual controls, as well as sharing best practices.

A score of 70 - 79 – Some Good Things Happening, but More Needs to be Done – Benchmark other organizations; attend conferences that present your best practices. Additional training may need to be done to assist employees to better understand additional Lean tools and concepts. Work with Human Resources and make Lean (or Six Sigma) part of the overall performance appraisal system for everyone.

A score of 60 - 69 – Not Much Happening to Keep Pace with Competition – Diligent efforts must be made on communicating the concepts of waste reduction and how the Lean tools apply. Must ensure 5S is implemented throughout the organization, and then quickly start the appropriate improvement projects. Focus energies on creating a "Lean Buzz!"

A score of <60 – Not So Good – Typically, not a passing or satisfactory grade. However, some good things may be happening. Acknowledge the positives and begin a 5S program immediately, as well as involve IT on all Lean projects. Communicate and educate all employees via web casts, blogs, monthly email blasts, newsletters, etc. with examples of Lean practices, as well as how the fundamental concepts apply. Acknowledge quick-adapters and allow them to assist in the training on Lean initiatives once they have shown success in their areas.

Once the Waste Audit has been performed and the overall concept of waste is understood thoroughly, it is time to conduct a Waste Walk to the area or process being examined.

Waste Walk

A **Waste Walk** is an activity when project team members visit a process area that is being considered for improvement, ask questions, and then identify the wastes on the current state value stream or process map. Many of the team members will be very familiar with the project area as it is their actual work area. Conducting this Waste Walk, the team members, along with their Lean Sigma training, will be viewing their areas with a fresh perspective as they look at the processes and work flows.

The Waste Walk accomplishes the following:

❖ Ensure everyone is aligned to the physical location of the processes being analyzed
❖ Ensure process workers are engaged in improvement activities
❖ Allow for all process workers to provide input
❖ Allow for open communications about the team's project
❖ Allow for discussions about the process to clear up any questions
❖ Allow for conveying wastes visually on a value stream or process map

Use the following steps when conducting a Waste Walk:

1. Educate the team members on the following wastes as well as suggested questions to detect waste.

Overproduction - *Producing some type of work prior to it being required is waste of overproduction.* Providing a quality product or service above and beyond what is needed is also considered overproduction. Overproduction is when too much of something is made or served. This is the greatest of all the wastes. Overproduction of work or services can cause other wastes.

To DETECT this waste ask:

❖ Is production or work required faster or slower than takt time (or demand)?
❖ Is there inventory (i.e., parts, materials, documents, reports, etc.) in a queue waiting to be processed immediately downstream?
❖ Is there a lack of one-piece or small lot work flow?
❖ Is work scheduled according to a schedule or production quota?
❖ Is a pull system being used?
❖ Is takt time or demand known?

To ELIMINATE this type of waste:

❖ Establish continuous flow in terms of product or service needed at the appropriate time to the downstream customer.
❖ Ensure information is only entered into one common database.
❖ Create checklists to ensure all necessary information is attained.
❖ Create visual controls and/or kanbans to prevent early processing of information or services.

Waiting (or Delay) - *Waiting for anything (people, signatures, information, etc.) is waste.* This waste of waiting is "low hanging fruit" which is easy to reach and ripe for the taking. Waiting means idle time and that causes workflow to stop. We often do not think of paper sitting in an In-basket or an unread email as waste. However, when looking for the item (document or email), how many times do we mull through that In-basket or the Inbox folder to try to find it? How many times do you actually touch something before it is completed? The finish it, file it, or throw it away system helps eliminate this waste.

To DETECT this waste ask:

- ❖ Am I just watching the same operation and not adding value or contributing to any improvements?
- ❖ Can something else be completed that is value-added while I am waiting?
- ❖ Is standardized work being following?
- ❖ Are there "buffers" between processes for a reason? If so, have there been any ideas on how the "buffers" can be reduced or eliminated?
- ❖ Are Kanbans being used effectively?
- ❖ Does the transport time for the product seem excessive?
- ❖ Are lead times being met?
- ❖ Are lead times being improved upon?

To ELIMINATE this type of waste:

- ❖ Review and standardize signature and approval requirements.
- ❖ Cross-train staff to accommodate changes in customer demands.
- ❖ Balance workloads throughout the day and ensure staff members are working optimally.
- ❖ Identify and eliminate constraints and/or bottlenecks.
- ❖ Ensure equipment and supplies are located in close proximity of their required use.
- ❖ Ensure work items are labeled and at point-of-use (as appropriate).

Motion - *Any movement of people, material, products, and/or electronic exchanges that does not add value is waste.* This waste is created by poor physical layout or design, faulty or outdated equipment, supply inaccessibility, and movement of information or data that does not add value. The waste of motion is insidious and is hidden in old procedures that have not been reviewed for continuous improvement initiatives. Regardless of the industry, motion waste may appear as someone who is looking "busy" but not adding value to the work or service. Lean Sigma tools will assist to identify, reduce, and/or eliminate this waste.

To DETECT this waste ask:

- ❖ Can walking or the excess movement of the work be reduced?
- ❖ Can body movement be reduced?
- ❖ Are shortcuts being used to reduce keystrokes for all data and information?
- ❖ Is the work area optimized for ergonomic reasons?
- ❖ Is there an active 5S program?
- ❖ Is standard work being followed and improved upon?
- ❖ Is cross-training being done?

To ELIMINATE this type of waste:

- ❖ Ensure supply areas are well organized utilizing color-codes and labels for quick access.
- ❖ Arrange Desktop PC files for easy retrieval (establish file naming conventions for the department).
- ❖ Establish standards of communicating process needs and method of work flow.
- ❖ Relocate staff, equipment, etc. to accommodate continuous flow where practical.

Transport - *Transport waste is the excess movement of materials, documents, information, etc. within an organization.* Excess transport affects the time of delivery of any work within an organization. Even with the Internet and email readily available, too often, or not often enough, documents (i.e., files) that provide little or no value are moved downstream regardless of need. Reducing or eliminating excess transport waste is important. Locating all work in sequential process operations and as physically close together as possible will help eliminate or reduce this waste. Transport between processes that cannot be eliminated should be automated as much as possible. Ask questions such as: "Is the physical layout optimal?" "Is the release and request for work automated?" and "Is IT aware of the problem and can they help?"

To DETECT this waste ask:

- ❖ Are parts, supplies, or any type of work being stored in inventory of some sort?
- ❖ Has the physical layout been improved upon given Lean concepts?
- ❖ Is the communication of work transfer automated and does it only move if the downstream process signals for it?
- ❖ Is a pull system being used?

To ELIMINATE this type of waste:

- ❖ Minimize distance for work to be moved.
- ❖ Use point-of-use for materials and tools.
- ❖ Create standard transport times (when transport is necessitated).
- ❖ Create standard process times.
- ❖ Consolidate electronic worksheets as much as possible.

Overprocessing - *Putting more effort into the work than what is required by internal or external customers is waste.* This waste is going above and beyond the needs and expectations of the internal or external customer and is very difficult to discover. Many people see this waste as improved quality, but it is not. Quality is meeting needs and expectations. Excessive processing does not add value for the customer and the customer will not pay for it.

To DETECT this waste ask:

- ❖ Is this a poor process design and what is its purpose?
- ❖ Are incorrect process capabilities specified?
- ❖ Is there a clear understanding of the customer requirements?
- ❖ Is someone doing the same process but differently?
- ❖ Is standard work defined?

To ELIMINATE this type of waste:

- ❖ Review all steps within a process and eliminate non value-added activities.
- ❖ Standardize work procedures to best practice and ensure customer specifications or requirements are met, no more, no less.
- ❖ Eliminate redundant information required on forms by consolidating forms (or information required).

Inventory - *Excessive piles of materials, parts, paperwork, computer files, and supplies are the waste of inventory, and cause extra time spent searching or other wastes.* They all take up space or require someone's time. If work is accumulating or backing up between processes, waste of inventory is present. Work-In-Process (WIP) may be an asset, but it can also be a waste.

To DETECT this waste ask:

- ❖ Are there queues throughout the value stream or processes?
- ❖ Are parts or materials purchased in larger quantities than what the customer demands?
- ❖ Is there obsolete inventory?
- ❖ Is the process capable?
- ❖ Is standard work being followed and improved upon?
- ❖ Is there too much variation in the process?

To ELIMINATE this type of waste:

- ❖ Produce or provide only the necessary information, supply, or service to satisfy the downstream customer.
- ❖ Use Kanbans or pull systems to standardize levels for supplies and keep organized.
- ❖ Audit the replenishment system to ensure correct levels of supplies are always available.
- ❖ Ensure work arrives at the next process on time.

Defects or Errors - *Defect waste refers to all processing required in creating a defect and the additional work required to correct a defect or error.* Defects and errors (either internal or external) result in additional processing that add no value to the product or service. It takes less time to do work correctly the first time than the time it would take to do it over. Rework or correction of work is waste and adds more cost to any product or service for which the customer will not pay. This waste can reduce profits significantly.

To DETECT this waste ask:

- ❖ What is the defect rate?
- ❖ What is the capability or sigma level for the process?
- ❖ Are there common reasons for the defects?
- ❖ Are defects hiding in inventory?
- ❖ Is there a lack of process capability for the machine, tool, or process?
- ❖ Is standardized work being followed?

To ELIMINATE this type of waste:

- ❖ Create visual controls to ensure work standards are met.
- ❖ Create work standards that meet best practice.
- ❖ Ensure preventive maintenance schedules are adhered to for all equipment.
- ❖ Ensure cross-training is conducted to accommodate increases in demand.
- ❖ Improve process capability by centering the process nominal or reducing variation.

People's Skills or Knowledge - *The underutilization of people is a result of not placing people where they can (and will) use their knowledge, skills, and abilities to their fullest potential in providing value-added work and services.* An effective performance management system will reduce this waste significantly. Use company policies and procedures to effectively place people where they will most benefit the organization. The employees performing the work tasks know the work the best. It is a waste of their knowledge not to listen to them and involve them in improvement initiatives.

To DETECT this waste ask:

- ❖ Are employees effectively cross-trained?
- ❖ Are employees encouraged to suggest improvements?
- ❖ Are new employees trained to best practice before they beging working?
- ❖ Are employees improving the work standard?

To ELIMINATE this type of waste:

- ❖ Develop a robust performance appraisal system.
- ❖ Ensure employees have a training and development plan and monitor it to ensure it is being followed.
- ❖ Challenge employees on performance objectives.
- ❖ Be flexible in allowing employees to try new ideas.

Unevenness - *Lack of a consistent flow of inputs/information/scheduled work from upstream processes causes many types of waste previously mentioned.* Waste of unevenness creates fluctuations in workload and unbalanced production and/or service on-time-delivery. This waste directly impacts customers and can cause frustration for employees.

To DETECT this waste ask:

- ❖ Are employees effectively cross-trained?
- ❖ Is work scheduled to the day or hour?
- ❖ Are employees aware of the next process requirements?
- ❖ Are there times when work piles up in front of a particular process?
- ❖ Have bottlenecks and/or constraints been identified?

To ELIMINATE this type of waste:

- ❖ Cross-train employees to accommodate fluctuations in workloads.
- ❖ Determine customer demand and create a visual leveling system for everyone to see.
- ❖ Create standards for how work should flow.
- ❖ Create continuous flow where possible.

Overburden - *Overburdening or overloading occurs when the capacity of the process is not known and/or is not adequately scheduled.* This typically causes other wastes to occur. Overburden must be handled as a separate waste; it can be identified easily during the value mapping process and is often expressed in terms of capacities of equipment or people. Usually this waste causes a great sense of frustration, anger, and job dissatisfaction on the part of the employee. This most likely would have a negative impact on the customer as well.

To DETECT this waste ask:

- ❖ Are employees effectively cross-trained?
- ❖ Is capacity known for all processes?
- ❖ Are we flexible when customer demand changes?
- ❖ Is work scheduled through multiple processes with standard times?
- ❖ Is standard work being followed for repetitive tasks?

To ELIMINATE this type of waste:

- ❖ Cross-train employees to accommodate fluctuations in workloads.
- ❖ Create value-added and non value-added analysis.
- ❖ Create a value stream map or process map to determine overall flow and then implement appropriate Lean tools.
- ❖ Create an Employee Balance Chart for the processes that are overburdened, brainstorm, and then reallocate duties as appropriate.

Environmental Resources - *As organizations become more sustainable or "Green," they have to make extra efforts to protect environmental resources.* Any waste that is generated by an organization that negatively impacts the environment, whether it is solid or liquid, is classified as environmental waste.

To DETECT this waste ask:

- ❖ Are employees aware of environmental waste?
- ❖ Are there supplies or materials that have recycled potential?
- ❖ Are there any forms of recycling being done now?

To ELIMINATE this type of waste:

- ❖ Train employees with examples on environmental wastes.
- ❖ Conduct a Waste Walk and focus on the environment.
- ❖ Create a team to continue research and find ways to conserve.

Social Responsibility - *Social Responsibility waste is broad and includes poverty, discrimination, malpractices, health and injuries, nutrition, literacy and education, office politics, and social media networking.*

To DETECT this waste ask:

- ❖ Are employees aware of company communication rules?
- ❖ Are social networks (Facebook, Twitter, etc.) being used to promote the products or services to the appropriate market segment?
- ❖ Are employees ethical in how business is being conducted (internally as well as externally)?
- ❖ Is training conducted regularly on diversification in the workplace?

To ELIMINATE this type of waste:

- ❖ Ensure each employee has read and signed the company standards for what is proper communication within the organization.
- ❖ Research competitor's social networking sites.
- ❖ Ensure each employee clearly understands what is acceptable and what is not acceptable in terms of business ethics and discrimination of any kind.

2. Communicate to the employees working in the prospective areas/processes/departments when you will be bringing the group through and explain your purpose using an "elevator speech." *An **elevator speech** is a brief, comprehensive verbal overview on the purpose and related activities regarding the product, process, or service being examined.* It should convey the following: *"Here's what our project is about..............," "Here's why it's important to do............," "Here's what success will look like.............," and "Here's what we need from you.......... ."*

3. Assign one person in each group to take notes. Use the Waste Walk sheet on the following page as a guide. This can easily be created in Microsoft Excel or Word. It is also available at www.TheLeanStore.com for a nominal fee.

4. Ensure the team has thought of questions to ask, including: What are some of the issues affecting your work? What could be improved? Do you help out when things get busy? If not, why? Do you know when you are behind schedule? Do you know when the work you provide is needed downstream (or the next process)? It is suggested you review the "To DETECT this waste ask:" parts for each waste and create a set of 3 – 6 questions.

5. Do not cause any disruption to the process. (e.g., If a Waste Walk is to be conducted through the Emergency Department of a hospital, if possible, schedule a walk during the least busy or slack time.)

6. If the group is larger than 5, break into smaller groups.

7. Start with the most downstream process and work backwards upstream.

8. Thank the people for their time.

9. Consolidate the information from the Waste Walk and update the current state value stream or process map with how these wastes can be reduced or eliminated through the use of Lean Sigma tools and concepts. List initial improvement ideas on the Meeting Information Form, PDCA Kaizen Activity Worksheet, or Action Item Log.

Kaizen Event	Waste Walk

Value Stream: _____ **Date:** _____

Department: _____ **Team Members:** _____

Type of Waste	Waste Observations
Overproduction Producing more material, information, or a service than is needed or used.	
Skills and Knowledge Not using people's minds and getting them involved.	
Transport Moving supplies, materials, documents, people, etc. excessively.	
Inventory Any unnecessary material, information, documents, etc. that resides between two processes.	
Motion Any unnecessary movement that does not add value.	
Defects or Errors Redoing work that has been done previously.	
Overprocessing Providing work or service that is not part of the customer requirement.	
Waiting or Delays The time spent waiting for material, information, people, etc.	
Overburden Work that is added with no additional support or resources.	
Unevenness Work that arrives without being scheduled and in varying amounts.	
Environmental Products, processes, activities, etc. that are not good for the planet.	
Social Communicating and networking via social networks that does not add value.	

Process Attributes

Process Name	Attributes	Process Name	Attributes

The following benefits can be obtained by conducting a Waste Walk:

- ❖ Provide additional insight into processes that are being examined
- ❖ Connect classroom value stream or process mapping to the actual processes
- ❖ Allow for everyone to "see" or walk the process flow to all be on the same page

Note: If program applications are being analyzed for electronic waste, consider either having the appropriate screen shots or the application available for the team to review.

The book *Today's Lean! Learning About and Identifying Waste* has the Waste Walk as a convenient 3.5" x 5.5" booklet for team members to reference and take notes in on their walk.

Please visit your favorite app store for the Waste Audit and Waste Walk apps from MCS Media, Inc. These apps are very interactive and informative to help your train employees in the identification of wastes.

What is Kaizen and Its Relationship to Lean Sigma

Kaizen means "kai" to "take apart" and "zen" to "make better." Kaizen is also synonymous with continuous improvement. Kaizen can be major organizational improvements directed to a value stream (i.e., integrating two business units' processes) or it can be something very simple (i.e., placing a Post-it Note on a signature page to make sure the document is signed in the correct location) – and everything in-between.

The **Kaizen Mindset**, also known as Lean Thinking, is for employees to be continually making incremental improvements in their work processes as well as be a contributor to larger, organizational change type projects. Start sowing the seeds of a "kaizen mindset" with employees by having them understand the following: Consider everything you are doing right now as the worst way of doing your job! Although this comment might sound extreme, please note that this is not designed to be a disparaging comment about you or the way you do your job. It is just a statement designed to get your mind into a "kaizen mindset" and to start seeing ways to streamline and improve your processes through one of the five types of Kaizen Events. This "kaizen mindset" is a state of belief that should progressively find its way into the deep roots of an employee's behavior thus allowing for a new organizational culture to emerge over time.

Strong upper-level management support for initiating and sustaining continuous improvement initiatives is crucial for any type improvement project. Ensure improvement initiatives maintain their focus on the strategic objectives of the business. The following may prevent upper-level management support:

- ❖ Poor communication of the objectives or anticipated outcomes
- ❖ Lack of understanding of the potential value and the level of commitment required
- ❖ A desire for a "quick fix " or " magic bullet"
- ❖ A poor or no implementation process or plan
- ❖ Insufficient controls
- ❖ Inadequate validation process or follow-up plan
- ❖ Loss of focus on the identification and elimination of waste - project too vague

The following can be done to eliminate the reasons just listed:

1. Schedule a "JIT" learning session with upper management. Use the session to spark their interest and entice them to become trained so that they can oversee or sponsor a Kaizen Event themselves. Make them part of the solution. Learn-by-doing is one of the most effective and eye opening teaching methods.

2. Invite upper management and executive project sponsors to routine project reviews. The reviews should include participation, not only from the process owner, but from those overseeing and sponsoring the project.

3. Ensure improvement project initiatives (PDCAs) always maintain their focus on eliminating waste and increasing value to the customer. The language of management is money, reducing costs to the organization, and ensuring employee safety and well-being. If leadership does not see these benefits reflected in providing value to the customer and improving the bottom line, they will question the validity and/or value of the Kaizen Event project.

4. Ensure a financial aspect of the project is discussed or addressed. This may mean working with the CFO.

5. Detail the implementation plan or methodology to be used. Provide examples of other departments or other organizations that have had success with this plan or methodology.

6. Ensure the plan has the follow-up details needed for sustaining any improvements.

These six activities will help ensure management commitment from the initial stages of the project through to creating the necessary standards to sustain it.

There may be an opportunity to generate interest and support from the middle or lower levels of the enterprise without the benefit of upper management support or even awareness. Gaining momentum bottom up does not happen very often, but it is possible. In this rare case, the impact trickles up and top management takes notice when significant dollars positively affect the bottom line. Suddenly, leadership wants to know what is causing this phenomenon and what it will take to get more. As a result, they come to you searching out the critical mass, and the project team that may have initially been viewed skeptically gains active, broad support to expand and deploy similar practices throughout the enterprise.

Identifying waste and training employees on the Lean Six Sigma tools, providing a proven structured approach for conducting an improvement project, ensuring sincere management involvement and commitment, and getting employees actively involved in process change will help to instill a "kaizen mindset" as a way of life within your organization.

The next section explains the various "X" factors that need to in place prior to initiating a Kaizen Event.

The X Factors for Kaizen Events

Engaging Today's Workforce

Today's workforce is more diverse than ever before. To lead and supervise this diverse and dynamic group, supervisors and leaders need to fully understand the workforce for maximum results in facilitating any type of Kaizen Event. The advent of social networking and the Internet adds an additional complexity on speed of communications and information transfers. Yet, the concept of doing more with less remains as a key driver for supervisor success. Productivity, efficiency, and effectiveness are key measures of success. To leverage or capitalize on this situation, leaders and supervisors will be well-served to study the key drivers and motivators for the individual groups or subsets that exist in the workforce. This section provides insights into the key drivers and motivators of today's workers as well as practical activities to better engage employees before, during, and after a Kaizen Event.

Reducing wastes and costs and improving the total customer satisfaction will lead to overall business growth and profitability. Growth and profitability are essential for any business to survive. Through implementing a Lean Sigma transformation, a business will survive, become stronger, and will be able to provide wage and earnings growth, and advancement in a safer, more stable work environment. But at the heart of any Lean Sigma transformation is to understand your people and engaging them into a pro-active role in continuous improvement.

There are four generations in the workforce today interacting on a day-to-day basis, each with different computer skills and work experiences. These differences, if not acknowledged and leveraged appropriately can give rise to frustration, clashes, and misinterpretation – all of which can contribute to a non-Lean Sigma work environment. However, utilizing each generation's positive work styles (i.e., technical and work experience skills) can also create a more creative and diverse atmosphere in which the organization can then excel and create a competitive advantage. It is imperative for managers, as well as the front-line workers, to understand these differences from both a generational and computer skills point-of-view. Working to improve communications between these generations will ultimately improve the quality of decision-making as well as improve the flow of information, products, services, etc. throughout the organization. Do not underestimate the importance of people's attitudes and generational attributes and how those can impact work processes within an organization.

The years that differentiate the generations in today's workforce, as outlined in this section, may be defined a bit differently due to a certain set of criteria used by various organizations. Keep in mind the bigger picture of the "groups" of people as a generation; these are generalizations. We do not mean to "categorize" a certain age group in any negative way. The intent is to recognize the differences that do exist and use those differences, along with the right balance of technology, to improve communications.

The following are the four working generations and some general attributes of each that exist in today's workforce (years and numbers referenced are for the United States):

The **Matures (Traditionalist, Veterans, and Silent)** *is the oldest generation in the workforce and these people were born between 1925 and 1945.* There are approximately 63.2 million Matures in the workforce. The Matures are currently retiring or facing retirement in the next few years. This group is also referred to as the "greatest generation of all time" mainly due to their experiences in the Great Depression (1929), World War II (1941 – 1945), and the Korean War (1950 – 1953).

- ❖ Value: respect for authorities, conformity, and discipline
- ❖ Key Word: loyal
- ❖ Their families are very traditional (nuclear)
- ❖ Education is typically seen as a dream
- ❖ Communicate in person (i.e., face-to-face)
- ❖ Deal with money by saving it, and when spent, paying with cash

The **Baby Boomer Generation** *is the second oldest generation in the workforce, and these people were born between 1946 and 1964.* There are roughly 76.8 million Baby Boomers in the workforce. The Baby Boomers are currently becoming empty nesters (i.e., having no children at home) and make up the largest segment in the workforce. These people grew up post World War II and have experienced Kennedy's Camelot years at the White House, Woodstock, and the Vietnam War.

- ❖ Value: being involved
- ❖ Key Word: optimistic
- ❖ Their family is disintegrating (divorce rates beginning to increase dramatically)
- ❖ Education is a birthright
- ❖ Communicate by phone and like to be called at anytime
- ❖ Deal with money by buying something now and paying for it later

The **Generation Xers** *are the people born between 1965 and 1980.* There are roughly 52.4 million Gen Xers in the workforce. These people are buying, if they can afford it, their first homes, waiting longer to start families, and beginning to move to higher-level management positions being vacated by the Matures and Baby Boomers. These people grew up in the decade after the Cold War and during the fall of the Berlin Wall.

- ❖ Value: fun and informality
- ❖ Key Word: skepticism
- ❖ Family is noticing latchkey kids (children home alone while parents working)
- ❖ See education as a way to get some place in life
- ❖ Communicate with cell phones and like to be called only when at work
- ❖ Deal with money by saving, conserving, and being cautious

The *Generation Y (Millenials)* are the youngest working generation in the workforce and these people are born between 1981 and 1999. There are roughly 7.6 million Millenials in the workforce now, with many more on the way - and they do not all reside in Chicago! These people are facing independence and moving out of their parent's homes after completing college and entering the workforce while seeking further academic degrees.

- ❖ Value: confidence, extreme fun, and being social
- ❖ Key Word: realistic
- ❖ Families are typically merged
- ❖ Education is seen as an incredible expense
- ❖ Communicate using text messaging and smart/4G devices
- ❖ Deal with money by earning it and then spending it

The following Pie Chart summarizes the current breakdown of workers in the U.S. workforce as of 2010:

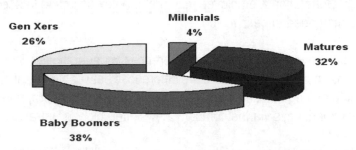

The emerging workforce born after 1999 is referred to as the "*Cyber Generation*." This group of young people is still in elementary and high schools and soon will have a profound effect on work environments. The potential number of workers in the Cyber Generation rivals that of the Baby Boomer generation, yet their childhood influences will be quite different. The Cyber Generation will have spent their entire lives with the constant availability and bombardment of real-time news, videos, communication, social-cyber interaction, and instant information and gratification. This group has watched military conflicts and world crisis unfold in real-time, and will expect the same of their business interactions and buying habits. As workers and consumers, their demands will far exceed those of any previous generation, and their respect for conformance and red tape will be intolerable. Qualities of this generation are:

- ❖ Never lived without an Internet connection
- ❖ Never lived without a cell/smart phone with instant text or messaging
- ❖ Never lived without laptops and small micro-computing tablets
- ❖ Angry and or feel helpless when out of 3/4G or WiFi communications
- ❖ YouTube and Wikipedia with instant learning opportunities
- ❖ Socially connected instantly
- ❖ Constant detailed world event news available
- ❖ Use of Facebook, FaceTime, Skype, Twitter, LinkedIn, cell/smart phones, tablets, texting, etc.
- ❖ Fear of loss of social contact
- ❖ Reality and social television on demand

The mix of workers in the workforce will be a continually changing dynamic, and leaders must continually adapt their strategy to achieve success.

The following 10 Tips to Help Bridge the Socio – Techno Gap will help foster an environment necessary to identify and eliminate waste:

1. *Communicate early and often*. All generations have a need to be included in any change; however, it is acknowledged that there are times when everyone cannot be part of the team that is initiating or designing the change. If that is the case, ensure communication from the manager is done early in the process as well as provide regular updates. Mistakes or reasons why things do not get completed on time may be due to miscommunication in the workplace.

2. *Be enlightening.* Show how diversity can benefit a company. Be positive when working toward eliminating the generational gaps. Discuss openly what could be some additional motivators for each generation. For example, the Baby Boomer employee may want additional time-off after the completion of a large project while a Generation X employee may prefer a flex-schedule to accommodate their lifestyle. Human Resources may need to be involved.

3. *Be open.* Have open conversations about the differences in generations. Share experiences and viewpoints in a safe environment. Knowing there are differences between generations is important, however, it is more important to manage these differences. When and where appropriate, have employees share work and technical experiences via the company newsletter, blog, or Intranet.

4. *Be flexible.* Create a work environment that all generations will like. If a Matures Generation employee likes title recognition then create an appropriate title. If a Baby Boomer wants a formal meeting, let that happen but limit the time to accommodate the Generation Y employees (Generation Y employees like short meetings). Utilize email, iPhones, and the Internet to accommodate the younger generation's communication style but also have formal meetings to accommodate the Baby Boomers and Matures.

5. *Be creative.* Be creative in providing rewards for people. Different generational employees like different rewards, therefore, research what rewards each generation likes and accommodate accordingly. For example, the Matures and Baby Boomer Generations would most likely prefer a certificate or monogrammed company sweater than a team lunch or gift certificate.

6. *Create learning opportunities for new software applications.* Ensure there is available training for new applications and make it optional. If at all possible have training made available in different platforms, such as traditional classroom, online, or self-paced. Having a learning or training opportunity on multiple platforms will not single out those less tech savvy.

7. *Create rules and standards.* Every generation wants to know what is expected of them as well as what is acceptable and what is not acceptable in terms of communication (i.e., all emails must be returned within 1 business day, receiving text messages or any type messages for non-emergency reasons while at work, etc.).

8. ***Create opportunities.*** When at all possible, promote employee's skills within the organization as well as communicate their successes via any and all organizational bulletin boards.

9. ***Understand generational differences.*** Always keep in mind that the Matures and Baby Boomer Generations value active participation and want their ideas to be heard or acknowledged. However, the Gen Xers and Millenials prefer less formal meetings and do not feel the need to have everyone's ideas heard.

10. ***Keep a balance.*** Since there exists these generations in the workforce, and as the next generation enters, try not to let one generational style dominate as that will lead to discernment and frustration on the part of the employee as well as the manager.

It is the responsibility of the leader to understand the differences in order to be effective. Leaders need to understand the differences and recognize that generational traits will influence the personality traits and team work. Using the previous information and adjusting communications and work assignments accordingly will improve the following:

- ❖ Employee satisfaction
- ❖ Communication problems
- ❖ Customer satisfaction
- ❖ Productivity

The following are a few examples of waste that can be eliminated by understanding each generation. Use these as a springboard to discuss other ways your organization can reduce and eliminate similar types of wastes that exist due to not understanding generational attributes and behaviors.

Overproduction – Example: A Matures generation employee phoning a Generation X or Y associate that they just emailed them the information. The phone call is waste.

Transport – Example: Meeting with a colleague for lunch just to answer a simple question when an email or text would suffice. Walking or driving to the destination and extra time spent on this meeting is waste.

Overprocessing – Example: Having everyone attend meetings when only certain people need to be present.

People Utilization – Example: Requiring everyone to receive training on a new application or functionality, whereas, some employees may learn it on-the-job.

Not adapting and adjusting your work style to these generational issues contribute to some of the following:

- ❖ Lack of standardization of processes and knowledge sharing
- ❖ Higher turnover among the X-Y Generation worker
- ❖ Lack of succession leadership

There are some overlaps with the various attributes between the generations; this is because some traits carry on for longer than one generation. For example, agreeing to hierarchy standards in companies was common in the first two generations, however, now people are becoming less interested in 'titles' and more focused on the task at hand and using people's talents given the situation, regardless of their title. Understanding these generational strengths and weaknesses in the workplace by managers and employees alike will give an organization a competitive advantage.

The following two charts summarize the generational personal and lifestyle characteristics, along with the workplace behaviors previously discussed and listed:

Workplace Behaviors				
	Matures 1925 - 1945	**Baby Boomers** 1946 - 1964	**Gen Xers** 1965 - 1980	**Millenials** 1981 - 1999
Work Ethic	Hard workers Dedicated to job	Workaholics Works efficiently	Eliminate the task	Whats next? Multi-taskers
Work is...	An obligation	An exciting adventure	A difficult challenge A contract	A means to an end Fulfillment
Leadership Style	Directive Command and control	Consensual Collegial	Everyone is the same Challenge others Ask why	TBD
Interactive Style	Individual	Team player Loves to have meetings	Entrepreneur	Participative
Communication	Formal Memo	In person	Direct Immediate	Email, Text Messages Voicemail
Feedback and Rewards	No news is good news Satisfaction in a job well done	Does not appreciate it Money Title recognition	Sorry to interrupt, but how am I doing? Freedom	Whenever I want it, or at the push of a button Meaningful work
Messages that motivate	Your experience is respected	You are valued and needed	Do it your own way and forget the rules	You will work with others who are bright and creative

Generational Personal and Lifestyle Characteristics				
	Matures 1925 -1945	**Baby Boomers** 1946 - 1964	**Gen Xers** 1965 - 1980	**Millenials** 1981 - 1999
Values	Respects authority Disciplined	Optimism Involvement	Skepticism Fun times Informality	Realistic Confidence Extreme fun Social
Family	Traditional Nuclear	Divorce Family members moving out	Latch-key kids	Merged families
Education	A dream	More plausible A right	A way to get someplace	Very expensive
Communication	One-on-one Formal memos	Touch-tone phones Call anytime	Cell phones Call at certain times	Internet iPhones, Text messages Email
Money	Save Pay cash	Buy, buy, buy and pay later	Cautious Conservative Save	Earn the money then spend

The following chart provides guidance on how to interact with the various generations in reference to Kaizen Events:

Kaizen Event Generational Coaching Tips, Do's and Don'ts				
	Matures 1925 - 1945	**Baby Boomers** 1946 - 1964	**Gen Xers** 1965 - 1980	**Millenials** 1981 - 1999
Kaizen Event Coaching Tips	Encourage them to talk about their experiences	Help them feel victorious	Prove you are on authority, nothing is a given	Become the provider of information
	Match your approach to a good experience	Be responsive to competition	Appear to enjoy your work	Demonstrate personal relevance, uniqueness
	Acknowledge their rules of engagement	Provide opportunities for more positive experiences	No hard answers	Highlight peer-to-peer examples
	Focus on quality/structure	Become a member of their team	Provide all details, options, alternatives up front	Recognize them as individuals
Do's	Allow Matures to set the "rules of engagement"	Help them use their time wisely	Put all options on the table	Offer customization - a project just for them
	Asked what has worked for them in the past - adapt	Access their comfort level with technology in advance	Be prepared to answer "why"	Offer peer level examples
	Let them define quality - fit your approach to that	Demonstrate the importance of a strong team	Present yourself as an information provider	Provide information and guidance
	Use testimonials from government, business, etc.	Customize your style to their unique needs	Use their peers as testimonials when possible	Be a coach
	Emphasize approach has worked in the past	Emphasize working with you will be a good experience	Appear to enjoy your work	Try to show them that work can be fun
	Respect their experience and ask about it	Communicate the long term benefits if possible	Convey this as an opportunity	Acknowledge their uniqueness
	Communicate sincerely and often	Communicate sincerely and often	Communicate sincerely and often	Communicate sincerely and often
Don'ts	Attempt to WOW them with data or newness	Assume you know or understand their needs	Try to underplay the challenge	Create a stressful environment
	Force the use of technology unnecessarily	Assume technology is the solution	View questions as an implied challenge	Forget the importance of their individuality
	Ignore their experiences	Be quick to judge their ideas	Expect them to have all the answers	Tell them what to do
	Show indifference	Show indifference	Show indifference	Show indifference

In summary, older generations are a natural match for their younger counterparts. Older workers are rich in experience and insight, younger workers can benefit from their successes and challenges. Combining that with the younger generation's enthusiasm and technical aptitudes, organizations can immensely benefit from this interaction in any type of Kaizen Event.

Managing Change

What is Change?

Most people express the emotion of fear – fear of the unknown when you mention or hint at change. Their mind jumps to fear of embarrassment, looking dumb, falling behind, not fitting in or being left out. These are some of the most common fears that come to mind.

This fear of change often raises the following troubling questions:

Is there a place for me? Will my job be eliminated? Will I be eliminated?

Before these issues are explored, "change" must first be defined to ensure a clear understanding of what is meant by change. Commonly, we all talk and moan and groan about it but can you define it?

Change *is a disruption; an intense human experience that requires individuals to experience loss or at least a letting go of the old way to make way for the new.* It is experienced individually. Change needs to be treated as a process - one that is ripe for continuous improvement efforts because very few organizations have gotten the change process "right" consistently as a fundamental business process.

People will react differently to any change. Leaders and managers tend to recognize that any type of significant change in an employee's work process is an emotional time for them and a "one size fits all" approach will not work.

"What do we mean by disruption?" We all work within some form of relationship - leadership/management, supervisors, and employees. These relationships are built on established expectations and agreements. Change can disrupt and alter these expectations, if not managed properly, which can and will hinder any type of Kaizen Event.

Each person experiences change to a different degree as well as at a different pace. It is a process that requires you to be aware that one person's experiences may differ from that of another. Change is a personal thing but your thoughts and fears are likely some of the same thoughts and fears that others (including your supervisor, manager, director, CFO ,CEO, etc.) may be losing sleep over. Being part of the process change that Kaizen Events bring may include some or all of the following fears:

- ❖ Too many stakeholders
- ❖ What sequence to bring on board?
- ❖ Tailoring messages takes time
- ❖ Competing for time with other project teams
- ❖ Geographical spread
- ❖ Lack of buy-in; denial of opportunity
- ❖ Lack of commitment

- Overcoming the skeptics/cynics
- Making the case that past learning will make a difference
- Providing enough information on the project without getting into solution mode
- Getting resources to assist during measurement
- Getting schedules aligned
- Overloaded with other things
- Getting trust of specialists where needed

Continuous improvement (Kaizen) is about change...change for the better. Things have to change in order to be able to improve. Status Quo management will not work with Kaizen. The following are some major challenges facing the leader, manager, or supervisor when bringing about change:

- How do you hang on to your good folks?
- How do you keep morale up and address resistance?
- Most important, how do you get the results senior leadership expects of your team?

Change is stressful and can fray everyone's nerves, if allowed. The following are the fundamental attributes regarding Kaizen Event change:

- No-one really has the power to change you. Others can influence you or exert pressure to encourage certain behaviors, but ultimately it is up to you. It is also true that you cannot change someone else. You can influence or exert pressure but ultimately it is up to the individual to change. You can only make it happen for yourself. So given this, a leader, manager, or team member must *influence* others to change their behaviors.
- Change management is concerned with making significant improvements succeed and making sure the business benefits are delivered quickly and smoothly. Change management focuses particularly on managing people through change to ensure that the behavioral benefits as well as the technical benefits are delivered - without these two any change (i.e., improvement) will not likely be sustained.

The road to change is bumpy and things do not always progress in a straight line. Organizations and individuals typically need to get down in the ditch before they can crawl out and onward. Having employees think and feel differently about any proposed changes will help leaders to better and more effective influence employee's behavior throughout the change process:

Thinking differently will help individuals to their change behavior and lead to better results by:

- Collecting data (not just numbers), and analyzing it
- Presenting the information logically to change people's thinking and not being afraid to address people's needs by outlining 'what's in it for them'
- Realizing that a change in thinking can lead to a significant change in behavior

---

Feeling differently can change behavior MORE and lead to different results by:

- ❖ Creating surprising, compelling and if possible, visual experiences
- ❖ Participating in the experience will change how people feel about the situation
- ❖ Realizing that a change in feeling can lead to a significant change in behavior

To have employees think and feel differently can be accomplished by the following:

- ❖ Discipline yourself to make contact face-to-face and address issues and the particular change
- ❖ Ask people for help
- ❖ Volunteer for new responsibilities
- ❖ Make people feel listened to
- ❖ Build relationships by confiding mutually
- ❖ Let people get the problem out – ask, do not prescribe or dictate
- ❖ Serve peoples' interests, do not "sell" them
- ❖ Help people become the solution
- ❖ Get supporters to carry the idea
- ❖ Deal directly and quickly with the resistors
- ❖ Deal with the people, the solution, and the events
- ❖ Communicate openly and honestly with the lukewarm stakeholders and the arguments against any proposed changes

People will change only if they:

- ❖ Believe they have the ability to accomplish the change goal
- ❖ Understand what is expected of them
- ❖ Want to make the change

The leader or contributing member of a Kaizen Event team is one of the change agents, who may or may not be the process owner. A successful change agent is a work-in-progress, a life-long learner constantly honing his/her personal skills to:

- ❖ Shape and share the vision so others can engage themselves in the "Big Picture"
- ❖ Create the need for change-"the wake up" call
- ❖ Identify and deal with any form of resistance
- ❖ Sustain or make change last by means of ongoing commitment and follow-through
- ❖ Measure change and monitor progress
- ❖ Work with others to identity and modify systems and structures as needed
- ❖ Inspire and mentor others

Kaizen Events will likely comprise employees that will easily accept any change to those that will be entirely against it. As a change agent in the Kaizen Event, ensure you understand what change is and how behavior can be influenced. Knowing that, as well as the next section *How to Manage Change*, will help ensure a successful Kaizen Event.

How to Manage Change

Peter Senge said, "People don't resist change. They resist being changed." This section will convey the basic principles of change as well as how to effectively manage change for all types of Kaizen Events. This will help ensure that employees don't just resist change, but move forward to accept it.

Managing change is the process of orchestrating the way improvements in the working environment are implemented and how to minimize disruption in the workforce. It is a key topic for leaders as well as employees to understand. In today's fast paced world, change and improvement is required for an organization to survive. Improper managing of change and/or natural resistance to change can cripple an organization. Proper management and understanding of change leads to a healthy, thriving, challenging and fun work environment.

Most people dread change, especially at work. At work, change means breaking with routine tasks in order to try things in a new way which forces employees out of their safety zone. This is one reason why many people are change-averse. Despite this resistance, change is necessary if a company wants to remain competitive. A good manager knows this and adapts their style of leadership and communication skills to define how the change is managed.

Fundamental to successful Kaizen Event in organizations is for leaders to cultivate a culture where change is good; that change or improvement to a process is imperative for the organization to grow and thrive. To do this, leaders must embrace change themselves, and continually communicate the need for changes before, during, and after the changes have occurred. One of a leader's responsibilities is to communicate the current realities for the organization and take a positive approach regarding the improvements or changes. If change takes this positive approach, the likelihood of the Kaizen Event to sustain any gains will be significantly increased.

The following steps or guidelines can be used to effectively manage change before, during, and after the Kaizen Event:

1. Help employees understand the answers to the following three questions:

Leadership Question	Answers
Why do we need change?	Explain the business reality. Educate people as to the global marketplace, competitors, customer needs and demands, and supplier issues. Present and benchmark information and data on productivity, quality, delivery, and people measures. People can handle the truth. Define the current state of affairs.
What do we need to do differently?	The leaders of the organization must create a shared vision. Explain and help people understand what a productive, high quality organization looks like. Define the future state vision and what the organization is trying to become. Give examples.
How do we change together?	Leaders must have a plan--what methods, people, measures, and the like will be deployed to achieve the future state. Provide a systematic, consistent approach to leadership, problem solving, and improvement. Don't hesitate to over-communicate. Explain, inform and involve people in the standard methods. This is what leadership is all about!

2. Understand resistance to change. Recognize that most resistance comes from deep rooted fears of the unknown that is typically related to a loss; fears of losing a job, losing pay or benefits, or status, or not being the expert, or of having to go back to school, or take a test. It is a natural human survival response. The objective then is for the leader or supervisor to address people's fears in a positive and constructive manner. The following table lists common resistance statements as well as responses that may be of value to the change agent or facilitator to address people's concerns in an appropriate way:

Common Resistance	Suggested Response
What problem? There is no problem here.	Check and confirm that the underlying problem is the real issue and has not gone away or morphed into something else.
Impracticality - It will never work!	Ask why and address objections one by one. Describe the basic features. Give it a try and then let's talk.
Jump to solutions.	Sell "we want to fix problems so that they stay fixed; Band-Aids or workarounds are no longer an option." To do this, we must try to understand, not assume, why things go wrong now. Collect data to support our position before moving to solutions.
Been there, done that - it didn't work...	Focus on small, achievable next steps to demonstrate that this experience is different and does work. Hold off on grand visions.
Attack	Remember the attack usually has nothing to do with you personally, although it may seem directed at you. Take a deep breath. Resist the temptation to fire back or walk away. Help the person work through it, if appropriate.
Confusion	Ask directly "what about this is confusing?" if they don't give you clues. Work back to the last point of understanding, then proceed more simply; include only key detail. Check for understanding.
Silence	Don't talk just to fill the silences. Think for a moment and then ask open ended questions that will provide you more information on where these folks are coming from. The open ended questions will prompt responses - good or bad; be sure to address each one.
Intellectualizing	Firmly guide the discussion back to practical next steps and accountabilities.
Blaming others	Focus on the process, not the people. Help the person identify the issue with the process and how he/she can contribute to improve the situation.
Passive-aggressive	If there is no resistance at all, get concerned. Make commitment requirements visible. Tie names to specific accountabilities in written plans, then refer to and share with key players and stakeholders.
Why do we have to do it this way? – Methodology objections	Work with your timekeeper to set a time limit to address method questions and any valid objection(s). Focus on outcomes, benefits, and the need for consensus to build momentum for the approach. WIIFM also proves helpful.
Wanting more detail.	Check and verify why more detail is needed. If you decide to provide more detail, be careful to make sure you do not remove the person's responsibility for the outcome.
Giving you too much detail.	Reconfirm the level of detail needed. Over thinking is a waste. Tie key points to "big picture" goals.
I don't have time for this!	Ask candidly what it would take for the person to prioritize this matter. Offer flexible meeting times, venues, assistance, etc.

Regardless of the type of Kaizen Event and throughout the Event answer questions employees ask, and try to understand their concerns. In business there are no guarantees, so do not over commit. Just tell people the truth, in a humane way. Open and honest dialogue is usually the best way to deal with all types of resistance.

For special cases, such as an extremely vocal resistor or resistance from other leaders, leaders need to develop more deliberate strategies. For vocal resistance, it may be appropriate to remove vocal individuals from the team by following your organizations performance management and disciplinary procedures. Leaders need to be clear that change and improvement is part of everyone's job.

3. Identify the specific type of change that will be required from each employee. How will their daily tasks change? Will there be additional training? How will each employee be measured in accepting the change or in his or her new duties? These questions must be considered when creating the specific improvement activities in a Kaizen Event.

4. Understand the managing change time line (below graph) and the following explanations for additional support. Use it to identify strategies to deal with resistance in the Kaizen Event.

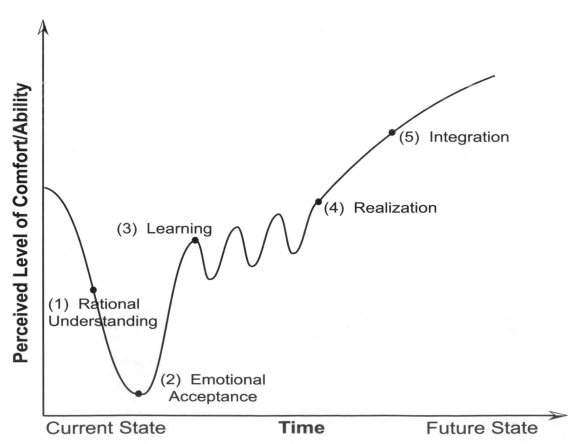

Kaizen Demystified

(1) *Rational Understanding* - This is the realization that there may very well be a need for change; the perceived competence decreases again. Employees focus on finding short term solutions, thus they only cure symptoms. There is no willingness to change one's own patterns of behavior. This stage may be met with *"I get it, but I am unsure where this will take me!"*

(2) *Emotional Acceptance* - This is also called the 'buy-in" phase and is the most important one. Only if management succeeds to create willingness for changing values, beliefs, and behaviors, the organization will be able to make real change happen. This stage may be met with *"It seems that it doesn't matter what I say or do!"* but evolves to a readiness to find out more and explore the opportunities.

(3) *Learning* - The new acceptance of change creates a new willingness for learning to make the best of the change. Employees start to try new behaviors and processes using the PDCA cycle. They will experience success and failure during this phase. It is the change managers task to create some early wins (e.g., by starting with easier projects, providing one-on-one support with certain employees, etc.); their perceived individual level of comfort and ability to perform required tasks increases. This stage may be met with *"I guess this change can't be all bad!"*

(4) *Realization* - This is when employees start to communicate in a positive way regarding the change. This communication has a feedback-effect. Employees begin to understand which behavior is effective in which situation. This, in turn, opens up their minds for new experiences. These extended patterns of behavior increase organizational flexibility; their perceived competency has reached a higher level than prior to change. This stage may be met with *"I can't believe I was so against this change. I can do that!"* Some may even acknowledge the benefits.

(5) *Integration* - Employees totally integrate their newly acquired patterns of thinking and acting. The new behaviors become routine and the organization has experienced a positive change. This stage may be met with *"I now understand how this change has benefited our organization. I am glad I was able to contribute to make it happen!"* Some may even go far to say *"I enjoy my job. It doesn't feel like hard work any more!"*

5. Look for subtle change in resistance behaviors and address them quickly. Keep communication channels open throughout the Kaizen Event, not only with the team members and managers, but those that will be part of the change or new process. This can be done via email updates, postings, face-to-faces, etc.

Keep in mind that cultural changes are not quick-fixes. Such changes take significant time and investment to hard-wire the new way of doing business with any Lean transformation. Kaizen Events, although can provide both significant and incremental improvements, are a new way of doing business, way outside the status quo for the vast majority of enterprises.

Kaizen Events can provide both significant and incremental improvements but they are a different way of doing business, which is significantly beyond the status quo for the vast majority of enterprises. This reality cannot be discounted or treated lightly. Although the tools are straight forward, the required fortitude, patience and perseverance needed to change the culture is what determines success with continuous improvement and sustainable outcomes.

Leadership and Coaching

First of all, we need to differentiate management from leadership (and coaching). It is a common practice for people to use these two terms interchangeably. However, they are very different. Stephen Covey defines the two terms by explaining that people manage things...data and information. People lead people. Therefore, with these two definitions behind us, this section of the book will concentrate on the dynamics behind people leading people for all types of Kaizen activities. Even though we will be primarily addressing the supervisor or manager (or process owner), team leader or facilitator (e.g., a Black Belt, Lean Sensei, or Continuous Improvement Specialist), team members would also find value in this information. It is from the team members that the "informal" leaders will arise and be a catalyst for not only the current event, but subsequent ones as well. Therefore, the Kaizen Event Leadership chapter will provide specific skills on how to effectively lead a Kaizen Event when dealing with those non-technical (or people) issues and problems.

If you take the personal aspect out of leadership, then you are leading only from a position of authority or title. A person who is abusing his or her authority, and accomplishing tasks using threats, may be considered to be leading the effort. However, very few people would consider this person to be exhibiting leadership qualities. This is because a true leader – a person exhibiting the qualities associated with effective leadership, leads through coaching, mentoring, and influencing.

To truly be a leader you must have people who are willing to follow. That is where the trust issue comes in. Trust is personal. Trust is the product of time spent between individuals or between the leader and his or her team. Trust is the product of a relationship between people and an essential component of effective leadership and quickly be a determining factor in the success of a Kaizen Event.

The critical issue surrounding trust is the understanding that trust must be earned. Additionally, the reality of trust is that it is something that may take a great deal of time to achieve and yet take only a matter of seconds to lose. This reality is what makes being a leader so difficult, as the leader must always be "on," to a degree, in the face of the follower.

The three leadership practices that will help ensure a successful Kaizen Event, if applied effectively, are as follows:

Effort

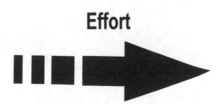

1. Leading from the rear
   - Let others lead
   - Assist those struggling
   - Be supportive
   - Coach
   - Mentor

2. Leading from within the team
   - Listen   - Assess
   - Watch   - Suggest
   - Engage   - Assist
   - Participate

3. Leading from the front
   - Vision
   - Direction
   - Proactive
   - Directing
   - Telling

The leader will be leading from the front by establishing the vision for the team and providing direction to the team to accomplish the tasks as defined by the Team Charter. In this case the leader is leading from the front. Then, during the team's execution of the task or project (the PDCA Implementation Phase), it is important that the leader monitor the effort – to listen, watch, and assess - in order to make timely and effective course corrections to the team. In this case the leader is leading from inside of the effort. He or she is, in effect, being an integral member of the team during execution of the task. Finally, effective leaders lead from the rear...allowing strong members of the team to exhibit their own leadership skills while taking time to work with those individuals who may be struggling as team members. Performing leadership from each of these positions will enhance team member's trust in the leader. This will help to ensure a successful Kaizen Event.

Note: For practical tips and tools for addressing those "people-issue" challenges within a Kaizen Event, read Chapter 5. Kaizen Event Leadership.

A3 Report

*The **A3 Report** is designed to help you "tell the story" in a logical and visual way with reference to a particular subject matter.* The A3 refers to size 11" X 17" paper, however, in today's applications it can be any type of medium that is easily viewed. The main types of A3 Reports are: Continuous Improvement and Problem Solving (or Project) - the focus of this section, Status, Proposal, and Strategic (or Hoshin) Planning. The A3 Project Report was originally developed by Toyota to represent a problem or improvement initiative in the field with paper.

There are typically eight steps or categories of the A3 Project Report type (the more common one that is used in Kaizen Events); however, there may be more or less of the steps depending on the project. For example, step 7. Verify Results (next page) may be divided into Pre-Metrics and Post-Metrics, or, step 1. Problem Statement may be renamed to Current Business Case, etc. The overall purpose of this tool is to efficiently display relevant information on one page (or Desktop/Tablet screen) in a logical sequence relative to an improvement project or problem solving activity as well as be a road map for your project. Relevant data or information should be represented on the A3, however if the information does not fit, additional sheets may be used and then referenced on the A3.

The A3 Project Report provides a consistent approach for learning and applying the Lean Six Sigma tools. It is simple and typically organized as a series of boxes in a template, which structures your problem solving or continuous improvement initiatives. It is used to help employees "think" Lean.

The following are the benefits that can be obtained by using the A3 Project Report:

❖ It provides a single, easy-to-use approach or methodology for any type of problem solving or continuous improvement project.
❖ It frees people up to focus on the root causes of problems - without needing to reinvent new ways of reporting.
❖ The A3 "thinking" or Lean thinking stimulates group dialogue and creative problem solving and builds consensus based on objective facts.
❖ Breaks people of the bad habit of jumping to solutions before defining the root causes.
❖ Instills an organizational culture of "learning to learn."
❖ Grooms new leaders and teams to solve problems in a scientifically repeatable (i.e., standard) way.
❖ Provides a systematic logical thinking process. It teaches people to see a problem or improvement opportunity, understand and "see" cause and effect relationships at-a-glance.

The main A3 Project Report sections are:

1. Problem Statement - Define the business problem, issue, or specific improvement project.

2. Current State - Describe the current state by completing a process or value stream map, a graph or chart denoting a negative trend, etc.

3. Improvement Opportunity - Identify the desired outcomes and targets.

4. Problem Analysis - Examine the process in detail using a Fishbone Analysis, Brainstorming, 5 Why Analysis, Impact Map, etc.

5. Future State - Create a future state free of waste.

6. Implementation Plan - The specific steps, Who, What, When, etc. for the process changes (referred to as PDCAs) and complete as planned.

7. Verify Results - Show before and after measurements using good charting methods.

8. Follow-Up - Create a plan for system-wide roll-out, if applicable, training, and possibly use SPC and Visual Management principles to monitor process changes.

The following A3 Project Report aligns Key Questions with the eight main categories of the A3:

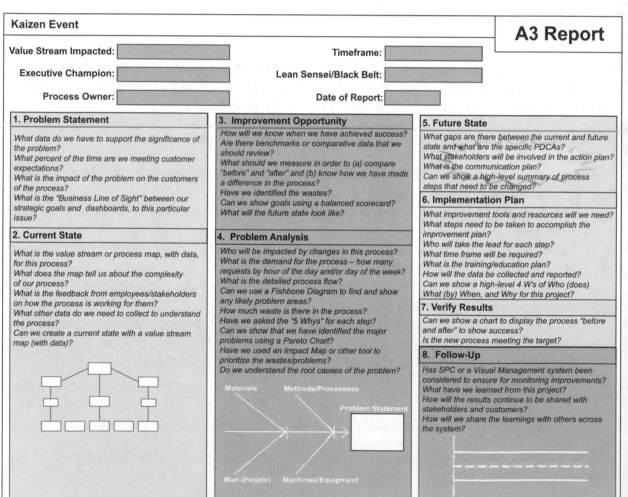

Note: The title A3 Project Report has been shortened to A3 Report or simply A3.

The following A3 Report aligns the main Lean Six Sigma tools with the eight main categories of the A3:

Kaizen Event | **A3 Report**

Value Stream Impacted: _____ Timeframe: _____

Executive Champion: _____ Lean Sensei/Black Belt: _____

Process Owner: _____ Date of Report: _____

1. Problem Statement

Charters
Team Selection and Buidling
Effective Meetings
Project Management

2. Current State

Value Stream and Process Maps
(w/ SIPOC Diagrams)

3. Improvement Opportunity

Waste Walk
VA versus NVA Analysis
Constraint Analysis
Demand Analysis Plots and Takt Time
VOC/QFD
MSA
Process Capability

4. Problem Analysis

Charting
Brainstorming
Cause and Effect (or Fishbone) Diagram
5 Whys
Interrelationship Diagram
Employee Balance Chart
Force Field Analysis
Impact Map

Materials   Methods/Processes

Problem Statement

Man (People)   Machines/Equipment

5. Future State

(Value Stream and Process Maps)
Kaizen Events
PDCAs

6. Implementation Plan

5S	Mass Customization
Visual Controls	Flow
Mistake Proofing	Quick Changeovers
Standard Work	Total Productive
Process or Work	Maintenance
Area Layout	Cross-Training

7. Verify Results

(Charting)

8. Follow-Up

Statistical Process Control
Visual Management
Standard Work for Leaders
Layered Process Audits

Please see *The Lean Six Sigma Pocket Guide XL, The Practical Lean Six Sigma Pocket Guide, Practical Lean Six Sigma for Healthcare,* and *The Practical Lean Six Sigma Pocket Guide for Healthcare* books for a detailed explanation for each of the tools listed as well as mini case studies and examples for each.

During any of the team-based Kaizen Events, the A3 (Project) Report can be used as a Storyboard to create an executive summary. The main activities for each of the three Kaizen Event phases will reference the specific A3 Report section that needs to be completed. Therefore, at the end of the Kaizen Event project, the completed A3 would be the formal project summary to be appropriately shared throughout the organization for a transfer of knowledge. It is highly recommended that the A3 Report be completed as you progress throughout the project to serve as a status-type report.

Note: See page 200 for an A3 Report example from a Standard 5 Day Kaizen Event.

What is Lean A3 Thinking?

A3 Thinking is basically Lean Thinking. It is looking and documenting a problem or improvement initiative in a standard format allowing for waste-free reporting and communications (i.e. sharing). Lean Thinking, as it applies to report writing, allows for an improved thought process of those individuals on the team, in that, problems/issues, etc. are condensed or seen as to what can be absorbed or solved easily - eliminating extraneous data or information. Through this process, the team member will start to "see" issues and problems more clearly as well as possible solutions. Using the A3 structure as a thought process will accelerate Lean Sigma implementation efforts.

Note: It is recommended each team member also receive *The A3 Pocket Handbook for Kaizen Events* to document team and individual activities. The book includes Lean Thinking Statements and Lean Thinking Questions that follows the A3 Report format to keep team members engaged in the project as well as be a repository for organizational knowledge.

Note: There is an Add-On for MS Office Excel called QI Macros that has over 90 charts and graphs for assisting in data presentation and analysis. It is a fill-in-the-blanks for chart and documentation templates (the A3 Report being one of them). Also, check your favorite app store for the Practical Lean Six Sigma for Healthcare Series - A3 Report app as well as other apps. Consider GoodNotes, QuickOffice, or comparable type application to interactively modify the A3 on your Tablet or smart device.

How to Select Your Kaizen Event Type

This section provides the information required for you to select the type of Kaizen Event that best fits your needs. A thorough and detailed description for each of five types of Kaizen Events, a Kaizen Event Decision Flowchart, Kaizen Event Summary Matrix, and a Kaizen Event Summary Checklist are contained in this section and should assist you in how to select your Kaizen Event.

Understanding Process Variation for Kaizen Events

Common causes of variation often lie hidden within the system, and are sometimes assumed to be unavoidable. Yet it is very possible, and often very rewarding, to improve processes and reduce common cause variation. Experience had shown that, amongst the people in and around the process, there are enough ideas for improvements to make a significant impact, even on a sound process. This means Near Zero or defect free processes. However, when a process is being affected by special causes of variation, it is called "unstable" or "out of control." Removing special causes when they are harmful (which is most of the time) or integrating them when they are beneficial (which is rare) is an important part of process improvement. Kaizen Events (or typically Lean or process improvement-type projects) may center around logistics, cycle time, flexibility/responsiveness, flow issues, delays, bottlenecks, or asset utilization problems (i.e., typically associated with special cause variation); however, if you are trying to reduce a 24 hour burn-in cycle by 85%, or you are trying to optimize anodizing schedules for a $22 million progressive assembly operation, or you are trying to strategically reduce your inventory in your distribution centers for quick response (i.e., typically associated with common cause variation) the quantitative analysis of the Six Sigma tools may provide the answers. This is not to say Lean tools will not be utilized in these scenarios; however, the main tool set of statistical analysis with Six Sigma may be a better fit when a process has to be redesigned. Kaizen Events are used to systematically implement the correct tool set for eliminating special cause and common cause variations from processes to ultimately increase the quality of the product or service at a lower cost with Total Employee Involvement.

Types of Kaizen Events

The five types of Kaizen Events are:

1. Standard 5 Day Kaizen Event (team-based)
2. Rolling Kaizen Event (team-based)
3. Web Based Kaizen Event (team-based)
4. Today's Kaizen Event (team-based)
5. Wiki (or Quick) Kaizen Event (individual-based)

Each Kaizen Event type will have three parts or phases. The three parts are:

Part 1. Planning Phase (or Determination Phase for the Wiki Kaizen Event Type)
Part 2. PDCA Implementation Phase
Part 3. Follow-Up Phase (or Sharing Phase for the Wiki Kaizen Event Type)

The following are the definitions and main attributes for each of the Kaizen Event types:

1. **Standard 5 Day Kaizen Events**, *also referred to as Kaizen Blitzes or Rapid Improvement Events (RIE), are targeted improvement activities (PDCAs) used by teams to implement improvements quickly in a specific area.* The Standard 5 Day Kaizen Event allows teams to implement significant improvements in a relatively short time-frame when the area or process is fairly easily accessible. This type of Event is typically used for major restructuring of an area, cell, or department.

The following are the attributes for this type of Kaizen Event (italics signifies main differences from the other types):

- ❖ *Team can physically meet in one place for 3 – 5 days*
- ❖ *Processes or areas immediately accessible*
- ❖ *Resources (facilities, equipment, employees) are immediately and physically available*
- ❖ *Process change (PDCAs) tested or implemented during the 3 – 5 days*
- ❖ *Immediate attention is required*
- ❖ *Problem not too complex to solve (or implement trial solutions) within the 5 days*
- ❖ *80% of the training is broad and 20% is specific**
- ❖ *Focus efforts during the 3 – 5 days with entire team, then sub teams to monitor*
- ❖ *High cost due to employees time being present during the 3 - 5 days*
- ❖ Process may require using experiments and/or statistical methods to determine root cause
- ❖ Large (typically more than 1 department) or small (changes only within the department) scope
- ❖ Team required
- ❖ Management involvement
- ❖ May require statistical analysis to determine root cause
- ❖ 5S may be implemented to demonstrate a "change" to the area or process, allowing for everyone in the area to be involved

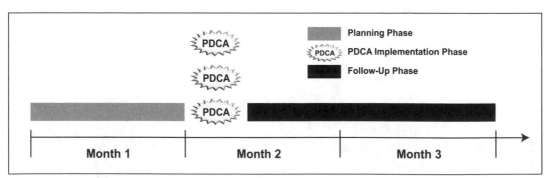

*Broad training is a comprehensive explanation of Lean and Six Sigma tools and concepts. The tools and concepts are thoroughly explained via PowerPoint presentation, examples, exercises, and a simulation. Specific training is presenting a comprehensive explanation of the "likely" tools and/or concepts that may be used.

2. **_Rolling Kaizen Events_** _are targeted improvement activities (PDCAs) used by teams to implement improvements or solve a problem in a specific area that can only be accessed in-frequently and/or the resources are not available for immediate use; therefore, resources and improvements must be allocated over time._

The following are the attributes for this type of Kaizen Event (italics signifies main differences from the other types):

- ❖ _Team can physically meet in small increments of time (1-2 hours)_
- ❖ _Processes or areas accessible over time_
- ❖ _Process changes (PDCAs) continuously applied over 3 months_
- ❖ _Complex problem that may need time to be resolved_
- ❖ _80% of the training is specific and 20% is broad_
- ❖ Large (typically more than 1 department) or small (changes only within the department) scope
- ❖ Team required
- ❖ Resources (facilities, equipment, employees) are immediately and physically available
- ❖ Process may require using experiments and/or statistical methods to determine root cause
- ❖ Regular meetings required throughout the 3 months
- ❖ Process change happens throughout the 3 month period
- ❖ Management involvement
- ❖ May require statistical analysis to determine root cause
- ❖ Medium-to-Low cost due to employees not being away from their work for any extended period
- ❖ 5S may be implemented to demonstrate a "change" to the area or process, allowing for everyone in the area to be involved

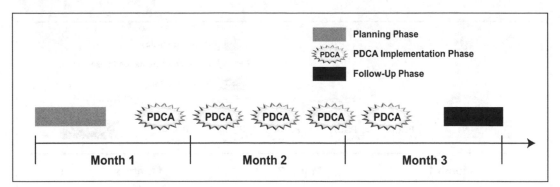

3. **Web Based Kaizen Events** *are targeted improvement activities (PDCAs) used by team members using emerging technologies to plan, implement, and sustain improvements or solve a problem over time.*

The following are the attributes for this type of Kaizen Event (italics signifies main differences from the other types):

- *Team cannot physically meet in one place*
- *Medium cost due to limited time commitment with employees; however, Web conferencing application may be costly*
- *Web-based conferencing tools (i.e., emerging technologies) used as main form of communications*
- Large (typically more than 1 department) or small (changes only within the department) scope
- Team required
- Process not immediately accessible
- Resources (facilities, equipment, employees) are not immediately and physically available
- Immediate attention is required
- Process changes (PDCAs) continuously applied over 3 months
- Complex problem that may need time to be resolved
- Root cause may or may not be known
- Process may require using experiments and/or statistical methods to determine root cause
- 80% of the training is specific and 20% is broad
- Numerous meetings required throughout the 3 months
- Process change happens throughout the 3 month period
- Management involvement
- May require statistical analysis to determine root cause

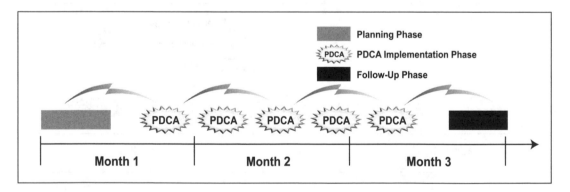

4. **Today's Kaizen Events** *are used by teams to find and implement solutions to a known problem or continuous improvement initiative within a short time period (less than four weeks).* Team members meet for a one day planning and brainstorming session with key stakeholders to build consensus on exactly what needs to be done. Teams use a variety of techniques to quickly generate ideas: round robin idea generating, idea mapping, brainstorming, etc. to work through solutions to barriers that the team has identified in this one day. This type of Kaizen Event is used due to an urgent problem that has arisen; root cause is known, and solution fairly apparent. This type of Event can also be used to implement a time-tested solution, such as 5S to an area requiring immediate organization, implementing a kanban system due to excess inventory, etc.

The following are the attributes for this type of Kaizen Event (italics signifies main differences from the other types):

- ❖ *Small (changes only within the department) scope*
- ❖ *Team initially required to detail subsequent activities and/or team involvement*
- ❖ *Process changes (PDCAs) applied within days or a few weeks after the 1 day meeting*
- ❖ *Root cause known*
- ❖ Process immediately accessible
- ❖ Resources (facilities, equipment, employees) are available
- ❖ Immediate attention is required
- ❖ 100% of the training is specific
- ❖ Management involvement
- ❖ Low cost due to limited time commitment with employees
- ❖ Duration is four weeks, with 1 day (or less) of the Planning Phase dedicated for a meeting with stakeholders to create the implementation plan

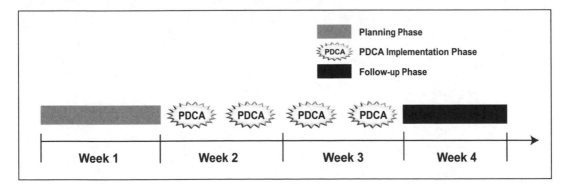

5. **Wiki (or Quick) Kaizen Events** *are quick, easy-to-implement improvements by the front-line worker that does not typically require any type of team collaboration or approval.* This type of Event is becoming popular due to emerging technologies that allow for sharing of information seamlessly and communicating with colleagues real-time, while encouraging employees to make improvements happen.

The following are the attributes for this type of Kaizen Event (italics signifies main differences from the other types):

- ❖ *Small (changes only within the department) scope*
- ❖ *Team not required*
- ❖ Process immediately accessible
- ❖ Resources (facilities, equipment, employees) are available
- ❖ Root cause known
- ❖ 100% of the training is specific
- ❖ Low cost

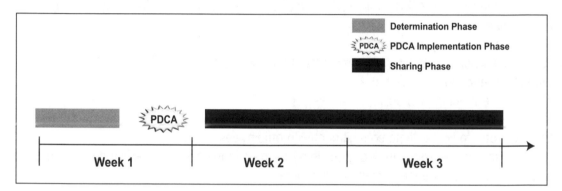

Kaizen Event Summary Matrix

The following Kaizen Event Summary Matrix is a compilation of the characteristics for each type of Kaizen Event.

Characteristic	Standard 5 Day	Rolling	Web Based	Today's	Wiki (or Quick)
Length of Project	3 - 4 Months	3 - 4 Months	3 - 4 Months	1 - 4 Weeks	1 - 2 Weeks
Large Scope (crosses departments)	YES	YES	YES	NO	NO
Small Scope (within the department)	YES	YES	YES	YES	YES
Immediate Attention Required	YES	NO	YES	YES	NO
Process Immediately Accessible	YES	NO	YES	YES	YES
Root Cause May Be Known	NO	NO	NO	YES	YES
Specific Training Required	YES	YES	YES	YES	YES
Broad Training Required	YES	YES	NO	NO	NO
Team Members Physically (Locally) Available	YES	YES	NO	YES	NO
Meeting Times < 4 Hours	NO	YES	YES	NO	YES
Process Change (PDCAs) Continuously Applied Over a Few Days	YES	NO	NO	YES	YES
Management Involvement	YES	YES	YES	YES	NO
5S Applied	YES	YES	YES	NO	NO
Training Costs a Factor	YES	YES	YES	NO	NO
Requires Detailed Planning Meetngs	YES	YES	YES	NO	NO
May Require Statistical Methods to Determine Root Cause	YES	YES	YES	NO	NO
Web-based Collaboration Application Main Form of Communication	NO	NO	YES	NO	NO
Team Required	YES	YES	YES	YES	NO
Value Stream or Process Map Required	YES	YES	YES	NO	NO
Will Impact Balanced Scorecard or Performance Dashboard Metric	YES	YES	YES	YES	NO
Team Charter Required	YES	YES	YES	NO	NO

Note: While the terms "YES" and "NO" are used for the Kaizen Event Summary Matrix characteristics, the word "YES" could be substituted for "LIKELY" and the word "NO" substituted for "UNLIKELY."

Use the Matrix as a guide to help select the Kaizen Event type that best fits your specific needs.

Kaizen Event Summary Quick Checklist

The following is a quick checklist to help select the appropriate Kaizen Event type:

Kaizen Event	Kaizen Event Summary Quick Checklist

Value Stream: [   ]

Department: [   ]

Key Questions to Ask	Yes	No
Is a team required?	Standard 5 Day Rolling Web Based Today's	Wiki
Can you physically meet in one place?	Standard 5 Day Rolling Today's	Web Based
Are the solutions known and just need to work out the details for planning the improvements?	Today's	Standard 5 Day Web Based Today's
Can a solution be piloted or implemented within 3 - 5 days with a dedicated team that is physically present?	Standard 5 Day	Rolling Web Based
Are team members only physically available for short periods of time regarding the problem?	Rolling	Standard 5 Day Today's

For immediate access to...	Go to page...
Standard 5 Day Kaizen Event	71
Rolling Kaizen Event	169
Web Based Kaizen Event	203
Today's Kaizen Event	249
Wiki Kaizen Event	269

Use the additional attibutes listed in this chapter to select the type of Kaizen Event that will be of most value.

Note: It is recommended you first read the Standard 5 Day Kaizen Event section (pages 71 - 141) and then proceed to the specific Kaizen Event.

Kaizen Event Decision Flowchart

The following flowchart is a quick reference to determine which type of Kaizen Event may best suit your needs. It provides a high-level decision tree for each of the Kaizen Event types.

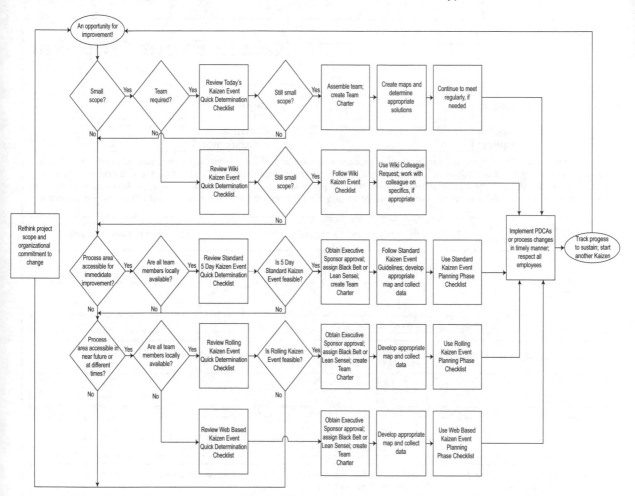

Each Kaizen Event type is comprised of similar tools, worksheets, and guidelines. However, for each type of Kaizen Event there will be a slightly different approach and possible use of the worksheets. It is suggested that all five Kaizen Event types be reviewed to see their commonality. Subsequently, determine the type or types of Kaizen Events that will provide the most value for your organization. If appropriate, customize them to fit your specific business needs.

Kaizen Event Proposal

The following Kaizen Event Proposal is used to communicate to upper management there exists an opportunity for an improvement:

Kaizen Event

Kaizen Event Proposal

Name: _____ **Department:** _____

Upstream Supplier: _____ **Downstream Customer:** _____

The Kaizen Event Proposal is a communication tool between the supervisor or manager of a department and the next level to determine the feasibiliy of an improvement project. The proposal may be initiated due to a problem or issue facing the employees in the department. The proposal will provide an overview of the issue or problem as well as the resources required. **It may also be used to verify or align improvement activities with departmental performance goals.**

Step 1: Describe the Problem or Opportunity.	Include photos, charts, and graphs, if necessary. Include current measurements.

Proposed Start Date: _____

Step 2: List Potential Benefits.	Be specific in terms of how the team's success will be measured. Use Balance Scorecard measures, if possible.

Proposed End Date: _____

Step 3: List Resources Required.	Include support needed from IT, HR, etc. Also, estimate the time commitment for each, if appropriate.

Type of Support	Estimated Hours Needed	Department/Colleague	Dates Requested

Step 4: Determine Feasibility and Next Steps.

❑ Approved As A Standard 5 Day Kaizen Event ❑ Approved As A Web Based Kaizen Event
❑ Approved As A Rolling Kaizen Event ❑ Approved As A Wiki Kaizen Event
❑ Approved As A Today's Kaizen Event ❑ Need More Information
❑ Currently Being Addressed

Sign-Off Date: _____

The Kaizen Event Proposal will be driven by the following needs or demands:

- ❖ Customer/market needs and requests for improvements which would include outside customers as well as internal customers
- ❖ Underperforming areas indicated by key metrics or performance outcomes/results
- ❖ Value stream or process maps indicating areas of wastes (and opportunities)
- ❖ Assessment scores or customer audits

Note: The Kaizen Event Proposal would not be prepared when the initiative is assigned to a manager or supervisor.

The Kaizen Event Proposal can be easily recreated in Excel or a Customer Relationship Management (CRM) application. It can also be created in Google Drive (as long as everyone has access to the Internet). The form can also be submitted in the text of an email or some other form of emerging technology. However, the information submitted should be standardized to what is required, where it is sent, and when a decision will be made.

Once the form is submitted the following should occur from the next level of management (Step 4 of the Kaizen Event Proposal) which will typically be a manager, director, V.P. or the process owner:

Approved As A Standard 5 Day Kaizen Event - Thank the manager, supervisor, and/or employee for the idea. Provide support and guidance if needed. Ensure you are committed to the project and establish a good line of communications.

Approved As A Rolling Kaizen Event - Thank the manager, supervisor, and/or employee for the idea. The issue confronting the department and organization may be lacking the necessary resources to commit the time, resources and/or energy now. However, the Rolling Kaizen Event would spread this commitment out over time, which would be a WIN-WIN for all.

Approved As A Today's Kaizen Event - Thank the manager, supervisor, and/or employee for the idea. Be specific as to what the next steps should be. Provide additional information as to why this should be undertaken as a Today's Kaizen event instead of as a Rolling Kaizen Event as requested.

Approved As A Web Based Kaizen Event - Thank the manager, supervisor, and/or employee for the idea. The issue confronting the department and organization may be lacking the necessary resources to commit the time, resources and/or energy now. However, the Web Based Event would spread this commitment out over time if employees are not local or physically present, which would be a WIN-WIN for all.

Approved As A Wiki Kaizen Event - Thank the manager, supervisor, and/or employee for the idea. The issue described may only require minimal resources and a formal team may not be required.

Need More Information - Thank the manager, supervisor, and/or employee for the idea. Let the submitter know if another type of measurable is needed under the List Potential Benefits section? Are the List Resources Required not clear enough?

Currently Being Addressed - Thank the manager, supervisor, and/or employee for the idea. Explain how a current program or project will address the issue that was identified in the proposal. If this is the case, better communication with the on-going project should occur throughout the organization. Consider having the manager or supervisor or someone from the department participate on the current team that is addressing the problem, or at least be an ad hoc team member that can provide input when needed.

Adapt the Kaizen Event Proposal to your organization. Many organizations may already have methods in place to propose projects. Determine if those methods or avenues of communication are being used, and if so, modify accordingly. Modification may be by simplifying the form, making the form Web-accessibility (e.g., Google Drive), or through a quick discussion using FaceTime or Skype. The overall intent of the Kaizen Event Proposal form is to standardize an improvement project proposal process.

Regardless of the selection in Step 4 of the Kaizen Event Proposal, the supervisor or manager should be notified of the decision within 1 – 2 business days, if at all possible. Or, at a minimum, a thank you for submitting the form should be done immediately (within 1 business day) with an expected time frame on the forthcoming response.

Chapter 2. Kaizen Event Types
Standard 5 Day Kaizen Event

This chapter is suggested to be read by everyone. You may also have identified your project as a Standard 5 Day Kaizen Event from the How to Select Your Kaizen Event Type (pages 59 -70).

Overview

Standard 5 Day Kaizen Events, *also referred to as Kaizen Blitzes or Rapid Improvement Events (RIEs), are targeted improvement activities (PDCAs) used by teams to implement improvements quickly in a specific area.* Teams use the Standard 5 Day Kaizen Event to implement significant improvements in a relatively short time-frame.

The following is the Standard 5 Day Kaizen Event Quick Determination Checklist to ensure this is the type of Kaizen Event required given your specific situation. Ensure the majority of Characteristics are checked as Yes or Likely in the Your Situation column.

Characteristic	YES or LIKELY	Your Situation	Characteristic	YES or LIKELY	Your Situation
Large Scope (crosses departments)	✔		Management Involvement	✔	
			5S Applied	✔	
Small Scope (within the department)	✔		Training Costs a Factor	✔	
			Requires Detailed Planning Meetngs	✔	
Immediate Attention Required	✔				
Process Immediately Accessible	✔		May Require Statistical Methods to Determine Root Cause	✔	
Root Cause Known					
Specific Training Required	✔		Web-based Collaboration Application Main Form of Communication		
Broad Training Required	✔		Team Required	✔	
Team Members Physically (Locally) Available	✔		Value Stream or Process Map Required	✔	
Meeting Times < 4 Hours			Likely Will Impact Balanced Scorecard or Performance Dashboard Metric	✔	
Process Change (PDCAs) Continuously Applied Over a Few Days	✔		Team Charter Required	✔	

Table title: **Standard 5 Day Kaizen Event Quick Determination Checklist**

A successful Standard 5 Day Kaizen Event must have following conditions present:

- ❖ Process or area available during the time period.
- ❖ Good communications with everyone involved.
- ❖ Nearly all team members are local and available.
- ❖ Resources such as time, training, other departments for support, etc. will be available.
- ❖ Management committed and engaged in the project.
- ❖ Process area employees' ideas are considered (as only a few will be on the team).
- ❖ All employees are treated with dignity and respect.

The Standard 5 Day Kaizen Event was very popular in the 1990s when Lean (i.e., The Toyota Production System) became a widespread improvement platform (outside of Japan). Manufacturing was implementing significant change in their production facilities by reducing inventories and consolidating floor space through the implementation of the Lean tools of cell layout, continuous flow and kanbans, visual controls, etc. This required a major physical change requiring a tightly controlled and focused effort in a relatively short time period. Also, management wanted to demonstrate a commitment to continuous improvement by dedicating resources and people. The Standard 5 Day Kaizen Event was a perfect platform to do this. However, this is not the case so much today; therefore, the "standard" Kaizen Event has evolved into these other types of Kaizen Events to meet today's demand for continuous improvement. The Standard 5 Day Kaizen Event is still considered a valuable tool for those organizations that require a significant change in a short period of time.

Steps and Forms

The following steps and forms should be used as a guide to customize a Standard 5 Day Kaizen Event to fit your organization requirements. There are many variables to consider, some of which are:

❖ Number employees that are part of the project team as well as the process area employees that require training in Lean and/or Six Sigma (which may require two levels of training)
❖ Number of Continuous Improvement Specialists, Black Belts, or Lean Senseis available for support in training and/or facilitating improvement projects
❖ Managers or supervisors ability to lead continuous improvement projects – they may be great as a departmental leader, but lack the facilitation skills to get employees effectively engaged
❖ Availability of time to be dedicated to a Kaizen Event
❖ How management will stay involved in the project, especially during the Standard 5 Day Kaizen Event of the event
❖ Team members' availability
❖ Complexity of the project
❖ How to address previous negative experiences with team projects
❖ How to effectively manage change
❖ Other departmental needs

The Standard 5 Day Kaizen Event is comprised of three phases:

Part 1. Planning Phase (spans 3 - 4 weeks)

Part 2. PDCA Implementation Phase (spans 3 - 5 days)

Part 3. Follow-Up Phase (spans 2 - 4 weeks)

Each of these will be explored in detail along with the recommended forms to be used.

The activities required for a successful Standard 5 Day Kaizen Event will be presented in a linear fashion; however, many of detailed activities listed can be completed at different times and/or in parallel. For example, the value stream mapping exercise that is listed as an activity in the Planning Phase – 3 Weeks Out could also be completed (or updated) in the Planning Phase – 2 Weeks Out or 1 Week Out. Or, if it is not a complex process, can also be done in Day 1 of the PDCA Implementation Phase.

There are "suggested" time frames for each of the phases. These time frames are general in nature and will require more or less time depending on the complexity of the process, Lean Sigma knowledge of the facilitator or Black Belt as well as the team members, activities that can be only done by certain team members, and availability of the team members.

Part 1. Planning Phase (spans 3 - 4 weeks/12 - 16 hours meeting time)

The foundation for success of any improvement project is determined by the amount of detail that goes into the plan. The saying, "the devil is in the details" certainly fits here. Employee's time is a valuable commodity, and even though they are getting paid whether sitting in a conference room working on a continuous improvement project or in their area working a daily routine, their time should be respected. The employees selected to be on a Kaizen Event team will most likely incur additional stress due to having to work a little extra before or after the entire Kaizen Event to catch up. This may include working overtime, evenings, during lunch, or taking work home with them. Therefore, the time that they are part of the Kaizen Event must be used wisely. This must start from the initial communications that occurs in the Planning Phase, up through and including all parts of the Follow-Up Phase. The energy, passion, and commitment to sustain the improvements from the team members will be predicated on how well they are treated and respected!

The Planning Phase is further segmented into 3 – 2 – 1 weeks leading up to the PDCA Implementation Phase.

Note: The Planning Phase includes all the activities prior to implementing the process changes. Keep in mind that these are guidelines and the various activities listed can be completed in different parts of this Phase, as well as, at times, be incorporated into the Part 2. The PDCA Implementation Phase.

3 Weeks (spans 4 hours before the PDCA Implementation Phase)

The following steps can be used as a guide:

1. Determine project scope. This is critical to align management expectations with the departmental manager or supervisor (or process owner) to ensure resources are used wisely. The process owner is the person who is responsible for the area or process. The responsibilities of a process owner would include such things as conducting performance reviews, attending management or departmental meetings, and being responsible for the group's work.

Determining project scope can be done in a variety of ways, some of which are:

a. Using the Balanced Scorecard, Performance, or Dashboard measurements that indicate a negative trend and root cause is not known. Immediate action is required.
b. Addressing customer mandates that require an immediate change in processes or their business may go elsewhere.
c. Addressing customer audits that indicate that change is required – soon.
d. Reducing costs to remain competitive.
e. Launching a new product or line that must be integrated into current processes.
f. Incorporating new governmental or environmental regulations that required significant process change.
g. Addressing an employee turnover problem for a specific department or job function. Human Resources have determined this in their exit interviews with high potential employees.

Top-level management must have honest dialogue with the process owner and the Black Belt, Lean Sensei, or Continuous Improvement Specialist regarding the scope of the project. Regardless of who leads the Kaizen Event, it is critical that the process owner be involved and on-board with the project. Otherwise, it will be a long, hard road for whoever is leading the project!

2. Gather initial data set. Before the initial team is determined and brought together, spend the necessary time to obtain the data set behind the Balanced Scorecard, Performance or Dashboard measurement or specific customer survey result that is under investigation, typically a trend that is of a concern. Obtain data that is one level down from what was defined by the project scope at this time. This may help determine the appropriate team members. Subsequent team activities will require further analysis of the data. The following are types of data that may be fairly easy to obtain:

Adjustment times	Number of people required
Batch sizes	Number of pieces of equipment
Change over times	Number of shifts
Customer requirements (specs)	Process times
Cycle times	Quality yield
Errors/Mistakes/Defects	Queue times
Delay times	Reference procedures (SOPs)
Delivery schedules	Rework percentages
Demand or takt time	Sigma value
Down times	Special packaging instructions
Efficiency percentages	Suppliers
Failure rates	Tools
Inputs	Total hours available
Lot sizes	Up times
Maintenance times	Value-added times
Mean time between failures	Warm up times
On-time-delivery performance	

3. Create high level value stream or process map. This would involve listing the main processes comprised of the value stream or main processes being examined and the high-level measurements such as total lead-time, total queue time, value-added time, quality issues, if known. If a value stream map is not practical, consider a type of process map (i.e., spaghetti diagram, macro or micro process map, deployment flowchart, etc.). The important point is to visually display the processes so the team, once assembled, can see the "big picture" or 30,000-foot view. The following are examples of high level value stream maps:

Current State Map for Classic Inc.

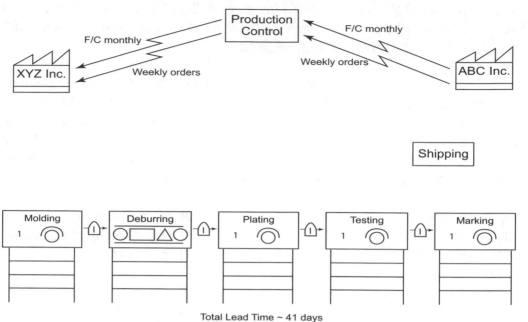

Total Lead Time ~ 41 days

The Order Entry Value Stream Current State Map

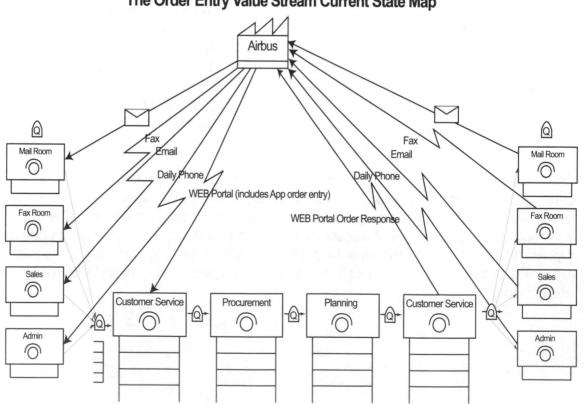

Subsequent team meetings will populate the needed information to help identify the wastes that exists in the process being examined as well as additional process attributes.

4. Determine initial team members. Selecting a group of employees and anyone outside the organization (i.e., consultant or supplier/customer) should be a fairly easy endeavor. The process owner and the person who will be facilitating the improvement should do this. This facilitator most likely will be the Black Belt, Lean Sensei, or Continuous Improvement Specialist within the organization. If the organization is not large enough to have a full-time employee for this position, then consider a supervisor or team leader that has exhibited leadership qualities or has led an improvement team in the past. With this book, a good knowledge of Lean and Six Sigma, and a willingness to listen and learn from the employees, will provide that supervisor or team leader a solid foundation upon which to conduct a Kaizen Event. If this supervisor or team leader does not have any experience in Lean Six Sigma tools and concepts, but has a good relationship with their work group, consider hiring an outside consultant to help lead the first Kaizen Event. The following are the definitions and activities for the various team members:

The *team champion (or executive sponsor)* has the authority to commit the necessary resources for the team. This person may or may not be the process owner; however, many times it will be. This will depend on the size of the organization and its reporting structure. The champion should "kick-off" the first meeting and then be updated regularly with appropriate reporting forms. Other duties of the team champion may include, but are not limited to:

- ❖ Continually being involved and communicating often with the team leader and/or process owner
- ❖ Refereeing cross-functional resource requests by removing barriers to project success
- ❖ Assisting to ensure the team is aligned with strategic goals
- ❖ Appointing the team leader
- ❖ Handling issues that the team leader and/or process owner cannot
- ❖ Providing team guidance when the team is struggling

The *team leader* is responsible for the day-to-day or week-to-week running of the team. Other duties of the team leader may include, but are not limited to:

- ❖ Scheduling and coordinating the meeting times (agenda and location)
- ❖ Communicating with team members and management (may be shared with facilitator)
- ❖ Making change happen through their level of responsibility and respect within the organization
- ❖ Having manager or supervisory authority, (if also the process owner)
- ❖ Believing in the project
- ❖ Suggesting additional team members
- ❖ Having an understanding of team dynamics
- ❖ Respecting others

The *facilitator* ensures that everyone at the meetings stays on task and everyone contributes. The facilitator should not have any vested interest in the project, one way or another - other than ensuring the meetings are effective. These duties include, but are not limited to:

- Keeping discussions focused on the topic (agenda item)
- Intervening if multiple conversations are occurring
- Preventing one person from dominating
- Being positive about any proposed changes
- Promoting interaction and participation
- Bringing discussions to a close
- Guiding the group in accordance with the Team or Project Charter

The *timekeeper* is responsible for ensuring the scheduled times (start, stop, breaks, topics, etc.) are followed. The timekeeper can manage the process and agenda. This frees everyone else to focus on contributing ideas. Other duties of the timekeeper may include, but are not limited to:

- Monitoring time with respect to the agenda
- Notifying team when it is behind schedule
- Updating the team on progress to time allocated
- Assisting with determining the appropriate time allocation for next meeting
- Contributing as a team member

The *scribe* records the notes of the meeting and distributes the information within a certain period, ideally within 24 hours of the meeting. Other duties of the scribe may include, but are not limited to:

- Capturing the group's thoughts on flip charts, black/smart boards, laptops, or tablet devices
- Representing the group's thoughts and actions without imposing his/her own interpretation
- Contributing as a team member

The *technical representative (tech rep)* is the person from IT (or someone with advanced computer application skills) who provides insights into the technology tools available. Other duties of the tech rep may include, but are not limited to:

- Providing the group with needed computer application support
- Providing information regarding new systems or programs that may be available in the near future that may impact the team's mission
- Contributing as a team member

The *informaticist* applies the tools of information theory to a specific discipline. This person will be responsible for organizing data and making it presentable. Note: The tech rep may also have this skill set.

Other duties of the informaticist may include, but are not limited to:

❖ Providing the team with easy-to-understand data sets and charts
❖ Assisting with visual measurement systems

The *Lean representative (Lean rep)* has a theoretical and practical knowledge of Lean and Six Sigma and is often referred to as a Black Belt, Lean Sensei, or Continuous Improvement Specialist. This person has previously conducted Kaizen Events.

Other duties of the Lean rep may include, but are not limited to:

❖ Train team members on the appropriate Lean Six Sigma tool required
❖ Support other team member roles through a positive approach and not be too demanding
❖ Be a conduit if multiple teams are working on different parts of the project and relay pertinent information

Note: The Lean rep typically has the Black Belt, Lean Sensei, or Continuous Improvement Specialist having broad responsibilities throughout the organization in terms of implementing continuous improvement. This person may or may not be the team leader, but more likely, be the facilitator.

The *team member* - the most important member of the team - is responsible for keeping an open mind, being receptive to change, and contributing ideas in a respectful manner.

Note: It is important that both the facilitator or team leader and scribe duties not be assigned to the same person. Some organizations will name the position of the team leader as a facilitator and the process owner taking a team leader role. The important point is to clearly identify the roles so there is no ambiguity or confusion as to who does what, when, and why.

5. Create the initial Team Charter. *The **Team Charter** details and documents the team structure, membership, and overall objectives, measures, and resources required for an improvement project to be successful.* It is usually developed by the process owner and/or team leader (if assigned) and subsequently reviewed and amended at the first Kaizen Event team meeting. The Team Charter fully defines the scope and resources required to complete an improvement project. The following is a generic template of a Team Charter.

Kaizen Event

Team Charter

Process Owner: [ ]   **Black Belt or Lean Sensei:** [ ]   **Start Date:** [ ]   **End Date:** [ ]

Value Stream: [ ]

Objective: [ ]

Team Members:

	Name	Dept/Site
Facilitator:		
Scribe:		
Team Leader:		
Team Members:		

Meeting Fequency:

Dates:	
Times:	

Lean Objectives: [ ]

Deliverables:

What are the specific metrics that will be improved?

[ ]

What are the specific opportunities for:

Growth?		Customer Satisfaction?	
Current:	Target:	Current:	Target:

Efficiency?		Quality (Defects or DPPMs, Errors, etc.)?	
Current:	Target:	Current:	Target:

Operational Excellence?		Dashboard or Performance Measure?	
Current:	Target:	Current:	Target:

What are any issues or concerns that may impact this team's objective?

Concerns: [ ]

Sign-Off:

Executive Sponsor:_____ Date:_____

Champion/Value Stream Manager/VP:_____ Date:_____
(maybe the same as Executive Sponsor)

Process Owner: _____ Date:_____

Deliverables to be included with this Charter:
- ❑ Value Stream or Process Map for the project
- ❑ Supporting High Level Data

The following are terms and definitions for various sections of the Team Charter:

Black Belt or Lean Sensei: represents the person who has experience in leading continuous improvement projects

Value Stream: the organizational process name that is being examined

Project Focus: a more specific process name from the Value Stream listed above

Note: The Value Stream and Project Focus could be identical, but may have different names according to organizational structure

Lean Objectives: the overall approach on how Lean (and Six Sigma) can be used for this project

Deliverables: the Current and Target for the various Balance Scorecard or other Performance Measurements

The following are additional aspects of a Team Charter:

❖ Ensure the specific project team provides input into the Team Charter and management reviews it to ensure alignment
❖ Customize the Team Charter for any internal or external issues that the organization may be facing
❖ Post or publish the Team Charter so it is available for everyone to view
❖ Refer back to the Team Charter if the team is struggling with direction or focus
❖ Update the Team Charter as changes occur

The following are the benefits that can be obtained by using a Team Charter:

❖ Allow teams to stay on-task and not attempt to do more than what is required (prevent scope creep)
❖ Ensure alignment between management and organizational improvements
❖ Provide communication at all levels
❖ Reduce stress

Once an initial Team Charter has been created, data collected, and initial team members determined, it would be time for the first team meeting

6. Assemble the team and conduct first meeting. The team members should be communicated to via email or phone call requesting their participation. At this time, the initial Team Charter and Meeting Information Form can be sent to the proposed team members. The following is a generic template of a Meeting Information Form.

Meeting Information Form

Meeting Title: _____ **Date:** _____

Time: _____

Place: _____

Distribution: **FYI Copies:**

Participants	Roles	Stakeholders	Roles

Agenda:

Time	Item	Who	Duration

Action Items: (to be completed by the next meeting or sooner)

No.	Action Item	Who	Start Date	End Date	Status

The following are terms and definitions for various sections of the Meeting Information Form:

Stakeholder: person, group, or organization with an interest in a project
Status (under Action Items): Open or Closed as to the particular Action Item listed

An **effective meeting** *is an efficient use of people's time when they are gathered together working to obtain a desired result.* Meetings, like any process, can be studied and improved upon. Meetings can be one of the most powerful business tools or one of the least. While many decisions can be made by phone, email, or in hallway discussions, there will be other times that people will need to meet (in person or through Web conferencing) and gain a consensus on an issue or problem that needs to be resolved. It is when this occurs that people gathered together need to meet effectively. Effective meetings are a key component for a successful Kaizen Event of any type.

Effective meetings provide a forum to make necessary decisions and solve problems without wasting time. If meetings are effective, they will produce a result. People will arrive on time, participate, offer information and ideas, and have a positive attitude. However, if meetings are not effective, people will show up late, be less likely to participate, and their attention and ideas will be less productive. To achieve effective meetings, treat meetings as processes, create standard rules to follow, and then adhere to those standards. The following are some basic guidelines (or standards) on how to conduct an effective meeting:

- ❖ Agree on a clear objective and agenda for the meeting.
- ❖ Choose the right people for the meeting and notify everyone in advance.
- ❖ Clarify roles and responsibilities for the meeting (i.e., facilitator, scribe, timekeeper, team member, etc.).
- ❖ Ensure everyone adheres to meeting etiquette (being on time, turning off cell/smart phones, text messaging only during breaks, etc.).
- ❖ Determine when face-to-face meetings are required, and, if and when additional meetings can be held via Web conferencing.
- ❖ Evaluate the meetings and improve the appropriate areas. All meetings can be improved!
- ❖ Provide the list of Action Items to participants within 24 hours after the meeting.

The following are the benefits that can be obtained by running effective meetings:

- ❖ Team members will be more likely to arrive on time and be engaged in the project
- ❖ Employees will be focused on the specific issue and "scope creep" will not occur
- ❖ The likelihood of project completion may be sooner than expected
- ❖ Less time will be involved in the actual meetings
- ❖ Stress will be reduced

Keep the first meeting to 4 hours or less. The following is a recommended agenda for the first kick-off meeting:

Time	Item	Duration	Who
1:00 – 2:05	Welcome and Reason for Team	30 minutes	Champion/Process Owner
2:05 – 2:20	Review/Update/Amend Team Charter	20 minutes	All
2:20 – 2:30	Assign/Agree on Team Roles	10 minutes	All
2:30 – 4:30	Conduct Overview of Lean (Simulation)	120 minutes	Team Leader/Facilitator
4:30 – 4:45	Review High Level Value Stream Map	30 minutes	All
4:45 – 5:00	Assign Action Items/Meeting Evaluation	30 minutes	All

Further breakdown and details of the above listed schedule is as follows:

Welcome and Reason for Team – this should include sharing the data that was used to determine that there exists an immediate opportunity for improvement as well as entertaining questions from the newly assembled team

Review/Update/Amend Team Charter – ensure the team believes the objective is doable within the scheduled meeting times and resources listed, reviewed dates to ensure team's availability

Assign/Agree on Team Roles and Ground Rules – ensure roles and meeting rules are agreed upon; determine if there needs to be anyone else added to the team, or if someone on the team feels that they will not add value given the Team Charter.

Conduct Overview of Lean - a simple simulation is highly recommended that conveys the main Lean principles of continuous flow, visual control, mistake proofing, etc. (See the Lean Six Sigma Training Set or consult with your Quality or Training Department for support in providing a simple 1 hour simulation.) Present previous Lean projects and successes from the organization. Ensure The Dirty Dozen Wastes are reviewed relative to the simulation as well as referencing previous Lean projects as examples.

Note: This Conduct Overview of Lean part of the Planning Phase can be expanded into a 4 or 8 hour Lean Basic Training program delivered by the Black Belt, Lean Sensei, or Continuous Improvement Specialist. If the organization does not have this resource and there is a need for this training, contact your local university or college, a trade association, a consultant, etc. to conduct the training.

Review High Level Value Stream Map – review the 30,000-foot view of the process and solicit input – agree on this high-level before further analysis of the processes with the team

Assign Action Items/Meeting Evaluation – ensure everyone understands the specific tasks that have been assigned by each person acknowledging their individual tasks; also, ensure the Effective Meeting Evaluation worksheet is completed and discussed at the beginning of the next meeting

The following activities may need to be completed prior to the next meeting:

- ❖ 1 - 2 team members review or gather more data to further populate the value stream map.
- ❖ Lean or Six Sigma training conducted, if needed.
- ❖ Team Charter, if modified, be approved by the executive sponsor, process owner, etc.
- ❖ Team Leader meet with process owner, if practical, to address any concerns.
- ❖ A team member research for similar-type projects within the organization and be prepared to share.
- ❖ 1 - 2 persons create a list of any additional resources that may be required.

Meetings are a process like any other and should be evaluated on a regular basis.

Use the following Effective Meeting Evaluation worksheet with your team to continuously improve your meetings. The team can review it as a group or each team member completes the evaluation. If each team member completes the score, then average the Total Score and address lower scoring items.

Kaizen Event

Effective Meeting Evaluation

Meeting Title: _____ **Date:** _____

Time: _____

Place: _____

Use the following 5 level Likert item scale for each statement:

1- Strongly Disagree
2- Disagree
3- Neither Agree nor Disagree
4- Agree
5- Strongly Agree

		Score
1	We stayed on the agenda.	
2	We focused on the right issues during the meeting.	
3	We focused on the issues and did not place blame.	
4	Time was used wisely.	
5	Information was presented accurately and clearly.	
6	Everyone participated.	
7	Action Items were assigned properly.	
8	The pace of the meeting was appropriate.	
9	Questions and concerns were addressed appropriately.	
10	All ideas were explored given the time element.	
	Total Score	

Scoring Guidelines

45-50 Doing Well - Keep up the good work.
40-44 Doing OK - Must make more effort during meeting.
35-39 Not So Good - Must improve dramatically.

Address any low scoring areas on the Effective Meeting Evaluation worksheet. The team leader, process owner, and/or facilitator should review team dynamics after the first meeting (did everyone seem to be on board with the project? do we have the right team members? do we foresee any issues or problems at this time?, etc.) are some self-team reflecting questions to consider. This may lead to some Kaizen Event Leadership (Chapter 5) tools that may need to be used.

Ensure at the first meeting, ground rules (i.e., proper etiquette) are discussed and a consensus is reached. These ground rules may be initially created by the team leader and process owner prior to the first meeting and then reviewed and agreed upon by the team at the beginning of the first meeting. These ground rules should be posted at the meeting location, distributed prior to the meeting, and/or reviewed at the beginning of each meeting session. Ground rules may include the following:

* *Attendance.* There should be placed a high priority on meeting attendance. There should be defined legitimate reasons for missing a meeting with a procedure to inform the team leader if a member cannot attend. The best way to ensure good attendance is to run effective meetings.
* *Timing.* Meetings should begin and end on time. This avoids wasting time and makes it easier on everyone's schedule. Meetings are sometimes shorter when this rule is enforced. Each team should create specific ways to enforce this rule.
* *Participation.* Every member can make a valuable contribution to the meeting. Emphasize the importance of speaking freely and listening attentively. If unequal participation is a problem, then the facilitator can structure the meeting so that everyone participates through various types of structured and unstructured brainstorming techniques.
* *Basic Courtesies.* Everyone, regardless of job description, should use basic conversational courtesies. Listen to what people have to say, do not interrupt, have only one conversation at a time, and respect others.
* *Breaks and Interruptions.* Decide when breaks for phone calls, text messaging, etc. are allowed, and when they are not.

Other ground rules (if appropriate). Decide on other ground rules that seem appropriate. What is OK to talk about and what is not? Is it OK to receive and/or send text messages during the meeting?

At the conclusion of the first meeting, thank everyone for his or her participation.

7. Complete A3 Report - Section 1. Problem Statement. Completing this part of the A3 should only take a few minutes, as it will be a most likely identical to the Project Focus with a little more detail, if available. The following Lean Thinking Questions should be reviewed by the team to ensure the Problem Statement is as complete as possible:

1. Problem Statement
What data do we have to support the significance of the problem? *What percent of the time are we meeting customer expectations?* *What is the impact of the problem on the customers of the process?* *What is the "Business Line of Sight" between our strategic goals and dashboards, to this particular issue?*
2. Current State

Address any other concerns or issues the team may have brought up.

The following are the deliverables that would be expected 3 Weeks Out for this type of Event:

(1) Determined project scope.
(2) Obtained initial data set.
(3) Created high level value stream or process map.
(4) Determined initial team members.
(5) Created initial Team Charter.
(6) Assemble the team and conduct first meeting.
(7) Completed A3 Report - Section 1. Problem Statement.

2 Weeks (spans 4 hours before the PDCA Implementation Phase)

The following steps continue as a guide:

8. Create a SIPOC Diagram, if needed. *A **SIPOC Diagram** is a tool used by a team to identify all relevant elements of a process improvement project or high level value stream or process map to ensure all aspects of the process are taken into consideration and that no key components are missing.* The SIPOC Diagram is the ideal tool to help layout the whole business process under review for improvement and assess "what" data is required and "how-to" proceed with data collection. SIPOC is an acronym for the Suppliers (the 'S' in SIPOC) of the process, the Inputs (I) to the process, the Process (P) that is under review, the Outputs (O) of the process, and the Customers (C) that receive the process outputs. It helps to create specific objectives from a complex project that may not be well-scoped or defined. The SIPOC Diagram provides a framework to help ensure relevant information is included in creating a more detailed value stream or process map. The following is a generic template of a SIPOC Diagram.

Kaizen Event			SIPOC Diagram	
Value Stream:			Date:	
Objective:				
Team Members:				
Suppliers (5)	Inputs (4)	Processes (1)	Outputs (3)	Customers (2)

Use the completed SIPOC Diagram to ensure all process inputs and outputs are well defined. This information can be very useful when creating a value stream or process map and for diagnosing abnormalities in the supply chain. Often new information, such as cause and effect relationship and communication gaps, can be discovered while completing the SIPOC Diagram.

Before starting the SIPOC Diagram, key questions to be asked are:

- ❖ Why improve the process?
- ❖ What are issues with the process?
- ❖ What is out-of-scope?
- ❖ Who are the suppliers and customers? What are their requirements?
- ❖ What metrics do you wish to improve?
- ❖ What data needs to be collected?

The following are the benefits that can be obtained by creating a SIPOC Diagram:

- ❖ Provides a clear vision of all the main processes
- ❖ Allows teams to document key data in an organized format
- ❖ Ensures a more accurate and useful value stream or process map

Note: Many times the SIPOC Diagram will be completed on a sub process within the larger-scale or high-level value stream or process map. Use the SIPOC Diagram to focus the team to the specific areas of the project that may be unclear or leave room for too much interpretation.

9. Create detailed current state value stream or process map. Once the main processes have been defined from reviewing the high level value stream or process map, list the next level of detail processes in a value stream or process map format. The value stream or process map will be used as the visual roadmap to collect (or populate if data is available) process attributes, identify wastes, and ultimately be updated to a future state map with the application of Lean and Six Sigma tools. At this point, only a "straw man" or "shell" of the map would be created to help identify what data and attributes need to be collected.

The following are examples of initial current state maps:

Current State Map for Classic Inc.

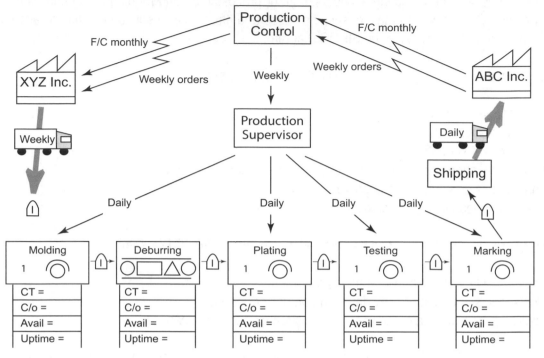

Total Lead Time ~ 41 days

The Order Entry Value Stream Current State Map

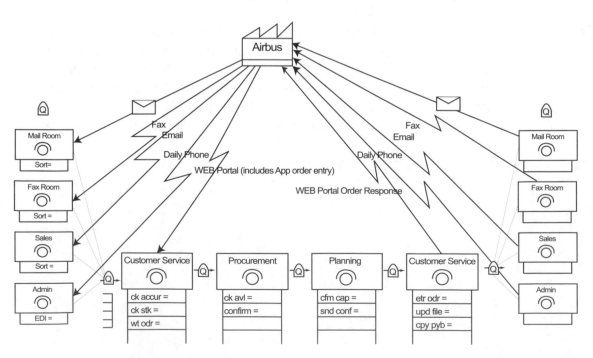

10. Create a Cycle Time Table (or appropriate method to obtain accurate cycle times). This may be created as an Action Item prior to the Kaizen Event Phase or completed during Day 1 of the Kaizen Event Phase. This data may also be available in the system; however, if it is, ensure the team reviews it. The following are generic templates of a Cycle Time Table and Document Tagging Worksheet to assist in standardizing the data collection process.

Kaizen Event

Cycle Time Table

Department: _____   **Data Collection Dates:** _____

Type: ☐ Historical (database)   **Totals:** _____
☐ Direct Observation (real-time)
☐ Voice of the Customer (survey)

Process Name			Process Name			Process Name		
Step	Description	Cycle Time	Step	Description	Cycle Time	Step	Description	Cycle Time
	Total			Total			Total	
Process Name			Process Name			Process Name		
Step	Description	Cycle Time	Step	Description	Cycle Time	Step	Description	Cycle Time
	Total			Total			Total	
Process Name			Process Name			Process Name		
Step	Description	Cycle Time	Step	Description	Cycle Time	Step	Description	Cycle Time
	Total			Total			Total	

Consider the following when using a Cycle Time Table:

❖ For each process step, determine the START and STOP points (from database retrieval, time stamps, observation methods, etc.) and record as the cycle time.
❖ Observe the process step at least 30 times, if possible, and average.
❖ If an individual process step takes less than 15 seconds, bundle it with the next (or previous) process step.
❖ Round up to nearest half-minute (30 seconds) or minute depending on the process.
❖ Include wait time between the agreed-upon START and STOP points in all of the process steps (referred to as in-process delay or wait).

Document Tagging Worksheet

Kaizen Event

Value Stream: _____

Department: _____

Start Date In: _____

Start Date Out: _____

Step	Process/ Dept.	In		Out		Task Activity	Delay/Wait Time from Previous Step	Cycle Time	Elapsed Time	Value-Added Time	Non Value-Added Time
		Date	Time	Date	Time						

Consider the following when using a Document Tagging Worksheet:

Delay/Wait Time is calculated by subtracting the In Time from the Out Time of the previous step.
Cycle Time is calculated by subtracting the beginning time of the step from the end time of the step.
Elapsed Time is the Delay/Wait Time plus the Cycle Time accumulated from each step (running total).
Value-Added Time is the time required to physically (or electronically) transform the product or service into value for the customer. It typically is the cycle time minus any delay or wait time (i.e., wastes) for that step.
Non Value-Added Time is calculated by adding the Delay/Wait Time plus any Cycle Time that does not add value (i.e., waste) to the customer.

Using the Document Tagging Worksheet is a different way to capture data than using the Cycle Time Table. The Document Tagging Worksheet focuses on ONE ELEMENT as it flows through the process, rather than all of the activities related to that process (i.e., using the Cycle Time Table). Remember, you will most likely not account for every single second or minute for the processes (or value stream) being examined. Do not let that deter your drive to gather this data. Be satisfied with 80% (or more) and move on!

Note: Whatever method is used to collect data, especially real-time, ensure each observer understands the true start and stop time for each task or activity being timed. If multiple team members will be observing at different times, consider using the tool Measurement System Analysis to ensure the data collection process is reliable. *Measurement System Analysis (MSA) is a specially designed experiment that seeks to identify the components of variation in the measurement.* All too often, measurements are not representative of the true value of the characteristic being measured. This may be because the measurement system is not accurate enough, not precise enough, introduces bias into the measurement, or is not properly being used by the worker or observer. Measurement System Analysis evaluates the test method, measuring instruments, and the entire process of obtaining measurements to ensure the integrity of data used for analysis and to understand the implications of measurement error for decisions made about a product or process. MSA is an important element of Six Sigma methodology and of other quality management systems.

Note: Everyone thinks they know the process steps and times, until you try to write them down. Use the appropriate amount of time so each process step is understood, from beginning to end. This will ensure an accurate current state value stream map, which will be the basis for creating and implementing the "doable" future state. Do not rush this step!

Typically, collecting this data will be an Action Item that assigns a few team members to obtain the needed data. When this data is collected, the team members should also collect any other process data attributes. You do not need the entire team to observe and collect this data!

11. Conduct a Waste Walk. (See the Introduction section pages 25 - 34 for a description of all the wastes as well as the detailed steps to conducting a Waste Walk.) A Waste Walk is an activity when project team members visit the process area that is being considered for improvement, ask questions, and then identify the wastes and other process attributes on the current state value stream or process map. Many of the team members will be very familiar with the project area as it is their actual work area. Conducting this Waste Walk, the team members will be viewing the area with a vision of what needs to be improved by knowing the deliverables from the Team Charter. At this time, they are not too close to the forest to see the trees!

The Waste Walk accomplishes the following: (Repeated from Introduction section.)

❖ Ensure everyone is aligned to the physical location of the processes being analyzed
❖ Ensure process workers are engaged in the Kaizen Event Phase
❖ Allow for all process workers to provide input
❖ Allow for discussions about the process to clear up any questions
❖ Allow for the collection of additional process attributes

To conduct a Waste Walk, consider the following:

❖ Communicate to the employees working in the prospective areas/processes/departments when you will be bringing the group through and explain your purpose using an elevator speech. An elevator speech is a brief, comprehensive verbal overview that describes the purpose and related-activities regarding proposed improvement. The name reflects the fact that an elevator pitch can be delivered in the time span of an elevator ride (say, thirty seconds or 100 - 150 words).

❖ Assign one person in each group to take notes.

❖ Ensure the team has thought of questions to ask, including:
    What are some of your issues affecting your work?
    What could be improved?
    Do you help out when things get busy? If not, why?
    Do you know when you are behind schedule?
    Do you know when the work you provide is needed downstream (to the next process)?

❖ Do not cause any disruption to the work area.

❖ If the group is larger than 5, break into smaller groups.

❖ Start with the most downstream process and work upstream.

❖ Thank the person(s) (and departmental manager/supervisor) for their time.

The following is a generic template of a Waste Walk form (identical to the one on page 33).

Kaizen Event

Waste Walk

Value Stream: _____   **Date:** _____

Department: _____   **Team Members:** _____

Type of Waste	Waste Observations
Overproduction Producing more material, information, or a service than is needed or used.	
Skills and Knowledge Not using people's minds and getting them involved.	
Transport Moving supplies, materials, documents, people, etc. excessively.	
Inventory Any unnecessary material, information, documents, etc. that resides between two processes.	
Motion Any unnecessary movement that does not add value.	
Defects or Errors Redoing work that has been done previously.	
Overprocessing Providing work or service that is not part of the customer requirement.	
Waiting or Delays The time spent waiting for material, information, people, etc.	
Overburden Work that is added with no additional support or resources.	
Unevenness Work that arrives without being scheduled and in varying amounts.	
Environmental Products, processes, activities, etc. that are not good for the planet.	
Social Communicating and networking via social networks that does not add value.	

Process Attributes

Process Name	Attributes	Process Name	Attributes

Once the Waste Walk Audit has been completed and the information is fresh in everyone's mind, relate the wastes and any process attributes collected to the current state value stream or process map. This is accomplished in the following ways:

- ❖ Distribute different color Post-it Notes to each group (if the team was divided into two groups to conduct the Waste Walk). It is suggested that groups be no larger than 5.
- ❖ Allow 15 minutes for each person to write the various wastes that were identified on the Waste Walk onto the Post-it Notes.
- ❖ Direct each group (individual) to place their Post-it Note on the area of the value stream or process map where they believe the waste is occurring. If this map was created via a laptop and LCD projection unit, project the map on a whiteboard so the physical placement of the Post-it Notes can be done on the image.
- ❖ Keep in mind that the wastes may be listed as process steps or specific activities instead of the exact name of the waste. If that is the case then the facilitator should attempt to relate those items listed to the actual waste to ensure that everyone understands the overall concept of waste.

Allow the team members some latitude in how they identify the wastes on the current state value stream or process map. Then work with the team members and gain a consensus to consolidate similar wasteful activities using a different colored Post-it Note.

Many teams have found it helpful to conduct the Waste Walk prior to detailing the current value stream or process map. This will depend on the following:

- ❖ Access to the process area and/or system
- ❖ Number of team members with good knowledge of the area
- ❖ Any security or safety concerns

12. Update current state value stream or process map. This will include adding the data from the Cycle Time Table, Document Tagging Worksheet, and any information gathered during the Waste Walk.

Note: Creating a detailed current state map, as well as listing all the various wastes (before even applying Lean tools), can take from 1 to 8 hours. This depends on the following:

❖ Team members' knowledge of the processes
❖ Complexity of the processes (which includes cross-departmental communications)
❖ Access to the information
❖ Availability of the process or area to obtain needed information (especially if direct observation is required)

The following are examples of detailed current state value stream, process, and hybrid maps from various industries:

Current State Map for Classic Inc.

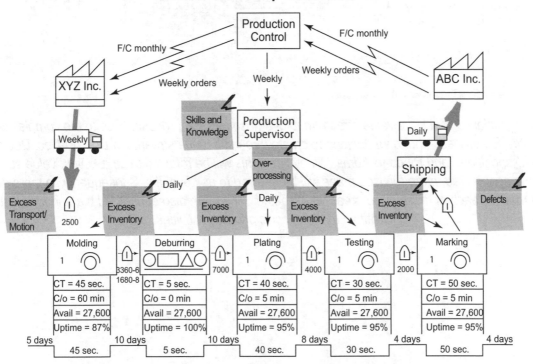

This is a traditional current state value stream map of 5 sequential processes noting the critical process attributes as well as the value-added and non value-added times as a step graph. This team also identified various wastes.

Oakview Hospital's ED Arrival to Inpatient Bed Current State Value Stream Map
Waste Audit Update

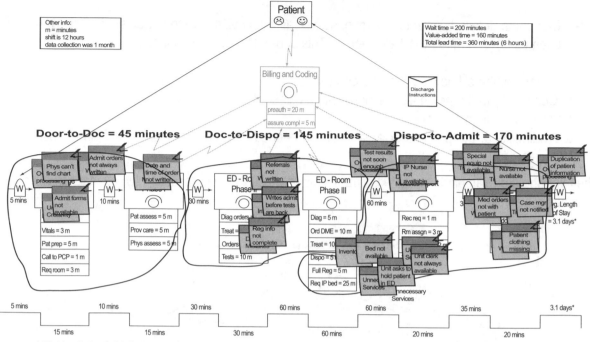

This is an initial current state value stream map of a hospital's ED process. Due to the complexity of the entire ED process, the team decided to create three sub-value streams of Door-to-Doc, Doc-to-Dispo (Disposition), and Dispo-to-Admit. Many times this will be referred to as a Level I value stream and the segmented, more focused maps will be referred to as Level II's. Subsequently, a more detailed map for each of those three areas was created. The team also connected the various wastes identified to the specific process activities.

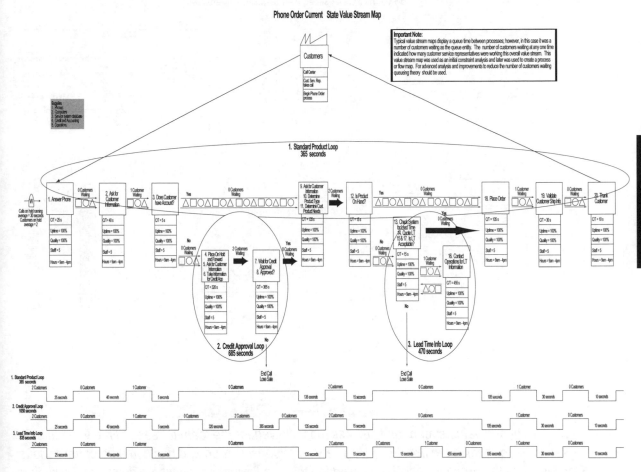

Phone Order Current State Value Stream Map

This current state phone order value stream map shows two additional paths or loops for the customer depending on if certain conditions are met or not. The step-graph at the bottom identifies these three loops as separate value streams. It is displayed in this format due to the sharing of common processes in the Standard Product Loop.

Note: See pages 150-151 for a larger image of this illustration.

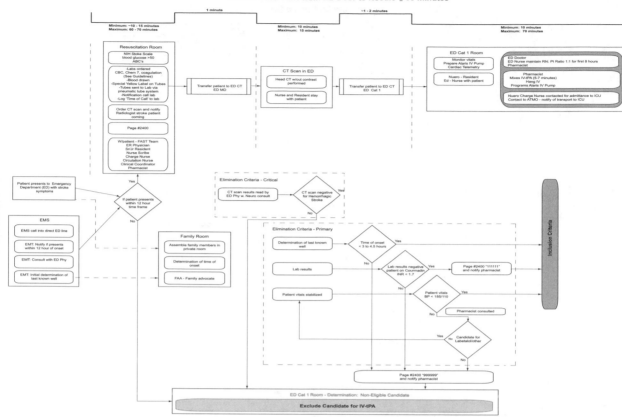

This current state hybrid value stream and process map allowed for the team to "see" all the various pathways for someone to receive the tPA drug. tPA is a very expensive drug and has some potential serious risks. Conveying all the process activities allowed the team to brainstorm on where delays and mistakes could occur and address them appropriately to ensure patient safety.

When mapping the process within a Customer Relationship Management program, or another type of system application, it may be helpful to print the various screen shots and post them on the map. As in this team's mapping process, it helped them see many "overprocessing" wastes (repeat data entry, unnecessary data, etc.). Mapping the processes can be a bit "messy," but it does shed light on the wastes!

Kaizen Demystified

Keep the second meeting to no more than 3 hours. The following is a recommended agenda for the second meeting:

Time	Item	Duration	Who
2:00 – 2:15	Review Action Items	15 minutes	Team Leader/Facilitator
2:15 – 3:00	SIPOC and Create Data Collection Tool	45 minutes	All
3:00 – 3:45	Conduct Waste Walk	45 minutes	All
3:45 – 4:45	Create/Update Detailed Current State Map	60 minutes	All
4:45 – 4:50	Review Issues or Problems	5 minutes	All
4:50 – 5:00	Assign Action Items/Meeting Evaluation	10 minutes	All

13. Complete A3 Report - Section 2. Current State and Section 3. Improvement Opportunity. The following Lean Thinking Questions should be reviewed by the team to ensure these sections are as complete as possible:

1. Problem Statement	3. Improvement Opportunity
What data do we have to support the significance of the problem? What percent of the time are we meeting customer expectations? What is the impact of the problem on the customers of the process? What is the "Business Line of Sight" between our strategic goals and dashboards, to this particular issue?	How will we know when we have achieved success? Are there benchmarks or comparative data that we should review? What should we measure in order to (a) compare "before" and "after" and (b) know how we have made a difference in the process? Have we identified the wastes? Can we show goals using a balanced scorecard? What will the future state look like?
2. Current State	**4. Problem Analysis**
What is the value stream or process map, with data, for this process? What does the map tell us about the complexity of our process? What is the feedback from employees/stakeholders on how the process is working for them? What other data do we need to collect to understand the process? Can we create a current state with a value stream map (with data)?	Who will be impacted by changes in this process? What is the demand for the process – how many requests by hour of the day and/or day of the week? What is the detailed process flow? Can we use a Fishbone Diagram to find and show any likely problem areas? How much waste is there in the process? Have we asked the "5 Whys" for each step? Can we show that we have identified the major problems using a Pareto Chart? Have we used an Impact Map or other tool to

Address any other concerns or issues the team may have brought up.

The following are the deliverables that would be expected 2 Weeks Out for this type of Event:

    (1) Created SIPOC Diagram.
    (2) Created initial current state value stream or process map.
    (3) Created a Cycle Time Table (or appropriate method to obtain accurate cycle times).
    (3) Conducted a Waste Walk.
    (4) Updated current state value stream or process map.
    (5) Completed A3 Report - Section 2 Current State and Section 3. Improvement Opportunity.

1 Week (spans 4 -8 hours before the PDCA Implementation Phase)

The following steps continue as a guide:

14. Conduct a Stakeholder Analysis. *Stakeholder Analysis is the technique used to identify the key people who have to be won over for a project implementation or change initiative.* You then use Stakeholder Planning to build the support that helps you succeed. Stakeholder Analysis is critical to the success of every project in every organization. By engaging the right people in the right way before, during, and after completion of a major initiative (i.e., business improvement project or a Kaizen Event) within an organization, can make a big difference to its success. Do not underestimate the importance of using this tool or some variation of it!

The benefits of using a Stakeholder Analysis are that:

❖ The opinions of the most powerful stakeholders to shape projects at an early stage are revealed. Not only does this make it more likely that they will support the project, their input can also improve the quality and likelihood of success of the initiatives.
❖ The support from powerful stakeholders can help obtain adequate resources - this makes it more likely that the project will be successful.
❖ Communicating with stakeholders early and frequently will help ensure that everyone fully understands what the project is about and its benefits.
❖ Anticipating people's reaction to a project will allow a leader to take early action to promote acceptance.

Note: When possible, include the key stakeholders in the analysis or ensure you solicit their input. The Stakeholder Analysis could have been done earlier in the Planning Phase; however, many times it will take a few meetings to have the project's focus defined at the level required to assure an accurate Stakeholder Analysis.

To conduct a Stakeholder Analysis, consider the following:

Identify the stakeholders. Conduct the Stakeholder Analysis to brainstorm who the stakeholders are in reference to the change that is about to occur or the project that is being considered. List all the people who are affected by the work, who have influence or power over it, or have an interest in its successful or unsuccessful conclusion.

Types of stakeholders are:

Primary stakeholders: are those ultimately affected (i.e., process area employees), either positively or negatively by an organization's actions. This group will continually be engaged throughout the Kaizen Event by the various tools and activities (e.g., Waste Walk interaction, 5S involvement, etc.) the team will be using.

Secondary stakeholders: are the intermediaries, that is, persons or organizations who are indirectly affected by an organization's actions. The Reporting and Communications Forms will address this group sufficiently.

Key management stakeholders: are those who control critical resources, who can block the change initiative by direct or indirect means, who must approve certain aspects of the change strategy, who shapes the thinking of other critical constituents, or who owns a key work process impacted by the change initiative. This is the group more analysis will be required for in this phase.

Some key questions the team leader or facilitator may ask the team at this step is:

   (1) Who is threatening the target of this project?
   (2) Who is most dependent on this project?
   (3) Has there been a similar project in the organization? If so, to what extent did it succeed? Who was in charge and how did local stakeholders respond?
   (4) Who possesses claims - including legal jurisdiction and customary use - over the project/resources at stake?
   (5) Are any government departments to be involved in this project?
   (6) Are there national and/or international bodies involved in this project because of specific laws?
   (7) Who are the people or groups most knowledgeable about the project?
   (8) Are the stakeholders and their interests' stable or is there any identifiable pattern that exists?
   (9) Are there major events/trends/activities currently affecting the stakeholders?

Prioritize the key management stakeholders. Map these stakeholders on a Power/Interest Grid as shown below and classify them by their power over and interest in the project. Color-coding can be used to easily identify (e.g., advocates in green and critics in red).

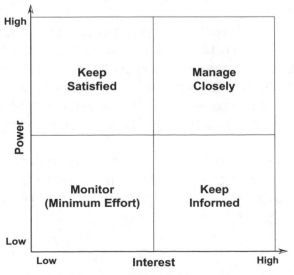

Standard

Discuss confidentially both objective evidence of where the individual is (e.g., "At the last staff meeting Bill clearly stated his unwillingness to assign a member of his group to the team.") as well as subjective opinion (e.g., "Betty is likely to be strongly supportive because of her unit's objectives in this area.").

It may be useful to first have each team member rate each stakeholder without discussion, and then tally individual ratings and discuss obvious differences. While it probably is not critical to strive for complete consensus, it is usually worthwhile to take the time to generally agree on whether each key stakeholder is in reference to the grid.

Some questions the team leader or facilitator may ask at this step are:

(1) Who is directly responsible for decisions important to the project?
(2) Who holds positions of responsibility in interested organizations?
(3) Who is influential in the project area?
(4) Who will be affected by the project?
(5) Who will promote/support the project, once they are involved?
(6) Who will obstruct/hinder the project if they are not involved?
(7) Who has been involved in the area in the past?
(8) Who has not been involved up to now but should have been?

Consider the following actions:

High power, high interested people: these are the people you must fully engage and make the greatest efforts to satisfy. For example, changing a technical process or method, highly skilled employees of a process or trade may fit into this category due to their technical expertise. Teams need their support for the success of the improvement.

High power, less interested people: put enough work in with these people to keep them satisfied, but not so much that they become bored with your message. For example, these individuals might be key organizational leaders in related areas that many people respect, trust, and follow. If these key people agree, many more people will find it easier to "buy-in."

Low power, high interested people: keep these people adequately informed, and talk to them to ensure that no major issues are arising. These people can often be very helpful with the detail of your project. For example, these individuals may be the people closest to the actual change or improvement. The change or improvement may affect the way they work; yet due to their position in the organization they have little power or control of the situation. These people are a key to success, in that if they "buy-in" they will do their best to achieve success for the initiative. It is important to listen and respond to their ideas and opinions to ensure success.

Low power, less interested people: monitor these people, but do not bore them with excessive communication. For example, co-workers in another area or different department often serve to influence other key groups. These folks may not see the changes as a big deal, and may help the other key people to relax and lower their resistance.

The more you know about the stakeholders, the better prepared you will be to handle their concerns regarding the project.

Some key questions the team leader or facilitator may ask at this step are:

(1) What financial or emotional interest do they have in the outcome of the project?
(2) What motivates those most of all?
(3) What information do they want or need?
(4) How do they want to receive information? What is the best way of communicating to them?
(5) What is their current opinion of the project? Is it based on good information?
(6) Who influences their opinions generally, and who influences their opinion of this project? Do some of these influencers therefore become important stakeholders in their own right?
(7) If they are not likely to be positive, what will win them around to support the project?
(8) For those that cannot be won over, how will their opposition be managed?
(9) Who else might be influenced by their opinions? Do these people become stakeholders?

A very good way of answering these questions is to talk to the key management stakeholders directly - people are often quite open about their views, and asking people's opinions is often the first step in building a successful relationship with them.

The importance of the process in planning and conducting successful collaborations cannot be overemphasized. Good-faith efforts are often derailed because the parties are not skilled in working together, and because insufficient attention is given to designing and managing it. Use an inclusive, transparent approach for the Stakeholder Analysis. It will help build ownership and commitment to the project from all sides. If it is not possible or realistic to have all key management stakeholders involved from the outset, then a process for gradual involvement may be needed.

15. Conduct specific Lean tool training. As the project is further defined, the team leader and/or facilitator should provide more detail on the likely Lean tools that may be implemented. This would involve the overall steps for that tool to be implemented, review the forms or worksheets, and provide and discuss actual applications or examples of that tool. Some key tools to consider are 5S, Standard Work, Mistake Proofing, Continuous Flow and Kanbans, Leveling (or Heijunka), Visual Controls, Visual Management, and Total Employee Involvement. See Chapter 3. Lean Six Sigma Tools for a brief description of the Lean Six Sigma tools.

Note: It is highly recommended that *The Lean Six Sigma Pocket Guide XL, The Practical Lean Six Sigma Pocket Guide, Practical Lean Six Sigma for Healthcare, or The Practical Lean Six Sigma Pocket Guide for Healthcare* be purchased for all team members. These books offer the most simple and basic explanation of over 50 Lean Six Sigma tools with step-by-step implementation guidelines, photos, and example worksheets. The books, including *Kaizen Demystified*, provide a consistent, standardized approach to the understanding, learning, and subsequent implementing Lean Six Sigma.

Keep in mind that many of the tools are inter-related. For example, if a visual control is needed for a process improvement that could also be considered a form of standard work. It is not so important as to label the tool correctly, it is more important to improve the process.

16. Determine specific improvement activities and use the Plan – Do – Check – Act (PDCA) format. In the context of the Kaizen Event, *PDCA is an interactive four-step problem solving and improvement process used to implement (or pilot/test) and validate business process improvements.* It is also known as the Deming or Shewhart cycle. It is also being referred to as the specific improvement activity or "mini" improvement within the Kaizen Event.

It is more than likely that many numerous mini-improvements (or PDCAs) will need to be implemented to meet the deliverables as defined in the Team Charter. These mini-improvements can be defined or proposed using the tools of 5S, Standard Work, Mistake Proofing, Flow Improvements, etc. as well as analysis tools such as Valued-Added versus Non Value-Added Analysis, Histograms, 5 Why Analysis, Brainstorming, Cause and Effect (or Fishbone) Diagram, Force Field Analysis, Impact Maps, Employee Balance Charts, Value Stream Mapping, Waste Audit, etc.

A PDCA is often referred to as an experiment or trial. The PDCA process will assist the stakeholders or employees from the area in the proposed change as well as help create a "buy-in" to the improvement activities. Often getting people to try something new is one of the more challenging parts of reaching an improved state. The PDCA experiment or trial is a short-term, controlled trial process used to capture data during any process change, learn about the process from those working the process, and adjust as necessary while keeping the improvement objective in mind. This approach helps people adapt to change more easily.

Once the team has a good understanding of the processes and a basic understanding of Lean tools and principles, the specific improvement activities should be listed. Most likely, many team members probably have expressed ideas on how the processes being examined could be improved during the Waste Walk or when creating the detailed current state value stream or process map, but it was important to not jump to any conclusions prior to having all the data.

The following are the benefits that can be obtained by following the PDCA process:

- ❖ Minimizes the possibility of error
- ❖ Allows for real-time corrective action and collaboration
- ❖ Optimizes the utilization of time
- ❖ Improves productivity immediately
- ❖ Engages process area employees

Note: Kaizen Events typically will require numerous PDCAs to meet the Team Charter deliverables. This is one of the main reasons a team was assembled: to help distribute the improvement activities as well as get buy-in to the process changes.

The following are additional guidelines for using PDCA:

Plan – define the specific improvement activity or experiment, what will be done, who will do it, and how it will be measured; this information should be well documented.

Other activities may include the following:

❖ Gathering additional data
❖ Communicating to the process area when/where there will be activities and solicit their input as often as possible
❖ Setting up any restrictions, conditions, barriers, etc. to ensure customers are not impacted
❖ Obtaining current Standard Operating Procedures and the updated procedures
❖ Obtaining any needed supplies, especially if 5S is part of the improvement
❖ Posting, publishing, or emailing the Team Charter and PDCA Kaizen Activity Worksheet to process area employees and providing a feedback mechanism for their input (highly recommended!)

The following PDCA Kaizen Activity Worksheet, also referred to as an Action Item Log in project management terms, can be used to help organize and prioritize improvement activities:

Kaizen Event			**PDCA Kaizen Activity Worksheet**		
Value Stream:			Date:		
Department:			Team Members:		
Process Name/Activity (as identified on the value stream, process map, etc.)	**Problem or Waste**	**Lean Tool**	**Specific Activities**	**Who**	**When**
Parking Lot Items or Wiki Kaizen Event Ideas					

Note: This is similar to the Action Items category in the Meeting Information Form. The PDCA Kaizen Activity Worksheet should be used to list the specific activities required to eliminate the wastes that were previously identified as well as with the Lean (or Six Sigma) tool being applied as defined in the Do step. If the team is experienced with Kaizen Events, then the Meeting Information Form (or appropriate project management reporting tool) could be used.

Do – implement the improvement plan or experiment. This will be carrying out the Specific Activities listed on the PDCA Kaizen Activity Worksheet.

Other activities may include the following:

- ❖ Being surgical in the process change, plan your work, and work your plan!
- ❖ Respecting individual work areas
- ❖ Not judging current processes when working in the area
- ❖ Ensuring EVERYONE in the process area is aware of why the process is being changed or modified as well as when it will occur
- ❖ Keeping an open mind for on-the-go type improvements as the team may have missed something, and may have become apparent during this "trial"

Check – ensure that the intended improvement was successful in terms of the measurements set forth in the Team Charter. Measure and discuss the results of the trial or experiment.

Other activities may include the following:

- ❖ Updating the process due to new information during the Do phase
- ❖ Monitoring the process for a certain period of time
- ❖ Supporting the new process with additional training, resources, and/or support
- ❖ Creating and updating the necessary Control Charts and/or Run Charts

Act – confirm that the improvement experiment worked with improved performance; act to standardize the new process. If the improvement experiment or PDCA trial did not provide the results expected or no improvement whatsoever, immediately reinstate the process to its original condition. Return back to the Plan stage incorporating what has been learned.

Other activities may include the following:

- ❖ Updating the Standard Operating Procedures
- ❖ Creating a sub team for a full-departmental or value stream roll-out of the new process
- ❖ Documenting and communicating the success of the activities to the full team
- ❖ Providing additional training before formal training can be conducted
- ❖ Implementing another PDCA for this area
- ❖ Appreciating those in the process area that were not part of the team, but contributed

In summary, even though most of these activities are completed in the Kaizen Event Phase, it was discussed in detail in this Phase to ensure that proper planning is conducted. This will help ensure an effective Standard 5 Day Kaizen Event Phase schedule.

17. Create a future state value stream or process map. Once the specific Lean activities have been listed in the PDCA Kaizen Activity Worksheet, the team can create a future state value stream or process map providing the visual vision for all the improvements. There are a number of ways to create the future value stream or process map. Some of which are:

Note: The following guidelines are typically used for creating future state value stream maps, however, the guidelines can also be used similarly for process maps. Keep the big picture in mind that in whatever type of mapping method is used, display, in simple terms, the improvement activities and proposed results. No two maps will be identical - just Google value stream or process maps!

❖ If working off the flip chart, use different colored Post-it Notes to identify the various Kaizen activities.

❖ When creating a digital version of the map, use the icon of a "burst" or "cloud" to represent the Lean tool name being used or the specific Kaizen activity (these terms would relate to the PDCA Kaizen Activity Worksheet). Include the Lean tool or Kaizen activity inside the "burst" or "cloud." Each of these icons should be placed near the process name on the current state value stream or process map.

❖ Create and appropriately label a new future state value stream map using common symbols for the Lean tools visually conveying the new and improved value stream or process. This map may also include the Kaizen activity or Lean tool icons.

❖ Create a legend on the future state value stream or process map noting the current and proposed future state measurements such as total lead time, total queue times, etc. This should be updated once all improvements have been implemented and sustained.

Note: Having the Lean tools and specific Kaizen activities identified on the current state value stream map may simply be renaming the future state map at this time.

The following are examples of detailed future state value stream, process, and hybrid maps from various industries:

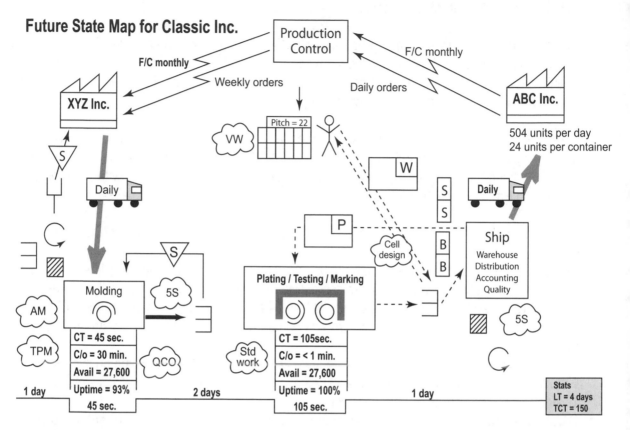

Future State Map for Classic Inc.

This future state map clearly indicates the physical changes as well as the flow of information changes using future state value stream mapping icons. The various Lean tools application is listed in the approximate physical locations as they were conducted. This team combined the various activities and conducted one Standard 5 Day Kaizen Event and one Standard "2" Day Kaizen Event.

The 30-Year Fixed Mortgage Application Future State Value Stream Map

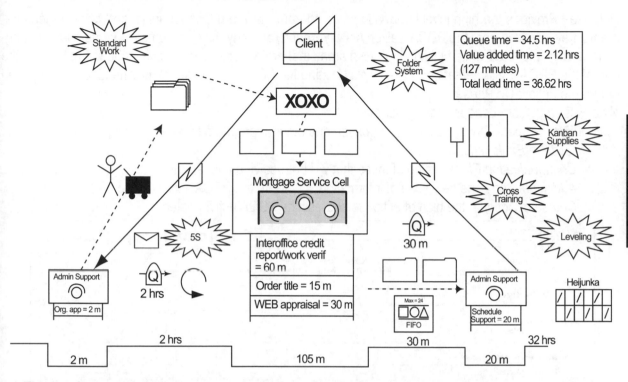

This is a future state value stream map of a financial services mortgage application cell. There were many changes incorporated into this future state value stream. This team made all the major changes using the Standard 5 Day Kaizen Event.

Note: Visio and Excel are common applications to create value stream and process maps. There are others such as SmartDraw, Smooth Flowcharter, FlowBreeze, ConceptDraw, SigmaFlow, iBrainstorming, etc. Many of these allow a 30-day trial prior to purchasing.

18. Create Reporting and Communication forms. The following forms can be used to communicate the status of the Kaizen Event before, during, and after the PDCA Implementation Phase. Use these to enhance your current reporting forms or modify accordingly to fit your Kaizen Event. A sub team may be formed by designating 1 – 2 team members to create/modify the appropriate forms.

The next four worksheets or forms can be used for the end-of-the-day debriefing that may be part of the Standard 5 Day Kaizen Event. The debriefing would be comprised of a 10- 15 minute meeting at the end of each day with key management personnel and the Kaizen Event team allowing management to gain a perspective on how the PDCA Implementation Phase is preceeding as well as provide support as needed.

Project Prep Status

Purpose: Provides the high level information derived from the Team Charter, initial and current measurements, key activities from the PDCA Kaizen Activity Report, and any major accomplishments and/or changes in what is expected while highlighting those areas that are not presenting a challenge to the team at the end of the PDCA Implementation Phase. This is listing the PDCA activities that may need to be completed during the Follow-Up Phase.

Who Fills Out: Team Leader and/or Facilitator

Distribution: Process Owner, Executive Sponsor, and other appropriate top-level managers

Additional Term Explanations:

❖ *Communication Plan* – listing of those that will be receiving this report

❖ *Additional Info* – the next level of information specific to the PDCA activity listed

❖ *Course of Action* – the plan of action to address the PDCA activity listed

Kaizen Event	**Project Prep Status**

| Process Owner: | | Black Belt or Lean Sensei: | | Start Date: | |
| | | | | End Date: | |

Objective:	

Communication Plan:	

Measurement:			
Initial Data:			
Current Data:			
Percent Improvement:			

What (PDCA Activity)	Additional Info	Measurement Impacted	Course of Action

Sign-Off: Process Owner: _____   Date:_____

Kickoff

Purpose: Provides the summary information derived from the Team Charter and future state value stream or process map. It is used to report out to management.

Who Fills Out: Team Leader and/or Facilitator

Distribution: Process Owner, Executive Sponsor, and other appropriate top-level managers

Additional Term Explanations:

- ❖ *Target % Change* – this will be the expected improvements as conveyed on the future state
- ❖ *Measurements* – the value stream, department, or process measurements

Kaizen Event		**Kick Off**

By: _____ **Date:** _____

Team Name: _____

Measurements	Target % Change

Objective: _____

Team Members	Job Function	Team Role

Daily Recap

Purpose: Conveys the daily results throughout the PDCA Implementation Phase
Who Fills Out: Team Leader and/or Facilitator
Distribution: Process Owner, Executive Sponsor, and other appropriate top-level managers
Additional Term Explanations:

❖ *Accomplishments* – list any milestones the team accomplished during the day as well as any issues

❖ *Issues/Plans* – convey if the team is on schedule and how it plans to address any issues that may have arisen

❖ *# Day 1* - measurements of the process before any PDCA activity

---

Kaizen Event

Daily Recap

By: _____ Date: _____

Team Name: _____

Measurement	# Day 1	# Day 2	# Day 3	# Day 4	# Day 5	# Target

Accomplishments:

Issues/Plans:

Accomplishments	Issues/Plans
	Issue:
	Plan:
	Issue:
	Plan:
	Issue:
	Plan:
	Issue:
	Plan:
	Issue:
	Plan:
	Issue:
	Plan:
	Issue:
	Plan:
	Issue:
	Plan:
	Issue:
	Plan:
	Issue:
	Plan:
	Issue:
	Plan:
	Issue:
	Plan:
	Issue:
	Plan:

Summary

Purpose: Conveys the results at the end of the PDCA Implementation Phase
Who Fills Out: Team Leader and/or Facilitator
Distribution: Process Owner, Executive Sponsor, and other appropriate top-level managers

Kaizen Event | **Summary**

By: _____   Date: _____

Team Name: _____

Measurement	# At Start	# Target	Target % Chg.	# At End	Actual % Chg.

Objective: _____

Team Members:

19. Create PDCA Implementation Phase schedule.

The following items need to be considered when creating the detailed PDCA Implementation Phase schedule:

❖ The amount of training that has been conducted and how the team has embraced any new tools and/or concepts from previous Kaizen Event training or Planning Phase training
❖ The amount and quality of data collected
❖ The process owner's involvement
❖ Acceptance of additional resources being allocated
❖ Availability of all team members
❖ Management availability
❖ Schedule of the process or area for the next phase (hours, people, times, etc.)
❖ Flexibility of the team member's time with the upcoming PDCAs

Note: Even though we have defined a Standard 5 Day Kaizen Event in this book, it is almost a certainty that the one you develop for your organization will be somewhat different. Therefore, spend the necessary time with the team and create a detailed schedule. Use the following schedule as a guideline. It will not be practical to list every activity at this time, therefore, acknowledge to the team that they will have to be somewhat flexible during the PDCA Implementation Phase. This "unknown" may be an issue for some team members, however, address as many of their concerns as possible.

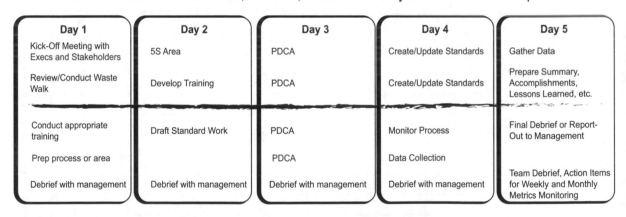

Day 1	Day 2	Day 3	Day 4	Day 5
Kick-Off Meeting with Execs and Stakeholders	5S Area	PDCA	Create/Update Standards	Gather Data
Review/Conduct Waste Walk	Develop Training	PDCA	Create/Update Standards	Prepare Summary, Accomplishments, Lessons Learned, etc.
Conduct appropriate training	Draft Standard Work	PDCA	Monitor Process	Final Debrief or Report-Out to Management
Prep process or area		PDCA	Data Collection	
Debrief with management	Debrief with management	Debrief with management	Debrief with management	Team Debrief, Action Items for Weekly and Monthly Metrics Monitoring

The detailed activities for each day will be conveyed in Part 2. PDCA Implementation Phase.

20. Communicate to Executive Sponsor and other managers the schedule. It is suggested the process owner, team leader, and Black Belt, Lean Sensei, or Continuous Improvement Specialist meet with the executive sponsor for 10 - 15 minutes to review the schedule. It will be very important to ensure the executive sponsor knows what is expected of them as well as how communications will occur throughout the Kaizen Event.

21. Complete A3 Report - Section 4. Problem Analysis, Section 5. Future State, and Section 6. Implementation Plan. The following Lean Thinking Questions should be reviewed by the team to ensure these sections are as complete as possible:

3. Improvement Opportunity	5. Future State
How will we know when we have achieved success? *Are there benchmarks or comparative data that we should review?* *What should we measure in order to (a) compare "before" and "after" and (b) know how we have made a difference in the process?* *Have we identified the wastes?* *Can we show goals using a balanced scorecard?* *What will the future state look like?*	*What gaps are there between the current and future state and what are the specific PDCAs?* *What stakeholders will be involved in the action plan?* *What is the communication plan?* *Can we show a high-level summary of process steps that need to be changed?*
4. Problem Analysis	**6. Implementation Plan**
Who will be impacted by changes in this process? *What is the demand for the process - how many requests by hour of the day and/or day of the week?* *What is the detailed process flow?* *Can we use a Fishbone Diagram to find and show any likely problem areas?* *How much waste is there in the process?* *Have we asked the "5 Whys" for each step?* *Can we show that we have identified the major problems using a Pareto Chart?* *Have we used an Impact Map or other tool to prioritize the wastes/problems?* *Do we understand the root causes of the problem?*	*What improvement tools and resources will we need?* *What steps need to be taken to accomplish the improvement plan?* *Who will take the lead for each step?* *What time frame will be required?* *What is the training/education plan?* *How will the data be collected and reported?* *Can we show a high-level 4 W's of Who (does) What (by) When, and Why for this project?*
	7. Verify Results
	Can we show a chart to display the process "before and after" to show success? *Is the new process meeting the target?*
	8. Follow-Up
	Has SPC or a Visual Management system been

Address any other concerns or issues the team may have brought up.

The following are the deliverables that would be expected 1 Week Out for this type of Event:

(1) Conducted Stakeholder Analysis.
(2) Continued with specific Lean tool training.
(3) Determined specific improvement activities and used the PDCA format.
(4) Created a future state value stream or process map.
(5) Created Reporting and Communication forms.
(6) Created PDCA Implementation schedule.
(7) Communicated to Executive Sponsor and other managers the schedule.
(8) Completed A3 Report Section 4. Problem Analysis, Section 5. Future State, and Section 6. Implementation Plan.

The following Standard Kaizen Event Planning Phase Checklist will help ensure all critical items are completed prior to Part 2. PDCA Implementation Phase. The Checklist is a listing of the main steps, main features for the steps, as well as the forms or worksheets suggested. This will help ensure a successful completion of this Phase. Use this as a guideline to customize a Checklist for your Event.

Kaizen Event	Standard Kaizen Event

Kaizen Event

Process Owner: _____ Black Belt or Lean Sensei: _____ Start Date: _____ End Date: _____

Objective: _____

Standard Kaizen Event Planning Phase Checklist

Weeks Denote Prior to Next Phase

3 Weeks (4 hour meeting time)

☐ **1. Determine project scope.**
Negative trends for Balance Scorecard or Performance Dashboard
Addressing customer mandates or audits that require immediate action
Reducing costs to remain competitive
Launching a new product line
Addressing employee turnover issues

☐ **2. Gather initial data set.**
Adjustment times, batch sizes, changeover times, cycle times, delay times, delivery schedules, down times, efficiency percentages, failure rates, quality yields, number of shifts, sigma value, value-added times, etc.

☐ **3. Create high level value stream or process map.**
It is the 30,000-foot view

☐ **4. Determine initial team members.**
Team Champion or Executive Sponsor, Team Leader, Facilitator, Timekeeper, Scribe, Technical Representative, Informaticist, Team Members

☐ **5. Create the initial Team Charter.**
Use Team Charter form
Aligns team to management
Allows team to stay on track and not have scope creep
Encourages communication at all levels
Reduces stress
Allows for project standardization

☐ **6. Assemble the team and conduct first meeting.**
Keep meeting to no more than 3 hours
Clarify roles and responsiblities
Conduct broad overview of Lean Sigma (simulation)
Ensure everyone commits to Action Items
Use Meeting Information Form
Use Effective Meeting Evaluation worksheet

☐ **7. Complete A3 Report - Section 1. Problem Statement.**

Other Activities:

☐
☐
☐

2 Weeks (4 hour meeting time)

☐ **8. Create a SIPOC Diagram, if needed.**
Supplier, Input, Process, Output, Customer identify suppliers, customers, and requirements
Helps ensure improvement project focus

☐ **9. Create detailed current state value stream or process map.**
Provides more detail than high level map
Provides visual to help determine what data may need to be collected
Maps come in all shapes and sizes

☐ **10. Create a Cycle Time Table (or appropriate method to obtain accurate cycle times).**
Ensure start and stop cycle times are understood by all
Be satisfied w/ 80% of data collected, but strive for more
Gather data process real-time
Consider Measurement System Analysis

☐ **11. Conduct a Waste Walk.**
Ensure process area employees know in advance of the Waste Walk
Assign one person to take notes
If group greater than 5, split into smaller groups
Start downstream and work your way upstream
Do not cause any disruption to the process area
Ensure questions are determined before the walk

☐ **12. Update current state value stream or process map.**
Use Post-it Notes to identify wastes on current state map
Consolidate similar wastes by reaching a consensus
Use data from Waste Walk, Cycle Time Table, etc.

☐ **13. Complete A3 Report - Section 2. Current State and Section 3. Improvement Opportunity**

Other Activities:

☐
☐
☐

1 Week (4 - 8 hours meeting time)

☐ **14. Conduct a Stakeholder Analysis.**
Ensure all key players are considered and proper communication occurs, before, during, and after the Event

☐ **15. Conduct specific Lean tool training.**
5S, Standard Work, Mistake Proofing, Continuous Flow and Kanbans, Leveling, Visual Controls, etc.
Distribute *The Lean Six Sigma Pocket Guide XL*s

☐ **16. Determine specific improvement activities and use the Plan – Do – Check – Act (PDCA) format.**
Consider Valued-Added versus Non Value-Added Analysis, Histograms, 5 Why Analysis, Brainstorming, Cause and Effect, etc.
Plan–define the improvement activity/experiment, what will be done, who will do it, and how it will be measured
Do–implement the improvement plan/experiment
Check–ensure that the intended improvement was successful in terms of the measurements set forth
Act–confirm that improvement experiment worked with improved performance; act to standardize the process
Document activities on PDCA Kaizen Activity Worksheet

☐ **17. Create a future state value stream or process map.**
Use different colored Post-it Notes for Lean tool application then create a future state map

☐ **18. Create Reporting and Communication forms.**
Project Prep Status, Kickoff, Daily Recap, Summary

☐ **19. Create PDCA Implementation Phase schedule.**
Be somewhat flexible in the schedule, everything cannot be planned out exactly on how it will go

☐ **20. Communicate to Executive Sponsor and other managers the schedule.**
Recommend face-to-face meeting
Keep all stakeholers informed

☐ **21. Complete A3 Report - Section 4. Problem Analysis, Section 5. Future State, and Section 6. Implementation Plan.**

Other Activities:

☐
☐
☐

Sensei Tips: Consider additional team members, use good project management skills, listen to employee's concerns, and use this Checklist.

The Standard Kaizen Event Planning Phase Checklist has proven helpful for teams in planning their Kaizen Events. However, the various activities listed under each of the three categories (3 Weeks, 2 Weeks, etc.) can be completed at different times throughout this phase (as well as some activities may also be completed on Day 1 of the PDCA Implementation Phase). For example, in the 2 Weeks section, (10) Create a Cycle Time Table could be completed in the 3 Weeks section, or, maybe the data is already easily accessible and the Cycle Time Table does not need to be created. Consider each activity listed as value-added or non value-added to the team's objectives. Also, be flexible to accept and use any other activities that team members might have experienced that may provide value to the team's objective. Use good project management techniques now and throughout the scope of the Event.

The following Action Item Log can be used in place of the PDCA Kaizen Activity Worksheet or some other project management tool can be used to schedule and document improvement activities. *The **Action Item (AI) Log** is used by the team to assign and follow-up on specific Actions Items agreed to throughout all three phases of the Kaizen Event.* The AI Log lists specific action items, the individual or group responsible to complete the action item, and when the action item is due to be completed. The AI Log can be used during regular team work sessions to follow-up on progress and to assign resources as necessary.

Kaizen Event

Action Item Log

Process Owner: [ ] Black Belt or Lean Sensei: [ ] On Schedule ☐ Delayed ■

Objective: [ ] Date: [ ]

Action Item - Task Description	Who	Start Date	Expected Completion	Completion Date	On Schedule or Delayed	Comments/Notes/Why

Once the Planning Phase has been completed, or at least 80% completed or addressed, then it would be time to begin the PDCA Implementation or "doing" Phase.

Part 2. PDCA Implementation Phase (spans 3 - 5 Days/24 - 40 hours meeting time)

There are many variables to consider when implementing the actual process changes (i.e., the PDCAs). Use the following as a guide during the PDCA Implementation Phase:

1. Review the following example on how one organization detailed their activities in their PDCA Implementation Phase.

Day 1

(1) Review team goals and objectives; train on additional Lean tools or more in-depth on most likely tools that will be used; review 5 day schedule.
(2) Review "before" data, documentation, and data collection methods and tools.
(3) Determine takt time/cycle time calculations and/or performance goals; use appropriate Standard Work Combination Table/Chart, Cycle Time Table, and/or Document Tagging Worksheet to obtain needed numbers.
(4) Review or update process or value stream map with Post-it Notes with any new information.
(5) Conduct a Waste Walk or modified Waste Walk if done previously, and take before photos.
(6) Identify value-added and non value-added activities.
(7) Review future state process or value stream map and modify accordingly.
(8) Meet with stakeholders to review plan.
(9) Plan 5S activities for Day 2.
(10) Complete Daily Recap and Kick Off documents and present or communicate to management at an end of the day meeting (there most likely will not be any change in the measurement on this first day).
(11) Review/adjust Day 2 schedule.

Day 2

(1) Review and discuss any information from Day 1.
(2) Create or review specific activities from PDCA Kaizen Activity Worksheet.
(3) Create plan for new process or work area layout.
(4) Meet with stakeholders and review proposed changes; solicit input, address concerns; be empathetic to their concerns and needs.
(5) Notify/confirm with ancillary support groups of time and place for any requested support services.
(6) Draft standard work of new process.
(7) Review PDCA of new process (if multiple processes are being modified, consider each a PDCA).
(8) Develop training plan for new process.
(9) Communicate training for affected stakeholders; determine start date for new process.
(10) Update Daily Recap document and present to management.
(11) Initiate 5S in process area, if appropriate.
(12) Review/adjust Day 3 schedule.

Day 3

(1) Review and discuss any information from Day 2.
(2) Create or review specific activities from PDCA Kaizen Activity Worksheet and modify accordingly.
(3) Conduct training stakeholders on new process.
(4) Continue PDCA improvements in process or area with stakeholders, includes training stakeholders and closely monitoring new process; commit 100% support during this time.
(5) Immediately correct any problems.
(6) Create or enhance visual controls.
(7) Work on 5S or any safety issues while PDCA is occurring, as time permits.
(8) Collect appropriate data with new process.
(9) Complete Daily Recap document and present to management.
(10) Review/adjust Day 4 schedule.

Day 4

(1) Review and discuss any information from Day 3.
(2) Continue PDCA activities and training stakeholders on new work layout and/or process.
(3) Fix any/all problems from Day 3.
(4) Continue support and data collection of new process.
(5) Adjust new process as necessary with input from stakeholders.
(6) Update with standard work procedures.
(7) Take after photos of new process.
(8) Conduct debriefing with stakeholders.
(9) Create visual management plan with stakeholders to monitor new processes and submit data weekly or make it available real-time.
(10) Complete Daily Recap document and present to management.
(11) Review/adjust Day 5 schedule.

Day 5

(1) Review and discuss any information from Day 4.
(2) Continue any final PDCA activities and ensure all stakeholders are thoroughly training on new work layout and/or process.
(3) Fix any/all problems from Day 4.
(4) Determine support role for sustaining and controlling improvements made (this may include additional support during Part 3. Follow-Up Phase.
(5) Create plan for enterprise roll-out of the new process, if appropriate.
(6) Prepare and present final presentation to management including the Daily Recap, Summary, Accomplishments, and Lessons Learned.
(7) Complete the To-Do List document for any activities that need to be completed during Part 3. Follow-Up Phase.
(8) Ensure each team member completes a Kaizen Event Participation Evaluation.

(9) Team Leader consolidates Kaizen Event Participation Evaluations and share with team and process owner; create plan for improvements based on evaluations.

(10) Ensure all critical documents (e.g., A3 Report) are completed as appropriate.

(11) Reward and recognize team members.

Note: Ensure the primary stakeholder is treated with the utmost respect. Remember that these stakeholders may be experiencing fear to this new process change. This may be due to new technical requirements or modified work procedures that may cause additional stress. Continually listen to their needs and concerns and make it a point to address each of them in a positive way.

Note: The Standard 5 Day Kaizen Event Part 2. PDCA Implementation Phase is detailed as 5 continuous, team activity days, but can be done in a 2, 3, or 4 day time period. This would depend on the availability of the team members, scope of the project, availability of the process area, ancillary support (e.g., IT, Facilities), etc.

2. Complete A3 Report - Section 7. Verify Results. The following Lean Thinking Questions should be reviewed by the team to ensure this section is as complete as possible:

7. Verify Results
Can we show a chart to display the process "before and after" to show success?
Is the new process meeting the target?
8. Follow-Up

The following are the deliverables that would be expected at the end of the PDCA Implementation Phase for this type of Event:

(1) Improved measurements as defined in the Team Charter.
(2) Reported progress to plan to management daily, or as required.
(3) Applied Lean Six Sigma tools to remove process waste and variation.
(4) Implemented 5S in process area.
(5) Communicated to all stakeholders throughout the project.
(6) Created new standards.
(7) Trained employees to new standards.
(8) Created a visual management plan.
(9) Presented final report out.
(10) Determined Lean Representative for continued support.
(11) Completed To-Do List.
(12) Evaluated the Kaizen Event.
(13) Created appropriate documentation to share results.
(14) Rewarded the team.
(15) Completed A3 Report Section 7. Verify Results.

The following Standard Kaizen Event PDCA (Implementation) Phase Checklist will help ensure all critical items are completed prior to Part 3. Follow-Up Phase. The Checklist is a listing of the main steps, main features for the steps, as well as the forms or worksheets suggested. This will help ensure a successful completion of this Phase. Use this as a guideline for customizing a Checklist for your Event.

Kaizen Event				Standard Kaizen Event

Standard Kaizen Event PDCA Phase Checklist

Kaizen Event

Process Owner: _____ Black Belt or Lean Sensei: _____ Start Date: _____ End Date: _____

Objective: _____

Day 1 (8 hour meeting time)	Day 2 (8 hour meeting time)	Day 3 (8 hour meeting time)	Day 4 (8 hour meeting time)	Day 5 (8 hour meeting time)
☐ 1. Review team goals.	☐ 1. Review/discuss info from Day 1.	☐ 1. Review/discuss info from Day 2.	☐ 1. Review/discuss info from Day 3.	☐ 1. Review/discuss info from Day 4
☐ 2. Review before documentation and data.	☐ 2. Create/review PDCA Kaizen Worksheet.	☐ 2. Create/review PDCA Kaizen Worksheet.	☐ 2. Continue PDCA activities and training stakeholders on new work layout and/or process.	☐ 2. Ensure all stakeholders are trained on new process.
☐ 3. Determine takt time or performance goal.	☐ 3. Create/review plan for new process or work area.	☐ 3. Conduct training with stakeholders.		☐ 3. Fix any/all problems from Day 4.
☐ 4. Review/update process or value stream map.	☐ 4. Meet with stakeholders.	☐ 4. Implement PDCA.	☐ 3. Fix any/all problems from Day 3.	☐ 4. Determine support roles.
☐ 5. Conduct or review Waste Walk.	☐ 5. Notify/confirm ancillary groups for support.	☐ 5. Correct problems as needed.	☐ 4. Continue support and data collection.	☐ 5. Create enterprise-wide roll out plan, if appropriate.
☐ 6. Take before photos.	☐ 6. Draft standard work of new process.	☐ 6. Create or enhance visual controls.	☐ 5. Listen to stakeholders and adjust as necessary.	☐ 6. Prepare and present final presentation to management.
☐ 7. Identify wastes.	☐ 7. Review PDCAs.	☐ 7. Work on 5S or safety issues.	☐ 6. Update with standard work.	☐ 7. Complete To-Do List.
☐ 8. Review maps and update.	☐ 8. Develop training plan.	☐ 8. Collect data on new process.	☐ 7. Take after photos of new process.	☐ 8. Ensure participants complete Kaizen Event Participation Evaluation form.
☐ 9. Meet with stakeholders.	☐ 9. Communicate training plan to stakeholders.	☐ 9. Update Daily Recap document; present to management.	☐ 8. Conduct debriefing with stakeholders.	☐ 9. Team Leader consolidate Participant Evaluations and appropriately shares.
☐ 10. Plan 5S activities for Day 2.	☐ 10. Update Daily Recap document; present to management.		☐ 9. Create visual management plan.	☐ 10. Share all documents (e.g., A3 Report).
☐ 11. Complete Daily Recap and Kick Off documents.	☐ 11. Initiate 5S in process area.		☐ 10. Update Daily Recap document; present to management.	☐ 11. Reward and recognize team members.
☐ 12. Review documents with management.				
Other Activities:	**Other Activities:**	**Other Activities:**	**Other Activities:**	**Other Activities:**
☐ _____	☐ _____	☐ _____	☐ _____	☐ Complete A3 Report - Section 7. Verify Results
☐ _____	☐ _____	☐ _____	☐ _____	
☐ _____	☐ _____	☐ _____	☐ _____	

Sensei Tips: Keep management informed, respect the process area employees, and use this Checklist.

The Standard Kaizen Event PDCA (Implementation) Phase Checklist has proven helpful for Kaizen teams in making the process changes in this phase. Consider each activity listed as value-added or non value-added to the team's objectives. Also, be flexible to accept and use any other activities that the team members might have experienced that may also provide value to the team's objective.

Once the PDCA Implementation Phase has been completed, or at least 80% completed or addressed, then it would be time to begin Follow-Up Phase.

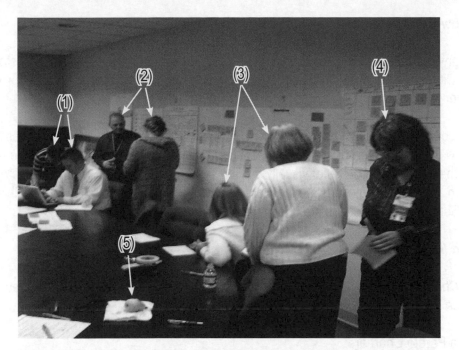

This team is in Day 2 of a Standard 5 Day Kaizen Event. Good project management techniques are demonstrated. Everyone has specific assignments. Note the following: (1) team members analyzing data and creating appropriate charts, (2) team members discussing where to take photos (typically done in Day 1), (3) team members reviewing the value stream map, (4) team member going to the process area, and (5) team member having left their healthy snack! This team is very productive and making great progress.

Part 3. Follow-Up Phase (spans 2 - 4 weeks/1 - 2 hours meeting time)

There are many reasons improvements from the PDCA Implementation Phase are not sustained over time. Use the following steps as a guide to help ensure the likelihood of the Kaizen Event improvements being sustained over time:

1. Continue communications. Ensure everyone, from various stakeholders to the process owner, understands how the improvements are being measured and the type of charting that will be used during this Phase. Charting is the process of visually making sense of the data. It is turning the "data" into useful information. The following charts are the more common ones that can be used during this Phase (or any Phase). Before and after charts are often created.

Pareto Chart (before and after)

The **Pareto Chart** is in a bar chart format that represents the Pareto principle which states that 20% of the sources cause 80% of the problems.

Attributes of a Pareto Chart are:

❖ Lists issues in descending order of importance
❖ Generally, tallest bars indicate biggest contributors to the problem
❖ Good for displaying before and after improvement initiatives

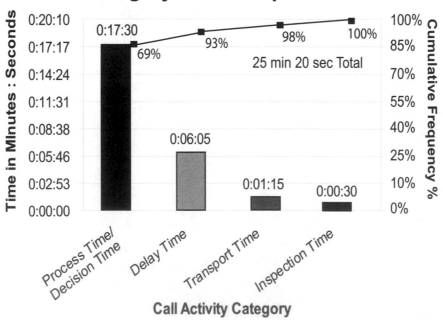

Paynter Chart (before and after)

The **Paynter Chart** *is a visual representation over time relative to the subgroups based on Pareto Chart information.* It is a further analysis of what is comprised on the bars of the Pareto Chart.

Attributes of a Paynter Chart are:

❖ Used to track defects over time relative to corrective action
❖ Similar to a Run Chart
❖ Paynter Chart goes beyond the Pareto by sub-grouping the Pareto bars relative to days, hours, etc.

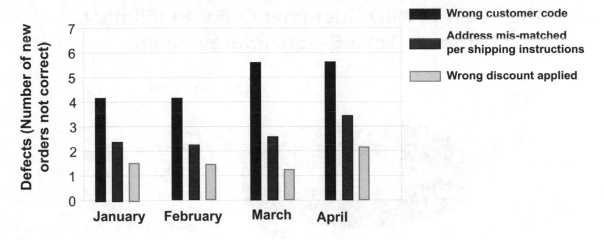

Pie Chart (before and after)

A **Pie Chart** *is a circular chart divided into sectors; each sector shows the relative size of each value.* Pie Charts and Pareto Charts basically illustrate the same data. Pie Charts are typically used to compare multiple sets of data, where comparing the size of one Pie Chart to another can illustrate a difference in size or magnitude of the situations.

Attributes of a Pie Chart are:

- ❖ Displays relative size of each category to each other
- ❖ Good for comparing multiple sets of data
- ❖ Illustrates a difference in size or magnitude of the data sets
- ❖ Allows for quick interpretation of the data

Pie Chart of New Customer Order Fulfillment Process Time Before Improvement

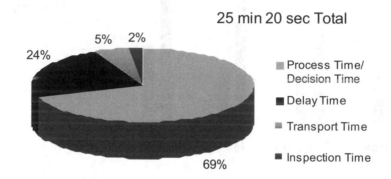

25 min 20 sec Total

- Process Time/ Decision Time
- Delay Time
- Transport Time
- Inspection Time

Scatter (and Concentration) Plots

Scatter (and Concentration) Plots *are used to study the possible relationship between one variable and another.* Through visual examination and additional mathematical analysis, problem solvers can determine relationships between variables.

Attributes of a Scatter (and Concentration) Plot are:

❖ Allows for trends (problematic areas) to be easily viewed
❖ Reveals relationship between variables
❖ Answers the question, are the variables related?
❖ Helps to identify the "outliers" which may need further investigation
❖ Provides data for a linear regression if there is a high degree of positive or negative correlation
❖ Provides data for a non-linear regression if there is a small degree of positive or negative correlation

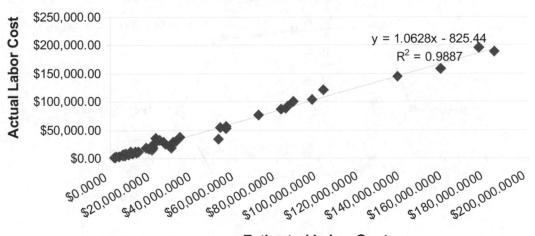

This Actual to Estimated Labor Cost Scatter Plot conveys that the Estimated Labor Costs are very accurate at predicting Actual Labor Costs for the project given the R² value is nearly 1 (0.9887).

Radar Chart (before and after)

A **Radar Chart**, also known as a Spider Chart or a Star Chart, because of its appearance, plots the values of each category along a separate axis that starts in the center of the chart and ends on the outer ring.

Attributes of a Radar Chart are:

❖ Allows for a visual representation of the before and after measurements in one view
❖ Allows for multiple data sets to be compared to one another if colors or some other indicators are used
❖ Provides a visual to get a "feel" for data

Call Center Key Performance Measures
Goal 100%

This Call Center Radar Chart displays their Key Performance Measures relative to their goal of 100%. The next step for the improvement team working on this project might be to determine why their customers are not satisfied (Customer Satisfaction Survey category) and why phone calls are going over 3.5 minutes (Target Call Length ≤ 3.5 Minutes category). The Radar Chart is a great visual tool.

Run Chart

A **Run Chart** is a method to display several data points over time. Because our minds are not good at re-membering patterns in data, a visual display will allow us to see the measurement(s) of an entire process.

Attributes of a Run Chart are:

- ❖ Allows improvements to be verified that they are working
- ❖ Assists to determine most effective long-term solutions
- ❖ Measures effectiveness of improvements
- ❖ Displays improvements relative to time

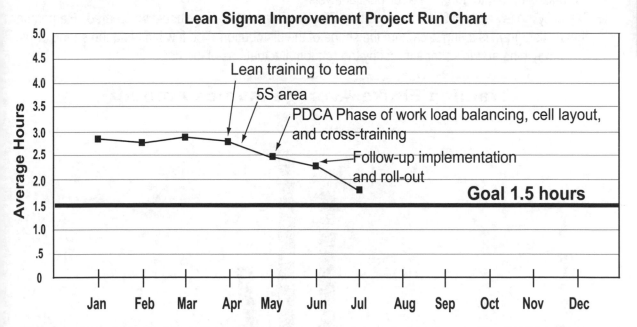

This Run Chart indicated that 5S had an initial impact to the goal of 1.5 hours. The PDCA Implementation Phase of work load balancing, cell layout, and cross-training has the trend going in the right direction.

Histogram (before and after)

Histograms *utilize measurement data and display the spread and shape of the distribution.* Histograms are simple bar chart representations of the range, amount, and pattern of variation for data (i.e., the population).

Attributes of a Histogram are:

❖ Displays the data showing peaks and valleys, clusters, and outliers (i.e., data points numerically different from the rest of the group)
❖ Allows visual representation of data sets
❖ Organizes data into "bins" for additional analysis
❖ Typically, no fewer than 5 and no more than 20 class intervals or bins should be created. Remember that a Histogram is trying to capture the shape of the distribution. Too few bins and the shape is lost. Too many bins and the shape is lost by the random fluctuations of the data.

Training Firm's Average Invoice Amount

	$ 0-100	$ 100-500	$ 500-1000	$ 1000-2000	$ 2000-3000	$ 3000-4000	$ 4000-5000	$ 5000-6000	$ 6000-7000	$ 7000-8000	> $ 8000
■ Series1	1	3	7	25	68	73	45	12	3	5	1

This sales team's Histogram indicates that the average invoice dollar amount is between $2,000 – $5,000. The sales team had a decrease in sales revenue for their area and used this information to assign additional marketing resources to target the higher-end clients (i.e., $7,000 - $8,000).

Statistical Process Control Charts

Statistical Process Control is a group of tools used to monitor and control process outputs. The idea behind SPC is to monitor processes to determine if they are in control, are developing trends, and/or when they go out of control. Processes are said to be in control if only natural or common cause variation is occurring. SPC Charts, also referred to as Control or Shewhart Charts, will identify when special cause variation has crept into the process. They are used to predict the future performance of a process.

Attributes of SPC Charts are:

❖ SPC Charts work with two types of data: variable data and attribute data. Variable data is data such as length, time, weight, etc. that is measured along a continuous scale. Attribute data assumes only two values (good or bad, pass or fail, etc.).

❖ 3 Standard Deviations (3 SD or 3 sigma) gives a "confidence level" which encompasses 99.73% of all events or 99.73% of ALL events will fall within +/- 3 SD. X-Bar plus 3 SD, referred to as the UCL, is the + 3 SD marker and X-Bar minus 3 SD, referred to as the LCL, is the -3 SD marker. This is used to recognize what is "normal" and what is "abnormal." Basically, as long as the individual plots are between the UCL and the LCL, the process is exhibiting "NORMAL" variation. However, 99.73% of events means that 0.27% of the points on the Control Chart would be outside the +/-3 SD control limits when the process is operating in control, and these would be false signals

❖ Based on these values, and calculated parameters for control limits, the control limits for the sample X-Bar and R values are established. Then the sample values are plotted on their respective charts. Any values or groups of values are deemed to be out-of-control if any of the following conditions occur:

  One point above the Upper Control Limit (UCL)
  One point below the Lower Control Limit (LCL)
  Any increasing run or trend of 7 consecutive points
  Any decreasing run or trend of 7 consecutive points
  Seven consecutive points above the X-bar
  Seven consecutive points below the X-bar
  Any point outside the range control limits
  Two out of three consecutive points in the outer one-third region of the control limits
  Four out of five points in the outer two-thirds region of the control limits

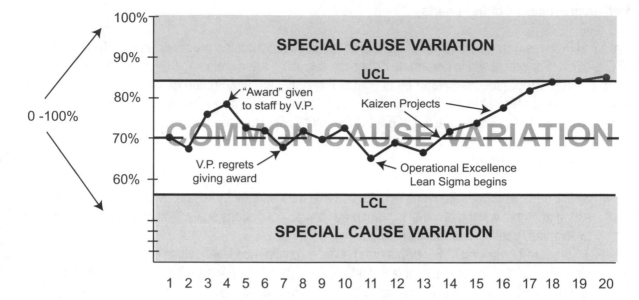

This customer service SPC Control Chart is for the question "I would recommend this organization's products and services to others." from their recently completed Customer Satisfaction Survey. Prior to a implementing Operational Excellence (a Lean Sigma program), the V.P. had prematurely given awards to employees and departments due to the improvements in scores (not remembering that this was most likely due to common cause variation). Upon initiating a formal program and having a few Kaizen Events completed, there was a significant improvement in the scores. This example clearly shows that prior to understanding Lean Sigma (and specifically Control Charts) managers had led by innuendos and rumors, not by statistically significant data. As the trend continued, the Upper and Lower Control Limits were recalculated.

2. Complete all PDCA activities. It is expected that 80 – 90% of all PDCA activity will be completed during the PDCA Implementation Phase. For those PDCA activities that could not be completed, consider the following actions:

  ❖ Assign any outstanding PDCAs and/or Action Items to specific team members. The final Action Item List should be maintained by the process owner with appropriate follow-ups and support.
  ❖ If for unforeseen reason, some major parts could not be done, consider extending the team with weekly with 1-hour meetings at an agreed upon time.
  ❖ Establish a new team if the Kaizen Event was a beta or pilot program, therefore, a company-wide roll-out will be expected. Keep 2 – 3 of the core team members of the new team. Consider using the Rolling Kaizen Event format for the company-wide roll-out.

3. Provide support after the Follow-Up Phase. This may be in the form of someone being designated (i.e., the Lean Sensei/Black Belt) from the core team that will be available as needed to the process workers where the changes occurred. This could also be someone from the intact work area that was part of the team, but now they must be available for any questions for a period of time, probably 30- 60 days, or until everyone is trained to the new standards.

4. Create and distribute the Kaizen Event Dashboards. This will align everyone on the process improvement relative to the measurements. There should be a review of the measurements on a weekly basis (if not done real-time or daily); however, if there are no issues, then a weekly review would be appropriate to ensure no negative trends are occurring. The following is a template of a 28 day follow-up (Weekly Project Dashboard) as well as a 4 month follow-up (Monthly Project Dashboard) report:

Kaizen Event

Weekly Project Dashboard

Type of Project:

Value Stream Impacted:

Executive Champion:

Process Owner:

Timeframe:

Lean Sensei/Black Belt:

Measurement	Project Start	Target/ Units	7 Day Date:	14 Day Date:	21 Day Date:	28 Day Date:	Project End
Process Yield %							
Performance compared to target %							

Dates

Key:
Green - Performance Meets or Exceeds Target
Yellow - Performance is Short of but close to Target
Red - Performance is Unfavorable to Target

Measurement	Project Start	Target/ Units	7 Day Date:	14 Day Date:	21 Day Date:	28 Day Date:	Project End

If the process metric is not meeting traget(s) the WWWWW (below) must clearly indicate how you plan to meet or exceed target.

What	Who	When (m/d/y)	Why	Comments/Status

Additional Notes:

Kaizen Event

Monthly Project Dashboard

Type of Project: [ ]

Value Stream Impacted: [ ]

Timeframe: [ ]

Executive Champion: [ ]

Lean Sensei/Black Belt: [ ]

Process Owner: [ ]

Measurement	Project Start	Target/ Units	Month 1:	Month 2:	Month 3:	Month 4:	Project End
					Dates		
Process Yield %							
Performance compared to target %							

Key:
■ Green - Performance Meets or Exceeds Target
■ Yellow - Performance is Short of but close to Target
■ Red - Performance is Unfavorable to Target

	Project Start	Target/ Units	Month 1:	Month 2:	Month 3:	Month 4:	Project End

If the process metric is not meeting traget(s), the WWWWW below must clearly indicate how you plan to meet or exceed target.

What	Who	When (m/d/y)	Why	Comments/Status

Additional Notes:

The Weekly Project Dashboard and the Monthly Project Dashboard should be maintained by the process owner, shared with the process area employees, and communicated to management.

5. Establish an avenue for stakeholders to provide feedback. This will most likely funnel from the stakeholders to a designee of the Kaizen Event team member, (i.e., the Lean Sensei or Black Belt), to the process owner. This cannot be taken lightly. It would be very easy for the employees to revert back to the old way of doing things, especially if the new process presents some unforeseen problems with no solutions. Again, many of these issues should have been discovered in the PDCA Implementation Phase. However, in those rare occurrences that something may have been missed provide the appropriate avenue for "continuous improvement" on the "continuous improvement" project!

The following are some suggestions on how the stakeholders can contribute ideas:

❖ A Kaizen Suggestion Box can be placed in the process area labeled appropriately. If this is done, ensure that the employees will target their suggestions to the recent improvement project.
❖ Employees can contribute ideas through a designated email address (i.e., KaizenProjectXX@CompanyABC.com). The email should be forwarded to the lean Sensei/Black Belt and the process owner. Items or suggestions should be responded to in a timely manner. All ideas and suggestions should be acknowledged with a thank-you.
❖ The Lean Sensei/Black Belt and/or process owner could designate a time each day to "walk" the new process, solicit input, and provide immediate feedback. (Highly recommended)
❖ The Lean Sensei/Black Belt or process owner could email each stakeholder and ask for a response for a limited time period. For example, a suggestion form of some sort could be placed on Google Drive. Employees who have access to the Internet could contribute. This could be set-up such that once someone contributes; an email will be generated from the Lean Sensei/Black Belt or process owner to the employee thanking them for their comments as well as ensuring them of a timely response.

6. Practice Gemba. **Gemba,** *(Japanese origin of genba) is a term meaning "the real place" or where the work is done.* It is commonly referred to as a Gemba Walk, much like Management By Walk-Around (MBWA). This is an activity that has the manager taking a pro-active approach to understanding and engaging front-line employees by visiting the process area while looking for waste and opportunities for improvement (through Kaizen). The Gemba Walk should be part of a manager's standard approach to interacting with their employees and not solely be part of a Kaizen Event. However, additional emphasis with a discussion of any past, current, or future Kaizen Event activity via the Gemba Walk would be of value.

Gemba activities for the manager are:

❖ Observe the area or process. Listen and watch. Engage the employees with positive comments when at all possible.
❖ Be as close to the customer (or process) as possible.
❖ Obtain firsthand information regarding the facts as to what is happening with the area or process.
❖ Be physically visible to the employees. Make eye contact.

Activities to avoid for the manager during a Gemba are:

- ❖ Arriving with prepared comments or speeches
- ❖ Solving issues or problems on the spot
- ❖ Staying for hours
- ❖ Acting on every single potential improvement that is observed

The following Going to the Gemba Checklist can assist leaders in their quest to become more aware of the issues facing their employees:

Kaizen Event	Going to the Gemba Checklist			
Your Name (optional): _____ Manager's/Director's Name: _____	Event Date(s): _____			

INSTURCTIONS: Use the following checklist to evaluate the area or process. Space is for comments.

	Questions to Consider	Yes	No	Comments
1.	Are the measures/metrics/scorecard updated, color-coded to standards, and have assignable causes been identified for unacceptable variations in any key areas?			
2.	Are there any positive performing areas to complement and/or thank the workers? (Go thank people, say you noticed, and tell them to keep up the good work!)			
3.	Are there poorly performing areas that need countermeasures and corrective actions? (Look for the beginning of trends as well. Use an A3 format to track improvement and countermeasure initiatives. Use the 5 Whys process and Pareto charts to drill down to root causes. Ask the workers for PDCA improvement ideas to try.)			
4.	Are the countermeasures and corrective action plans, with dates, names and status, clearly identified on the scorecard or A3?			
5.	Is there evidence that the workers are getting involved and continuing to learn and use Lean methods and tools?			
	Additional Notes and Comments			

The following are additional considerations when practicing Gemba:

- ❖ Arrive to the Gemba with a specific purpose. This could include checking on the progress of a Kaizen Event, new standard work procedures, or quality, cost or delivery performance measures? The leader is going to Gemba to check on some aspect of the team's work. This is not meant to be a micro-manager tool!
- ❖ Review and comment on the visual systems that are being used. These visual systems (performance dashboards, metrics, storyboards, etc.) provide a good avenue to "coach."
- ❖ Ensure the team or area continues to own the problems. A leader should not take it upon them to say, "Let me take care of that for you." Instead, provide support and encouragement - ownership is what you want your employees to have. Do take the responsibility away from the team.
- ❖ Engage all levels of management, when and where appropriate. It is recommended to not let higher level managers arrive and ask questions, etc. if the manager for that area is not present.

- ❖ Communicate to the area that you will be visiting at a particular time. The employees should know you are coming and the purpose. Do not overwhelm the team. Take notes as appropriate as you listen. Provide support and guidance as needed. Somehow acknowledge the employees with a thank-you after the visit. This may be an email that is posted, or an email blast to those employees.
- ❖ Build upon each Gemba. Keep good notes and show the employees that you remembered the last visit as well as acknowledging their progress.
- ❖ Request that the Black Belt, Lean Sensei, or Continuous Improvement Specialist, as well as the manager for the area, is present with the leader during their visit.

7. Apply Kaizen to the Kaizen Event. Use the following Kaizen Event Participation Evaluation form to identify areas for improvement in the next Kaizen Event.

Kaizen Event

Kaizen Event Participation Evaluation

Your Name (optional): [ ]   Event Date(s): [ ]

INSTURCTIONS: Please 'X' the appropriate response to each question.

How satisfied were you...	Strongly Disagree	Disagree	Neither Agree nor Disagree	Agree	Strongly Agree	Comments
1. ...that the pre-event team meetings provided adequate instruction and planning to ensure a successful event?						
2. ...that the current state value stream or process map and baseline data provided the team enough information to begin assessing the areas for improvement?						
3. ...that the majority of process wastes were identified?						
4. ...that the quality of the recommendations developed by the team were good?						
5. ...that the action planning process resulted in specific, measurable PDCA plans?						
6. ...That the facilitation supported achievement of objectives?						
7. ...that the Kaizen Event overall was successful?						
8. Which part of the Kaizen Event added most value? Why?						
9. Which part of the Kaizen Event could be improved? How?						
10. Would you like to participate in another Kaizen Event? Why or Why not?						
❑ Yes ❑ No						

For the team members that signed their name and had suggestions or selected Strongly Disagree on any of the statements, consider talking to them directly to gather additional information as they may rather talk in person about what could be improved. The form could also be modified to identify those that may have an interest to assist, lead, facilitate, and /or for subsequent Kaizen Events. Probably the most important question is number 10 - Would they like to participate in another Kaizen Event? If this is your first Kaizen Event, work it like any process, use the data from this evaluation and make appropriate changes.

8. Reward and recognize the team. The Kaizen Event team members should be rewarded and recognized by a senior manager, process owner, executive sponsor, or team champion. The recognition may be in the form of a simple thank-you at the closing meeting, then followed-up by an email noting some specific accomplishments of the team. Common types of rewards are as follows:

- ❖ Gift certificates (retail or restaurant), gift checks, cash equivalents
- ❖ Verbal recognition (announcements at company meetings)
- ❖ Parties, lunches, dinners
- ❖ Awards, written recognition (employee of the month, newsletter articles, blogs, Web pages, etc.)
- ❖ Tickets to entertainment venues (theater, movies, concerts, sporting events, etc.)
- ❖ Corporate gifts with the company logo (gold pens, calendars, T-shirts, golf balls, etc.)
- ❖ Time off
- ❖ Symbolic statues/items (something that may play on the company's name)
- ❖ Coffee or lunch with the CEO, V.P., or high-level director
- ❖ Greens fees
- ❖ Other simple and low-cost rewards that leaders can leverage to encourage Kaizen and create an environment rich in continuous improvement and problem solving thinking and doing

Rewarding each of the team members does not have to be identical; however, for the Kaizen Event team members, ensure if all team members are not receiving an identical item, ensure the value is the same.

9. Complete A3 Report - Section 8. Follow-Up. The following Lean Thinking Questions should be reviewed by the team to ensure this section is as complete as possible.

8. Follow-Up
Has SPC or a Visual Management system been considered to ensure for monitoring improvements? What have we learned from this project? How will the results continue to be shared with stakeholders and customers? How will we share the learnings with others across the system?

The following are the deliverables that would be expected at the end of the Follow-Up Phase for this type of Event:

(1) Continued communications.
(2) Completed all PDCAs.
(3) Provide support after the Follow-Up Phase.
(4) Created and distributed the Kaizen Event Dashboards.
(5) Established an avenue for stakeholders to provide feedback.
(6) Practiced Gemba.
(7) Applied Kaizen to the Kaizen Event.
(8) Rewarded and recognized the team.
(9) Completed A3 Report Section 8. Follow-Up.

The following Standard Kaizen Event Follow-Up Phase Checklist will help ensure all critical items are completed prior to starting another Kaizen Event. The Checklist is a listing of the main steps, main features for the steps, as well as the forms or worksheets suggested. This will help ensure a successful completion of this Phase. Use this as a guideline for customizing a Checklist for your Event.

Kaizen Event	**Standard Kaizen Event Follow-Up Phase Checklist**	
Process Owner: ___ Black Belt or Lean Sensei: ___	Start Date: ___ End Date: ___	
Objective: ___		

Follow-Up Activities		Comments/Notes
☐ 1. **Continue communications.** Consider the following charts: Pareto Chart Paynter Chart Pie Chart Scatter (Concentration) Plots Radar Chart Run Chart Histogram Statistical Process Ctrl. Charts	☐ 6. **Practice Gemba.** Observe the process Informally ask questions Show concern Arrive with a purpose Comment on visuals Notify the area Include different mgmt levels Build upon each Gemba Thank employees for their efforts	
☐ 2. **Complete all PDCA activities.**	☐ 7. **Apply Kaizen to the Kaizen Event.** Kaizen Event Participation Evaluation form	
☐ 3. **Provide support after the Follow-Up Phase.** Lean Sensei/Black Belt		
☐ 4. **Create and distribute the Kaizen Event Dashboards.** Weekly Kaizen Dashboard Monthly Kaizen Dashboard Maintained by process owner	☐ 8. **Reward and recognize the team.** Verbal recognition Gift cards Lunches, dinners, etc. Recognition letters, awards, etc. Corporate gifts Time off Green fees	
☐ 5. **Establish an avenue for stakeholders to provide feedback.** Kaizen Suggestion Box Emails Walk and talk Google Drive	☐ 9. **Compete A3 Report - Section 8. Follow-Up** Share appropriately	
Other Activities:	**Other Activities:**	
☐	☐	
☐	☐	
☐	☐	
☐	☐	

Sensei Tips: Ensure all PDCAs are completed, share results throughout the organization, and reward and recognize team members and any other employees that contributed.

The Follow-Up Phase Checklist has proven helpful for Kaizen teams in sustaining the gains made in the PDCA Implementation Phase. Consider each activity listed as value-added or non value-added to the team's objectives. Also, be flexible to accept and use any other activities that the team members might have experienced that may also provide value to the team's objective.

Once the Follow-Up Phase has been completed, or at least 90% completed or addressed, then it would be time to begin another Kaizen Event!

Case Study

The following case study demonstrates many of the tools explained in this section as well as some of the "people-side" issues that are encountered by the facilitator, team leader, process owner, or team member. As with any improvement project, you too would select only the appropriate activities (i.e., tools, worksheets, forms, etc.) to meet your specific Kaizen Event requirements for planning, implementing, and reporting.

Kate Mason, the new President and CEO of Tinker Town, Inc., softly replaced the telephone just as Jeff Stauer, the CFO, walked into her office.

"Well," Kate said, "That was the Baby Bundles purchasing manager and they're not renewing their order for Bright Baby Bears. 'Too many problems with their most recent order, mostly dealing with invoicing problems and deliveries to their stores,' they said. That was a custom design for their chain of stores and their not continuing with using us really hurts."

"What'd you expect, given how our customer satisfactions rating for Theme Bears and our on-time-delivery performance have dropped in the last two quarters?" Jeff asked.

"What do you know that I don't know?" she asked.

"Nothing other than I actually read the reports I produce." he said.

"Our business is cyclical. You're new with the company. Look, there are always wobbles in customer satisfaction."

"This isn't a wobble. It's a ski slope." Jeff said. "The second monthly decline was predictable since we didn't do anything to correct the negatives that showed up in the preceding monthly report. The decline in the Theme Bears has a direct impact on our overall Customer Satisfaction Survey results."

Kate kept her temper in check. It's already been a bad morning. Baby Bundles' rejection had stunned her and what Jeff had said was true. She hadn't paid enough attention to the reports. She needed to get control of this situation and fast.

"You're right, Jeff. Could you please get me copies of those reports and any other information that relates to any customer service issues?"

Tinker Town, Inc. is a small manufacturer of all types of Teddy Bears, from the Standard Teddy Bear to customize or Theme Bears for birthdays, holidays, country-type, and sports. The company is located in Santa Claus, Indiana, and the southern part of the state. Tinker Town, Inc. has been in existence for over 50 years with an excellent name in the market place for quality. The Standard Teddy Bear was the original Teddy Bear and is still the most popular one to date, however the Theme Bears line has been steadily increasing over the past year. Tinker Town had always prided itself on high customer survey results - typically averaging over 95% throughout the years. The industry benchmark had been 85%.

Approximately three months ago, Tinker Town, Inc. decided to go global and created a merchant account for their web site which allowed them to receive orders via the Internet. This involved installing a new order fulfillment system. They also participated in the Google AdWords program giving them immediate access to customers throughout the world.

Kate met with Rita, the Quality Manager, and they went over Jeff's reports.

"I don't know what's happened," Rita said. "I know that's a poor statement from a quality manager but I'm mystified. I'll get right on this. Let me talk to Chris (the customer service manager) and get on this right away."

"First, I'm not blaming you or Chris. Second, I want us to demonstrate to the organization that we are committed to continuous improvement and that we need to get our employees involved in this process. Total Employee Involvement is something that we did quite well at my previous company. From what I understand, what has been working well here is that typically management had been implementing solutions to problems with little input from the employees. Now I want to get our employees involved in the improvement and problem solving process. Therefore, I want us to conduct a Kaizen Event and use this situation as our launching point for a new way to improve our business processes – I believe we can not only fix this problem for the Theme Bears, and since many of the processes are similar, I would expect the improvements to provide a new level of customer service. This will serve as an example in our organization as we move forward. Go ahead and meet with Chris and let me know what I need to do. You have my full support. I want this to be a top priority."

Tinker Town, with 150 employees, did not have someone dedicated to continuous improvement, therefore, Rita, the quality manager, assumed the role for this project as the facilitator. Rita had been trained a few years ago as Black Belt and more recently had training on Lean. Rita had an outgoing personality, was well respected within the organization, and had been with the company a little over 7 years. Chris, the customer service manager, is the process owner and would be the Team Leader. Chris has just returned from a 2 week vacation and was not expecting this type of "welcome back." However, Chris was well-aware of last month's negative trend and thought it was just a blip and would improve as time went on. However, that was not the case. Chris was on-board to getting employees involved in this project.

Tinker Town's Part 1. Planning Phase (spans 3 - 4 weeks)

3 Weeks (spans 4 hours before the PDCA Implementation Phase)

Within a week, Chris gathered additional data, created an initial Team Charter and process map, as well as assembled the team. Chris and Rita had numerous 1-on-1 meetings to ensure they were aligned with specific activities that needed to be completed. The following Performance Dashboard and supporting charts were presented at the first meeting, making the business case for the project.

Note: The Quality - % Returns - Defects - Theme Bears measurement includes for any reason the product is returned or there was a problem with the order (over quantity, wrong discount applied, etc.).

Tinker Town Performance Dashboard

Customer Service

Customer Satisfaction Survey - All Bear Types

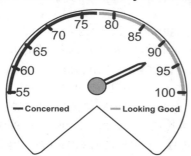

Customer Satisfaction Survey - Theme Bears

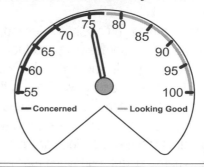

Quality

% Returns - Defects - All Types

% Returns - Defects - Theme Bears

Sales

Monthly Total Sales - All Types

Domestic Orders for May - All Types

Metric	Value	Goal	% to Goal - YTD
Total Ordered	222,382	400,000	56%
Avg Order Amount	110.53		
Total # of Orders	2012		

Notice to All:

We wil be starting an improvement project to address the Customer Service and Quality concerns as noted on the Dashboard. If you have any suggestions please email Kate.Moss@TinkerTown.com. We will be communicating to you, as well as asking for your assistance, as we work on these areas.

Sales are ahead of goal and quarterly bonuses will be distributed at the next pay period!

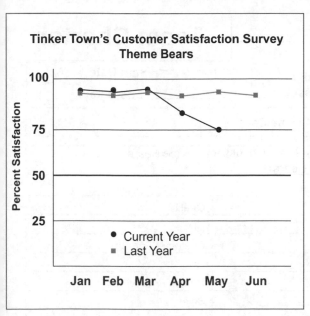

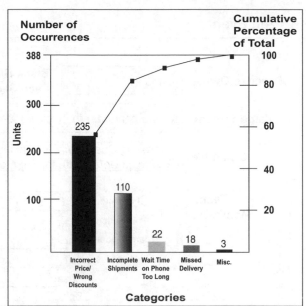

The Line Chart on the left displays the current decline in the Customer Service Satisfaction Survey for Theme Bears compared to last year. The Pareto Chart on the right displays the main reasons why customers are currently dissatisfied with their level of customer support and service, specifically for the Theme Bear product line. This provided the team with much-needed information.

When the Lean team met for the first time, Juan Gonzales, the HR Manager and team member, asked Kate, "Okay, so what do you want us to do? Usually meetings regarding improvements have been just implemented without meetings."

Kate answered, "I don't have the answers but I think working as a group, we can come up with them. We can't just throw a bunch of people together and expect them to know how to function effectively as a team. We need to understand some basic principles about teaming, meeting effectively, and how Lean can be a valuable asset in our organization going forward."

Kate continued, "While the Lean tools and problem solving tools are obviously important, the key to Lean success is people working effectively together as a team. I will support the changes this team recommends and will be available anytime. As I stated with Rita and Chris, this is a top priority for us going forward."

Kate handled a few questions and then concluded, "Please work with Rita, your facilitator for this project and Chris as the process owner and team leader. They are excited to be working with you in what we are calling our first "formal" Kaizen Event. The Kaizen Event will involve numerous planning meetings, followed by 3 days of implementation referred to as PDCA Days. After the 3 days a sub team will be formed to monitor the process changes and make any necessary adjustments. Also, in the training you will learn all about Lean and Kaizen. Rita and Chris will ensure your time is used wisely for this project. Have a good first meeting!"

Rita continued to explain the team roles; Juan volunteered to be the scribe. Since someone from IT was not originally on the team, it was decided at the next meeting that someone from IT would be present. The following Team Charter was reviewed and everyone quickly agreed to its focus, objectives, and deliverables.

Kaizen Event

Team Charter

Process Owner:	Chris	**Black Belt or Lean Sensei:**	N/A	**Start Date:** 6/2 **End Date:**

Value Stream: Customer Order to Invoicing for Theme Bears

Objective: Improving Customer Satisfaction Survey results for Theme Bears
Reducing Defect rate for Theme Bears

Team Members:

	Name	Dept/Site
Facilitator:	Rita	Quality
Scribe:	Juan	HR
Team Leader:	Chris	Customer Service
Team Members:	Jeff	IT
	Susan	Customer Service
	Bob	Sales
	Carly	Customer Service
	Aubrey	Warehouse (added)

Meeting Frequency:

Dates: PDCA Phase, 6/22-6/25
Times: 7:30 am - 3:30 pm

Lean Objectives: Use the Standard 3 Day Kaizen Event approach to create the necessasry changes that will improve the Customer Satisfaction Survey results and Defect rate.

Deliverables:

What are the specific metrics that will be improved?
Customer Satisfaction Survey scores to improve at or above 95%
% Defects to be reduced to <1.25%

What are the specific opportunities for:

Defects?		Customer Satisfaction?	
Current: 2.4%	Target:<1.25%	Current: 75%	Target: 95%

Efficiency?		Communications?	
Current:	Target:	Current:	Target:

Operational Excellence?		Dashboard or Performance Measure?	
Current:	Target:	Current:	Target:

What are any issues or concerns that may impact this team's objective?

Concerns: If orders increase beyond the demand forecast, may impact PDCA Phase dates.

Sign-Off:

Executive Sponsor: Kate _____ Date: 6/2 _____

Champion/Value Stream Manager/VP: Chris _____ Date: 6/2 _____
(maybe the same as Executive Sponsor)

Process Owner: Chris _____ Date: 6/2 _____

Deliverables to be included with this Charter: ☑ Value Stream or Process Map for the project
☑ Supporting High Level Data

The following high-level process map was also reviewed by the team at this first meeting.

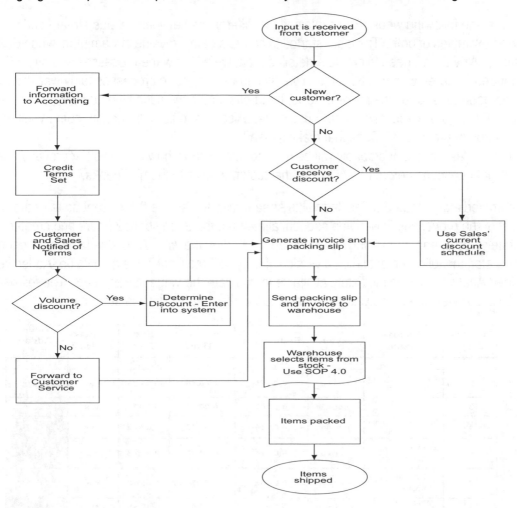

The team acknowledged that the high-level flowchart was not exactly how the customer service phone order process flowed. The new phone system and recent process changes were not incorporated into this flowchart. Rita appreciated their input and said that at the next meeting they will create a detailed flowchart or value stream map.

Rita spent the last 60 minutes providing an overview of Lean and Six Sigma. She focused on what a Kaizen Event is, and how this meeting is part of it. She explained the three different Phases of a Standard 5 Day Kaizen Event and that this particular Kaizen Event will only have 3 days in the PDCA Implementation Phase. She also noted that Lean is about involving the employees to make change happen. Rita conducted a simple 30-minute Lean simulation demonstrating continuous flow and kanbans, visual controls, takt time, and 5S. Everyone seemed to have a basic understanding of Lean.

At the end of the first team meeting, Chris said, "I want to thank everyone for your ideas and positive attitudes. We all have some actions items assigned, please ensure they are completed before our next meeting. I appreciate Rita's work in keeping us on schedule as our facilitator. We should be able to do quite a bit next week. Also, remember to schedule those 3 days for the PDCA Implementation Phase."

2 Weeks (spans 4 hours before the PDCA Implementation Phase)

The team met the following week. Rita explained the differences between a value stream and process map and showed examples of both. The team started to create a detailed value stream map, when Susan asked the question, "Why do we need to create a detailed map, we all know the processes and steps?"

Rita responded, "I agree with you Susan that we all know our specific processes fairly well, however, it will probably be good to "see" all the process flows, hand-offs, and how much time customers are waiting. We want to ensure we are responsive to our customers. Also, it should help identify some wastes that exist between groups or processes. Does that make sense?"

Susan replied, "Yes it does. It probably will be good for me to know how the Credit Approval process works as I always get questions before I have to turn the customer over to them. Thanks."

The team immediately created a detailed value stream map to capture the current state of the processes. Since most of the processes flowed in a sequential manner, the team spent 2 hours and created a detailed current state value stream map using flip chart paper taped on the wall. Also, due to the new phone system report generator, the following data (i.e., a version of a Cycle Time Data Table as a Value -Added versus Non Value-Added Analysis) was immediately available to populate the value stream map. The following is their VA versus Non Value-Added Analysis data, Bar Chart of the data, and value stream map.

Process Step	Process Name	Type	Begin Time	Operation Time	End Time	Value-Added?	Value-Added Total
1	Answer Phone	Process	0:00:00	0:00:25	0:00:25	Yes	0:00:25
2	Ask for Customer information	Process	0:00:25	0:00:40	0:01:05	Yes	0:01:05
3	Does Customer have Account?	Process	0:01:05	0:00:05	0:01:10	Yes	0:01:10
4	Place on Hold and Forward	Transport	0:01:10	0:01:15	0:02:25	No	0:01:10
5	Ask for Customer Information	Process	0:02:25	0:00:20	0:02:45	No	0:01:10
6	Take Information for Credit App	Process	0:02:45	0:03:45	0:06:30	Yes	0:04:55
7	Wait for Credit Approval	Delay	0:06:30	0:06:05	0:12:35	No	0:04:55
8	Approved?	Decision	0:12:35	0:00:00	0:12:35	Yes	0:04:55
9	Ask for Customer Information	Process	0:12:35	0:00:40	0:13:15	No	0:04:55
10	Does Customer have Standard Product?	Process	0:13:15	0:00:05	0:13:20	No	0:04:55
11	Determine Product Needs	Process	0:13:20	0:01:30	0:14:50	Yes	0:06:25
12	Is Product on Hand?	Process	0:14:50	0:00:15	0:15:05	No	0:06:25
13	Check System for Lead Time	Process	0:15:05	0:00:10	0:15:15	No	0:06:25
14	Quote Lead Time to Customer	Process	0:15:15	0:00:05	0:15:20	No	0:06:25
15	Is Lead Time Acceptable?	Process	0:15:20	0:00:00	0:15:20	No	0:06:25
16	Contact Operations for LT Information	Process	0:15:20	0:07:35	0:22:55	No	0:06:25
17	Is Lead Time Acceptable?	Process	0:22:55	0:00:00	0:22:55	No	0:06:25
18	Place Order	Process	0:22:55	0:01:45	0:24:40	Yes	0:08:10
19	Validate Customer Ship Info	Inspect	0:24:40	0:00:30	0:25:10	No	0:08:10
20	Thank Customer	Process	0:25:10	0:00:10	0:25:20	Yes	0:08:20

In a quick review of the VA versus NVA Analysis, it can be seen that there are opportunities for improvement given Value-Added Total time of 8:20 when the End Time total is 25:30.

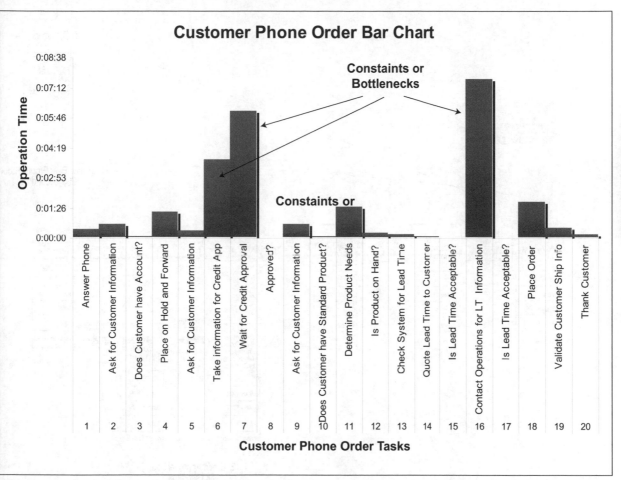

The Bar Chart of the data set indicates three potential bottlenecks or constraints. Discussions and the following detailed value stream map provided additional insights into these areas for possible elimination or reduction of them in the PDCA Implementation Phase.

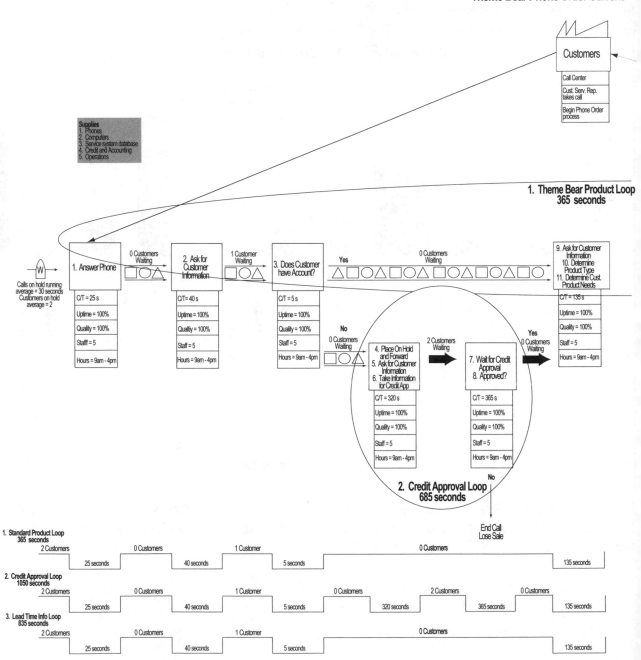

Theme Bear Phone Order Current

Customers

| Call Center |
| Cust. Serv. Rep. takes call |
| Begin Phone Order process |

Supplies
1. Phones
2. Computers
3. Service system database
4. Credit and Accounting
5. Operations

1. Theme Bear Product Loop
365 seconds

W

Calls on hold running
average = 30 seconds
Customers on hold
average = 2

1. Answer Phone

| C/T = 25 s |
| Uptime = 100% |
| Quality = 100% |
| Staff = 5 |
| Hours = 9am - 4pm |

0 Customers
Waiting

2. Ask for Customer Information

| C/T = 40 s |
| Uptime = 100% |
| Qualtiy = 100% |
| Staff = 5 |
| Hours = 9am - 4pm |

1 Customer
Waiting

3. Does Customer have Account?

| C/T = 5 s |
| Uptime = 100% |
| Quality = 100% |
| Staff = 5 |
| Hours = 9am - 4pm |

Yes

0 Customers
Waiting

9. Ask for Customer Information
10. Determine Product Type
11. Determine Cust. Product Needs

| C/T = 135 s |
| Uptime = 100% |
| Quality = 100% |
| Staff = 5 |
| Hours = 9am - 4pm |

No
0 Customers
Waiting

4. Place On Hold and Forward
5. Ask for Customer Information
6. Take Information for Credit App

| C/T = 320 s |
| Uptime = 100% |
| Quality = 100% |
| Staff = 5 |
| Hours = 9am - 4pm |

2 Customers
Waiting

Yes
0 Customers
Waiting

7. Wait for Credit Approval
8. Approved?

| C/T = 365 s |
| Uptime = 100% |
| Quality = 100% |
| Staff = 5 |
| Hours = 9am - 4pm |

2. Credit Approval Loop
685 seconds

No

End Call
Lose Sale

1. Standard Product Loop
365 seconds

| 2 Customers | | 0 Customers | | 1 Customer | | 0 Customers | | |
| 25 seconds | | 40 seconds | | 5 seconds | | | 135 seconds |

2. Credit Approval Loop
1050 seconds

| 2 Customers | | 0 Customers | | 1 Customer | | 0 Customers | | 2 Customers | | 0 Customers | |
| 25 seconds | | 40 seconds | | 5 seconds | | 320 seconds | | 365 seconds | | 135 seconds |

3. Lead Time Info Loop
835 seconds

| 2 Customers | | 0 Customers | | 1 Customer | | 0 Customers | | |
| 25 seconds | | 40 seconds | | 5 seconds | | | 135 seconds |

State Value Stream Map

Important Note:
Typical value stream maps display a queue time between processes; however, in this case it was a number of customers waiting as the queue entity. The number of customers waiting at any one time indicated how many customer service representatives were working this overall value stream. This value stream map was used as an initial constraint analysis and later was used to create a process or flow map. For advanced analysis and improvements to reduce the number of customers waiting queueing theory should be used.

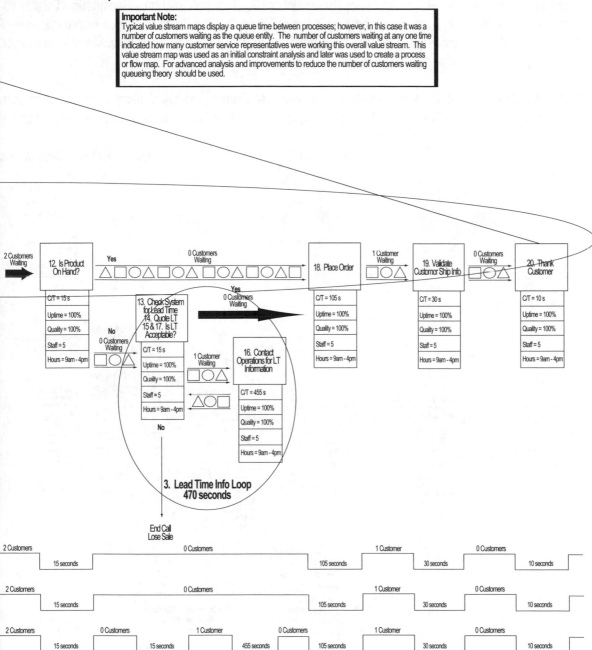

Note: Not all the data shown in the above current state value stream map was populated during this 4 hour meeting. Two team members were assigned to complete the map after this second meeting using all the data that was provided. It would be available at the next meeting (1 Week Out).

The team was surprised at some of the numbers. The team conducted a Waste Walk to solicit input from the process area employees as to any other issues that may be affecting the Customer Satisfaction Survey results. During the Waste Walk, many of the employees mentioned that the delay for Credit Approval, as well as obtaining accurate lead times, as reasons customers would complain and want to speak to a manager. This was the type of information the team needed.

Once the team got back in the room, Rita asked everyone to use Post-it Notes and place on the value stream map the various process activity wastes. The following is their updated current state value stream map.

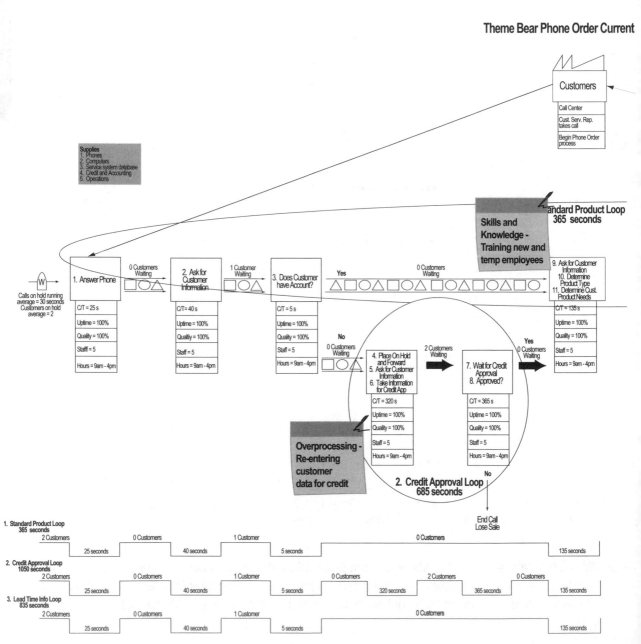

Kaizen Demystified

State Value Stream Map

Important Note:
Typical value stream maps display a queue time between processes; however, in this case it was a number of customers waiting as the queue entity. The number of customers waiting at any one time indicated how many customer service representatives were working this overall value stream. This value stream map was used as an initial constraint analysis and later was used to create a process or flow map. For advanced analysis and improvements to reduce the number of customers waiting queueing theory should be used.

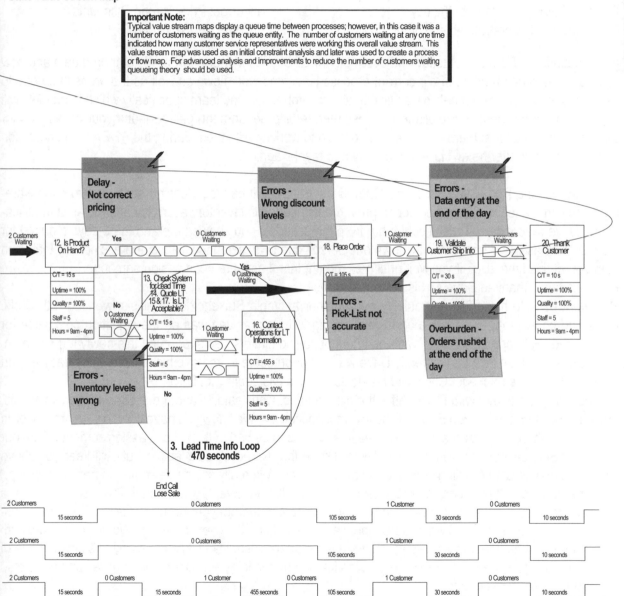

Rita further guided the team to connect the wastes that were identified with the various categories listed in the initial Pareto Chart.

Waste	Pareto Category to Impact
Overprocessing – Re-entering customer data for credit	Wait Time on Phone Too Long
Skills and Knowledge – Training new and temp employees	Wait Time on Phone Too Long
Errors – Not correct pricing	Incorrect Price/Wrong Discounts
Errors – Inventory levels wrong	Incomplete Shipments/Missed Deliveries
Errors – Wrong discount levels	Incorrect Price/Wrong Discounts
Errors – Pick-List wrong	Incomplete Shipments/Missed Deliveries
Errors – Data entry – end of the day	Incorrect Price/Wrong Discounts
Overburden – Orders rushed end of the day	Incorrect Price/Wrong Discounts

Rita concluded, "We did a lot today and again I thank all of you for your efforts. We gathered data and now have a great understanding of our current process times and work flows as well as the areas that need to be improved. At our next meeting we will use all this information and learn specifically which Lean tools will improve the processes. For those in the customer service department, please thank your colleagues for their input today and let them know we look forward to working with them during the PDCA Implementation Phase, the week after next. Have a good day and thanks again!"

After the meeting Rita asked Dave, the Operations Manager, if he would assign someone from the warehouse to join the team due to expected improvements needed in inventory accuracy and Pick-List modifications. Dave responded, "I wish I could, but from the schedule you showed me and the 3 days required for the PDCA Phase, and I am currently down one person due to an extended illness, there is no way that I can help you at this time. But, if you wait until next month, then I am sure I can assign someone."
Rita reluctantly thanked Dave for his honest response.
Rita went back to her office and quickly put together a simple Stakeholder Analysis, working with Chris. Chris had known that Dave had a good relationship with Jeff, as Jeff was on the selection committee for hiring Dave. Rita approached Jeff with the intent of having him discuss supporting this newly formed team. Also, Chris informed Rita that currently Dave was under pressure to improve his inventory accuracy as part of his performance package. Chris said he would discuss this again with Dave.
The next day, Chris met with Dave. After the pleasantries, Chris said, "Dave, I don't know if you know this, but a big focus for this Kaizen Event will be inventory accuracy. We know you have trained your group well in this area. Is there any way that you can release someone to be part of this? I can assign someone from our Customer Service group to fill in during that time. I know they will not be as effective, but it will keep you above water and they would be willing to work overtime if need be. We really could use someone from your group."
Dave responded, "Chris, I can commit to two days of the Kaizen Event, even though I was scheduled for a long weekend during that time, I will forgo it, and with someone from your group replacing the person I assign, and we should be OK. I will assign Aubrey and she will be at the next meeting. Would you ensure I am copied on the schedule and any reports that are generated? Also, I would like possibly to sit in on some of this Event, as I too need to make some process improvements fairly soon in my other areas and this would be a good learning experience."
Chris responded, "I knew there was a reason we hired you. Thanks."
They both smiled.

1 Week (spans 4 hours before the PDCA Implementation Phase)

Rita welcomed Aubrey to the team and said they were sure her input would be a great contribution. Rita continued with reviewing the specific Lean tools of 5S, Standard Work, Continuous Flow and Kanbans, and Visual Controls. She also conveyed how improvements using the PDCA model would be implemented.

The team proceeded to narrow down the lists of wastes to either Invoicing or Order Fulfillment problem. It was believed that Order Fulfillment would directly relate to Incomplete Shipments/Missed Deliveries from the previous Pareto Chart. The team then brainstormed on all possible causes of these issues or problems. The following were the issues from their 15 minutes of brainstorming:

- New fulfillment system not working correctly
- New bar code readers
- New sales manager
- New computers in Shipping
- Customer Service Representatives not trained
- New product line of Teddy Bears with multiple discounts
- Customers not using current system correctly
- Discount schedules not updated regularly
- Quantity discounts for new products not immediately known
- Current customer discounts always changing
- New shipping vendor not connected to system
- Four retirements
- Customer Service Representatives entering wrong info
- Customer Service Representatives working overtime (OT) and making more mistakes
- Customer Service Representatives not receiving orders until end of the day
- No avenue for customer order when sales info is not available (product item or quantity is not available for quantity discounts)
- A customer entering wrong information and order is accepted by the system
- Supervisors not checking orders
- Orders over $5000 not following free shipping process
- Customers entering wrong discount and new system not verifying it
- Orders shipped short
- Pick-List for customers not accurate
- Items names on pick-list does not match exactly with inventory shelf labels
- Quantity in inventory not up-to-date
- Sales and marketing not filling out paperwork for free samples they send to customers
- New merchant account not transferring order information correctly
- Part time employee in customer service not trained adequately

The brainstorming went well. Many of the items listed were either more descriptive analysis of what was already defined or the problem restated. Rita suggested the Cause and Effect (or Fishbone) Diagram would be a good tool to narrow down these ideas into something more manageable. Even though the team realized that Incorrect Price and Wrong Discount were inter-related, they wanted to focus only on the Incorrect

Price for their first Fishbone. Subsequent Fishbone Diagrams were completed for Wait Time on Phone Too Long, Wrong Discounts, and Incomplete Shipments/Missed Deliveries. The following is their Fishbone Diagram for Incorrect Pricing.

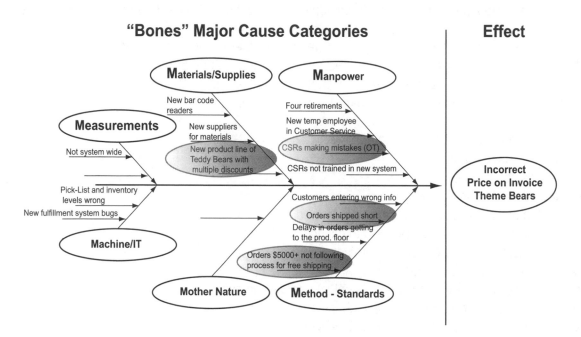

The team further identified the top 5 areas to attack in the PDCA Implementation Phase (identified as the shaded areas on the Fishbone Diagram) and conducted a 5 Why Analysis as shown below:

5 Why Analysis			
Problem: Incorrect Prices on Invoices for Theme Bears			
Cause CSRs making mistakes (OT)	**Cause** Orders shipped short	**Cause** Orders over $5000 not following process	**Cause** New product line with multiple discounts
Why? Always had large group of orders at the end of the day	**Why?** Not enough inventory to meet demand	**Why?** Orders were not separated	**Why?** Software not configured properly
Why? Intl orders processed at 1:00 pm daily and CSRs could not adapt to large orders	**Why?** Production did not have up-to-date inventory levels	**Why?** Sales informed shipping to ship regardless of credit	**Why?** Did not include account special information as well as new customer fields
Why? New system was not updated and only CSRs were trained in new system	**Why?** New fulfillment system only updates bi-weekly	**Why?** Sales knew that new system would cause delays	**Why?** No one was assigned to ensure information would work in new fulfillment system
Why? IT was not aware of Intl orders being processed only at 1:00 pm daily	**Why?** Standard feature on new fulfillment system	**Why?** Sales wanted to ensure customer demand be met	**Why?** Four retirements caused workers to absorb as much work as possible
Why? IT did not realize this batching of orders and being short in CS caused addl OT	**Why?**	**Why?**	**Why?**

Looking at only one column of the 5 Why Analysis, the Tinker Town team discovered that mistakes were being made by the customer service department - Why? 1) Because the Customer Service Representatives (CSRs) had large group of orders in the afternoon - Why? 2) Because International orders were processed at 1:00 pm and CSRs could not adapt to any large orders - Why? 3) New system was not updated and CSRs were the only ones trained on the new system - Why? 4) IT was not aware that this was a problem for customer service - Why? 5) IT was not aware this batching of orders and being short-staffed in customer service caused the additional OT. This 5 Why Analysis assisted the team to determine the root cause of why the issue or problem was occurring. This information would be used to help apply the right Lean tool to the right process for the right reason.

The team was on a roll and created the following PDCA Kaizen Activity Worksheet indicating the specific activities that would be implemented during the PDCA Implementation Phase.

Kaizen Event

PDCA Kaizen Activity Worksheet

Value Stream: Customer Order to Invoicing for Theme Bears

Date: 6/16

Department: Customer Service

Team Members: Rita, Juan, Chris, Jeff, Susan, Bob, Carly, Dave, Aubrey

Process Name/Activity (as identified on the value stream, process map, etc.)	Problem or Waste	Lean Tool	Specific Activities	Who	When
(12) Product on Hand (18) Place Order	Errors - Not Correct Pricing, Missed Deliveries	Standard Work, Mistake Proofing	1. Update new fulfillment system. 2. Create new sales update program. 3. Create real-time discount system.	Chris, Jeff, Susan, Aubrey	Day 2
(12) Product on Hand (18) Place Order	Errors - Not Correct Pricing, Missed Deliveries	Cross-Training, Work Load Balancing	1. Create and conduct training. 2. Implement pitch, orders to shipping. 3. Balance work loads.	Chris, Jeff, Susan, Aubrey	Day 2
(18) Place Order (19) Validate cust. ship info	Errors - Data Entry - at end of the day	Visual Mgmt., Scheduling/ Leveling	1. Post visual production board. 2. Create new schedule. 3. Create standard work.	Chris, Jeff, Susan, Aubrey	Day 1
(12) Product on Hand (18) Place Order	Errors - Not Correct Pricing, Missed Deliveries	Standard Work, Mistake Proofing	1. Create online checklist. 2. Training all on new checlist. 3. Desktop screen FIFO Lane indictor.	Chris, Jeff, Susan, Aubrey	Day 3
(12) Product on Hand (13-16) Check System, Contact Operations	Errors - Inventory Levels Wrong	Standard Work, Mistake Proofing	1. Conduct manual audit. 2. Create new Pick-List form and train. 3. Create standards for Pick-List.	Rita, Bob, Carly, Dave	Day 1,3
(4-8) Place on Hold - Approved	Overprocessing - Reentering customer data for credit	Standard Work, Mistake Proofing	1. Create link for customer data. 2. Train CSRs on new process. 3. Publish standards.	Rita, Bob, Carly, Dave	Day 1,2
(1-20) Answer Phone -Thank Customer	All types	5S	1. Implement 5S in CSR department. 2. Implement 5S in warehouse. 3. Implement 5S for electronic files.	Rita, Bob, Carly, Aubrey	Day 1,3

Parking Lot Items or Wiki Kaizen Event Ideas

Tinker Town's Part 2. PDCA Implementation Phase (spans 3 days)

At the beginning of the PDCA Implementation Phase Rita spent about 5 minutes and summarized the PDCA Kaizen Activity Worksheet, along with an explanation of the Lean tools that were going to be being used. Rita also noted additional items from the Waste Walk that the team did not address during the last meeting. The following is a summary of her presentation:

5S - Organizing the customer service department because all CSRs had their own filing system for customer orders and quotes (both in electronic form as well as many still kept hardcopy as backup). Also, in the production/manufacturing area, it was apparent that aisle ways were not marked, workers were not consistent in placement of their tools - people were always looking for something - and that equated to waste of travel, motion, etc.

Standard Work - Sales had many different methods in which to give customers large discounts and that information was not being entered into the new fulfillment system in a timely manner.

Continuous flow - The new fulfillment system did not accommodate real-time international orders due to the merchant account system of PayPal, so information was not Just-In-Time.

Visual controls - The Customer Service Manager had no idea until 3:00 - 4:00 pm each day that the department had to work overtime.

Work Load Balancing - It was apparent, as Rita walked through the sales and customer service departments, that everyone may not be as busy as they could be, and that some work load balancing could be of value.

Mistake Proofing - There were many errors due to the customer discount and pricing information was not easily accessible and was not up-to-date.

Rita reflected, "WOW, how do we have any customers with all these problems. It's great we finally are doing something about it! I think we pretty much have a good plan from last week. So, let's spend the next 10 -15 minutes and review our plans before we separate into our two smaller work groups."

The following are some additional activities that the team addressed during the 3 days:

It was determined that the incorrect invoices were reflected throughout all customer orders. The team created a Distribution Report to delineate the three value streams that comprised all invoicing and the work that was associated with each. There were additional value streams in administration and manufacturing, however, only these three were related to the problem.

Distribution Report

| Department | Customer Service | | Date | March 1 - May 31 |

Value Streams	March	April	May	Total
Orders - domestic (Theme Bears)	2140	2328	2012	6480
Orders - international	344	266	248	858
Quotes - domestic	146	158	178	482

The Orders – domestic value stream (Theme Bears) has a 5 minute takt time. The 5 minutes represents how often customer orders are arriving for this specialty line.
Available hours of operation: M-F 8 am – 5 pm = 9 hours/day (with CSRs taking staggered lunches)
Total hours for one week = 45 hours
Twelve weeks March - May (average) x 45 hours week = 540 available hours per three month period.

Takt time = Available daily work time = Time (T) / Total daily volume required Volume (V)
Takt time = 540 hours or 32400 minutes / 6480 domestic orders takt time = 5 minutes
The takt time for Orders Intl is 540 hours or 32400 minutes / 858 = 37.76 or approx. 40 minutes.

The takt time for Quotes – domestic is 540 hours or 32400 minutes / 482 = 67.22 minutes or approx. 70 minutes.
This information assisted the team in determining exactly how much work was being done by the customer service department.

It was realized that a true pull system could not be attained in this situation; however, a FIFO (First-In First-Out) Lane was used to ensure all orders were processed in a timely manner from Sales to Customer Service to Shipping. Also, having the Intl orders updated regularly greatly assisted the flow of information. This resulted in the customer service department working less overtime and thereby reduced the likelihood of a data entry error on an invoice. The following illustrates the work flow of the orders.

Pull - Lean - FIFO Lanes

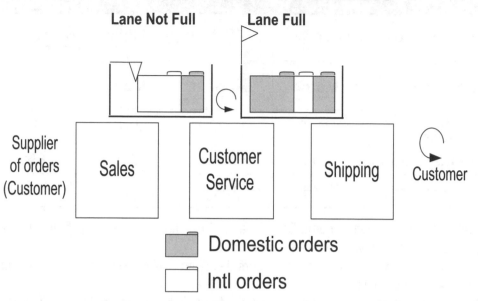

Each FIFO Lane was designated for 2 hours' worth of orders based on the 5 minute takt time, which comprised of 24 domestic orders. Pitch was determined to be 2 hours (takt time of 5 minutes multiplied by 24 domestic orders = 120 minutes) from Sales to Shipping. This time was initially set as a trial and further modifications would be made as the team went forward. Once pitch had been established for the orders – domestic value stream - then the other value streams could be added.

The two FIFO Lanes were represented by a graphic displayed on the CRM screen (Fulfillment System program). Jeff was instrumental in working with the team in creating this signal system. If more than 40 domestic orders at any time accumulated in the "system," the FIFO Lane Desktop icon would flash "red" indicating there was a bottleneck at the process (i.e., Shipping, Customer Service, or Sales). The team had one person cross-trained (initially) so they could assist the downstream process when indicated by the icon. After the pilot, everyone was cross-trained for assisting in the domestic order fulfillment process due to the success of the trial.

Note: The team only considered the domestic orders for Theme Bears at this time due to the complexity of international orders and the stability of the Standard Teddy Bear product line; however, after the Follow-Up Phase, it was suggested that international orders be integrated into this FIFO Lane system.

The following illustration is the fulfillment system standard work procedures. They used a Just-In-Time symbol to represent the immediate flow of information to the next step or process. The stop signal represented a delay in the process meaning that certain conditions must be met before the information or order can process to the next process. This particular form (i.e., standard) great assisted the team ensuring orders that were being shipped short had the correct price reflected on the invoice.

Standard Work Procedures Customer Ordering w/Discount

Item	Activity Description	Responsibility	Process Symbol
1	Place information from order into gateway.	IT	
2	Index Team record date, value, customer name, customer code, and release to queue.	CSR	
3	Order is picked off queue by CSR.		
4	Check RFS to see if customer has existing file.		
5.1	Do a search on Opening Screen to confirm customer ID is on file.		
5.2	A Select the copy customer info on both Screens, or		
5.3	B Select cancel option on both Screens, or		JIT
5.4	C Check current details, match auto populated details, or		
5.5	D Enter customer details on Screen 1.		
5.6	If more than 1 customer, repeat steps 4 to 5.4.		
5.7	Enter "0" in the number of company searches required (Screen 2).		
5.8	Enter details for multiple site shipments.		
5.9	Complete all details on Screen 5 for each order.		
5.10	Link discounts to orders on Screen 6.		
5.11	Enter standard discount details for each order on Screen 6.		
6.1	Validate and save information, then select Process Screen which will trigger Credit Reports to be generated.	Accounting	
6.2	Close the Fast Trace Summary from process Screen. Press Edit on the process Screen to re-enter credit details.		⊘
7.1	Assess all supporting information in line with credit policy.	Accounting	
7.2	Confirm, update credit information for customer file.		
7.3	Update Screen 2 with data from report generation.		⊘
7.4	Save and validate information. Review and email to CSR.		
8.1	Conduct order fulfillment from Screen 4.	CSR	
8.2	Note! Check any special notes on top of screen.		
8.3	Update order checklist on Screen 5.		JIT
8.4	Create pick list and submit to shipping on Screen 7.		
9.1	Obtain customer Pick-List.	Shipping	
9.2	Fill order to Pick-List and ship. Use SOP 4.2 for shipping instructions.		JIT
JIT ⊘	Just-In-Time information - this denotes information is immediately processed once it is received. Hold - work cannot proceed until conditions are met.	Takt time = 5 minutes	

For the Credit Application process, the CSRs had territories assigned to each of them. They created a process flowchart to better understand the various functions for international orders, which had an impact on the domestic orders for the Theme Bears. IT worked with CSR to streamline some of the credit checks so the CSR could initiate them as soon as the new customer for Intl orders was received. Cross-training was determined to be required to help alleviate the CSR workloads. The Intl orders and all quotes were creating backlogs for all orders, therefore, the team decided to balance the quotes as part of this Kaizen Event; however, it was not included in establishing a pitch at this time.

The team, with considerable support from IT, created an automatic Sales update program that once the discounts were entered by the Sales representative (given certain conditions made by the Sales manager) they would automatically be accessed by the customer service representative. They ensured that the discount that was quoted for Theme Bears would be exactly what would be invoiced.

The team created an online visual control system for customer orders to ensure mistakes would not occur. It would not allow the Pick-List to be printed unless all fields were completed, which would have the field area turn green. This ensured the discount schedule would be checked to the customer ID prior to fulfillment. Each CSR had a checklist that listed each of the customer requirements displayed on their screen. For each Theme Bear order, and as information was completed, a check mark was placed in the appropriate box alongside the requirement.

The PDCA Implementation Phase went fairly well; in 3 days all the main activities listed in the PDCA Kaizen Activity Worksheet, as well as some additional improvements, were completed. Kate had visited the conference room area a few times and also went to the various areas to see how things were progressing (her Gemba Walk). The team members appreciate her showing an interest.

Kate, Jeff, and other managers attended the final report out. There was much discussion on the various process changes and the team was confident that the Customer Satisfaction Survey scores would improve. The team presented some of the standard work changes as well as what changes were made to the Pick-List.

Even though the Kaizen Event was not officially over due to completing the Follow-Up Phase with some continuing Action Items, the bulk of the team's efforts and time for those five days were recognized. The team met at TGI Friday's that Friday for recognition. Kate provided each team member with a company golf shirt and a sleeve of golf balls which they appreciated.

Tinker Town's Part 3. Follow-Up Phase (spans 2 - 4 weeks)

There were two Action Items assigned to Susan, an experienced Customer Service Representative who contributed as a team member that was carried over from the PDCA Implementation Phase. When Rita and Chris meet to review and discuss the results, and since these particular Action Items were not completed, they could not validate the success of the team.

Chris went to Susan and asked, "Susan, we noticed those two Action Items from last weeks' Kaizen Event were not completed as scheduled. Is there a reason why?"

Susan responded, "No. I remember you or Rita stating at that last meeting that you would follow up with sending out a detailed list of the Action Items, and I had not received anything. Therefore, I thought it was taken care of. Do they still need to be done, as I remember Jeff from IT said he could take care of it. Let me know."

After further investigation, and talking to Jeff, he did say something about finishing those Action Items up, but nothing was set in stone.

Chris and Rita realized they had dropped the ball on the Follow-Up Phase communications. Rita immediately sent out an email with the Action Items to be completed. Within one day, Susan had completed them. Within the next week, the results were posted and success was achieved.

Chris used the Weekly Project Dashboard and the Monthly Project Dashboard to report to Kate each week for the first month, then monthly updates. The final A3 Report is as follows:

A3 Report

Kaizen Event

Value Stream Impacted: Customer Service to Invoicing Theme Bears

Timeframe: 6/2 - 8/30

Executive Champion: Kate

Lean Sensei/Black Belt: Rita

Process Owner: Chris

Date of Report: 1 Sep

1. Problem Statement

Customer Satisfaction Survey - All Customers / Customer Service / Customer Satisfaction Survey - All Bear Types / Customer Satisfaction Survey - Theme Bears / Quality / % Returns - Defects - All Types / % Returns - Defects - Theme Bears

2. Current State

Theme Bear Phone Order Current State Value Stream Map

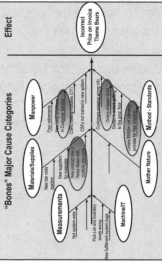

4. Improvement Opportunity

Customer Satisfaction Survey scores to improve at or above 95%
% Defects to be reduced to <1.25%

4. Problem Analysis

"Bones" Major Cause Categories

Manpower — Four retirements; New hires inexperienced in Customer Service; CSRs training deficiencies (OJT); CSRs not trained in new system

Materials/Supplies — New bar code readers; New suppliers for materials; New product line Teddy Bears with multiple discounts

Measurements — Not system wide; Pick-list and inventory levels wrong; New fulfillment system bugs

Machine/IT

Method - Standards — Customers placing wrong info; Orders shipped soon; Deliveries shipped correct to the prod. floor; Sales $5500+ in billing process for free shipping

Mother Nature

Effect: Incorrect Price on Invoice Theme Bears

5. Future State

Pricing is correct.
No data entry errors.
Accurate inventory levels.
Credit process simplified.

6. Implementation Plan

PDCA Kaizen Activity Worksheet

Kaizen Event

Value Stream: Customer Order to Invoicing

Department: Customer Service

Date: 6/16

Team Members: Rita, Juan, Chris, Jeff, Susain, Bob, Carly, Dave, Aubrey

Process Name/Activity (as identified on the value stream, process map, etc.)	Problem or Waste	Lean Tool	Specific Activities	Who	When
(12) Product on Hand (18) Place Order	Errors - Not Correct Pricing, Missed Deliveries	Standard Work, Mistake Proofing	1. Update new fulfillment system.	Chris, Jeff, Susain, Aubrey	Day 2
(18) Product on Hand (18) Place Order	Errors - Not Correct Pricing, Missed Deliveries	Create-Training, Work Load Balancing	2. Onsite new sales update program. 3. Create real-time discount system. 4. Create and conduct training. 5. Standardize work methods to efficiency. 6. Balance work loads.	Chris, Jeff Susain, Aubrey	Day 2
(18) Place Order (19) Validate cust. ship info	Errors - Data Entry - at end of the day	Visual Mgmt., Scheduling-Leveling	7. Post visual workstation board 8. Create metrics tracking	Chris, Jeff, Susain, Aubrey	Day 1
(12) Product on Hand (18) Place Order	Errors - Not Correct Pricing, Missed Deliveries	Standard Work, Mistake Proofing	9. Create standard work. 10. Create inspection checklist. 11. Create online checklist.	Chris, Jeff Susain, Aubrey	Day 3
(12) Product on Hand (13-16) Check System, Contact Operations	Enorm - Inventory Levels Wrong	Standard Work, Mistake Proofing	12. Balance of on new schedule. 13. Create daily workstation audits indicator. 14. Conduct manual audit.	Rita,Bob, Carly,	Day 1,3
(4-5) Place on Hold - Approved	Overprocessing Reentering customer data for credit	Standard Work, Mistake Proofing	15. Create new Pick-list form and logic. 16. Create link for customer data.	Rita, Bob, Carly,	Day 1,2
(1-20) Answer Phone -Thank Customer	All types	5S	17. Train PSRS on new process. 18. Implement 5S in CSR department. 19. Implement 5S in warehouse. 20. Implement 5S for electronic files.	Rita, Bob, Carly, Aubrey	Day 1,3

7. Verify Results

Measurement Theme Bears	Initial	Target	Results	% Improved
Customer Satisfaction Survey	75%	95%	95%	22%
% Defect	2.4%	<1.25%	1.2%	50%

8. Follow-Up

The following is a summary of the Lean, Six Sigma, and Leadership tools used in this case study:

Issue or Improvement Opportunity in Case Study	*Lean, Six Sigma or Leadership Tool Used*
Unknown delays/bottlenecks	VA versus NVA Analysis, Bar Chart (pgs. 148-149)
Current processes not mapped accurately	Detailed value stream map (pgs. 150-151)
Errors, not correct pricing and missed deliveries	Standard Work, Mistake Proofing (pgs. 160-161)
Missed Deliveries	FIFO Lane, Standard Work (pgs. 160-161)
Wrong Inventories	Standard Work, Cross-Training (pgs. 160-161)
Info and orders do not flow	FIFO Lane (pg. 160)
Lack of participation/not engaged	Meeting Leading (pg. 145)
Lack of support from other departments	Stakeholder Analysis (pg. 154)

Note: Measurements or results are shown on the previous page, A3 Report, Section 7. Verify Results and Section 8. Follow-Up.

Sensei Tips

Note: Many of the following Sensei Tips can be used or applied in the other Kaizen Events, where and when appropriate.

- ❖ Open the initial meeting with enthusiasm, excitement, and some type of fun activity.
- ❖ Have t-shirts for team members, if appropriate, for when they are "out-and-about."
- ❖ Ensure each team member has a folder with any pre-created forms, worksheets, layouts, etc.
- ❖ Ensure each team member has *The Lean Six Sigma Pocket Guide XL, The New Lean Pocket Guide, The New Lean Office Pocket Guide, The Practical Lean Six Sigma Pocket Guide,* etc. for reference as well as this book. The other books provide additional examples of Lean and Six Sigma tools.
- ❖ Take a group photo of team members at the initial meeting and photos of the process area before and after improvements, as well as some impromptu (appropriate) photos throughout the event.
- ❖ Provide everyone with contact numbers if phones are turned off during any parts of the meeting.
- ❖ Provide refreshments throughout the Event as well as healthy-type snacks and lunches.
- ❖ Consider non-team members from the organization to participate and learn the process (they may provide some invaluable insights).
- ❖ Do not schedule more than two long evenings in a row, if at all possible.
- ❖ Ensure WiFi or printer access at specific areas - organizations are not paperless yet!
- ❖ Ensure all forms include the company logo.
- ❖ Provide name tags for everyone, if not an exclusive work group.
- ❖ Ensure all supplies are available (paper, Post-it Notes, flip chart paper, etc.)
- ❖ Communicate the Event at least 1 week prior to forming the team on as many platforms as possible. Consider a visual "countdown" via an email reminder, text message, or posting something on the company intranet or bulletin board; something that is professional and appropriate (not irritating).
- ❖ Hold an informative meeting with the process area employees (i.e., the stakeholders) that are not part of the Kaizen team.
- ❖ Send out appropriate communications to all team members well in advance.
- ❖ Post locations of first-aid kits, aspirin, tweezers, Band-Aids, etc., or stock them in meeting room.
- ❖ Ensure meeting times are adhered to as well as creating ground rules for the Event.
- ❖ Include a team roster at the first meeting if participants are from remote areas or from other departments - include name, position, email, phone number, etc.
- ❖ Ensure facilities are aware of your meeting times to schedule appropriate cleaning (but don't leave the area a mess). Practice 5S as a team in the meeting areas you will be using.
- ❖ Arrange mid-day breaks to allow employees to check-in or answer messages.
- ❖ Create a bulletin board to communicate information for the week as well as post any photos.
- ❖ Ensure all team members attend the Report-Outs at the end of the day.
- ❖ Ensure all team members contribute something to the final Report Out, if conducted.
- ❖ Keep the team balanced with new employees as well as with experienced employees.
- ❖ Share the success through the Report-Out as well as any Storyboards or A3 Reports within the organization. Establish a best practice intranet site for this sharing or some other easy-to-access platform.
- ❖ Ensure team members are recognized and rewarded for their work.

- ❖ The Planning Phase is critical to a successful Kaizen Event. Ensure resources of people's time, process area availability, etc. are scheduled appropriately. Plan the work, then work the plan!
- ❖ Keep management informed of progress-to-date. Especially keep them informed if something unexpected happened that will be eventually hear about. Do not hide issues or problems with management. However, in these rare occurrences, provide recommended solutions with a risk analysis, if appropriate.
- ❖ Ensure flexibility in the PDCA Implementation Phase schedule for those things that are unexpectedly encountered.
- ❖ Have the attitude that all meetings and Kaizen Events can be improved upon, if this is your first Kaizen Event or your one-hundredth!
- ❖ Keep the PDCA Implementation Phase moving along. If the schedule has to be modified, do so. If all team members accomplished their tasks for the day, conclude for the day. Do not waste time with "busy work" to keep them there.
- ❖ If one or a few team members are not participating, analyze with them privately early on. Attempt to address their concerns. As a leader or facilitator, you may have to "lead" from within and set the example by helping team members with specific Action Items.

Notes

Kaizen Demystified

Rolling Kaizen Event

You have identified your project as a Rolling Event Event from the How to Select Your Kaizen Event Type (pages 59 -70)

Overview

Note: It is suggested the Standard 5 Day Kaizen Event section be read first to fully understand the basic structure and activities required that comprise all types of Kaizen Events (to some degree). The Rolling Kaizen Event is a take-off or modification of the Standard 5 Day Kaizen Event and, therefore, will have similar activities. This section will only *reference* the activities that are unique to this Kaizen Event type.

Rolling Kaizen Events *are targeted improvement activities (PDCAs) used by teams to implement improvements or solve a problem in a specific area that can only be accessed in-frequently and/or the resources are not available for immediate use; therefore, resources and improvements must be allocated over time.* The Rolling Kaizen Event may start off with a 2 - 4 hour meeting, and then meet weekly for 1 - 2 hours throughout the course of the Kaizen Event (typically 3 months).

The following is the Rolling Kaizen Event Quick Determination Checklist to ensure this is the type of Kaizen Event required given your specific situation. Ensure the majority of Characteristics are checked as Yes or Likely in the Your Situation column.

Rolling Kaizen Event Quick Determination Checklist					
Characteristic	**YES or LIKELY**	**Your Situation**	**Characteristic**	**YES or LIKELY**	**Your Situation**
Large Scope (crosses departments)	✔		Management Involvement	✔	
			5S Applied	✔	
Small Scope (within the department)	✔		Training Costs a Factor	✔	
Immediate Attention Required			Requires Detailed Planning Meetngs	✔	
Process Immediately Accessible			May Require Statistical Methods to Determine Root Cause	✔	
Root Cause May Be Known					
Specific Training Required	✔		Web-based Collaboration Application Main Form of Communication		
Broad Training Required	✔		Team Required	✔	
Team Members Physically (Locally) Available	✔		Value Stream or Process Map Required	✔	
Meeting Times < 4 Hours	✔		Will Impact Balanced Scorecard or Performance Dashboard Metric	✔	
Process Change (PDCAs) Continuously Applied Over a Few Days			Team Charter Required	✔	

Rolling

A successful Rolling Kaizen Event must have following conditions present:

- ❖ Process or area available for only short periods of time.
- ❖ Good communication with everyone involved.
- ❖ Team members available for limited lengths of time (typically 1 - 2 hours a week).
- ❖ The Just-In-Time concept utilized for all activities.
- ❖ Management committed and engaged in the project.
- ❖ Process area employees' ideas are considered (as only a few will be on the team).
- ❖ All employees are treated with dignity and respect.

The Rolling Kaizen Event can be thought of as the One-Minute Manager for meetings on steroids. In that regards, the team must look at everything (i.e., meetings, improvements activities, gathering data, creating reports, etc.) in time "buckets." These time "buckets" or "meeting and activity standards" will be determined by the team or by the team leader, process owner, facilitator and/or Black Belt, Lean Sensei, or Continuous Improvement Specialist at the beginning of the Event. Typically, these buckets will be 1, 2, or 4 hours. (Or, if team members are experienced in Lean Sigma concepts and this is not their first improvement project using these tools, then time buckets can be in 15 or 30 minute increments.) Regardless of the type or amount of time buckets used, the key point is to think of all activities in slices of time. In so doing, it will create a good foundation for the subsequent meetings. For this type of Kaizen Event, all activities for each of the Phases should have very definitive time buckets.

All types of Kaizen Events require creating a schedule (time buckets) to train, brainstorm, pilot improvements, etc. However, for the Rolling Kaizen Event there is a renewed focus to succinctly use the Just-In-Time concept for all activities. For example, many times during a Standard 5 Day Kaizen Event, all the Lean (and Six Sigma) tools may be briefly reviewed as well as additional activities such as simulations, daily report outs, teaming exercises, etc. will be conducted. Activities such as these likely will not be part of the Rolling Kaizen Event, or if they are, they will exist in a condensed version. Therefore, categorizing as many activities as possible in these time buckets will make for a successful Rolling Kaizen Event.

If the team decided to use 1 hour buckets and an improvement activity requires 4 hours, then that would entail 4 buckets. Organizing and conducting a Kaizen Event in this manner allows the team to start thinking in "standard" times to maximize all resources. Each phase of this Kaizen Event will provide suggested times for the various activities required. However, the more experience the process owner, team leader, Lean Sensei, Black Belt, etc. has with these activities, and the easier it will be to "right-size" your time buckets.

As with any Kaizen Event staying on schedule is crucial, but even more so for the Rolling Kaizen because of the shorter time bucket "windows" that the team has to conduct its work as well as the frequency of the team meetings. Time lines should be drawn up for meeting activities and adhered to by the team. Buckets of time should be specifically scheduled for each activity and the sequence of meeting events should be planned prior to the meeting and put into the meeting agenda to keep the team accountable for maintaining the time line. No meeting should be conducted without a written agenda. Ultimately, it is the team leader's responsibility to ensure that all the activities that need to get done are completed in a timely fashion, but the team leader should also elicit the help of the team in this regards. Assigning roles such as timekeeper and scribe to team members will help to keep the meetings flowing.

As with any meeting, some flexibility needs to be built into the schedule. The less experienced the team, particularly the team leader and/or facilitator, the greater the amount of flexibility that should be factored into how long it will take the team to accomplish its necessary tasks. Initially, the team leader should try to determine how much time each activity will take and prepare the schedule for about half to three quarters of the allotted meeting time which will allow some "slack" to make up for unexpected events and activities taking longer than expected. As the team grows in its knowledge and experience, the team leader will gradually be able to accurately schedule about ninety percent of the team's time (always leaving some flexibility for unforeseen events and needed discussions). At the end of each meeting, the leader should review progress with the team and assign the specific Action Items to team members or small subgroups of the team (referred to as sub teams). The Action Items should be completed prior to the next scheduled Kaizen Event meeting.

One of the key differences in the Rolling Kaizen Event over the Standard 5 Day Kaizen Event is that the process changes (PDCAs) happen over a longer period of time (for the Rolling Kaizen Event), not 80% of the process change (or pilot) occurring within a 3-to-5 day time period as in the Standard 5 Day Kaizen Event. The Rolling Kaizen Event is becoming the more common type of Kaizen Event for organizations today because of the time constraints for most employees. Many of the activities comprised in this type of Event will be allocated to groups of 1 – 2 team members (sub teams) to be completed between meetings. This type of Kaizen Event goes beyond just using a detailed project management program due to the following:

❖ Lean and/or Six Sigma tools are understood and used, as needed.
❖ Training is conducted, as needed.
❖ Team members and process area employee's ideas are part of the Lean approach to continuous improvement and engaged as necessary.
❖ Management is involved.
❖ Project duration limited to approximately 3 months.

Note: The forms and worksheets provided in this book can be used in conjunction with your current project management program and documents. The communication of schedules, meeting, activities, etc. between all team members must be effective across the board to ensure Kaizen success. There is NO one method of communication that will work for all teams all the time. The more Kaizen Event experience employees at all levels of the organization acquire, the more effective the Kaizen Event will be. Use the combination of the forms and worksheets provided in this book, your current documents that complement and support the overall Kaizen Event approach, and use "team common-sense" to conduct a Rolling Kaizen Event for your organization.

Steps and Forms

The following steps and forms should be used as a guide to customize a Rolling Kaizen Event to fit your organization requirements. There are many variables to consider, some of which are:

❖ Number of employees with Lean and Six Sigma or problem solving experience
❖ Root cause is unknown
❖ Change management principles applied
❖ Process availability (The process is not immediately available for process change)
❖ Team members' availability
❖ Complexity of the project
❖ How to address previous negative experiences with team projects
❖ How to effectively manage change
❖ Other departmental needs

The Rolling Kaizen Event is comprised of three phases:

Part 1. Planning Phase (spans 1 - 2 weeks)

Part 2. PDCA Implementation Phase (spans 4 - 6 weeks)

Part 3. Follow-Up Phase (spans 2 - 4 weeks)

The three phases and activities (steps) for each of the phases are identical to the Standard 5 Day Kaizen Event Phases; however, the difference will be that many of the activities will be streamlined into 1-hour (or less) time "buckets" (or what you have deemed to be the time segment). Since there will not be as much concentrated time together as a team, many of the activities will be assigned as Action Items that will need to be completed by designated team members (sub teams) prior to the next meeting. This will allow for specific training to occur when it is needed (Just-In-Time). The following three phases will be detailed as to an expected time frame for each activity, who should be mainly responsible, and what training, if any, should be made available. This will allow you to customize the Rolling Kaizen Event to meet your specific project requirements on meetings times, training topics, PDCA implementations, etc.

Note: The Planning Phase includes all the activities prior to any process change. Keep in mind that these are guidelines and the various activities listed can be completed in different parts of this Phase, as well as, at times, be incorporated into another Phase.

Part 1. Planning Phase (spans 1 - 2 weeks/8 - 10 hours meeting time)

The Planning Phase will provide the team members with the structure to move forward ensuring that time will be well-managed when everyone meets. Since the team members have time constraints, it will be important to gain a consensus at the first meeting to the following:

- ❖ Meeting times in reference to specific dates, times, and durations
- ❖ That tasks will be evenly allocated to team members and will require Action Items to be done between meetings
- ❖ Consensus on the deliverables, including completion date

Note: The Planning Phase and the PDCA Implementation Phase may run in parallel for some of the activities. Meeting structure and standards are important in this Event as well as the other types; however, allow common sense and team consensus to prevail. The important point is to establish a schedule with the team and stick to it – getting done what needs to be done at the appropriate time.

The Planning Phase is comprised of the same activities as in the Planning Phase of the Standard 5 Day Kaizen Event; however, these activities are not segmented into 3 weeks out, 2 weeks out, etc. The activities can be allocated at the first team meeting and the activities can be completed by creating sub teams. Or, if the Team Leader, Black Belt, or Continuous Improvement Specialist has previous experience running a Kaizen Event, then many of the activities can be done prior to the first meeting and then reviewed by the team members.

During this part of the Planning Phase use the following steps as a guide:

1. Gain an understanding of the main tools that can be used in this Phase. This type of Event requires specific Lean tool training Just-In-Time. The broad training will consist mostly of an 1 hour (or less) overview of Lean and Six Sigma. The Team Leader, Black Belt, or Continuous Improvement Specialist should have a good handle of these tools which will help the team in determining the ones that may be used. If the process owner is conducting that Rolling Kaizen Event and does not have a lot of experience with Lean and/or Six Sigma and/or running a Kaizen Event, consider the following:

   - ❖ Solicit a team member that is pro-active about change that can assist in co-facilitating the project
   - ❖ Provide all team members with *The Lean Six Sigma Pocket Guide XL, The Practical Lean Six Sigma Pocket Guide* (non-healthcare industries), *Practical Lean Six Sigma for Healthcare, and The Practical Lean Six Sigma Pocket Guide for Healthcare* and ensure appropriate sections are read prior to the meeting. Other books that may be helpful are: *The New Lean Pocket Guide, The New Lean Office Pocket Guide, Lean Office Demystified II, The New Lean Healthcare Pocket Guide*, and the *Today's Lean!* series of books available at TheLeanStore.com or your favorite bookstore.
   - ❖ Acknowledge to the team that you are learning-as-you-go. Be a good conduit for ideas and suggestions, and not defensive. More time must be allocated at the meetings for discussions.
   - ❖ Participate in any type of Kaizen Event prior to running your own, if at all possible.
   - ❖ Solicit assistance from a colleague that has conducted a Kaizen Event or contract with an experienced consultant from your local university or trade group association affiliation.
   - ❖ Most importantly, be honest with team members about your Kaizen Event experience.

This following list of tools can be used as a quick-reminder as to the array of tools that may be considered for use in the Planning Phase (typically the Define, Measure, and Analysis Phases of the Six Sigma methodology). Please see Chapter 3. Lean Six Sigma Tools for a description for each of these tools.

Define Phase	**Measure Phase**	**Analyze Phase**
Performance Dashboard	Voice of the Customer (VOC)	Value-Added (VA) versus
Project Management	Quality Function Deployment	Non Value-Added (NVA) Analysis
Project Charter	(QFD)	Pareto and Pie Charts
Teaming	Value Stream and Process	Constraint or Bottleneck Analysis
Effective Meetings	Maps	Demand Analysis Plots and Takt
Team Charter	Supplier-Input-Process-Output-	Time
Action Item (AI) Log	Customer	Histograms, Ogive Charts,
Issues and Opportunities (IO)	(SIPOC) Diagram	and Cumulative Frequency
Log	Key Metric Data Profiles	Cause and Effect (or Fishbone)
	Check Sheet and Frequency	Diagram
	Chart	Brainstorming
	Run Chart	5 Why
	Measurement System Analysis	Radar Chart
	(MSA)	Scatter Plot
		Process Capability
		Force Field Analysis
		Interrelationship Diagram
		Impact Map
		Work Load Balancing

2. Establish the time buckets that all activities will be measured against (e.g., 15 minutes, 30 minutes, 1 hour, 2 hours, etc.). Typically, not as much broad training will be conducted in this type of Kaizen Event; therefore, appropriate training activities may need targeted to the area or process being addressed. This will save time at the first team meeting and then the team members' "process knowledge" can better be utilized. The following is a list of the main steps in the Planning Phase as well as "suggested" time buckets.

Steps/Activities for Planning Phase	***Suggested Time Allocation***
1. Determine project scope.	1 hour
2. Gather initial data set.	2 hours
3. Create high level value stream or process map.	1 hour
4. Determine initial team members.	15 minutes
5. Create the initial Team Charter.	30 minutes
6. Assemble the team and conduct effective meeting.	2 hours
7. Complete A3 Report - Section 1. Problem Statement	15 minutes
8. Create a SIPOC Diagram, if needed.	30 minutes
9. Create initial current state value stream or process map.	2 hours
10. Create a Cycle Time Table.	2 hours

Steps/Activities for Planning Phase	Suggested Time Allocation
1. Determine project scope.	1 hour
2. Gather initial data set.	2 hours
3. Create high level value stream or process map.	1 hour
4. Determine initial team members.	15 minutes
5. Create the initial Team Charter.	30 minutes
6. Assemble the team and conduct effective meeting.	2 hours
7. Complete A3 Report - Section 1. Problem Statement	15 minutes
8. Create a SIPOC Diagram, if needed.	30 minutes
9. Create initial current state value stream or process map.	2 hours
10. Create a Cycle Time Table.	2 hours

Rolling

3. Determine which activities can be completed *prior to* the first full team meeting and which ones can be addressed by the entire team *at* the first full team meeting. Establish a concise time line and complete the activities as needed. Use the following Rolling Kaizen Event Planning Phase Summary to review the time buckets, team representations, etc. that are unique to this type of Event.

Kaizen Event				**Rolling Kaizen Event Planning Phase Summary**	
Process Owner:		**Black Belt or Lean Sensei:**	**Start Date:** **End Date:**		
Objective:			**Team Representation:** TL - Team Leader PO - Process Owner ES - Executive Sponsor	BB - Black Belt/Lean Sensei, or Continuous Improvement Specialist ATM - All Team Members (highlighted) STM - Sub Team Members	

Steps	# of 1 Hour Time Buckets	*Team Representation	Additional Representation	Lean, Six Sigma or Project Management Tool	Comments/Notes
1. Determine project scope.	1	TL, PO, ES, BB	Customer or supplier, if applicable	Balanced Scrorecard, Performance Dashboard, Customer Survey results, Pareto Chart, etc.	
2. Gather initial data set.	2	TL, PO, BB		Take time, cycle times, quality yields, value-added times, etc.	
3. Create high level value stream or process map.	1	TL, PO, BB		Value stream or process map; use appropriate mapping software	Microsoft Excel, Visio, or PowerPoint can be used.
3. Determine initial team members.	.25	TL, PO, BB			
5. Create the initial Team Charter.	.5	TL, PO, BB		Team Charter	
6. Assemble the team and conduct effective meeting.	2	ATM	Trainer, consultant	Lean and/or Six Sigma overiew (include waste), Effective Meeting Evaluation Worksheet	Conducting a Lean simulation would be helpful.
7. Complete A3 Report - Section 1 Problem Statement	.25	TL, PO, BB		A3 Report	To be posted and shared with team.
8. Create a SIPOC Diagram.	.5	STM		SIPOC Diagram, value stream or process map, Post-it Notes	
9. Create initial detailed current state value stream or process map.	2	STM			
10. Create Cycle Time Table.	2	STM	Informaticist	Document Tagging Worksheet, Cycle Time Table, Database Reports, Pareto Chart, Run Chart, etc.	Consider MSA if multiple sources are collecting data.
11. Conduct a Waste Walk.	1	ATM		Waste Walk Audit, Elevator Speech	Do not disrupt the process!
12. Update current state value stream or process map.	0.5	ATM		Post-It Notes, good facilitation, value stream or process map	Make the mapping process visual so everyone is involved.
13. Complete A3 Report - Section 2. Current State and Section 3. Improvement Opportunity	0.25	TL, PO, BB		A3 Report	To be posted and shared with team.
14. Conduct a Stakeholder Analysis.	0.5	STM		Stakeholder Analysis	Ensure all types of stakeholders are included.
15. Continue with specific Lean tool training.	1	ATM	Trainer, consultant		Directed to potential solutions to guide the team.
16. Determine specific improvement activities and use PDCA format.	2	ATM	Trainer, consultant	5 Why Analysis, Impact Map, Fishbone Diagram, Brainstorming, PDCA Kaizen Activity Worksheet.	Do not rush this step!
17. Create a future state value stream or process map.	1	STM		Value stream or process map; use appropriate mapping software; Post-It Notes (various colors)	Microsoft Excel, Visio, or PowerPoint can be used.
18. Create Reporting and Communication forms.	1	TL, PO, BB		Project Prep Status, Kick Off, Weekly Recap, Summary, etc.	Use current forms and update with Lean focus.
19. Create PDCA Implementation Phase schedule.	2	ATM		Project timeline, PDCA Kaizen Activity Worksheet or Action Item Log	Be flexible and work with team.
20. Communicate to Executive Sponsor and other managers the schedule.	0.25	TL, PO, BB		Reporting and Communication forms	Meet face-to-face if at all possible.
21. Communicate A3 Report. Problem Analysis, Section 5. Future State, and Section 6. Implementation Plan	0.25	TL, PO, BB		A3 Report	To be posted and shared with team.

* If multiple representation is listed, it can be one or all, depending on the experience of the individuals.

Kaizen Demystified

When determining your activities and Team Representation, keep in the mind the following:

- ❖ After the first full team meeting (Number 6 from the previous Rolling Kaizen Event Planning Phase Summary), it is expected that the sub teams (STM) will complete many of the expected activities, with the assistance of the Black Belt, Lean Sensei, or Continuous Improvement Specialist. However, the process owner, if knowledgeable in the Lean Six Sigma tools can also be part of the sub teams - but NOT always. Team members must obtain ownership quickly.
- ❖ If there are team members that have participated in previous Kaizen Events, ensure to utilize their experience on the sub teams as well as in the full team meetings. You may not need a Black Belt, Lean Sensei, etc. to be part of every sub team; however, they would provide continuity between all the activities which may be of value.
- ❖ If the position of Black Belt, Lean Sensei, or Continuous Improvement Specialist does not exist within the organization, solicit someone from the quality department, another colleague in the organization that has Kaizen Event experience, or hire an experienced consultant, to assume that role.

Team Representation can be any one of the titles listed in the Rolling Kaizen Event Planning Phase Summary or a combination thereof. Not everything has to be done as a team! However, the team should be made aware of what has been done and/or what is being planned.

Rolling

4. Use the following Rolling Kaizen Event Planning Phase Checklist to help ensure all critical items are completed prior to Part 2. PDCA Implementation Phase. The Checklist is a listing of the main steps, suggested time elements, as well as the main team members involved. This will help ensure a successful completion of this Phase. Use this as a guideline for customizing a Checklist for your Event.

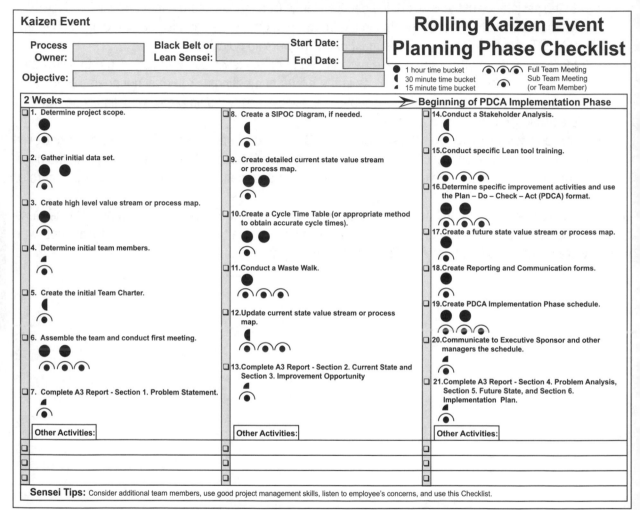

The following icons can be used to communicate the steps for the Planning Phase:

1 hour (or 30, 15 minutes) – represents a suggested time bucket for the step

Full Team Meeting– represents full team meeting

Sub team Meeting (or Team Member) – represents either a sub team or a single team member to complete the step

Note: The icons for the various steps are only guidelines for this Checklist, as each team will create their own. The purpose of this for the Rolling Kaizen Event is to ensure time buckets are assigned to the various steps. The steps are identical to the Standard 5 Day Planning Phase Checklist (page 118), however, icons were used to make this a "quick" checklist. For a detailed explanation of each of these steps, please read the particular section in the Standard 5 Day Kaizen Event section (pages 74 - 119).

The Rolling Kaizen Event Planning Phase Checklist has proven helpful for Kaizen teams in planning their Kaizen Events. Consider each activity listed as value-added or non value-added to the team's objectives. Also, be flexible to accept and use any other activities that the team members might have experienced that may also provide value to the team's objective.

Once the Planning Phase has been completed, or at least 80% completed or addressed, then it would be time to begin the PDCA Implementation or "doing" Phase.

Part 2. PDCA Implementation Phase (spans 4 - 6 weeks/weekly 2 hours or less meeting time)

There are many variables to consider when implementing the actual process changes (i.e., the PDCAs). Use the following as a guide during the PDCA Implementation Phase:

1. Gain an understanding of the main tools that can be used in this Phase. This following list of tools can be used as a quick-reminder as to the array of tools that may be considered for use in the PDCA Implementation Phase (typically the Improve Phase of the Six Sigma methodology). Please see the Tools section for a description for each of these tools.

Improve Phase
5S
Visual Controls
Mistake Proofing
Standard Work
Process or Work Area Layout
Mass Customization
Flow
Quick Changeovers (QCO)
Total Productive Maintenance (TPM)
Cross-Training

Note: The Black Belt, Continuous Improvement Specialist, etc. can provide mini-learning lessons on these tools. This could be recommending Lean apps, selecting reading sections from *The Lean Six Sigma Pocket Guide XL*, *The Practical Lean Six Sigma Pocket Guide*, *Practical Lean Six Sigma for Healthcare, or The Practical Lean Six Sigma Pocket Guide for Healthcare* or providing links to YouTube videos on appropriate topics. This will depend on the depth of knowledge that the team members have on Lean Sigma tools and the complexity of the problem at hand. These tools could also be reviewed in the Planning Phase, however, that would depend on how many of the Planning Phase tools/activities had to be learned and applied. It is not so important as to the "number" of tools or concepts learned, but rather if the tools or concepts are understood by all the team members and appropriately used in the Kaizen Event. As noted in the Planning Phase, this type of Event requires specific Lean tool training Just-In-Time.

2. Review the following guidelines that connect the various wastes (i.e., identified in the Waste Walk or other activity) with "likely" tools to be used to eliminate those wastes.

Note: The below listed *Lean Tools for Consideration* is a starting point for using a particular tool or concept to eliminate a waste. Many Lean tools inter-relate. For example, if it was determined in the Planning Phase that the cycle time for a particular process was quite varied among employees, then the tool of standard work may be of value. However, with standard work, this would most likely include a takt time (or demand or goal to meet) as well as some type of visual control. It is not so important to use the correct Lean name or label, it is more important to eliminate the process waste with a common sense approach. The Lean tool name can be a starting point. And, then work with the team in its application to the issue or waste.

Waste Category	*Lean Tools for Consideration*
1. Overproduction	Flow and Kanbans, Pull Systems, Demand Analysis, Takt Time, Visual Controls, Leveling/Heijunka
2. Waiting (or Delay)	Flow and Kanbans, Pull Systems, Quick Changeovers, Cross-Training, Leveling/Heijunka
3. Motion	5S, Standard Work, Cross-Training, Work Load Balancing, Process or Work Area Layout
4. Transport	5S, Standard Work, Flow and Kanbans, Pull Systems, Process or Work Area Layout, Cross-Training
5. Overprocessing	Mass Customization, Standard Work, Cross-Training
6. Inventory	Flow and Kanbans, 5S, Pull Systems, Quick Changeovers, Visual Controls, Leveling/Heijunka
7. Defects or Errors	Mistake Proofing, Standard Work, Total Productive Maintenance, Visual Controls
8. People's Skills and Knowledge	Cross-Training, Standard Work, Work Load Balancing
9. Unevenness	Flow and Kanbans, Pull Systems, Leveling/Heijunka, Cross-Training, Work Load Balancing
10. Overburden	Work Load Balancing, Cross-Training, Standard Work
11. Environmental Resources	Mistake Proofing, Flow and Kanbans, Mass Customization
12. Social Responsibility	Standard Work, Cross-Training

Note: There are other tools and concepts that also can be used to eliminate wastes. For example, using SPC and Process Capability studies can help to eliminate Defect or Errors with appropriate process changes or new standard work procedures. Also, the Team Charter, Meeting Minutes, etc. (tools typically used in the Planning or Define Phase) help to eliminate Overburden and People's Skills and Knowledge wastes. As often stated throughout this book, keep in mind the overall objective of the team, respect team member's ideas, and use common sense to process changes, and the wastes will be eliminated.

3. Establish the time buckets for implementing the various tools identified in (2). Gain a consensus with the team on your time buckets relative to the PDCAs. Often times, after understanding the Lean tool, the team may list the specific process change and the time element for implementation (and not the specific Lean or Six Sigma tool). Even though you may regularly meet weekly in 1 or 2 hour meetings, the PDCAs will be implemented by sub teams at other times. The following are some guidelines for establishing time buckets for the Lean tools:

Improve Phase	Time Bucket Guidelines (hours)
5S	4
Visual Controls	2
Mistake Proofing	1
Standard Work	2
Process or Work Area Layout	4
Mass Customization	1
Flow	2
Quick Changeovers (QCO)	1
Total Productive Maintenance (TPM)	2
Cross-Training	1

Note: The time associate with each Lean tool is a starting point. Your time buckets may be very different from these. For example, implementing Leveling/Heijunka as part of the Flow tool may require 8 hours of demand analysis, creating standards, visual controls, etc. 5S has a 4 hour time bucket, but your project may not even require 5S. As stated above, focus on the process change required and then work with the team to gain a consensus on how long in your defined time increments those process changes (PDCAs) would require.

Rolling

4. Determine, schedule, and implement the improvements (PDCAs) using the Rolling Kaizen Event PDCA Phase Time Bucket Matrix as a guide. There will be a variety of methods in which to implement the improvement activities for a Rolling Kaizen Event. It is nearly impossible to provide all the various options on what tool should be used, how long it takes to implement, etc.

Kaizen Event

Rolling Kaizen Event PDCA Phase Time Bucket Matrix

Process Owner: _____

Black Belt or Lean Sensei: _____

Start Date: _____
End Date: _____

Objective: _____

	Tools	1 Hour Time Bucket Expectations	Limitations	Minimum Number of Team Members	Additional Lean and/or Six Sigma Tool Support	Comments/Notes
☐	5S	4	None.	3 - 4, or entire team	Creates awareness of waste as well as allows everyone in the department or process area to be involved.	Sort - establish sort guidelines (30 minutes); Set-In-Order - create labels, markings, etc. (60 minutes); Shine - clean area (30 minutes); Standardize - create and train everyone to standards (60 minutes); Sustain - create audit and establish audit team (30 minutes)
☐	Visual Controls	2	May require assistance from Facilities or IT.	1 - 2, or entire team	Nearly all Lean tools have some form of visual control.	Ensure the team understands the four levels of visual controls.
☐	Mistake Proofing	1	May require assistance from Facilities or IT.	1 - 2, or entire team	Tied closely with Visual Controls Level 4.	Can eliminate and/or reduce errors significantly.
☐	Standard Work	2	Must have access to SOPs.	1 - 2, or entire team	Standard Work Combination Table and Chart can be used to document procedures and times.	All process should be standardized; it is the basis for continuous improvement.
☐	Process or Work Area Layout	4	May require assistance from Facilities.	3 - 4, or entire team	Spaghetti Diagram can be used to map before and after work flows.	Remove barriers of all kinds for improved work flow. Think in terms of continuous flow.
☐	Mass Customization	1	Familiar characteristics are required.	3 - 4, or entire team	Brainstorming, Data/Demand Analysis can be used to determine if this is practical.	May be difficult to apply at times, but can provide significant cost savings.
☐	Flow	2	Other departments may need to be involved.	1 - 2, or entire team	Consider continuous flow, paced, or scheduled flow to improve processes. Use pitch if appropriate.	Focus on removing bottlenecks and delays.
☐	Pull Systems	2	Requires use of signals.	1 - 2, or entire team	Consider kanbans, supermarkets, and FIFO Lanes. Use pitch and visual controls as needed.	Requires good communications with upstream and downstream processes.
☐	Quick Changeovers	1	Requires variety of products and/or services.	1 - 2, or entire team	Allows organization to provide Just-In-Time products and/or services.	Allows for smaller batches of products and/or services.
☐	Total Productive Maintenance	2	Requires critical equipment to the process.	1 - 2, or entire team	Requires reliability studies and standard work.	Equipment must be critical to the value stream or process.
☐	Cross-Training	1	Should include everyone.	1 - 2, or entire team	Training on problem solving skills and additional Lean Six Sigma may be of value.	This importance of this is usually underestimated.

Notes:

The Rolling Kaizen Event PDCA Phase Time Bucket Matrix main category descriptions are:

1 Hour Time Bucket Expectations – the number of hours typically required to implement the tool; use this only as an estimate, it will depend greatly on the team leader's, facilitator's, etc. experience level

Limitations – typically what is required for this tool to be successfully used

Additional Lean and/or Six Sigma Tool Support – identifies other possible alignments with Lean Sigma tools

5. Schedule and implement the specific improvement activities using the PDCA Kaizen Activity Worksheet (page 107) or Action Item Log (page 119) discussed in the Standard 5 Day Kaizen Event over the next 4 - 6 weeks. It is the detailed listing of Who does What, When.

6. Use the following Rolling Kaizen Event PDCA (Implementation) Phase Checklist to help ensure all critical items are completed prior to Part 3. Follow-Up Phase. Consider each activity listed as value-added or non value-added to the team's objectives. Also, be flexible to the regularly scheduled meeting times, in that, more or less time may need to be scheduled. This will help ensure a successful completion of this Phase. Use this as a guideline for customizing a Checklist for your Event.

Rolling Kaizen Event PDCA Phase Checklist

Kaizen Event

| Process Owner: | Black Belt or Lean Sensei: | Start Date: |
| | | End Date: |

Objective:

- ● 1 hour time bucket
- ◖ 30 minute time bucket
- ◢ 15 minute time bucket
- ◉◉◉ Full Team Meeting
- ◉ Sub-Team Meeting (or Team Member)

Week 1 (2 hours)
☐ 1. Understand specific Lean tools and continue to apply as needed:
5S
Visual Controls
Mistake Proofing
Standard Work
Process or Work Area Layout
Mass Customization
Flow
Quick Changeovers (QCO)
Total Productive Maintenance (TPM)
Cross-Training
● ◉◉◉

☐ 2. Update Kaizen Activity PDCA Worksheet.
Rolling Kaizen Event Time Bucket Matrix
PDCA Kaizen Activity Worksheet
● ◉◉◉

Week 2 (2 hours)
☐ 1. Review/discuss PDCA implementations (Action Items).
◖ ◉◉◉

☐ 2. Update PDCA schedule.
◉◉◉

☐ 3. Evaluate sub-teams implementation with appropriate metrics.
◢ ◉◉◉

☐ 4. Create Action Items.
◖

☐ 5. Update timeline for sub-teams implementation of PDCAs.
◢ ◉◉◉

Week 3 (2 hours)
☐ 1. Review/discuss PDCA implementations (Action Items).
◖ ◉◉◉

☐ 2. Update PDCA schedule.
◉◉◉

☐ 3. Evaluate sub-teams implementation with appropriate metrics.
◢ ◉◉◉

☐ 4. Create Action Items.
◖

☐ 5. Update timeline for sub-teams implementation of PDCAs.
◢ ◉◉◉

Week 4 (2 hours)
☐ 1. Review/discuss PDCA implementations (Action Items).
◖ ◉◉◉

☐ 2. Update PDCA schedule.
◖ ◉◉◉

☐ 3. Evaluate sub-teams implementation with appropriate metrics.
◢ ◉◉◉

☐ 4. Create Action Items.
◖

☐ 5. Update timeline for sub-teams implementation of PDCAs.
◢ ◉◉◉

Weeks 5+ (2 hours)
☐ 1. Review/discuss PDCA implementations (Action Items).
◖ ◉◉◉

☐ 2. Update PDCA schedule.
◉◉◉

☐ 3. Evaluate sub-teams implementation with appropriate metrics.
◢ ◉◉◉

☐ 4. Create Action Items.
◖

☐ 5. Update timeline for sub-teams implementation of PDCAs.
◢ ◉◉◉

Other Activities:
☐
☐
☐

Sensei Tips: Keep management informed, respect the process area employees, and use this Checklist.

The Rolling Kaizen Event PDCA Phase Checklist has proven helpful for Kaizen teams in making the process changes in this phase. Consider each activity listed as value-added or non value-added to the team's objectives. Also, be flexible to accept and use any other activities that the team members might have experienced that may also provide value to the team's objective.

Once the PDCA Implementation Phase has been completed, or at least 80% completed or addressed, then it would be time to begin Follow-Up Phase.

Part 3. Follow-Up Phase (spans 2 - 4 weeks/1 - 2 hours meeting time)

Use the following as a guide during the Follow-Up Phase:

1. Gain an understanding of the main tools that can be used in this Phase. This following list of tools can be used as a quick-reminder as to the array of tools that may be considered for use in the Follow-Up Phase (typically the Control Phase of the Six Sigma methodology). Please see the Tools section for a description for each of these tools.

Control Phase
Statistical Process Control (SPC)
Visual Management
Standard Work for Leaders
Performance Management
Layered Process Audits (LPA)

2. Establish the time buckets for implementing the various tools identified in (1). Gain a consensus with the team on your time buckets relative to what needs to be done in the next 2 - 4 weeks. The following Rolling Kaizen Event Follow-Up Phase Time Bucket Matrix provide guidelines for establishing time buckets for these tools as well as the type of Team Representation recommended.

Kaizen Event

Rolling Kaizen Event Follow-Up Phase Time Bucket Matrix

Process Owner: _____ Black Belt or Lean Sensei: _____ Start Date: _____ End Date: _____

Objective: _____

Tools	1 Hour Time Bucket Expectations	Limitations	Team Representation	Additional Lean and/or Six Sigma Tool Support	Comments/Notes
Project Management	1	May require assistance from IT for appropriate software use.	Team Leader, Process Owner	The A3 Report can be used to relay project completion as well as be a guide for the overall project. Gantt Charts can be used to detail the activities or the CRM program may have options available.	Additonal detailed listing throughout the scope of the project will need to be done to ensure action items are completed on time. This is critical for the success of this type of Kaizen Event.
Statistical Process Control	1	May require assistance from the Quality.	Black Belt or equiv., Process Owner	Allows for monitoring processes to determine if they are in control or if trends are developing.	Helps to determine when special cause variation has crept into the process.
Visual Management	3	Must have access to data.	Process Owner, Sub-Team Member	Storyboards can be used to convey project success. Department performance charts should be up-to-date.	Can improve productivity and quality immensely.
Standard Work for Leaders	2	Must have access to job requirements of leaders.	Team Leader, Process Owner	Need leaders to agree to a schedule to meet with employees and share information regularly.	Regularly scheduled short morning or afternoon meetings can help sustain improvements.
Performance Management	2	May require assistance from Human Resources.	Team Leader, Process Owner, Sub-Team Member	Individual, group, and department measurements should all tie together. This is essential to sustain process changes for the long term.	Use SMART Goals of: Specific Measureable Assigned Realistic Time-Bounded
Layered Process Audits	2	Need to have system in place that everyone has bought into.	Team Leader, Process Owner, Sub-Team Member	Need to define standard work and expectations from all levels of the department. Audit recommended.	May seem redundant with Visual Management and Performance Measurements, but can provide value if done with buy-in by all employees..

Notes:

3. Establish a concise time line and ensure the following activities are completed as needed. Keep in mind that not everything has to be done as a team! However, the team should be made aware of what still may need to be done.

   (1) Appropriate type of charts (i.e., Run, Pareto, SPC, etc.) used to monitor process changes.
   (2) Completed all PDCAs.
   (3) Lean Representative assigned.
   (4) Continued feedback about process changes from primary stakeholders.
   (5) Updated the A3 Report (or similar report) and shared appropriately within the organization.
   (6) Gemba practiced.
   (7) Kaizened the Rolling Kaizen Event process with the Kaizen Event Participation Evaluation and subsequent analysis.
   (8) Rewarded and recognized the team.

4. Use the following Rolling Kaizen Event Follow-Up Phase Checklist to help ensure all critical items are completed prior to starting another Kaizen Event. The Checklist is a listing of the main steps, main features for the steps, as well as the forms or worksheets suggested. This will help ensure a successful completion of this Phase. Use this as a guideline for customizing a Checklist for your Event

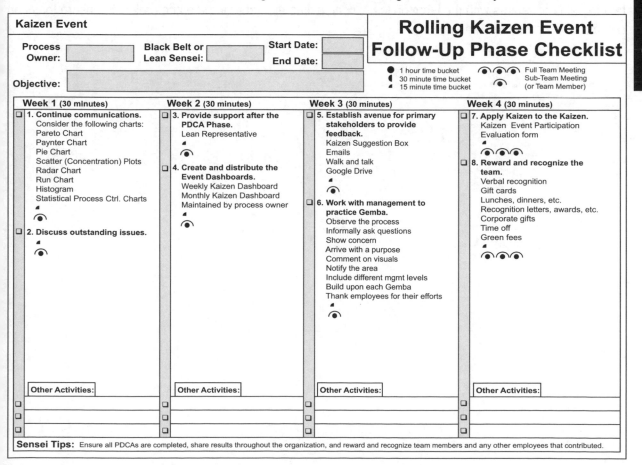

The Follow-Up Phase Checklist has proven helpful for Kaizen teams in sustaining the gains made in the PDCA Implementation Phase. Consider each activity listed as value-added or non value-added to the team's objectives. Also, be flexible to accept and use any other activities that the team members might have experienced that may also provide value to the team's objective.

Once the Follow-Up Phase has been completed, or at least 80% completed or addressed, then it would be time to begin another Kaizen Event!

As you noticed, the activities comprised of the Rolling Kaizen Event are identical to the Standard 5 Day Kaizen Event. Keep in mind that the overall objective for the Rolling Kaizen Event is to allocate the meetings, process changes, and training over a period of 3 months, with most of the process changes happening over a period of 4 - 6 weeks. Again, this will depend on the size of the team, the complexity of the project, the time employees make available for implementing the actual process changes, and how well the entire Rolling Kaizen Event is managed.

Even though the Rolling Kaizen Event defined in this book is for a 3 month period of time, it is common for these types of events to be 1 month or 6 months, with larger-scale projects going even longer. It is important to gain consensus with the team on the expected time element for the entire project to ensure they can commit to the proposed time period.

Case Study

The following case study demonstrates many of the tools explained in this section as well as some of the "people-side" issues that are encountered by the facilitator, team leader, process owner, or team member. As with any improvement project, you too would select only the appropriate activities (i.e., tools, worksheets, forms, etc.) to meet your specific Kaizen Event requirements for planning, implementing, and reporting.

KAP Manufacturing is the sole source supplier of blenders and other small kitchen appliances for Lean Chef, a global firm specializing in small kitchen and cooking appliances. KAP Manufacturing is vertically integrated, in that, they not only assemble the products such as blenders, choppers, and knife sharpeners, but they also produce most of the metal and plastic components that make up the units. KAP operates metal stamping and plastic molding presses, and associated cleaning and processing equipment for parts produced on these machines.

KAP produces three models of blenders in a various colors for each model of blender. A summary of the models and colors is shown below.

Master Chef - This is the high-end blender designed for commercial applications, and comes with a Black, Silver, or White base.
Lean Chef – This is the signature mid-level line designed for serious at home cooks, and has fewer features, and a slightly less powerful motor than the Master Chef model. This model comes with a white, red, or tan color base.
Gemba Chef – The Gemba Chef model is an entry-level blender designed for a low consumer price point. This blender has only basic features and a smaller motor than the other models and comes with a black or white base.

The KAP plant is a large sprawling plant with more than 250,000 sq ft under one roof. They are traditionally organized by department. The plastic molding machines and tool storage are in a contained area at the North end of the building. The metal stamping and finishing is near the South end of the facility, with certain specialty areas located in isolated areas throughout the plant. As KAP grew, they were forced to put equipment where they had space. They have work-in-process (WIP) inventory scattered near work centers throughout the plant as well. Assembly and sub-assembly lines are centrally located, not too far from the 12 shipping and receiving docks. Their finished goods (FG) inventory is located in a random rack storage area, and their shipping personnel pick and ship to the daily schedule and hot list every day.

From a scheduling aspect, KAP receives a weekly pull from their parent customer's Distribution Centers (DC's) and must ensure orders are shipped by the end of the following week. Recently their FG's inventory has been increasing at an alarming rate. Tim, the Operations Manager, believes the inventory levels have increased because each of the 5 DC's have increased their normal demand inputs due to a recent late delivery problem experienced by KAP. Their On-Time-Delivery performance was at 96.3, well below their goal of 99% for the Lean Chef product line. Also, the rework at Final Assembly for the Lean Chef product line was at 7.2%, again well below their target of <1%. The late deliveries for this product line were due to a few weeks of excessive reworks and down time at the final assembly lines caused by some quality problems with the metal parts. Regardless, Tim wanted to get to the bottom of this and reduce inventory levels for good. Additionally, The V.P. of Sales indicated that the Lean Chef product line (or value stream) are expecting to add another large retail outlet and is predicting future demand to increase approximately 30% in the next 3 - 6 months. Tim is being pressured by the management team to meet this increasing demand with existing resources in terms of physical plant space, equipment, and people, as well as resolve the delivery problem before this new retail customer looks for another source.

KAP's Part 1. Planning Phase

Tim is feeling a bit stressed over the entire situation. It appeared that the Lean Chef product line was experiencing a perfect or "super" storm of quality, delivery, and inventory problems. It is a business challenge of a life time, and Tim is determined to meet the challenge. Tim believes the plant is currently too busy to be able to stop production or take production employees away from their jobs for an improvement team that a Standard 5 Day Kaizen Event requires. However, the sense of urgency was there. Tim contacted a local training and consulting firm looking for help, and a first meeting was arranged with Tony, their Lean Six Sigma expert.

Tim explained to Tony what has been happening within the organization regarding their current issues. With Tony's experience with Kaizen Events, he described the Rolling Kaizen Event to Tim. The Rolling Kaizen Event reduces the downtime impact to a production process that might be caused by a Standard 5 (or 3) Day Kaizen Event. For a Rolling Kaizen Event, in Part 1, the Planning Phase activities such as data collection, planning, mapping, and training are completed by the process owner or team leader several weeks before any process changes are proposed. Improvement teams meet in small increments of time (less than four hours at any one meeting with them typically requiring two hours or less). Then during the Part 2. PDCA Implementation Phase, the Action Items are completed by sub teams or individual team members prior to the next meeting. A Rolling Kaizen Event may span over several months, but typically last 2 - 3 months through all three phases. Therefore, with this type of Event, production can keep running. Tony outlined the Rolling Kaizen Event target areas and worked with Tim to draft the Team Charter and a Rolling Kaizen Event Planning Phase Summary as shown in the following two illustrations.

Kaizen Event

Team Charter

Process Owner:	Tim	**Black Belt or Lean Sensei:**	Tony	**Week of:**	6/1 Wk 40

Value Stream: Lean Chef

Objective: 1. Reduce rework at the final assembly line   2. Reduce inventory   3. Improve On-Time-Delivery

Team Members:

	Name	Dept/Site
Facilitator:	Tony	SC College
Scribe:	Doug	Quality
Team Leader:	Tim	Production
Team Members:	Brenda	Planning/Scheduling
	Mack	Production
	Doug	Production
	Bud	Production
	Susan	Production

Meeting Fequency:

Dates:	6/15,6/22,/6/29,7/6,7/13,7/20,7/27,8/4
Times:	Tuesday's, 1:00 - 2:30 - Training Center

Lean Objectives:
1. Improve throughput by 10% in 3 months.
2. Reduce rework at Final Assembly from ~6-9% to <1% in 3 months.
3. Improve OTD to >99% in 3 months.

What are the specific metrics that will be improved?

Deliverables: Tuesday's, 1:00 - 2:30 - Training Center

What are the specific opportunities for:

Productivity/Cost?	**Quality?**
Current: 1500 U/P/D **Target:** 1650 U/P/D	**Current:** 7.2% rework **Target:** <1% rework

Delivery?	**People?**
Current: 96.3 OTD **Target:** >99% OTD	**Current:** Good **Target:** Train in tools

Customer?	**Financial?**
Current: Potential new business **Target:** New business awarded	**Current:** 200 hrs/week overtime **Target:** <100 hrs/week overtime

What are any issues or concerns that may impact this team's objective?

Concerns: None at this time.

Sign-Off:

Executive Sponsor: _Gary_____   Date: _6/2_____

Champion/Value Stream Manager/VP: _Tim_____   Date: _6/2_____
(maybe the same as Executive Sponsor)

Process Owner: _Tim_____   Date: _6/2_____

Deliverables to be included with this Charter: ☐ Value Stream or Process Map for the project
☑ Supporting High Level Data

Rolling

Rolling Kaizen Event
Planning Phase Summary

Kaizen Event

Process Owner:	Tim	Black Belt or Lean Sensei:	Tony	Start Date:	6/1
				End Date:	8/26

Objective: 1. Improve On-Time-Delivery | 2. Reduce inventory | 3. Reduce rework at the final assembly line

■ Highlights All Team Members (ATM)

Steps	# of 1 Hour Time Buckets	Team Representation	Additional Representation	Lean, Six Sigma or Project Management Tool	Comments/Notes
1. Determine project scope.	.25	Gary, Tim		Balanced Scorecard	Obtain new business for Lean Chef!
2. Gather initial data set.	.5	Tim		OTD, Quality Dashboard, Rework metrics, create charts for team review	
3. Create high level value stream or process map.	1	Tim, Tony	Brenda	Value stream map (Visio)	Work with Brenda to verify inventories.
3. Determine initial team members.	.25	Tim, Tony			
5. Create the initial Team Charter.	.5	Tim, Tony		Team Charter	
6. Assemble the team and conduct effective meeting.	2	ATM		Lean and/or Six Sigma overview (include waste). Effective Meeting Evaluation Worksheet	Conduct Cups simulation, review wastes, 5S benchmark in Master Chef speed cell.
7. Complete A3 Report - Section 1 Problem Statement.	.25	Tim		A3 Report	To be posted and shared with team.
8. Create a SIPOC Diagram.	N/A	N/A	N/A	N/A	N/A
9. Create initial detailed current state value stream or process map.	1	Tim, Tony, Mack	Brenda	Value stream map (Visio)	Work with Brenda to update map.
10. Create Cycle Time Table.	1	Tim, Bud		Cycle Time Table (MRP report)	Consider MSA if multiple sources are collecting data.
11. Conduct a Waste Walk.	.5	ATM		Waste Walk Audit form	Everyone understand the wastes.
12. Update current state value stream or process map.	.5	ATM		Value stream map	Use flip chart paper for main areas of map so everyone is involved.
13. Complete A3 Report - Section 2. Current State and Section 3. Improvement Opportunity.	0.25	Tim		A3 Report	To be posted and shared with team.
14. Conduct a Stakeholder Analysis.	N/A	N/A	N/A	N/A	N/A
15. Continue with specific Lean tool training.	1	ATM		Mistake Proofing, Visual Controls, 5S, Flow, and Standard Work	Use examples from Master Chef product line.
16. Determine specific improvement activities and use PDCA format.	2	ATM		Use Action Item Log.	Do not rush this step!
17. Create a future state value stream or process map.	1	Tim, Tony, Mack	Brenda	Value stream or process map; use appropriate mapping software; Post-It Notes (various colors)	Microsoft Excel, Visio, or PowerPoint can be used.
18. Create Reporting and Communication forms.	1	Tim		Project Prep Status, Kick Off, Weekly Recap, Summary, etc.	Use current forms and update with Lean focus.
19. Create PDCA Implementation Phase schedule.	2	ATM		Project timeline, PDCA Kaizen Activity Worksheet or Action Item Log	Be flexible and work with team.
20. Communicate to Executive Sponsor and other managers the schedule.	.25	Tim		Reporting and Communication forms	Meet face-to-face if at all possible.
21. Communicate A3 Report. Problem Analysis, Section 5. Future State, and Section 6. Implementation Plan.	.25	Tim		A3 Report	To be posted and shared with team.

The preliminary areas of focus are a 50% reduction in total inventory and a 30% improvement in (through-put) T/P or units per person per day (U/P/D) with the existing Lean Chef lines. A tall order, but achievable!

Tim and Tony established an initial time line plan as well as they created a high level current state value stream map and are graphically shown below.

Rolling Kaizen Work Session Schedule Plan - Lean Chef													
Phase/Activity	Month 1 Planning			Month 2 PDCA				Month 3 PDCA				Month 4 Follow-Up	
Rolling Kaizen Work Sessions: On-Time-Delivery and Quality Improvement	4		4	2	2	2	2	2	2	2	2	1	1
	4	0	4	2 = 10	2	2	2	2 = 8	2	2	2	2 = 8	0 1 0 1 = 2

Current State Map for KAP Manufacturing

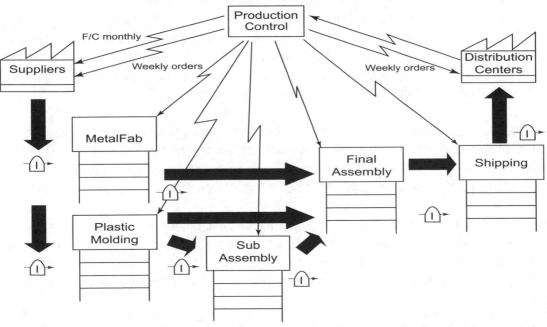

Tony conducted a brief overview of Lean Six Sigma methods and tools at the first four hour meeting. Tony reviewed the high level value stream map and requested that the team populated the map with process attributes. Tony had the team break into smaller groups to conduct a Waste Walk and collect process attributes to subsequently complete a more detailed value stream map. The following areas would be mapped.

Plastic Molding
Metal Fab
Sub Assembly
Final Assembly

Upon returning from the Waste Walk, Mack quickly stated, "It's amazing. We did this exact thing about a year ago. We made suggestions as there was this big push to get our ideas, and then nothing was done." Rita, realizing that this may be what other team members are thinking, responded, "Mack, I do remember something similar last year. However, let me point out some differences. First, Tim is fully on board as has a commitment to this project, as he stated at the beginning of our meeting. Also, last year we just treated it as a typical project and this time we hired a professional facilitator to lead us on how to conduct an effective Kaizen Event. We do not want to waste anyone's time. We know you were on something like this last year Mack and that is why we selected you. I am sure your input will be invaluable as we proceed. Also, we will be evaluating our meetings and will work to make your time here most valuable. We will also be incorporating an audit process to ensure the changes are sustained. This is not to say we will not have some issues or problems, but the resources have been committed to make necessary changes that need to be done. Please continue to express any and all concerns as we move forward. Did I address your question?" Mack concluded, "Sure. I will do what I can, but I do hope it is different this time as you say." Rita responded, "Fair enough!"

The information gathered was used to represent the entire material and information flow for KAP for the Lean Chef product line. By breaking the mapping into smaller "chunks," the team was able to more clearly "see" opportunities for improvement. It was apparent that inventory was clearly a problem (i.e., waste). The value stream map indicated that the typical lead time was 30 days, while the actual processing time including VA and NVA, and was only 0.88 days. When the organization is producing to demand, these should be nearly identical. The preliminary conclusions were that Tim had to somehow do a better job of linking actual demand/consumption/sales to production, and ensure the lines could respond quickly enough. To do this Tim had to smooth out the production delivery problems.

At the second four hour meeting demand analysts and supply chain planners were in attendance as extended team members to discuss the issue. It was determined that the delivery problems were stemming from quality and throughput problems in operations. The team decided that this was the root cause for poor overall performance and made the quality and throughput improvements their top priorities.

In a Lean Six Sigma improvement initiative, quality must always be improved first, or all other systems will remain at risk of added wastes, therefore, the rework had to be addressed first. If the team improved the Final Assemble line speed (U/P/D) without improving quality first, they would only make rejects faster. In general, Tony indicated that a Lean Six Sigma improvement approach address issues or opportunities in the following order.

1.   Improve quality
2.   Improve flow
3.   Create pull

Tim showed the team the following Pareto Chart:

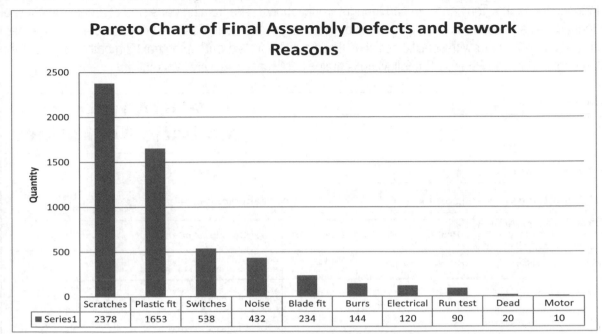

The last 30 minutes of the second four hour meeting the team brainstormed and created the following Fishbone Diagram:

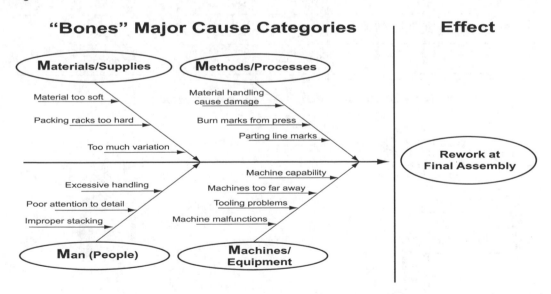

The team used this Fishbone Diagram to better understand the potential causes and agreed to gather more data on the major causes before the next meeting. Each person agreed to gather data on a different major potential cause and report out at the next work session.

The final two hour meeting in the Planning Phase consisted of 1 hour of Lean training on 10 of the main Lean tools (those that Tony and Tim had thought would apply). The training consisted of a brief overview of the tool as well as numerous examples many of which were from their Master Chef product line. The team continued in the 2nd hour with specific activities that would be "rolled-out" in the next 2 months as part of the PDCA Implementation Phase. The following is their PDCA Kaizen Activity Worksheet:

Kaizen Event			PDCA Kaizen Activity Worksheet		
Value Stream: Lean Chef			**Date:** 6/22		
Department: Production and Planning			**Team Members:** Tony, Doug, Tim, Brenda, Mack, Bud, Susan		
Process Name/Activity (as identified on the value stream, process map, etc.)	**Problem or Waste**	**Lean Tool**	**Specific Activities**	**Who**	**When**
Metal Fab - Stamping	Handling scratches	Mistake Proofing	Design and test a collection bin that reduces part on part scatching	Mack, Bud	15 Jul
Metal Fab - Stamping	Motion	Cell Design	Move the stamping machines into a cell with finishing area	Doug, Tim, Susan	1 Aug
Metal Fab - Lapping/Finishing	Handling scratches	Mistake Proofing	Design and test transport bins that reduces part on part scatching	Mack	15 Jul
Plastic Molding - Molding	Corrections and rework	Problem Solving, DOE, and SPC	Develop Design of Experiments to determine why plastic parts are defective	Bud, Tim, Susan	1 Aug
Plasic Molding - Molding	Corrections and rework	Check Sheets	Monitor the reasons for defects as they occur	Brenda	1 Jul
Plasic Molding - Finishing	Corrections and rework	PDCA	Implement trial actions to prevent defects from reaching Final Assembly	Susan, Tim	15 Jul
Sub Assembly	Corrections and rework	Check Sheets, Pareto Charts, Problem Solving	Collect data to determine and detail the volume and type of defects due to switches. Work with supplier.	Tim, Bud	15 Jul

Future State Map for KAP Manufacturing

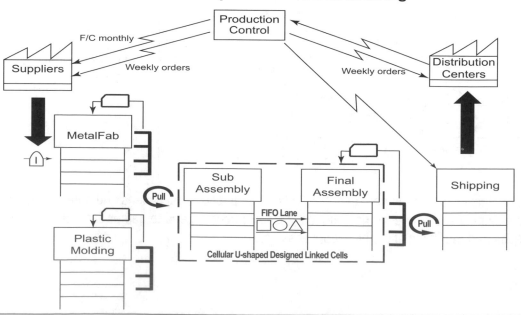

The next day, the following A3 Report as well as the PDCA Kaizen Activity Worksheet were posted at the various visual bulletin boards located in the areas being addressed. A note was posted next to the documents soliciting ideas from any employees. This communicate the team's progress as well as providing an avenue to get more employees engaged in this Lean initiative.

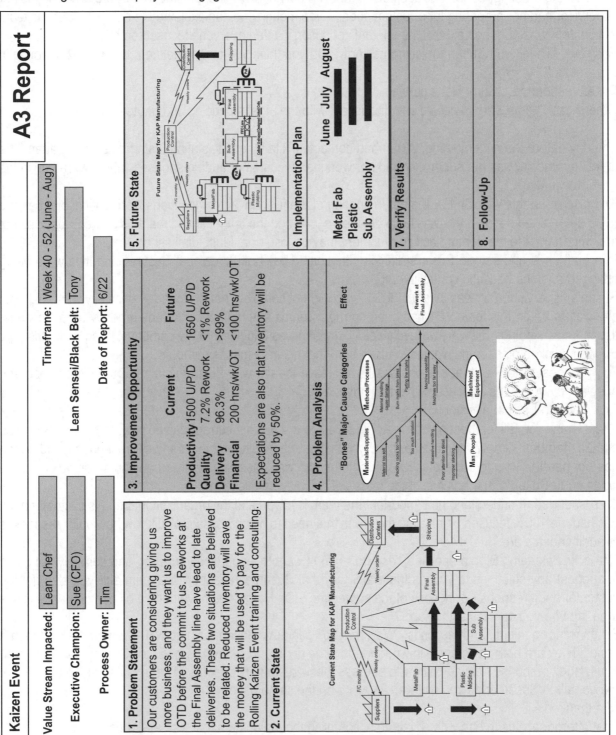

KAP's Part 2. PDCA Implementation Phase

At the first two hour meeting, 30 minutes had been scheduled for Susan to review new fixed inventory locations. At the meeting, Susan had apologized that she did not have enough time to prepare anything, as her supervisor had her preparing for a custom audit. Even though she had explained to her boss that this team Action Item was due, he said that the V.P. of Production wanted everyone focused on this audit.

Rita said, "Thank you Susan for letting us know. Do you think you can complete it by our next meeting in two weeks?"

Susan responded. "Sure. Not a problem."

Other Action Items were reviewed and discussed, with the meeting ending 30 minutes early.

The day before the next meeting, Susan had contacted Rita by email, stating that she could not attend the meeting tomorrow, as her supervisor had her working on customer audit responses, which were due in the next two weeks.

Rita discussed this with Chris. The determination of the fixed inventory locations were critical and needed to be determined soon. If this was to be delayed again, and the team sensed that this entire Event was not that important, the momentum and commitment may be lost, or at least, diminished.

Rita and Chris understood Susan's difficult situation. They both knew that Susan's priorities were being changed and she had little control over it.

Susan's supervisor, Bill, was aware that Susan could not complete her assigned and initially was "told" that she was to be on this team. Bill had been on many teams and did not sense any urgency regarding what this team was doing. Bill was two levels below Tim and was fairly new to the company, hired 9 months ago. Bill was quick to please and wanted to make sure that his area met its numbers.

Tony suggested to Rita that she or Chris have a face-to-face with Bill to explain the team's purpose and answer any questions or concerns he may have.

Rita met with Bill that afternoon.

Rita, "Thank you Bill for meeting with me. I just want to discuss our current Kaizen project that has Susan as a team member. I know you have been busy with the recent customer audit and the responses, and Susan has not had the time to complete the Action Items she was assigned. Is there anything I or we can do to help you or Susan? She has one of the more critical roles on this team."

Bill responded, "I understand how important the team is to you and the organization, but this customer audit has had me 100% focused on meeting the areas that need to be addressed. You know how quick responses to audit findings are."

Rita acknowledging Bill's response, "Yes I do. I don't want to jeopardize your area and certainly not going to suggest any solutions to you. Is there any way that Susan can support this team and you also get the customer audit response work done at the same time? Or, I know you have quite a bit of experience in this area, maybe you can assist this team?"

Bill thinks for a minute and responds, "Well, maybe I can have Susan team up with Greg for the next month or so. They are both well versed in what needs to be done. This might be good for Greg to get some customer audit response training on how to address these customer concerns. That should free up Susan. Let me go talk to Susan and Greg and we can all be on the same page."

Rita thanked Bill.

That afternoon, Susan had worked late to accomplish the Action Item that was assigned.

This part of the Rolling Kaizen Event required detailed project management and communication to ensure that the improvement tasks got completed on time. This is critical for a Rolling Kaizen Event team's success. New items were continually added to the Action Item Log and/or PDCA Kaizen Activity Worksheet list as new discoveries were made in the PDCA process. The team could see continuous incremental improvements through the weekly metrics.

Note: Even though the full team would meet for the next 4 - 6 weeks in the implementation of these activities, there were numerous sub team meetings.

The team used several Lean tools to develop the future state. They were able to use kanban signal systems to streamline both the Plastic molding and the Metal Fabrication processes. To do this, the improvement team first had to establish fixed inventory locations and containers for several of their larger volume parts. With this complete, kanban cards were created, and additional training conducted regarding how to produce and respond to kanban signal cards. The workers were able to quickly understand the simple kanban signals and even believed it was easier than following a schedule that was always changing!

During the third two hour meeting, Mack and Brenda were discussing what the inventory levels should be. They were the only two really engaged in the topic and discussion. After about 5 minutes of dialogue Tony had suggested a break for the team.
After the break, Tony said, "There was some good discussion from Mack and Brenda regarding what the inventory levels should be. Does anyone else have any ideas?"
No one responded. Tony continued, "If you do, please email Mack or Brenda and give them your thoughts.
"I believe, correct me if I am wrong, that this may be something we should assign a sub team to further investigate before our next meeting. How about it? Mack and Brenda, can you take that as an Action Item and provide us with a conclusion to your discussion?"
Brenda and Mack agreed, they too knew that their discussion was not benefiting the team at this time.

The team also employed U-shaped cell design concepts and line balancing in the Sub and Final Assembly areas. The team conducted a "quick train" session with the assembly teams, and the teams redesigned their areas to improve flow and reduce wastes. This allowed for the work teams to better see the quality issues earlier, and take appropriate corrective action to reduce rework. More importantly, the team felt they were getting the things they needed for success. The re-location of the raw materials, the reduced distance between the machines, and the missing tools identified in the Fishbone Diagram were finally getting addressed! All these improvements, combined with regular, effective meetings, had the delivery, quality, and inventory measurements improve.

KAP's Part 3. Follow-Up Phase

The overall improvement trend was looking good, which meant the team's improvement action items were succeeding! The Run Chart for rework is shown below and clearly shows and improvement trend.

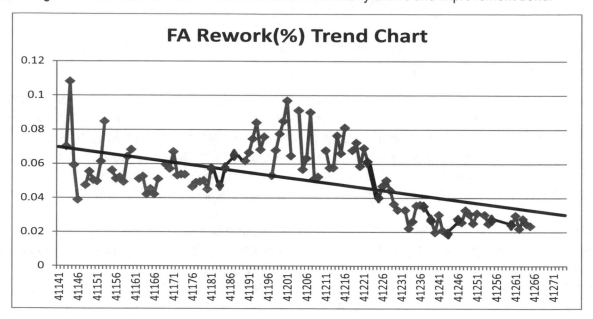

The following Line Balance chart shows the current and future states.

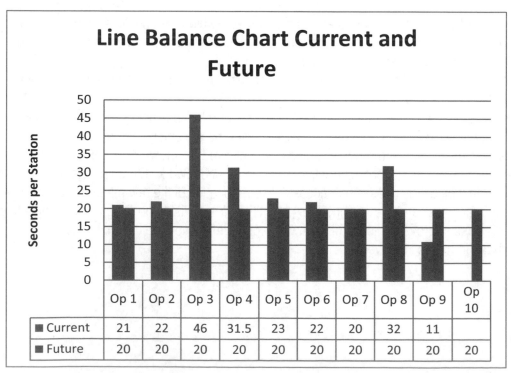

	Op 1	Op 2	Op 3	Op 4	Op 5	Op 6	Op 7	Op 8	Op 9	Op 10
Current	21	22	46	31.5	23	22	20	32	11	
Future	20	20	20	20	20	20	20	20	20	20

Note: Line balancing does not always balance exactly, and unbalanced time should continue to be reviewed for improvements.

The balancing of the line not only reduced wastes, but enabled the team to work toward one piece flow (OPF). Moving to OPF dramatically improved the throughput and reduced WIP inventory for the line, as shown below.

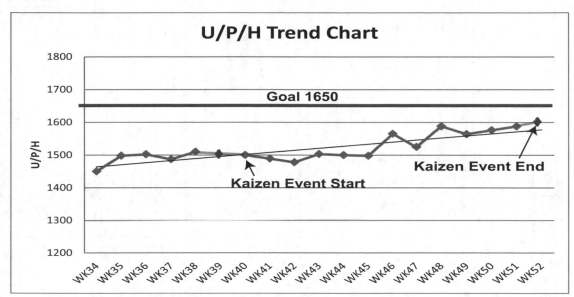

The increased production requirements could now be handled by the current line operators. This in itself was a huge success.

As the Rolling Kaizen Event team made their improvements in quality and throughput, OTD was also achieved. The graph below shows the OTD tracked over the life of the Rolling Kaizen Event. The team was very pleased with this unintended consequence, and so was the boss! (The perfect storm was weathered!)

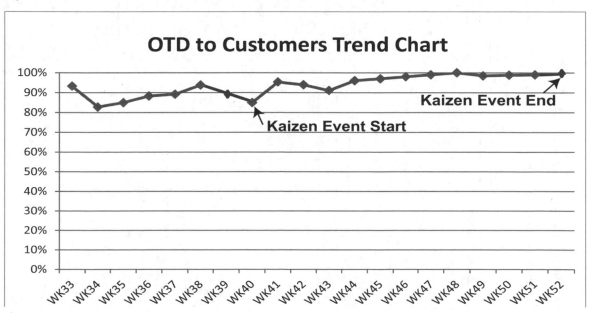

The final A3 Report is shown as follows as was shared within the organization:

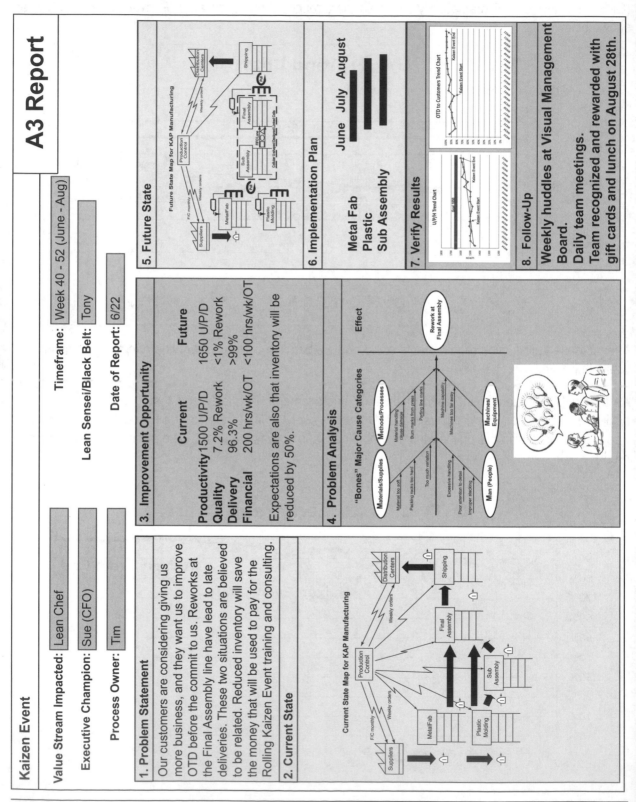

Kaizen Demystified

For the KAP company and improvement team, the Rolling Kaizen Event with its series of several shorter 2 hour work sessions worked very well, and conserved precious resources. The overall project took nearly 3 months and enabled the team to accomplish significantly more than a Standard 5 Day Kaizen Event would have allowed. The results spoke for themselves.

The following is a summary of the Lean, Six Sigma, and Leadership tools used in this case study:

Issue or Improvement Opportunity in Case Study	*Lean, Six Sigma or Leadership Tool Used*
Customer compaints and quality problems	Value Stream Mapping, Problem Solving, Mistake Proofing (pgs. 192-193)
Too much inventory	Kanban System (pg. 197)
On-Time-Delivery issues	Line Balancing, U-Shaped Cell Design, Problem Solving (pgs. 195-197)
Excessive rework and scrap	Problem Solving, Pareto Charts, Check Sheets, Data Collection, Mistake Proofing (pgs. 195-197)
Lack of confidence in sustaining changes	Layered Process Audits, Meeting Leading, Trust Building (pg. 192)
Lack of support from other departments	Communications (pg. 196)
1-2 people dominating meetings	Meeting Leading (pg. 197)

Rolling

Sensei Tips

Note: Many of the following Sensei Tips can be used or applied in the other Kaizen Events, where and when appropriate.

❖ Make all attempts to allocate Action Items equitably among the team along with the expected completion date. Often those activities (Action Items or PDCAs) will be a starting point for other activities.

❖ Create sub teams as needed. During the 1 - 2 weeks between meetings, having 2 (or 3 people) assigned to an Action Item will greatly increase the odds of that Action Item being completed.

❖ Meetings typically are scheduled for two hours, therefore, keep the meeting on track and if the meeting agenda gets completed ahead of schedule, end the team meeting. Team members will appreciate that type of meeting efficiency and respect for their time.

❖ Keep team members engaged in team meetings by having an activity or something fun during the two hours (something that lasts no longer than 1-2 minutes). At the one hour mark, this could be a brain teaser, someone sharing a hobby, a funny cartoon (politically correct), having dancing monkeys arrive (not really), etc. Be creative. A little light-heartedness can break the tension and re-energize the team.

❖ Avert any length discussions that are known to cause problems. Those discussions should be done before or after the meeting. However, there will be those value-added discussions. As a Kaizen Event leader, decide when it's appropriate to table a discussion for the good of the team.

❖ Try not to schedule the two hour meetings at the end of the work day. Team members will be anxious to leave and also may feel obligated to go back and check their emails, messages, etc. thereby not giving the last part of the meeting their undivided attention.

❖ Make sure to clearly document the Team or Project charter, what is in scope and what is out of scope, and communicate this regularly with the team, and organizational leaders for full alignment.

❖ Use the A3 tool, and other Kaizen Event forms to help facilitate and reconnect the team Rolling Kaizen Event at each new session. This keeps the focus aligned with a strong sense of purpose.

❖ Use outside resources such as Lean Sensei's and facilitators to train, and to facilitate the process, but do not rely on them to do the heavy lifting of making the improvements. This is the responsibility of the organization and team.

❖ Do not get caught up in trying to use too many Lean Six Sigma tools. Only apply the Lean Six Sigma tools that apply to the situation, and will help eliminate wastes.

❖ Regularly review the Rolling Kaizen Event process to identify additional wastes, and update the appropriate forms as new wastes and opportunities are identified.

❖ It may help to identify and schedule a specific time to meet each week to keep the momentum up during a Rolling Kaizen Event. A weekly session at a specific time and location will help to maintain the continuity of the improvement effort.

❖ When the Event is concluded, document the lessons learned, and formally close the Rolling Kaizen Event or project. Thank the team for their efforts, celebrate the successes, and learn from the failures.

Web Based Kaizen Event

You have identified your project as a Web Based Event Event from the How to Select Your Kaizen Event Type (pages 59 -70)

Overview

Note: It is suggested the Standard 5 Day Kaizen Event section be read first to fully understand the basic structure and activities required that comprise all types of Kaizen Events (to some degree). The Web Based Kaizen Event is a take-off or modification of the Standard 5 Day and Rolling Kaizen Event and, therefore, will have similar activities. This section will only *reference* the activities that are unique to this Kaizen Event type.

Web Based Kaizen Events *are targeted improvement initiatives with team members using emerging technologies to plan, implement, and sustain improvements or solve a problem over time.* The Web Based Kaizen Event may start off with a 2 - 4 hour meeting via a Web conferencing and/or emerging technology platform, then continue to meet weekly online for 1 - 2 hours throughout the course of the Kaizen Event (typically 3 months).

The following is the Web Based Event Quick Determination Checklist to ensure this is the type of Kaizen Event required given your specific situation. Ensure the majority of Characteristics are checked as Yes or Likely in the Your Situation column.

Web Based Kaizen Event Quick Determination Checklist					
Characteristic	**YES or LIKELY**	**Your Situation**	**Characteristic**	**YES or LIKELY**	**Your Situation**
Large Scope (crosses departments)	✔		Management Involvement	✔	
			5S Applied	✔	
Small Scope (within the department)	✔		Training Costs a Factor	✔	
Immediate Attention Required	✔		Requires Detailed Planning Meetngs	✔	
Process Immediately Accessible	✔		May Require Statistical Methods to Determine Root Cause	✔	
Root Cause May Be Known					
Specific Training Required	✔		Web-based Collaboration Application Main Form of Communication	✔	
Broad Training Required			Team Required	✔	
Team Members Physically (Locally) Available			Value Stream or Process Map Required	✔	
Meeting Times < 4 Hours	✔		Will Impact Balanced Scorecard or Performance Dashboard Metric	✔	
Process Change (PDCAs) Continuously Applied Over a Few Days			Team Charter Required	✔	

A successful Web Based Kaizen Event must have the following conditions present:

- ❖ Team members have access to Web conferencing tools.
- ❖ Team leader or facilitator proficient in Web conferencing tools and/or other emerging technologies.
- ❖ Good communication standards for everyone involved.
- ❖ Team members available for limited lengths of time (typically 1 - 2 hours weekly).
- ❖ The Just-In-Time concept for training, meetings, etc.
- ❖ Management committed and engaged in the project.
- ❖ Process area employees' ideas are considered (as only a few will be on the team).
- ❖ All employees are treated with dignity and respect.

This chapter demonstrates proven techniques to effectively and efficiently analyze and present information on improvement activities to direct reports, colleagues, and higher-level managers or executives in an online, Web-based collaborative environment. In this chapter you will learn how to:

- ❖ Provide team members with access to Web conferencing tools.
- ❖ Create a project "workspace" in a Web-based conferencing application for conducting a Kaizen Event.
- ❖ Invite project participants to a Web Based Kaizen Event.
- ❖ Establish project tasks and due dates for a Web Based Kaizen Event.
- ❖ Conduct effective meetings for a Web Based Kaizen Event.
- ❖ Create a platform for having participants collaborate on documents for a Web Based Kaizen Event.
- ❖ Sustain improvements for the Web Based Kaizen Event

Implementing these concepts in the Desktop and networking environment may require input from the entire department as well as the other departments. It may also involve 'buy-in' or support from IT. This type of Kaizen Event will require a significant portion of the time in the Planning Phase to ensure effective communications via a Web-based collaborative application. A team's motivation and potential for success can be severely compromised when they feel their time is being wasted due to the Web-based collaboration platform or app not being used effectively.

Note: Even though this chapter focuses on the non-physical face-to-face communications to conduct a Kaizen Event, it must be recognized that there are advantages to physical face-to-face meetings. One advantage is when people meet face-to-face they can bounce ideas back-and-forth in brainstorming sessions through both verbal and non-verbal cues. You can also approach them on a personal level that can be helpful in those more difficult situations. Even though instant messaging is available, it is not the same. However, the speed at which business decisions need to be made, the physical face-to-face meetings may not always be practical and feasible.

The distinction between "Web-based" sharing and "Desktop" sharing is: with Web-based, you are sharing a Web-based application simultaneously with many users and you are (all) looking at screens/updates located on a remote secure server or Cloud, which allows you to meet "online" rather than in person, and ensures you still have a structured and productive 'virtual' meeting. With Desktop sharing, the aim is to view (for example) a presentation on the screen of a single user who might be providing an update to an audience that has access to view the screen of that single user for the duration of the presentation. Now, in reality, many of the applications listed below use both Web-based and Desktop sharing technologies (sometimes simultaneously) to ensure effective communication.

Team meetings using the Web can save time, resources, and money. With today's ever growing demand for an integrated supply chain network for products and services, and employees and suppliers working in locations throughout the world, the Web Based Kaizen will undoubtedly be the future for continuous improvement projects. It allows everyone to be on the same page at the same time regardless of their physical location. Or, if they cannot be present for the Web Based Kaizen Event Web-conferencing (online) meeting, they will have the ability to review the meeting and contribute their ideas at a later time because most Web-based conferencing applications include a recording option.

The Web Based Kaizen Event can have the same results as any other type of team-based Kaizen Event if the technology is used effectively. The virtual collaborative team can brainstorm, review, edit, or modify presentations, documents, applications, etc. on their Desktop computer screens and smart phones/devices in real-time – just as if everyone were sitting in a conference room. By doing this, more can be done in less time when there is a need to collaborate on a business issue.

If this is the first time conducting a Web Based Kaizen Event or the Web-based conferencing tool is new to many of the participants, consider the following:

❖ Ensure each location (i.e., Desktop user) has some practice time with the Web-based conferencing application or emerging technology platform prior to the first meeting with the main features expected to be used (i.e., video, audio through the computer or phone lines, etc.). *The team leader or facilitator may have to conduct several mini-training sessions.*

❖ Coordinate someone from IT to be available in case there are technological difficulties at the first meeting. Subsequent support may or may not be needed depending on that first meeting. It is frustrating for a group of people that must wait for that one person who is having a technical issue. Work on any technological issue no more than 2 or 3 minutes during any full team meeting. Acknowledge the problem and what course of action that will be done. Respect everyone's time.

❖ Develop alternative plans if one aspect or feature of the Web-conferencing application is not working. For example, if the videos of all the participants are online except one person; make a decision and have them contribute using only audio. Or, if audio is not working for one person, consider having them use the land line or have them stay in the meeting and use instant chat. Be flexible, but keep the meeting moving forward.

❖ Use the reminder feature that many of the applications have to "remind" or "alert" participants via email, text message, etc. 5 minutes before the scheduled meeting start time (or whatever time frame is deemed appropriate) that the meeting is about to occur.

Before making your selection of the appropriate Web-based application, it is suggested you write a list of key features and functions the Web-based application (and the collaborate team) must have. Use the Web Based Collaboration Matrix (next page) to create your own list to assist you and your IT department to select the appropriate application and options for your Kaizen Event.

The following is a sample checklist for selecting a Web-based communication application:

- ❖ Ability to set/prioritize/filter tasks by deadline, ownership, milestones, and dependencies
- ❖ Ability to import files (e.g., Word, Excel, Project, as well as other pictures or diagrams)
- ❖ Access to a centralized, secure, and encrypted data storage
- ❖ Access to a centralized calendar system and integration with standard email/calendar applications (e.g., MS Outlook, Lotus Notes)
- ❖ Ability to create a unique/distinct project "space" and assign/restrict user access
- ❖ Access to secure "chat" room environments for decision making and brainstorming
- ❖ Ability to view and track project time line and send 'upcoming' task alerts to users
- ❖ Access to easy 'internal' information sharing (read and/or write access) and ability to publish externally via a simple URL for viewing by external public "groups"
- ❖ Ability to record and retrieve Web meetings
- ❖ Access to "at-a-glance" status dashboards to provide quick updates for busy users/managers
- ❖ Ability to integrate with phone systems and launch conference calls
- ❖ Ability to create, publish, and edit "wiki" pages for information sharing and training purposes
- ❖ Ability to do search queries to find specific information

There are numerous applications that help facilitate the three phases of a Web Based Kaizen Event. To improve the 'art of communication' and information sharing in a complex, fast-paced, multi-site office environment, we will be comparing some Web-based and Desktop sharing applications. The common Web-based and Desktop sharing applications are: Infinite Conferencing, InterCall, Basecamp, TeamLab, ProjectSpaces, WebOffice (WebEx), ClickMeeting, Adobe ConnectPro, MegaMeeting, GoTo Meeting, Huddle, etc. Many of these have monthly or user fees depending on the features required (e.g., video conferencing, document collaboration real-time, etc.). Other options to consider are the free applications of Drive.Google.com (previously known as Google Docs) and TeamLab. Both of these have similar features of the fee-based apps, however, video conferencing as well as other features are not currently supported at time of this printing.

The following Web Based Collaboration Matrix is a listing of the key features and functions of Web-based collaboration applications:

Kaizen Event	Web Based Collaboration Matrix

Characteristic	Vendor				
	TeamLab	Infinite Conferencing	ProjectSpaces	WebOffice (WebEx)	Huddle
Cost	Free	Price not listed Must call for quote	7 Membership opt-ions available	Price depends on # of users	Price not listed Must call for quote
Can you create calendars?	Yes - user can cre-ate/share calendar	No	Yes - user can cre-ate/share calendar	Yes - user can cre-ate/share calendar	Yes - user can cre-ate/share calendar
How do you manage tasks?	Create/Share to-do lists	Cannot create/ share to-do lists	Create/Share to-do lists	Create/Share to-do lists	Create/Share to-do lists
Are there reminders for tasks that have been assigned?	Yes - notifications sent via email	N/A	Yes - notifications sent via email	Yes - notifications sent via email	Yes - notifications sent via email
Can you share files with others? (MS Office?)	Yes	Yes	Yes	Yes	Yes
How does communication occur?	Open blogs and forums or IM	Private or open chat room/discussion	Onsite email	Open blogs and forums or IM	Onsite email or discussion forums
Is video conferencing available?	No	Yes- extra fee applied	No	Yes- extra fee applied	Yes
Other useful features	Time Tracker, Report Creater	Polling, Audio Conferencing	Ability to assign tasks to people	Whiteboard feature, assign tasks	Whiteboard feature, assign tasks
Can site be customize for your business?	Yes - change color scheme/layout	No	Yes - change color scheme/layout	Yes - change color scheme	Yes - custom URL, add logos
Can you make certain documents private?	Yes	Yes	Yes	Yes	Yes
Can you share your Desktop?	No	Yes	No	Yes	No
Is there a free trial?	N/A	Yes - 10 day free trial	Yes - 30 day free trial	Yes - 30 day free trial	Yes - 14 day free trial
Access to secured storage and data retrieval database system (cloud)?	Yes - allows cloud storage	Yes - allows Cloud storage	Yes - allows Cloud storage	Yes - allows Cloud storage	Yes - allows Cloud storage
Access to secured chat room environments	Yes	Yes	Site offers onsite e-mail-not chat rooms	Yes	Yes
Does the site offer collaborative file sharing in real-time?	Yes	Yes	No - cannot edit in real-time	Yes	No - cannot edit in real-time
Does the site support mobile devices?	Yes - supports Droid and iOS phones	No	No	Yes - supports Droid and iOS phones	Yes - supports Droid and iOS phones

The applications listed are constantly being updated with new features and pricing terms. Ensure the application of choice is supported by your business platform, system, or environment (i.e., Windows, Mac, Solaris, Linux, UNIX, and smart devices). Web-based collaboration applications are not inexpensive: therefore, completing a matrix ensures the most cost-effective features will be selected.

Note: Many Web-based collaboration applications will offer lower, initial prices, however, there will only be minimum feature accessibility at this lower price.

Web Based

The following techniques should be communicatee to that participants of a Web Based Kaizen Event:

❖ Participation plays an important role in a Web Based Kaizen Event. Participant or team member comments, questions, and suggestions on the technology platforms chosen are needed to make the Kaizen Event successful.

❖ Spend time exploring and navigating the Web-based collaboration application. Visit any and all Web pages that your facilitator advises and add these pages as bookmarks (Netscape) or favorites (Internet Explorer) because you may need to refresh some aspect of the application or quickly access a document that was posted/published previously.

❖ Be persistence and patience in the Web-based environment. Technical issues may arise or other questions will come up from time to time during the course of the Event. Do not wait to deal with these difficulties at the full online meeting. Send a note to the facilitator immediately upon encountering a technical issue.

❖ The Web-based environment restricts the ability to see the smile when you or someone makes a sarcastic comment or hears the anger in your voice because you are upset by someone's comments or actions. Use emoticons to help us know what you are thinking. An example of an emoticon is :-). A site that has a listing of emoticons can be found at Netiquette.

❖ When you send email, text, or place a comment on the bulletin board, remember that there is a person on the other side. It is alright to disagree with someone's ideas in this type of environment, but do it respectfully. Do not forget that a phone call may be needed. Just because it is a Web Based Kaizen Event, it does not mean that you cannot communicate via phone or face-to-face.

❖ Determine exact dates and times for the full team Web-based meetings, which may or may not include video conferencing. Keep these meetings to less than 1 hour if at all possible. Longer than that, participants will be checking their emails, texting, etc. while you "think" they are there (online).

❖ Set communication standards for acknowledging meeting times, Action Item assignments, or any other type of communications occurring between team members.

❖ Determine the type of communications (text, email, or phone) for quick-response questions. These are questions that require a Yes or No or one sentence response. When Action Items are assigned, team members may need to bounce an idea off another team member before completing the Action Item.

❖ As the facilitator, consider the following approaches when dealing with fellow team members on this type (or any type) of Kaizen Event: communicate high expectations, provide prompt feedback to team members, respect diverse talents and ways of learning, and recognize and appreciate the diversity of team members and their learning needs.

Steps and Forms

The following steps and forms should be used as a guide to customize a Web Based Kaizen Event to fit your organization's requirements. The activities and structure follow the Standard 5 Day and Rolling Kaizen Event formats with the main difference being that the full team meetings need to be conducted via a Web-based conferencing application. Also, when 1 - 2 team members are assigned a task, they most likely will be using a form of emerging technology to communicate. There are many variables to consider when using this platform, some of which are:

- ❖ Number employees that are part of the project team as well as the process area employees that require training in Lean and/or Six Sigma (which may require two levels of training)
- ❖ Number of team members that have experience with Web-based collaboration applications
- ❖ Number of Continuous Improvement Specialists, Black Belts, or Lean Senseis available for support in training and/or facilitating improvement projects through Web-based collaboration programs
- ❖ Managers or supervisors ability to lead continuous improvement projects remotely – they may be great knowing their business application platform, but lack the experience and practice with Web-based collaboration programs
- ❖ Availability of time to learn a Web-based collaboration application
- ❖ How management will stay involved in the project, given the technology being used
- ❖ Team members' availability and willingness to participate remotely
- ❖ Complexity of the project
- ❖ How to address previous negative experiences with team projects
- ❖ How to effectively manage change

Note: If this is the first Web Based Kaizen Event for an organization or department and someone within the department has experience with a Web-based conferencing application, consider having that person facilitate, or help facilitate, the Event.

Note: Google Drive can also be used as a "poor man's" version of a Web-based conferencing application.

The Web Based Kaizen Event is comprised of three phases:

Part 1. Planning Phase (spans 1 - 2 weeks)

Part 2. PDCA Implementation Phase (spans 4 - 6 weeks)

Part 3. Follow-Up Phase (spans 2 - 4 weeks)

The three phases and activities are similar to the Rolling Kaizen Event Phases and activities; however, the difference is many of the activities are streamlined into 1- hour time "buckets" and many of the activities are conducted as an online meeting via a Web-based conferencing application. Also, since there will not be as much concentrated time together as a team online, many of the activities will be assigned to team members as Action Items to be completed prior to the next full team online meeting. Therefore, team leaders must

Web Based

recommend specific training avenues and topics for the team members as determined by their need (i.e., Just-In-Time training). This can include book suggestions (hardcopy or Ebooks), YouTube videos on a certain Lean Six Sigma tool, Lean Six Sigma apps to view, etc. For example, if 1 - 2 team members are tasked with creating a value stream map, there is no reason for the entire team to be trained on that tool.

Three phases will be detailed with an expected time frame for each activity, who should be mainly responsible, and what training, if any, should be made available. This will allow you to customize the Web Based Kaizen Event to meet your specific project requirements for presentations, document sharing, brainstorming, sharing Desktops, etc. - all critical components to a successful Kaizen Event.

Part 1. Planning Phase (spans 1 - 2 weeks/1 - 2 hours meeting time or training on Web app)

This section is designed to primarily highlight how Kaizen projects have evolved to include Web-based collaboration. The focus will be reviewing the activities required in running a successful Kaizen Event online, not reviewing the micro details on "how-to" apply and use Lean methods and tools. The key actions (i.e., critical success factors) in the execution of this type of Kaizen Event are as follows:

- ❖ Assemble a strong cross-functional team with leaders, followers, agitators, and peace-makers, where members are associated with the various processes that need improvement.
- ❖ Determine project scope.
- ❖ Seek feedback on the Project/Team Charter. Gain consensus. Gain favorable project sponsorship from CEO/COO/CIO.
- ❖ Communicate with senior managers who will be directly or indirectly affected by resources that have been allocated to the Kaizen Event.
- ❖ Create a comprehensive project list of tasks and activities. Seek feedback from team members. Gain consensus. Publish tasks and Action Items.
- ❖ Create a current state and future state value stream or process map for the relevant work flows. This will include electronic and paper-based work flow. Capture how the processes are currently operating and use this as a baseline to identify problems or areas where waste can be eliminated.
- ❖ Populate value stream or process maps with process data collected at the 'gemba' (using surveys, frequency charts, one-on-one discussions, etc.).
- ❖ Select high impact, high payback 'hot spots' (i.e., areas of waste) to ensure you can visibly demonstrate the impact of using Lean methods to a wide audience and help facilitate project buy-in. Share successes and struggles within the organization.
- ❖ Ensure the IT department is part of selecting a Web-based conferencing application. Ensure team members are adequately trained in the use of the Web-based conferencing application.
- ❖ Establish meeting dates, times, Web-accessed application, user accounts (if applicable), etc.

The following is the Web Based Kaizen Event Planning Phase Checklist to help ensure all critical items are completed prior to Part 2. PDCA Implementation Phase. The Checklist is a listing of the main steps, main features for the steps, as well as the forms or worksheets suggested. This will help ensure a successful completion of this Phase. Use this as a guideline for customizing a Checklist for your Event.

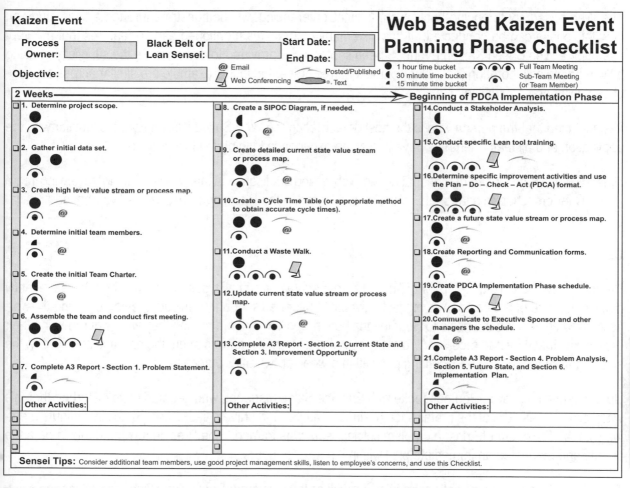

The following icons can be used to communicate the steps for the Planning Phase:

Email – represents sending attachments, links, communicating specifics, etc.

Web Conferencing– represents full team meeting using video, audio, etc.

Posted/Published – represents the document posted or published on the Cloud or elsewhere

Text– allows for quick communication, where appropriate and needed

Note: The icons for the various steps are only guidelines for this Checklist, as each team will create their own. The purpose of this for the Web Based Kaizen Event is to ensure the information collected in this Phase is made available to all team members on the appropriate technology platform. The steps are identical to the Standard 5 Day Planning Phase Checklist (page 118), however, icons were used to make this a "quick" checklist. For a detailed explanation of each of these steps, please read the particular section in the Standard 5 Day Kaizen Event section (pages 74 - 119).

Once the Planning Phase has been completed, or at least 80% completed or addressed, then it would be time to begin the PDCA Implementation or "doing" Phase.

Part 2. PDCA Implementation Phase (spans 4 - 6 weeks/weekly 1 hour meeting times)

The Web-based conferencing application, InfiniteConferencing, will demonstrate through a case study on how this phase can be conducted. It has (like many others sites mentioned earlier) features that are very useful for a Web Based Kaizen Event. Screen shots will be provided to demonstrate the simplicity of using a Web-based collaboration tool. Many of the features presented in this example are similar across all Web-based collaboration applications.

It is expected that the person who is the host or facilitating the Web Based Kaizen Event is familiar with the application and all team members have had some experience logging in at least once.

Note: Even though we are demonstrating the Web-based application in this phase, training, reviewing Team Charters, sharing charts, etc. could be completed in the Planning Phase with a Web-based application.

Case Study

Heather Eisle, the Quality Manager of Arias, Inc. (a manufacturer of all types of running shoes), was recently notified that one of the company's biggest university buyer has suddenly decided against renewing their orders. Upon delivering the news to Heather, the buyer reported that the reason they were not renewing their orders was that they had received "too many complaints" from customers about the product, specifically, the stitching from around the heel coming part within a week or two after purchase.

Upon hearing this news, Heather spoke with Eric, the Sales Manager, who seemed quite disturbed that this was occurring, as 40% of their retail shoe business was through universities. After a quick five minute meeting with the President of Arias, a problem solving team was formed. The President wanted this to be a top priority and requested an immediate plan within the next 24 hours.

To comply with everyone's hectic schedules, as well as the Customer Service and Operations Manager visiting key leather suppliers out-of-state, Heather looked into meeting with the team online, using a Web-based conferencing application. Heather was familiar with Infinite Conferencing from her previous employer.

Heather was aware of the three phases of the Kaizen Event and wanted to make sure no important part was missed. She immediately created a Team Charter detailing the overall plan for conducting a Web Based Kaizen Event and streamlined the three phases into six weeks. The Team Charter and overall plan was immediately approved by the President of Arias. Heather notified prospective team members and provided them with the Team Charter as well as how this type of Kaizen Event would occur. She collected the appropriate data and created an initial Fishbone Diagram. She proceeded to provide each team member with a link to InfiniteConferencing for them to create their accounts and go through the online tutorial (demo). Heather followed-up with a phone call within the next day to ensure everyone completed their online tutorial and was ready for their first online meeting.

Heather visited the infiniteconferencing.com site as shown below.

From the site's home page, Heather selected to **Sign Up**, an option listed at the top of the page. She followed the instructions as they appeared on her screen and created a new account. Now back at the site's home page, Heather selected to Log In, an option listed at the top of the page. After selecting to **Log In**, the following screen was shown.

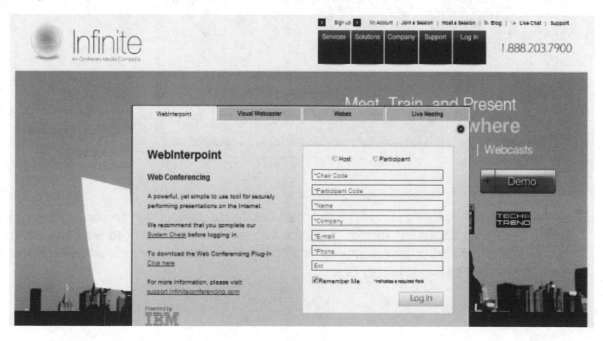

Heather selected Host on the log in screen and entered the *Chair Code* and *Participant Code* she was provided with upon creating her new account. She entered her *Name*, *Company*, *Email*, and *Phone number* and was ready to log in. After logging in, the following screen appeared.

Before beginning the first meeting Heather wanted to re-familiarize herself with the site. She checked out all the options or features she could use. Heather reviewed the options listed in the following screen appeared.

Note: Even if you have had experience with a particular Web-based collaboration application, ensure you review the current application as most likely the features and user interfaced will have changed. Always, always, always practice and become familiar with the application before training others or conducting your Web Based Kaizen Event.

After familiarizing herself with the site, Heather was now ready to start conferencing. Heather clicked on the green *Start* icon in the window to open a new conference. The following pop-up appeared on the screen.

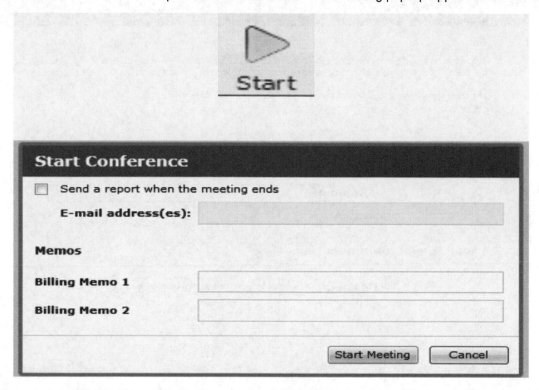

She realized this window is not to invite others to conference but simply to offer her the option of having a billing memo or a report sent to her own personal email after the end of the meeting. To do so, she would simply enter her email into the space listed and click *Start Meeting*. However, to opt out of this option, she left the spaces empty and chooses *Start Meeting*.

To invite the participants to the meeting, she clicked *Invite...* listed on the top left side of the window.

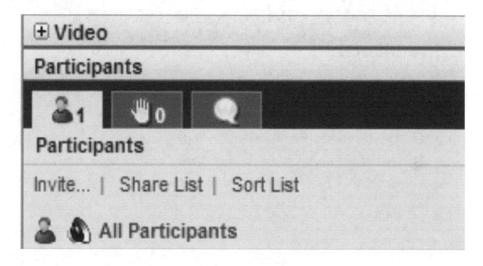

After selecting *Invite...* the following pop-up appeared on her screen.

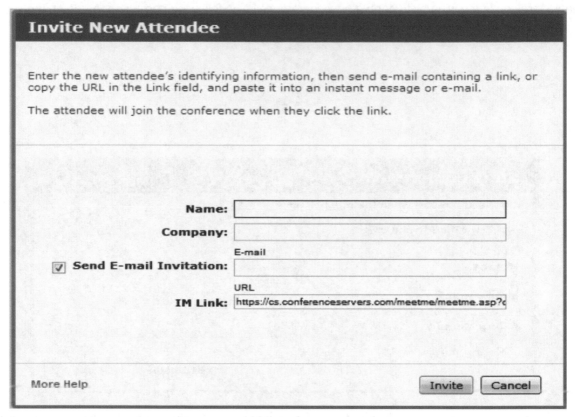

Heather entered the name and email addresses of the employees she wanted to invite into the conference. She then hit *Invite*. As people begin to check their emails and accept the invitation to the conference, their names appear in the window on the right side of the screen.

As members started joining the conference, Heather wanted to send out a message via Infinite Conferencing's chat room to introduce the purpose of the meeting and the problem the company is currently facing. Heather clicked on the last icon on the right side of the screen and chose to send the message to **All** members of the conference at the bottom of the screen.

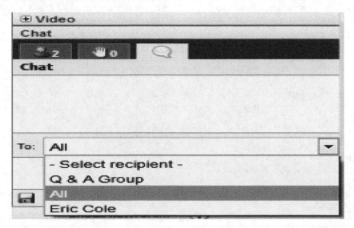

After selecting the appropriate chat options, all members of the conference can type in the text box at the bottom of the chat screen and hit **Send** to send their message to all other members.

After introducing the situation to the team Heather had assembled, the team needed to be trained in Lean to help discover the root causes of the recent problems as well as solutions to fix the problems. Heather had put one of the members of the team, Eric, in charge of Lean training. Eric attended a few Lean seminars and had put together a Lean presentation to present to the rest of the team over Infinite Conferencing. However, the presentation was saved on Heather's Desktop as she made some modifications to it. To allow Eric to present the PowerPoint presentation to the rest of the team, Heather had to first publish the PowerPoint to Infinite Conferencing. The first step to publishing a document to Infinite Conferencing is to simply select the **Publish** icon in the options bar at the top of the screen.

After selecting *Publish*, the following screen appeared.

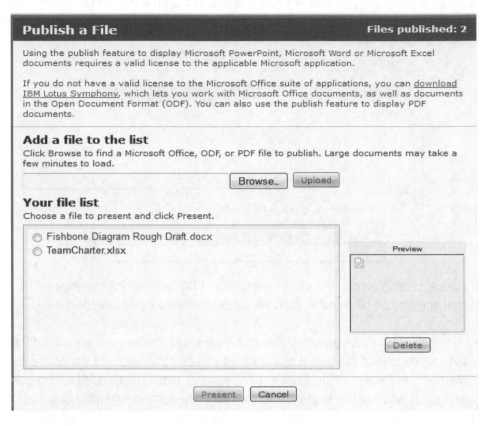

Once at this screen, simply select *Browse* to search for the document of the computer Desktop, select the file, and then *Upload*. Once the file is uploaded it will appear on the screens of the host and the other members of the conference. (An example is shown in the image below.)

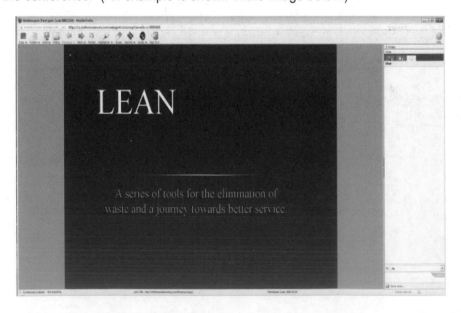

From this point, only the host can control the presentation. However, Heather wanted to transfer control of the meeting at this point over the Eric so he can present to the team the Lean presentation he put together. Heather clicked on the 'participants' icon on the right side of the screen to allow the names of other members of the meeting to appear. She clicked on the name of who in the meeting to transfer control to and scrolled down and chose **Make Presenter.** This gave another member control of the meeting and allowed him/her to access the controls of the host.

By making another member of the team a presenter, this allowed them to upload documents and files from their own Desktop to share with the group. Therefore, throughout the meeting, other members, besides the host, can easily share work they have done with the rest of the team. Once they are done sharing, they can easily restore control back to the original host.

Once the team was trained in the basic principles of Lean by Eric, Heather was ready to brainstorm and collaborate with the team on the Team Charter, Fishbone Diagram, and other data that she had available. To collaborate on a document in real-time with other members of the conference, the host must engage in a process called Application Sharing. To begin Application Sharing, the host must choose the option of **Sharing** at the top of the screen.

After selecting *Sharing* the following screen appeared.

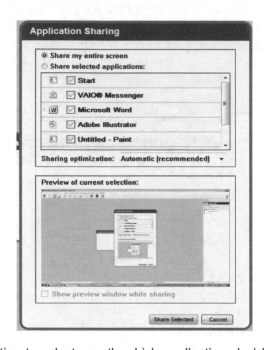

This provided the host the option to select exactly which applications he/she would like to share with the other members of the meeting. The host has the option to *Share my entire screen* or *Share selected applications*. Heather shared only the applications valuable to the team by checking them individually and clicking on *Share Selected*. At this point, each of the members can now see the available documents on their own screen and can see any changes and alterations the host might make to the documents. To allow other team members to make changes as well, and to collaborate with each other and the host in real time, the host can click on the name(s) of the member(s) he/she wants to allow to edit the documents and scroll down to click *Give Control*.

Once the host gives control to other members, each of the members can together edit and collaborate on (previously made or blank) documents, files, presentations, etc. all in real-time. To stop using this feature, the host can simply choose to **Stop Sharing** on the following screen that appears in their Infinite Conferencing window.

In order to speak to the other members of the team during the conference, Heather had to set up an audio conference. Heather clicked on the **Audio** icon at the top of the screen.

The following screen appeared.

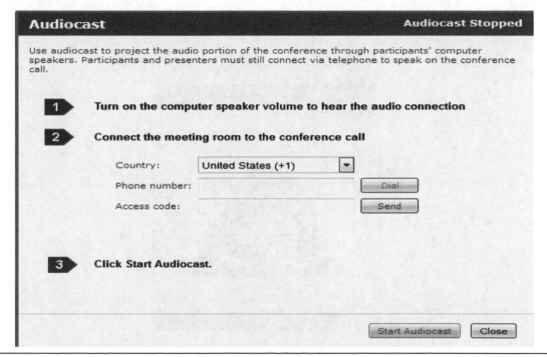

To configure the audiocast, Heather entered her phone number into the appropriate spot and clicked **Dial**. This called the phone number she entered and allowed Heather to speak into the phone and let the audio be heard through the computer's speakers. Heather then clicked **Start Audiocast**. This prompted the host to mute their computer speakers and notified the other members of the meeting that the host has now enabled audiocast. To end the audiocast, the host can simply hang up the phone line connected to the host or any of the members of the meeting can choose the option to **Stop Audio** listed at the top right side of the screen.

The host can also choose to configure a video conference in which the members of the conference can view the host. The host clicks on the option **+Video** at the top right side of the screen. The host can then click **Start Video** and a live video feed should be streamed through their Webcam for the other members to see.

Kaizen Demystified

Note: Only the host can make a video available for others to view. Similarly, only the host can set up an audiocast, and be the only one heard. However, the host can make someone else the presenter during a meeting giving them the control to do so as well.

During one of the meetings, Heather shared charts with the team. While collaborating on documents, the host and the members also have the following options to highlight or edit a certain piece of information.

Anyone can use the Pointer or Highlighter to draw attention to a certain spot. They can also use the Eraser to get rid of unnecessary information. These are just a couple of the added extra tools to facilitate collaboration.

Another important feature is that at any time during a conference the host of the meeting can send a document privately to any member(s) of the meeting by clicking on their name on the left side of the screen, and scrolling down to select the option to **Send File**. From there they can fill out the following box and hit **Send File**.

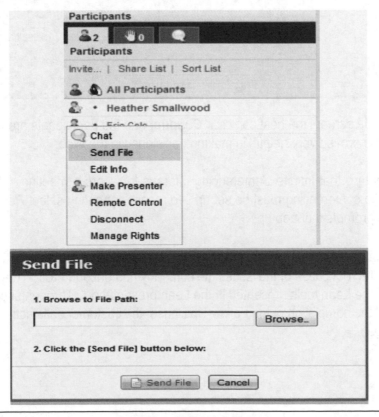

Throughout the meetings, Heather continually asked questions to gain a consensus on some of the action items being discussed. Through Infinite Conferencing, the host of the meeting can poll the members of the meeting to get their feedback and opinion on certain questions or concerns. To do so, the host must choose the Polling icon at the top of the screen and fill out the window shown below.

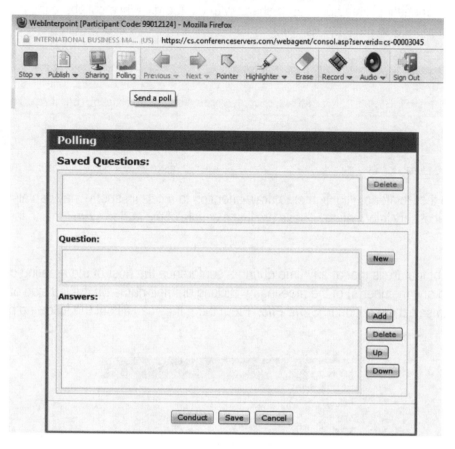

After filling out the above screen, the host can click **Conduct** and the participants are notified and asked to submit an answer. This proved very helpful in making decisions via the Web.

One last important feature that Infinite Conferencing offers is to record a meeting. However, to record a meeting, audio or video conferencing must be set up. To record a meeting select **Record** at the top of the screen and follow the prompts that pop up.

The PDCA Implementation Phase meetings were done through Infinite Conferencing, the Lean team Heather put together found the root cause of the issues the company had encountered. They moved forward and implemented some of the Lean tools presented in the Lean presentation. Through successful implementation of these tools and the completion of the Follow-Up Phase, the customer satisfaction ratings rose to their normal levels once again.

The following Web Based Kaizen Event PDCA (Implementation) Phase Checklist to help ensure all critical items are completed prior to Part 3. Follow-Up Phase. Consider each activity listed as value-added or non value-added to the team's objectives. Also, be flexible to the regularly scheduled meeting times, in that, more or less time may need to be scheduled. This will help ensure a successful completion of this Phase. Use this as a guideline for customizing a Checklist for your Event.

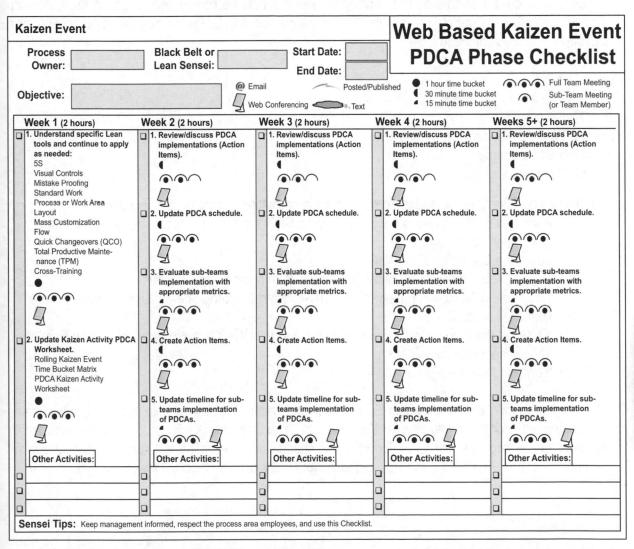

The Web Based Kaizen Event PDCA Phase Checklist has proven helpful for Kaizen teams in making the process changes in this phase. Consider each activity listed as value-added or non value-added to the team's objectives. Also, be flexible to accept and use any other activities that the team members might have experienced that may also provide value to the team's objective.

Once the PDCA Implementation Phase has been completed, or at least 80% completed or addressed, then it would be time to begin Follow-Up Phase.

Part 3. Follow-Up Phase (spans 2 - 4 weeks/15 minutes meeting time)

Use the following as a guide during the Follow-Up Phase:

1. Gain an understanding of the main tools that can be used in this Phase. This following list of tools can be used as a quick-reminder as to the array of tools that may be considered for use in the Follow-Up Phase (typically the Control Phase of the Six Sigma methodology). Please see the Tools section for a description for each of these tools.

Control Phase
Statistical Process Control (SPC)
Visual Management
Standard Work for Leaders
Performance Management
Layered Process Audits (LPA)

2. Establish a concise time line and ensure the following activities are completed as needed.
    (1) Appropriate type of charts (i.e., Run, Pareto, SPC, etc.) used to monitor process changes.
    (2) Completed all PDCAs.
    (3) Lean Representative assigned.
    (4) Continued feedback about process changes from primary stakeholders.
    (5) Updated the A3 Report (or similar report) and shared appropriately within the organization.
    (6) Gemba practiced.
    (7) Kaizened the Web Based Kaizen Event process with the Kaizen Event Participation Evaluation and subsequent analysis.
    (8) Rewarded and recognized the team.

3. Use the following Web Based Kaizen Event Follow-Up Phase Checklist to help ensure all critical items are completed prior to starting another Kaizen Event. The Checklist is a listing of the main steps, main features for the steps, as well as the forms or worksheets suggested. This will help ensure a successful completion of this Phase. Use this as a guideline for customizing a Checklist for your Event.

Kaizen Event

Web Based Kaizen Event Follow-Up Phase Checklist

Process Owner: _____

Black Belt or Lean Sensei: _____

Start Date: _____
End Date: _____

Objective: _____

@ Email
Web Conferencing
Posted/Published
Text

● 1 hour time bucket
▮ 30 minute time bucket
▲ 15 minute time bucket

Full Team Meeting
Sub-Team Meeting (or Team Member)

Week 1 (30 minutes)	Week 2 (30 minutes)	Week 3 (30 minutes)	Week 4 (30 minutes)
☐ **1. Continue communications.** Consider the following charts: Pareto Chart Paynter Chart Pie Chart Scatter (Concentration) Plots Radar Chart Run Chart Histogram Statistical Process Ctrl. Charts	☐ **3. Provide support after the PDCA Phase.** Lean Representative	☐ **5. Establish avenue for primary stakeholders to provide feedback.** Kaizen Suggestion Box Emails Walk and talk Google Drive	☐ **7. Apply Kaizen to the Kaizen.** Kaizen Event Participation Evaluation form
☐ **2. Discuss outstanding issues.**	☐ **4. Create and distribute the Event Dashboards.** Weekly Kaizen Dashboard Monthly Kaizen Dashboard Maintained by process owner	☐ **6. Work with management to practice Gemba.** Observe the process Informally ask questions Show concern Arrive with a purpose Comment on visuals Notify the area Include different mgmt levels Build upon each Gemba Thank employees for their efforts	☐ **8. Reward and recognize the team.** Verbal recognition Gift cards Lunches, dinners, etc. Recognition letters, awards, etc. Corporate gifts Time off Green fees

Other Activities:

Sensei Tips: Ensure all PDCAs are completed, share results throughout the organization, and reward and recognize team members and any other employees that contributed.

The Web Based Kaizen Event Follow-Up Phase Checklist has proven helpful for Kaizen teams in sustaining the gains made in the PDCA Implementation Phase. Consider each activity listed as value-added or non value-added to the team's objectives. Also, be flexible to accept and use any other activities that the team members might have experienced that may also provide value to the team's objective.

Once the Follow-Up Phase has been completed, or at least 80% completed or addressed, then it would be time to begin another Kaizen Event!

The activities comprised of the Web Based Kaizen Event are identical to the Standard 5 Day Kaizen Event and Rolling Kaizen Event. Keep in mind that the overall objective for the Web Based Kaizen Event is to allocate the meetings, process changes, and training over a period of 3 months using emerging technology due to team members' availability and location.

Case Study

The following case study demonstrates many of the tools explained in this section as well as some of the "people-side" issues that are encountered by the facilitator, team leader, process owner, or team member. As with any improvement project, you too would select only the appropriate activities (i.e., tools, worksheets, forms, etc.) to meet your specific Kaizen Event requirements for planning, implementing, and reporting.

Stephanie works for a successful niche $30 million dollar company called "Call Response Solutions, Incorporated." CRS's head office is based in Atlanta, Georgia (U.S.) and provides outsourced customer service (call center) solutions to firms across the east coast of the United States. CRS has three additional offices (call centers) in key global regions of Europe, Asia, and South America primarily to ensure that CRS maintains a 24-hour call-center response service to those clients that require a 24/7 service.

Stephanie reports to the Chief Financial Officer (CFO). Stephanie is one of several key employees that directly work for the CFO and her role is to maintain 'real-time' visibility of CRS's profit and loss position as well as other key financial metrics.

For a successful multi-million dollar company with an "off-the-shelf" financial management system, CRS still struggles to produce accurate, on-time financial reports that display the salient financial metrics required by the CFO for compliance and reporting purposes. The financial management system (FMS) has a number of standard reports that lack the detail needed by CRS, and now with the FMS over 7 years old, is several versions behind the latest update.

As a result, over the years, the Finance department has progressively developed financial reporting sheets (spreadsheets) that sit 'outside' the FMS. These Excel spreadsheets are commonly referred to as 'work-around' tools that nearly every company develops over the course of time. There always seems to be a lag between what a Customer Relationship Management (CRM) system, for FMS in this case provides, and what is currently needed to ensure the timely information is provided to make business decisions.

In CRS's situation, the Finance department has progressively developed a comprehensive suite of Excel-based financial reporting spreadsheets that are distributed to the field offices at the end of the month. These spreadsheets are required back by the 2nd working day of the next month. The Excel spreadsheets are consolidated and analyzed in Excel, before they are finally (re)keyed into the FMS and presented to the CFO and other senior executives via the standard 'high-level' financial reporting tools in the FMS.

Some of the key issues encountered by Stephanie and her team during the End of Month /Start of Month data consolidation and reporting phase include:

- ❖ Unanticipated workload spikes due to poor management of the reporting process
- ❖ Inefficiencies in having a spreadsheet that exists in multiple locations at same time
- ❖ Incomplete, inaccurate data, requiring double/triple handling and re-entry
- ❖ Late submissions by the field offices
- ❖ Poor version control (i.e., confusion as to if the Finance department has the "latest copy")
- ❖ Lack of edit restrictions, resulting in spreadsheets that are (re)formatted incorrectly

- Multiple users trying to access a single spreadsheet, with changes failing to "save"
- Lack of centralized control
- Use of office email system to transfer/receive spreadsheets, causing lost emails
- Users unable to open/read spreadsheets due to incorrect file security settings
- Different time zones make discussion groups and information sharing difficult
- Office staff becoming "document masters" instead of process managers

CRS's Part 1. Planning Phase

Stephanie was aware that the Web was increasingly being used to centralize data management processes and that an array of web sites had emerged to enable disparate users to share, collaborate, and control information in a secure environment. After reviewing a number of web sites, Stephanie decided to use the Google Drive application. Google Drive is a free service offered by Google that allows you to store and share files online. It is used as a collaboration tool to create and edit files and documents with others, all online, and all stored in one central location. This would enable her and the team to create a secure centralized 'work space' to manage the monthly financial reporting process. She discussed this with the IT department and they approved the use of the Google Drive application.

Stephanie wanted to ensure this first "virtual" or Web Based Kaizen Event was successful and she knew that all projects needed to be grounded in measurements. The following were the key metrics:

- 'On-time' submission from all field offices of all financial reports (monthly): 72.4%
- Data integrity (correct data) from field offices: 54.2%
- 'On-time' completion of financial month-end reporting obligations: 83.3%

Stephanie understood the basics of Lean and Six Sigma and realized that "standardizing" the reporting process would reduce the errors (data integrity) and "standardizing" the workflow will improve the 'On-time' submission and 'On-time' completion metrics for the financial reporting.

Stephanie first downloaded the free software, Google Drive to her computer. Once the software was installed, the following screen appeared.

Note: Screen shots and steps may be different depending on the version of Google Drive.

To actually begin using the tools provided by Google Drive, Stephanie had to sign in using an already existing Gmail account (at URL: drive.google.com).

Note: To login to Google Drive, use the same email address and password needed to login to your Gmail account. If you do not have a Gmail account, you cannot use Google Drive until one is created. To create a Gmail account, go to gmail.com and follow the instructions to sign up. Because Google Drive is linked to your Gmail account, you can also access Google Drive by simply logging into your Gmail account, without ever visiting drive.google.com. To do so, go to Gmail.com, Login using your account information, and at the top left corner of the browser there will be a bar listing a series of pages all linked in to your Gmail account (e.g., Google Play, YouTube, Google Images, etc.). This is where you will see the option to go to "Drive."

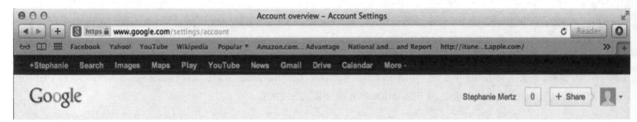

Once you click on Drive you will be taken into Google Drive and you will be ready to use your account.

Now logged in to Google Drive, Stephanie wanted to become more familiar with the Web-based system. The following is the initial screen shot after logging in to Google Drive.

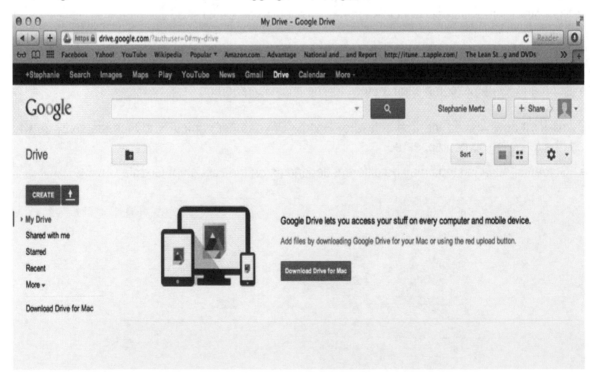

Stephanie formed a team comprised of all the field office managers and this was to be their first use of emerging technology platform for an improvement project. Stephanie initially decided to start small with a goal of improving the End of Month P&L process. She wanted everyone to get familiar with this type of improvement event and everyone having a positive experience. She carefully drafted a communication bulletin, which equated to a modified Team Charter, to all field offices stating the need for improving the End of Month P&L process. She also created a first pass Cause and Effect (or Fishbone) Diagram. She wanted the team members to access these documents, comment on them, and provide feedback within Google Drive. Once they became familiar with Google Drive in this Planning Phase, then the PDCA Implementation Phase or process changes would be easier. Even though Stephanie had known what improvement she required, she also knew how important it was to engage the users or those working the process in any changes. Even though this process of creating this team would take a bit longer, Stephanie believed the long term value of getting input and feedback for any changes would benefit not only this project, but subsequent ones.

In addition to uploading, editing, and collaborating on a pre-existing file, Google Drive also gives their users the option to create a new file directly from the Google Drive home page. Once logged in, you could click Create on the left hand side of the page, and choose between creating any of the following: Document, Presentation, Spreadsheet, Form, or Drawing. These are very similar to the actions one could perform using Microsoft Word, PowerPoint, Excel, etc. The image below shows how to create a new file, a Fishbone Diagram, and share accordingly.

Stephanie decided to utilize this "Create" feature to, together with her team, make and collaborate on a Fishbone Diagram to further visualize some of the issues affecting their End of Month /Start of Month data consolidation and reporting phase.

To do so, as shown above, Stephanie went into her Google Drive account and after clicking **Create** and bringing up the options list, she clicked **Drawing**.

Stephanie was shown the following blank drawing document in Google Drive.

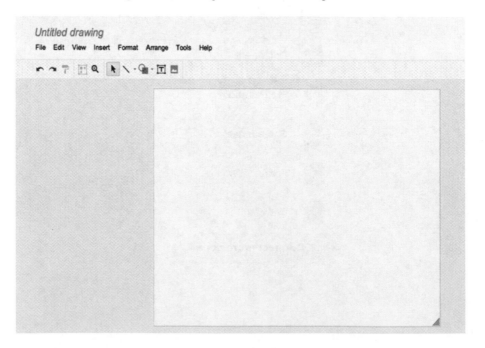

The first thing Stephanie did was retitle the Untitled Document. To do so she simply clicked on the current title, "Untitled Drawing" in the top right corner and was presented with the screen below in which she entered and saved a new title for the document.

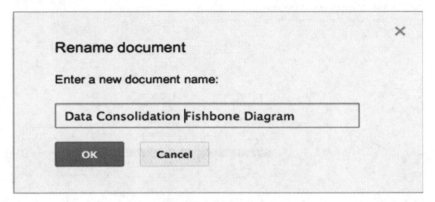

Stephanie used the tools offered in the tool bar underneath the document title, specifically the Insert option.

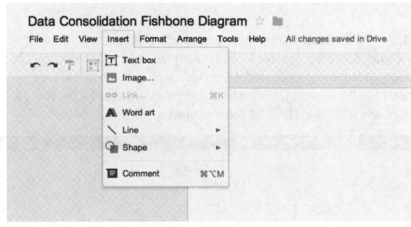

Using these tools, Stephanie created the basic outline of a Fishbone Diagram.

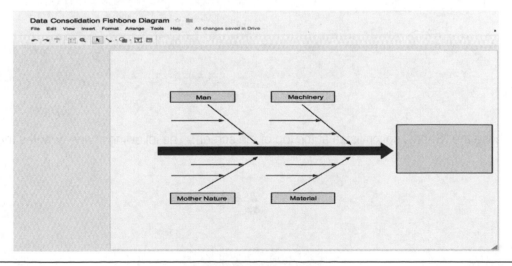

The work Stephanie does on any document is automatically saved in here Drive. After creating an initial Fishbone she saved the file.

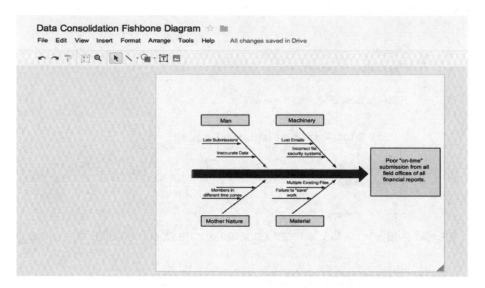

After Stephanie had created the basic Fishbone Diagram and a modified Team Charter, she needed to share the files with fellow employees/team members. To share a file in Google Drive, Stephanie returned to the home page of her Google Drive account. Under the "My Drive" section of the page, all of the documents created and/or uploaded to her Google Drive account are listed. To share a file with others, Stephanie first selected the document she wished to share as shown below.

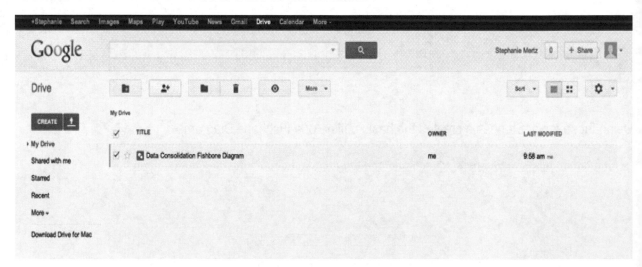

Next, she chose the "Share" option listed at the top of the screen. The following image denotes the "Share" icon.

After selecting the "share" option, the following screen appeared.

Using this prompt, Stephanie added the email addresses of each of her fellow employees with whom she wished she share this document, as a list, under the heading "Add people:." Once email addresses are added, the option to "Add a message" is offered as well. The following image shows an example of the screen you should see after adding all the necessary information to share a document.

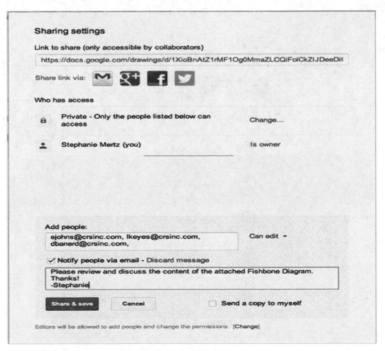

Once this information is added, simply select "***Share & save***" and the file, along with the optional message, will be sent through email to the people listed. By sharing this document, Stephanie gave each team member full access to the documents allowing multiple people, including Stephanie, to access the document at the same time and engage in real-time collaboration. Everyone Stephanie granted access to can pull up the document at any time and all begin editing/adding to the document - with each change made appearing on everyone's screens in real-time. She sent an email to the team requesting their input within the next business day on this Fishbone Diagram. It would be unlikely that two people would be working on the Fishbone at the same time; however, Google Drive was set up for those situations. If multiple people work on the document simultaneously, the changes made by each person will appear on the other's screen as they are making them. For the Team Charter, she requested any recommendations be sent via email or text message and then those would be posted and discussed to ensure alignment going forward.

All team members responded as requested on their first assigned Action Item on providing input to the Fishbone Diagram. Stephanie sent a message to all team members thanking them for such a quick response. (For this case, there were numerous other documents shared during the Planning Phase to ensure alignment and consensus before the next phase began.)

Note: Only a subset of the tools and worksheets are being presented in this part of the Kaizen Event case study. The purpose is to demonstrate the practicality of using this emerging technology to improve communications in an improvement project.

CRS's Part 2. PDCA Implementation Phase

After the team reached agreement on the new process, Stephanie created a folder by clicking ***Create*** and scrolling down to ***Folder***.

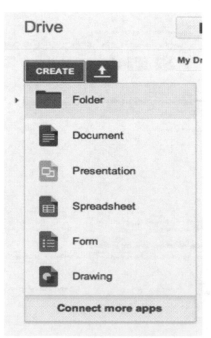

Stephanie was then able to create a "title" and click **Create**.

Stephanie had a P&L spreadsheet (that was already in use with all field offices) as shown below.

		Insert months of data for current year				4		
PROFIT AND LOSS - HISTORICAL & PROJECTION								
Call Response Solutions - Europe	Jan	Feb	Mar	Apr	**Current Full Year Estimate**			
TOTAL SALES in your Region	624,865	559,914	621,042		$7,601,721			
Sales Growth		-10%	11%					
COST OF GOODS SOLD								
Call Centre Wages and Salaries	20,000	20,000	20,000		$240,000			
Call Centre oncosts	4,000	4,000	4,000		$48,000			
Call (Phone) Costs	4,500	5,700	4,230		$62,340			
Subcontractor(s) Costs	12,000	11,000	12,300		$134,400			
Other Direct Costs	6,561	3,456	5,123		$69,129			
TOTAL COGS	47,061	44,156	45,653		553,869			
GROSS TRADING PROFIT	677,804	515,758	575,389		$7,047,852			
EXPENSES								
Depreciation	10,890	10,040	12,000		$139,092			
Rent	2,456	2,456	2,456		$29,472			
Management Wages and Salaries	14,564	14,564	14,564		$174,768			
Management oncosts	3,641	3,641	3,641		$43,692			
Advertising & Marketing Expenses	2,378	2,20	3,400		$43,401			
Other Operating Expenses	7,108	6,298	8,391		$90,588			
TOTAL OPERATION EXPENSES	41,037	39,199	44,452		$521,013			
EBIT (Earnings Before Interest & Tax)	536,767	476,559	530,937		$6,526,839			
Other Income	1,200	1,428	1,428		$16,668			
Other Expenses								
Interest Paid	800	721	720		$8,913			
Other Expenses	670	950	753		$11,487			
Total Other Expenses	1,470	1,671	1,173		$20,400			
TOTAL NET PROFIT	536,497	476,316	531,192		$6,523,107			
Net Profit Growth		-11%	12%					

Europe / Asia-Pacific / South America / Consolidated

This Excel spreadsheet required the field offices to select the correct tab (at the bottom of the spreadsheet). In this example, the Europe call center tab is displayed. In the past, the financial controller in the Europe office would normally receive the spreadsheet via email, and then fill in all the orange fields (shown as dark grey), and resubmit the Excel spreadsheet back to Stephanie's team via email.

Web Based

Stephanie had the P&L spreadsheet that she wanted to upload into Google Drive; Stephanie clicked the *Upload* button as shown below. After selecting the upload button, Stephanie followed the screen prompts starting the upload process.

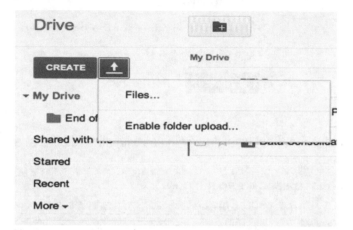

Stephanie selected the option "*Files...*" and was able to upload a document from her desktop. After doing so, Google Drive would then indicate when the upload was complete.

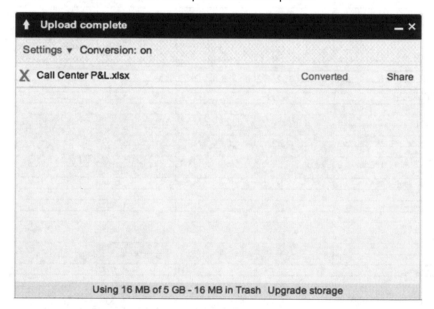

Back at the main menu, the P&L spreadsheet was now loaded into Stephanie's "My Drive" work area as shown below.

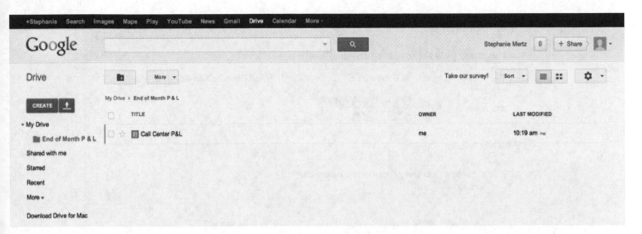

Stephanie now needed to share the P&L spreadsheet, and ensure that it was visible to the appropriate field offices (i.e., team members). By clicking the Share button, and following the prompts, Stephanie was able to share the P&L with all team members (who already had their Gmail accounts and could access Google Drive).

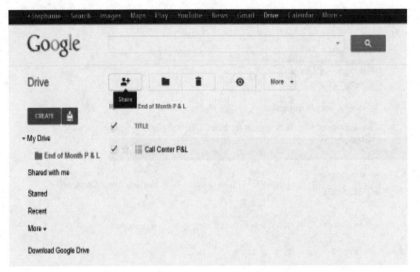

Stephanie was able to add individual users as shown below.

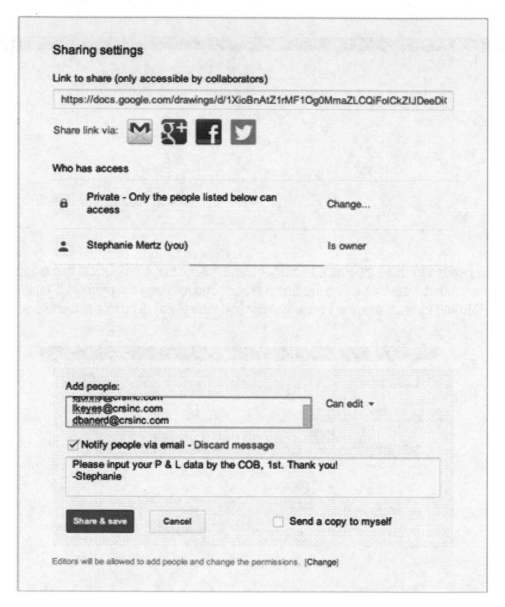

Kaizen Demystified

Every month, the new standard stated that the P&L spreadsheet would be loaded and visible to authorized users 1 week before End of Month. The P&L spreadsheet (in Google Drive) could now be accessed from anywhere around the world, by anyone who was authorized by Stephanie to view the P&L spreadsheet (and had an internet connection). On the 1st work day of the new month, field office staff (from Finance) would log into Google Drive and go to the "My Drive" area and bring up the Monthly P&L spreadsheet. The following screen shot shows Europe completing their P&L spreadsheet portion on Google Drive.

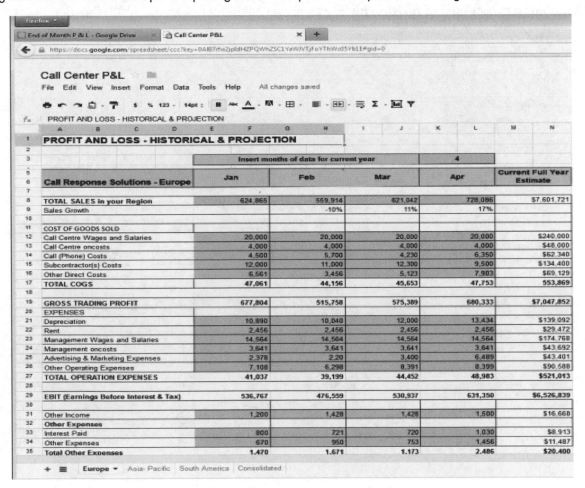

PROFIT AND LOSS - HISTORICAL & PROJECTION

Call Response Solutions - Europe	Jan	Feb	Mar	Apr	Current Full Year Estimate
TOTAL SALES in your Region	624,865	559,914	621,042	728,086	$7,601,721
Sales Growth		-10%	11%	17%	
COST OF GOODS SOLD					
Call Centre Wages and Salaries	20,000	20,000	20,000	20,000	$240,000
Call Centre oncosts	4,000	4,000	4,000	4,000	$48,000
Call (Phone) Costs	4,500	5,700	4,230	6,350	$62,340
Subcontractor(s) Costs	12,000	11,000	12,300	9,500	$134,400
Other Direct Costs	6,561	3,456	5,123	7,903	$69,129
TOTAL COGS	47,061	44,156	45,653	47,753	553,869
GROSS TRADING PROFIT	677,804	515,758	575,389	680,333	$7,047,852
EXPENSES					
Depreciation	10,890	10,040	12,000	13,434	$139,092
Rent	2,456	2,456	2,456	2,456	$29,472
Management Wages and Salaries	14,564	14,564	14,564	14,564	$174,768
Management oncosts	3,641	3,641	3,641	3,641	$43,692
Advertising & Marketing Expenses	2,378	2.20	3,400	6,489	$43,401
Other Operating Expenses	7,108	6,298	8,391	8,399	$90,588
TOTAL OPERATION EXPENSES	41,037	39,199	44,452	48,983	$521,013
EBIT (Earnings Before Interest & Tax)	536,767	476,559	530,937	631,350	$6,526,839
Other Income	1,200	1,428	1,428	1,500	$16,668
Other Expenses					
Interest Paid	800	721	720	1,030	$8,913
Other Expenses	670	950	753	1,456	$11,487
Total Other Expenses	1,470	1,671	1,173	2,486	$20,400

Europe ▼   Asia-Pacific   South America   Consolidated

After entering in the appropriate P&L information, Google Drive automatically saves the new work and all that has been edited. After adding the information, a message will appear at the top of the screen letting the user know that all changes have been saved and that the user can now close out of the window.

To see a specific list of who made what changes to the document and when, Stephanie can click on the specific file and bring up the page. From there, Stephanie can go to *File* in the top right corner of the screen, and scroll down to click on *See revision history* as shown below (or use shortcut "Alt+Ctrl+G").

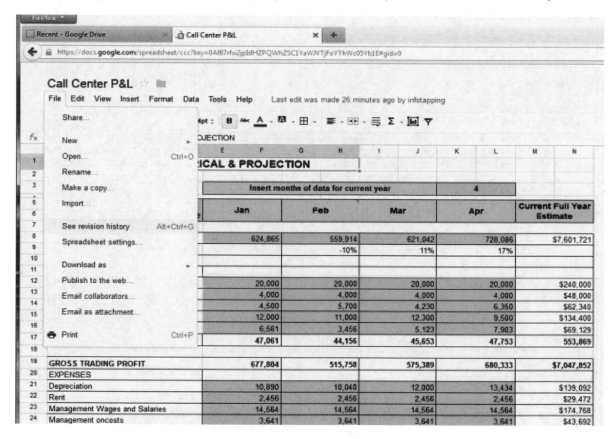

After selecting "See revision history" a window will pop up in the left side of the screen showing a complete list of all changes made to the document, who the changes were made by, and the option to change back by selecting "Restore this Revision." You can click on any of the changes listed that were previously made, and see the changes on the document itself. Refer to the image below.

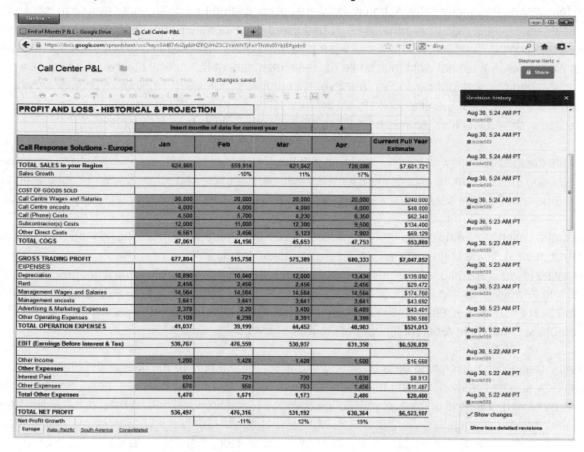

By the 2nd work day of the month, all field offices had completed the P&L spreadsheet and had saved their changes to the centralized Google Drive application.

The Planning Phase had went well for Stephanie. However, during the first part of the PDCA Implementation Phase, only one in five of the Action Items were completed on time. This meant, since everyone had at least one Action Item, four of the five team members did not complete their assignment and there was no communication indicating that there were any problems. At the next Web Conferencing meeting, Stephanie asked for reasons why many of the Action Items were not completed (not calling out any one person). The responses were, "I just didn't have the time" "I had some questions that I needed answered and did not know who to contact." and a few others that were similar in nature. Stephanie thought the responses (excuses) were lame, but did not want to alienate the team members at this critical stage. She also knew that this was the beginning of forthcoming Kaizen Events to further streamline their global customer service response levels. Therefore, Stephanie had to set the foundation for getting the team members more engaged and excited in the project (excited was probably a wishful dream at this time for Stephanie).

Stephanie decided to work with each of the team members' managers to determine what, if any, incentives could be done to ensure more engagement for team members, for now and future Kaizen Events. After two days or emails and phone calls, there were two areas that each of the various regions would address:

1. Communication to all employees that the percent of bonus for participation will include the words "active participation in daily assignments as well as Kaizen Event teams."
2. Overtime issued (or comp time) for those members of Kaizen Event teams that must get their work done and had to work late while contributing to the Kaizen Event team activities or any Action Items assigned. Team Leaders of all Kaizen Teams will follow-up with a report on team member participation was well as a log of the Action Item report at the end of the Kaizen Event.

Stephanie thought that this could be a bit strong and allocated the first 10 minutes at the next meeting to discuss how she had worked with the managers to assist this team and future type teams. She began the meeting by saying, "I wish to thank everyone for being logged in on time and getting most of the Action Items completed before this meeting. As the person who reports directly to the CFO, we wanted to make sure your participation on teams is a positive and rewarding experience; therefore, we wanted to ensure compensation for those that needed to work extra during the Kaizen Event time. Also, we reignited the bonus program to ensure those that do participate on these type teams are rewarded. By doing this, we believe the organization will reap the benefits of the improvement efforts due to your extra effort during this time? Does anyone have any questions?"

Juan, the field office manager from Mexico City, asked, "I am not sure being part of this team has any benefits for me as the manager. I cannot take the time off that I currently have on the books."

Stephanie responded, "Juan, I understand as a manager it is more difficult to give yourself time-off. We make these changes to ensure all employees, especially those that work for you, to contribute more to team activities. We will ensure at the next Kaizen Event we will include one or two of your employees."

Juan concluded, "That makes sense and I am sure they will appreciate it."

No one had any other questions or statements.

Henceforth, each of the managers completed all Action Items on time, realizing they will be initiating teams of their own as well as participating on other events, and wanted to lead by example.

CRS's Part 3. Follow-Up Phase

CRS's first Web Based Kaizen Event had successfully increased the productivity level of Stephanie's department. The CFO was impressed how Stephanie had used this type of event to streamline what clearly was an inefficient and time consuming Month-End business process. Some of the key benefits for Stephanie's department were:

❖ Reduced workload for Stephanie's team (no need to email, follow-up, correct errors, etc.)
❖ Single centralized copy of P&L spreadsheet eliminated version control issues
❖ Eliminated need to collaborate with attachments
❖ Eliminated active spreadsheets at multiple locations
❖ Updates/amendments controlled by users
❖ No more lost/late emails or spreadsheets
❖ Ability for Stephanie's team to log into Google Drive and quickly assess job status
❖ No need to consolidate multiple spreadsheets/work books
❖ Eliminated need for email system to send/receive spreadsheets
❖ Eliminated double/triple-handling
❖ Ability for users to access a single spreadsheet from anywhere, anytime
❖ Real-time collaboration (edit files and see changes as they are typed)
❖ Ease of transfer (move files between Desktop environment and Google Drive)

The following are the measurements before and after this Web Based Kaizen Event.

Pre-Web Based Kaizen Event Metrics

❖ 'On-time' submission from all field offices of all financial reports (monthly): 72.4%
❖ Data integrity (correct data) from field offices: 54.2%
❖ 'On-time' completion of financial month-end reporting obligations: 83.3%

Post-Web Based Kaizen Event Metrics

❖ 'On-time' submission from all field offices of all financial reports (monthly): 84.7%
❖ Data integrity (correct data) from field offices: 76.2%
❖ 'On-time' completion of financial month-end reporting obligations: 99.7%

As the months passed, Stephanie and the team progressively moved more documents, spreadsheets, and other files onto the secure confidential Google Drive platform to improve efficiencies and streamline work flows.

Note: Google Drive may not support the importing of macros from a MS Excel spreadsheet. You should carefully test any spreadsheet to ensure it functions correctly within Google Drive (or any other collaborative application).

The following is a summary of the Lean, Six Sigma, and Leadership tools used in this case study:

Issue or Improvement Opportunity in Case Study	*Lean, Six Sigma or Leadership Tool Used*
Multiple spreadsheets with similar data	Standard Work (pgs. 236-243)
Incomplete or wrong data entered	Standard Work (pgs. 236-243)
Late submissions of reports	Visual Control (pgs. 236-243)
Version control problems	Standard Work (pgs. 236-243)
Errors to reporting format for spreadsheet	Visual Control (pgs. 236-243)
Lack of participation, not engaged/ Not completing Action Items	Performance Management and Goal Setting, Reward and Recognition (pg. 244)

This case study demonstrated the power of standardizing work documents via a Document Management System (or some other emerging technology document control app). Creating a "standard" document with specific fields for specific individuals can improve work flow, reduce the likelihood of errors, and maintain file and version control. But with any technology improvement, ensure the employees are recognized and their input solicited, much like how Stephanie conducted herself in her first Kaizen Event. Many times the issue will not be the technology (or Lean Sigma tool) being implemented or used, it will be dealing with those "softer" or "people" issues.

Sensei Tips

Note: Many of the following Sensei Tips can be used or applied in the other Kaizen Events, where and when appropriate.

❖ Try to meet physically at least once if at all possible. This may help smooth over rough areas that the team may encounter down the road. It is good as the leader to get to know all team members personally as well as professionally.

❖ Adhere to structure and ensure everyone agrees to it. Many times a virtual team member may need to "feel" included for a variety of reasons. They may have physically been part of a on-site Kaizen team, but received little recognition or their ideas were not heard. It is easier to "sit on the sideline" on a virtual team if a stringent structure of communications and reporting is not established in the Planning Phase.

❖ Be specific to task assignments and continually follow-up and coach. Even though everyone has agreed to the goals and objectives (via the Team Charter), it is difficult at times to see the link between the smaller improvements or PDCAs that are needed to meet the deliverables. The team leader must be the cheer leader for the team at times. Once the shared vision is apparent and everyone has bought-in, then the team members will "make-things-happen."

❖ Gain consensus on the type and frequency of communications. This is especially important for virtual or Web Based teams. Create a matrix and type of communication each team member prefers, as well as rules (i.e., standards) for responding to other team members' requests. Work with the team early on and establish a standard communications platform.

❖ Build team unity through communications. This can be done with regular short, 2-3 minute updates provided via Web Conferencing or a recorded a message for everyone to view. Keep the virtual team momentum going by providing regular updates.

❖ Create a "thread" for discussing team issues. Team members may be working on their Action Items at different times of the day or night, which is one of the beauties of virtual teams. Keep avenues of communication open for team members to post ideas, thoughts, issues, when and where they occur.

❖ Provide links on how the project will be tracked. This allows team members to view progress to date as well as serve as friendly competition to complete Action Items. The team leader should reward and recognize those team members that excel. This can be monitored by creating a the virtual team project dashboard.

❖ Work to establish a pull system for Action Items. Create links or provide information to team members to assist them to find solutions. At times, for the full team meetings, it may be good to let an experienced team member run the meeting.

❖ Respect and encourage team members at all times. Whether face-to-face in a conference room, or through some emerging technology platform, team members will "sense" if their work and effort are being respected and used. Emerging technology platforms, and how the particular communication occurs, can be impersonal. Take the time and ensure all team members are appreciated in their team duties.

Web Based

❖ Record the meetings to have available if someone cannot attend. A team member should communicate to the team leader, process owner, or facilitator if they cannot be present for the virtual meeting. There should be agreement if the team member cannot attend (baring any family emergency type reason).

❖ Communicate verbally as much as possible. Continue to solicit input from all remote locations throughout the meeting. This helps keep everyone engaged.

❖ Create activities that all team members can work together on during the meeting. Do not make the meeting having everyone "watch" and listen to a presentation. If that is needed, then record it and present a link to all team members to view it by a certain date. Engage employees by editing or viewing a shared document, brainstorm virtually in chat or on a whiteboard, or suggest an idea and take real-time polls. These activities help team members feel engaged and enhance their ability to feel in control.

❖ Consider and address team members' needs, whether in person or working from a virtual environment.

Kaizen Demystified

Today's Kaizen Event

You have identified your project as a Today's Event Event from the How to Select Your Kaizen Event Type (pages 59 -70)
Overview

Note: It is suggested that the Standard 5 Day Kaizen Event section be read first to fully understand the basic structure and activities required that comprise all types of Kaizen Events (to some degree). The Today's Kaizen Event is quite versatile in how it can be used. This section will only *reference* the activities that are unique to this Kaizen Event type.

Today's Kaizen Events are used by teams to find and implement solutions to a known problem or continuous improvement initiative within a short time period (less than four weeks). Team members meet for a one day (or less) planning session with key stakeholders during the Planning Phase to build consensus on exactly what needs to be done. These types of events are used by management when the root cause of a problem is known and/or the continuous improvement project has been clearly defined.

The following is the Today's Kaizen Event Quick Determination Checklist to ensure this is the type of Kaizen Event required given your specific situation. Ensure the majority of Characteristics are checked as Yes or Likely in the Your Situation column.

Today's Kaizen Event Quick Determination Checklist					
Characteristic	**YES or LIKELY**	**Your Situation**	**Characteristic**	**YES or LIKELY**	**Your Situation**
Large Scope (crosses departments)			Management Involvement	✔	
			5S Applied		
Small Scope (within the department)	✔		Training Costs a Factor		
Immediate Attention Required	✔		Requires Detailed Planning Meetngs		
Process Immediately Accessible	✔		May Require Statistical Methods to Determine Root Cause		
Root Cause Known	✔				
Specific Training Required	✔		Web-based Collaboration Application Main Form of Communication		
Broad Training Required			Team Required	✔	
Team Members Physically (Locally) Available	✔		Value Stream or Process Map Required		
Meeting Times < 4 Hours			Likely Will Impact Balanced Scorecard or Performance Dashboard Metric	✔	
Process Change (PDCAs) Continuously Applied Over a Few Days	✔		Team Charter Required		

A successful Today's Kaizen Event must have following conditions present:

- All key stakeholders actively involved.
- Root cause or solution known.
- Planning the known solution can be completed in one day.
- Management committed and engaged in the project.
- Process area employees' ideas are considered (as only a few will be on the team).
- All employees are treated with dignity and respect.

A team of experienced, knowledgeable people with a stake in the issue is chartered to develop solutions and action plans for a known problem. The team is empowered to proceed with implementation (or is given a clear reason for not proceeding or a specific direction for further study) and is accountable for follow-up of the action plans.

Note: If the project team's has had previous experience with Lean and Six Sigma initiatives, then the one day planning session may be less than the typical eight hours.

Steps and Forms

The following steps and forms should be used as a guide to customize a Today's Kaizen Event to fit your organization requirements. There are many variables to consider, some of which are:

- ❖ Immediate need for an improvement plan or problem solving team to meet and determine solutions
- ❖ Root cause or Lean tool application is known
- ❖ Change management principles applied
- ❖ Process availability
- ❖ Team members' buy-in
- ❖ Resource availability
- ❖ How to address previous negative experiences with team projects
- ❖ How to effectively manage change
- ❖ Other departmental needs

The Today's Kaizen Event is comprised of three phases:

Part 1. Planning Phase (spans 1 week)

Part 2. PDCA Implementation Phase (spans 1 - 2 weeks)

Part 3. Follow-Up Phase (spans 1 - 2 weeks)

Each of these will be explored in detail in reference to developing solutions and actions to a known problem or opportunity.

Today's

Part 1. Planning Phase (spans 1 week/8 hours (or less) meeting time on day 5)

The Planning Phase is primarily a modified subset of the Planning Phase activities that comprise the other three types of team-based Kaizen Events. The following conditions must be present for a successful Planning Phase:

* ❖ All potential team members are aware of the problem or issue as well as the urgency
* ❖ An experienced facilitator is available for the eight hour planning session
* ❖ All team members are available for the eight hour planning session

Use the following steps as a guide for the Planning Phase which usually takes place within a few days prior to the team planning day meeting:

1. Determine project scope.
    Use negative trends for Balance Scorecard or Performance Dashboard.
    Identify what is not in scope to keep the team aligned.
    Address customer mandates or audits that require immediate action.
    Launch a new product line.
    Address employee turnover issues.

2. Review data set.
    Support project with data (i.e., adjustment times, batch sizes, changeover times, cycle times, delay times, delivery schedules, down times, efficiency percentages, failure rates, quality yields, number of shifts, sigma value, value-added times, customer survey results, audit reports, etc.).

3. Determine team members.
    Ensure team members have responsibilities or key technical input for process changes.

4. Communicate to team members date for full team meeting.
    Ensure confirmation.
    Provide supporting data in condensed form (i.e., chart) from (2).

5. Conduct Stakeholder Analysis.
    Address potential road blocks with department and people early.

6. Conduct specific Lean tool training.
    Provide readings, links, etc. to Lean Sigma tools and concepts that may be the likely ones to be used.
    Ensure everyone understands the basics of Lean and this type of Kaizen Event.

7. Create Reporting and Communication forms.
    Use current Performance Scorecard or Dashboard.
    Use A3 Report, if needed.

Kaizen Demystified

8. Communicate to Executive Sponsor and other managers the schedule.
   Request Executive Sponsor to kick-off meeting.

9. Prepare for full day meeting.
   Confirm facilitator, conference room, etc.
   Send out confirmation 24 hours before.

The main focus in the Planning Phase is the full day meeting. This will have decision-makers in a highly intense and fast moving, but productive eight hours (or less) meeting. The following is a recommended agenda and details for the eight hours (maximum times are listed):

Review the problem. (30 minutes)

Even though everyone is aware of the problem and has had some type of communication prior to this meeting, the overall problem should be thoroughly reviewed. This may be in the form of presenting the supporting data in a Pareto Chart, Pie Chart, Histogram, Control Chart, or some type of audit report or assessment score. The Balanced Scorecard could also be used. This data will be used as the basis for making decisions the entire day. At the conclusion of this step, write the problem statement in a flip chart of whiteboard to ensure everyone is in agreement to the exact nature of the problem. Be careful to not jump to solutions with the team at this time.

List issues and barriers. (30 minutes)

Problems or barriers are defined as the current issues that may be or are impacting the problem, process, or department (typically addressing special cause variation issues). Issues and barriers may include some of the following:

❖ No overtime mandate
❖ Budgetary issues
❖ Supporting resources not available when needed
❖ Requires extra transportation
❖ Supplies not available
❖ Supplies cannot be found
❖ Training never done
❖ Not receiving information soon enough to do anything with it
❖ Equipment capacity (downtime)

This is the listing of any and all the main elements that may or actually have an impact on the problem. Further investigation to the main issues and barriers will be required.

Create second and third level Pareto Analysis. (1 hour) (includes break)

Obtain data to further analyze the main issues and barriers to determine exactly which ones are impacting the problem. If 80% of the main issues and barriers are identified, it is likely the solution will likely address the other ones.

Determine potential solutions. (2 hours)

Albert Einstein famously said "You cannot solve a problem with the same mind that created it." When determining solutions be logical and rely on factual-based or proven solutions. For this type if Kaizen Event, the root cause is known and the solution is fairly clear. Therefore, the team should "review" the solution(s) and develop the implementation specifics using brainstorming, Cause and Effect Diagrams, etc.

Assess specific solutions. (1 hour)

*The **Impact Map** allows teams to identify and select solutions most likely to have the greatest impact on the problem with the least effort.* (The Impact Map will be used for **Assess specific solutions** and **Select solutions**.) Opportunities that have a high impact on the organization and are easily completed should take top implementation priority. Opportunities that have a high impact and take more time and effort to accomplish should be targeted next. Ideas that have little impact, but are easily completed should be done as time permits. Finally, projects or ideas that have a low potential impact on the organization and are difficult or expensive to implement could be considered at a later date. In summary, teams should reach a consensus on the EASE of implementation, as well as the IMPACT that it will have on the result.

Make sure the team considers low cost or no cost solutions first and advocates "creativity before capital" for any and all solutions. Also, protect the customer and the organization by minimizing the risk of a proposed improvement not working. Ensure that the team can return the process or area to the "original" state if any solution fails - following the PDCA Implementation process.

Teams should develop the Impact Map in a participative manner so everyone has the opportunity to express their thoughts and opinions. Dialogue and discussion are used to reach consensus on specific implementation priorities. Team members develop a high commitment and ownership to improvement activities only when they have an influence on projects. Impact Maps also provide an excellent communication vehicle for communicating the plan within the organization.

Select solutions. (1.5 hours) (includes break)

The following steps can be used to create an Impact Map and assess and select specific solutions:

   a) List all potential implementation solution activities in a chart.
   b) Use team consensus and assign a score for each using the following:
         IMPACT of the result (1 - Very Low to 10 - Very High)
         EASE of achieving (1 - Very Difficult to 10 - Very Easy)
   c) Create a graph with the vertical-axis denoting IMPACT: 1 is at the bottom (label as LOW) and 10 at the top (label as HIGH). Create the horizontal axis denoting EASE with the left as 1 (label as VERY DIFFICULT) and the far right as 10 (label as VERY EASY).
   d) Divide the graph into four quadrants and label appropriately.
   e) Assign each item listed in step b to an area of the map.
   f) Determine which items have the greatest impact with the least amount of effort. Consider these (and any others that may be practical to implement) as improvement activities.

Impact Map

IMPACT of the result (1 - Very Low to 10 - Very High)
EASE of achieving (1 - Very Difficult to 10 - Very Easy)

No.	Potential Implementation Solution Activities	EASE	IMPACT
1.			
2.			
3.			
4.			
5.			
6.			
7.			

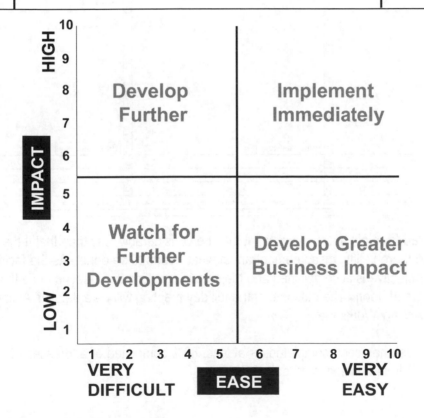

Create implementation plans. (1.5 hours)

Create specific implementation plans, Who does What, by When, and Why. Create a Project Dashboard or Scorecard to monitor implementation activities.

Today's

The following is the Today's Kaizen Event Planning Phase Checklist to help ensure all critical items are completed prior to Part 2. PDCA Implementation Phase. The Checklist is a listing of the main steps, main features for the steps, as well as the forms or worksheets suggested. This will help ensure a successful completion of this Phase. Use this as a guideline for customizing a Checklist for your Event.

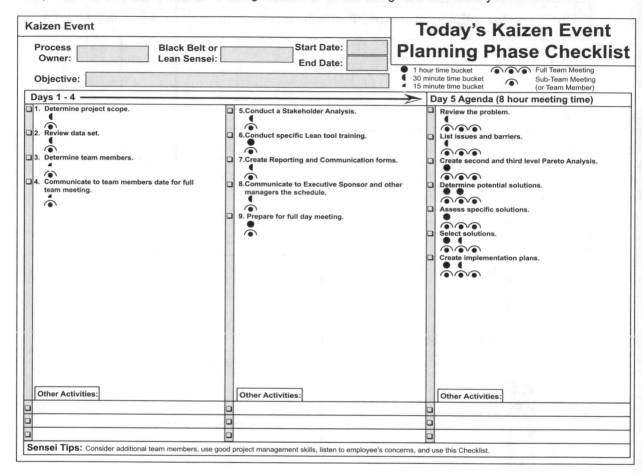

The Day 5 is scheduled for eight hours, however, it may be considerably less than that if the solutions are quickly agreed to and there is little disagreement about what needs to be done. As the facilitator or team leader, ensure each objective is accomplished and then move on. End the meeting once the implementation plan has been agreed upon. The outcome of the full day meeting will be a detailed Action Item Log or Kaizen Event PDCA Activity Worksheet.

Once the Planning Phase has been completed, or at least 80% completed or addressed, then it would be time to begin the PDCA Implementation or "doing" Phase.

Part 2. PDCA Implementation Phase (spans 1 - 2 weeks/no full team meeting times scheduled)

Once the Action Item Log or Kaizen Activity Worksheet is completed, it will be the responsibility of the team members to follow-through with those specific improvement activities (PDCAs). The facilitator or team leader should follow-up on a regular basis and be available for support, if needed. The purpose of this type of event is to quickly implement those proven solutions, typically within 1 - 2 weeks after the full day meeting.

The following Today's Kaizen Event PDCA (Implementation) Phase Checklist will help ensure all critical items are completed prior to Part 3. Follow-Up Phase. The Checklist is a listing of the main steps, main features for the steps, as well as the forms or worksheets suggested. This will help ensure a successful completion of this Phase. Use this as a guideline for customizing a Checklist for your Event.

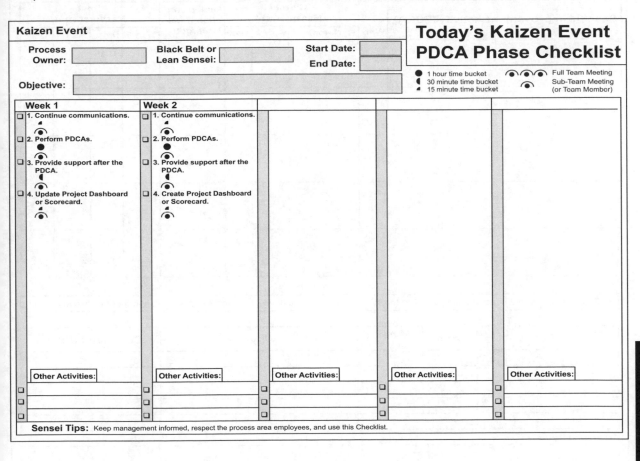

The following is a Today's Kaizen Event Project Scorecard that could be used as a guideline for your organization:

Kaizen Event			Project Scorecard	
Type of Project:		Start Date:		
		End Date:		
Value Stream Impacted:				
Executive Champion:		Lean Sensei/Black Belt:		
Process Owner:				

Specific Improvement Activity (PDCA)	Who	Current Measurement			Implementation Date/ Target	Post Measurements			
		Name	% or #	Date		% or #	Date	% or #	Date

If the measurement is not meeting traget(s) the WWWWW (below) must clearly indicate how you plan to meet or exceed target.

What	Who	When (m/d/y)	Why	Comments/Status

Additional Notes:

Part 3. Follow-Up Phase (spans 1 - 2 weeks)

All team members should be apprised on when the specific improvements are completed. If a Project Dashboard or Scorecard had been created, it should be posted/published for all team members to view. Also, if an A3 Project or Status Report was created to be shared within the organization that too should be made available. There should be a formal closure to the Kaizen Event even though the team may have only met once in the Planning Phase.

Use the following Today's Kaizen Event Follow-Up Phase Checklist to help ensure all critical items are completed prior to starting another Kaizen Event. The Checklist is a listing of the main steps, main features for the steps, as well as the forms or worksheets suggested. This will help ensure a successful completion of this Phase. Use this as a guideline for customizing a Checklist for your Event.

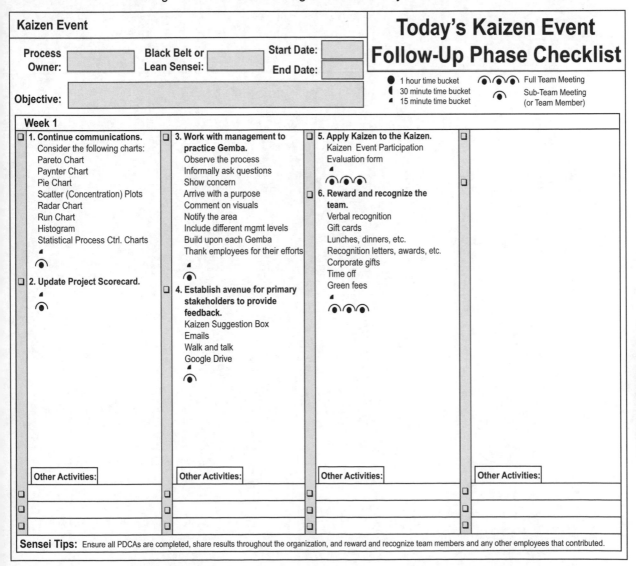

The Today's Kaizen Event Follow-Up Phase Checklist has proven helpful for Kaizen teams in sustaining the gains made in the PDCA Implementation Phase. Consider each activity listed as value-added or non value-added to the team's objectives. Also, be flexible to accept and use any other activities that the team members might have experienced that may also provide value to the team's objective.

Keep in mind that the overall objective for the Today's Kaizen Event is to agree to proposed implementation activities to a known problem with proven solutions in the one day planning session followed up with implementation within the next 3-4 weeks. Again, this will depend on the size of the team, the complexity of the project, the time employees make available for implementing the actual process changes, and how effective the full day meeting was.

Case Study

The following case study demonstrates many of the tools explained in this section as well as some of the "people-side" issues that are encountered by the facilitator, team leader, process owner, or team member. As with any improvement project, you too would select only the appropriate activities (i.e., tools, worksheets, forms, etc.) to meet your specific Kaizen Event requirements for planning, implementing, and reporting.

Granger Aerospace, Inc. is a manufacturer of high pressure hoses and fittings for the aerospace industry. They have been around since the 1950s and have over 400 employees in two separate plants located about 10 miles apart. Their business has been steadily increasing due to the Defense Departments demands. However, the profitability has been slowly declining from 6.5% last year to 5.9% this year.

Granger had been involved in an Operational Excellence program for nearly five years; however, management believes they need a new program as the old one seems to have been flat over the past two years. There used to be project bulletin boards, team activities, large project kick-offs, etc. and now all of that has come to a standstill.

Part 1. Planning Phase (spans 3 days/4 hour meeting time on day 3)

John Adams, the operations manager for the past two years, had just hired two new shift supervisors in the assembly area. They both came from the automotive industry. During the interview process they both had a plant tour, subsequently commenting (politely as they were still in the interviewing phase) on how the plant could be better organized in certain areas (tooling, quality, etc.) as well as they both had noticed no Visual Management (or Production) Boards. Both interviewees noted that the employees mentioned that there had been some 5S or Lean program started a few years ago but had taken a back seat to production issues. This was something John had known, but did not find the time to make it a priority, until today. John decided to re-initialize the Operational Excellence program with an immediate emphasis on 5S and Visual Management Boards. And, since there was to be a major customer audit next month this was a perfect opportunity!

John had a timeline of four weeks to re-launch Operational Excellence. John met with the Continuous Improvement Specialist, Renee, to do a walk-around the plant to get an idea on how things currently were operating. The following was concluded:

1. No formal structure or standard to the current bulletin boards (or Visual Management Boards)
2. 5S was not practiced as they both noticed tooling all over the place, employees stating that during the day they are constantly searching for tooling
3. Many times the "kits" that comprised the gauges, prints, special tools, etc. were not complete
4. No employee acknowledging working on any type of team-based improvement project
5. Numerous minor safety violations were apparent

When John and Renee returned to John's office, John quickly stated, "I'm upset. I cannot believe these supervisors let their areas get so bad. We need to have a meeting tomorrow and get them onboard. Heads may roll. I know I may be to blame, but these supervisors should have done better than this. I am surprised those two new supervisors wanted to work here at all."

Renee, who has been with the company over ten years, responded, "I agree that the areas are bad on the initial walk-around, but consider that we have been consistently recognized by our customers on great quality and customer service. Sure our audits indicated we could improve our housekeeping, but no customer has reduced or taken business away from us because of this. I know that is not an excuse, I just feel the supervisors have been under the gun to get the parts out the door as well as try to improve their processes. I remember five years ago, your predecessor started the Operational Excellence program with a big push, project teams started in all areas, etc. only to have it dissipate within a year."

John continued, "I understand that it has not impacted our business, but I cannot believe if we continue down this road and not address it, that someday it will impact us to some degree. Now is the time to do something as I want our customer audit next month to reflect some significant housekeeping improvements. I know this may be a lot, but our supervisors know what needs to be done, we just need to provide them with the right incentive and support. And, most importantly, this will be the way we continue to operate and THIS will NOT be a program of the month because of one customer audit next month."

Renee concluded, "I agree. I will put an agenda out for a meeting in two days for all the supervisors and managers for production. Does that work for you?"

John added, "Sure, but also include the managers for our administrative processes. I want this program to be throughout this facility. 5S, Visual Management, and Lean is for everyone! Also, I think due to the training everyone has had, we can get everything done in four hours."

Renee agreed and left.

Two days later, a four hour meeting was held with the appropriate supervisors and managers in attendance. Renee facilitated the meeting that comprised the following.

Review the problem. (10 minutes)

John kicked the meeting off stating how he appreciated everyone being on time and the current trends in the Balanced Scorecard. He continued to state that he wanted to re-initialize the Operational Excellence program with an immediate emphasis on 5S and Visual Management Boards. He mentioned the customer audit in a few weeks and this would be good target to make some noticeable visual improvements. After the 5S and Visual Management Boards were established, John stated he would support meaningful projects regarding problem solving and continuous improvement. Starting with 5S at least everyone could get involved and it would most likely have a positive impact on productivity. John asked for any input or ideas.

Gary, the engineering manager, asked, "I agree that we should get this going, as Lean and Six Sigma will improve and quality and reduce costs, however, this sounds exactly what we did five years ago. I know you were not here, but I know that we also got our employees excited and involved, only to let it die a slow death. What will be different this time?"

John responded, "Good question Gary. What will be different this time? Well, I believe that nothing I can say or do right now will change employee's attitudes. I will tell you that I have already committed to doing walk-arounds on a weekly basis with each of you in your department. I believe that, along with recognizing employees as they participate on teams will get the ball rolling. I do plan on allocating 5 minutes at our monthly meetings to review and discuss Operational Excellence progress. Also, I will solicit input from all of you what more I can do to support you and everyone's efforts as we go forward. Did I answer your question, Gary?"

Gary concluded, "Yes. I just want to say that our department will do what is necessary as well as support any of your work not only for this 5S program, but once we start to engage those more difficult quality and production process issues."

"Thanks Gary. Any other questions or concerns at this time?" John summarized.

List issues and barriers. (10 minutes)

Renee continued to facilitate the meeting. She had provided all participants with some links as well as readings on 5S and Visual Management. Everyone was well aware of these tools. She facilitated a discussion on any barriers and the following list was compiled:

1) Will overtime be approved to work on these initiatives?
2) Need standardization for a 5S program as well as the Visual Management Board layout
3) Need 5S supplies (floor tape, labels, paint, etc.)
4) Training new employees on Lean

Address issues and barriers. (10 minutes)

John, with Renee facilitating, addressed each of the issues and barriers:

1) Will overtime be approved to work on these initiatives: If necessary.
2) Need standardization for a 5S program as well as the Visual Production Board layout: Will be done in this meeting.
3) Need 5S supplies: Renee will coordinate after this meeting.
4) Training new employees on Lean: Renee will coordinate after this meeting.

Create implementation plans. (1.5 hours)

This part was divided into two parts, one to address 5S and one to create the standards for the Visual Production Board.

Renee continued to facilitate the implementation plans.

1) The group suggested a sixth S, Safety, be added and everyone agreed; however, they decided to name it 5S Plus 1 to keep the commonality of the previous Operational Excellence 5S program intact. Renee would update the previous 5S Audit with Safety, and forward it to everyone for review as well as get input from the Safety Committee.
2) A time line was established for each S, one week per S. Each department would initiate a 5S team within the next few days. Renee would assist with any support required.
3) Communication regarding the benefits of 5S to all employees would be done. Renee had already purchased some posters and would post them in the cafeteria.
4) It was agreed upon to track the waste of motion and transport for two areas and make a business case for additional tools (a sub-team was formed to collect the data, specifically the time spent searching for tools and supplies) before the second 2 - Set-In-Order was complete.

5) Renee will create one 5S Audit team comprised of hourly and salaried employees. Audit will start in four weeks. Renee will coordinate a benchmarking trip for the team within the next two weeks.
6) Renee suggested the following Visual Management Board to be used as a standard. Departments/areas can modify accordingly, but the overall look should remain similar.

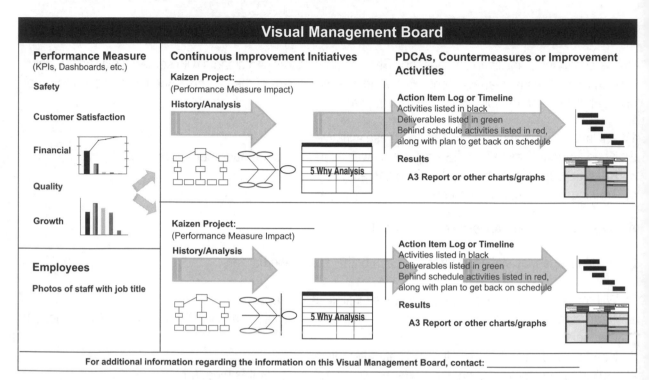

The meeting went very well and was concluded in three hours. John thanked everyone for their attention and forthcoming efforts. He also thanked Renee for facilitating the meeting and getting everything completed in less than the allocated four hours.

Part 2. PDCA Implementation Phase (spans 1 - 2 weeks/no full team meeting times scheduled)

Each supervisor and manager promptly initiated small teams (2-4 employees). The teams diligently met for the next three weeks making progress each time. Each meeting lasted no more than 30 minutes; however, additional time was allocated for some of the work (sorting parts, creating labels, cleaning, etc.). Each team realized that an audit team would be visiting their areas after the 3rd week to prepare for their first customer audit. The following had occurred during this time:

1. The teams appreciated Renee's enthusiasm and efficiency in getting supplies so quickly.
2. Renee and John immediately began to have weekly walk-arounds the departments to note the changes.

3. Visual Management Boards were created and/or updated with current information and each had a similar look and feel. This current 5S project was listed under Continuous Improvement Initiatives.
4. Team members received no negative feedback from employees.
5. Individual areas for both the front office and shop floor were much better visually organized.
6. A business case was made for a new high pressure tester given the data presented to John regarding wastes of motion and transport.

Part 3. Follow-Up Phase (spans 1 - 2 weeks)

The audit team created the following Sustain Audit sheet for the shop floor area (a similar one was created for the administrative areas):

5S Plus 1 Audit for Shop Floor

Purpose: To help the Audit Team maintain the 5S Plus 1 standards.

Who should fill it out: The Audit Team by consensus.

Directions: The best way to use this tool is to follow these steps:
1. Review the questions.
2. Reach consensus on the Item questions and score on the following five-level Likert item scale.

Audit Date: _____
Area Audited: _____
Auditors: _____
_____

1 - Strongly Disagree
2 - Disagree
3 - Neither Agree nor Disagree
4 - Agree
5 - Strongly Agree

Safety
There are no pallets, debris, etc. creating work hazards. _____
Employees are wearing protective clothing. _____
Entrance ways, fire extinguishers, and/or pathways are clear. _____
There are no trip hazards (cords, wires, tools, etc.) in the area. _____
Machine guards are being used or are firmly in place. _____

Sort
Only necessary items (tooling, parts, etc) are in the area. _____
Tooling, parts, supplies, etc. are sorted and organized. _____
Personal belongings are properly stored. _____
There is only necessary equipment, tooling, etc. in the area. _____

Set-In-Order
Aisles and walk ways are clearly marked. _____
Work areas are clearly identified. _____
Tools, equipment, supply areas are clearly identified. _____
Supply, equipment, tooling, etc. are in their proper location. _____
Storage areas are well-organized. _____

Shine
Cleaning materials are accessible. _____
Work areas are free of grease and grime. _____
The area has been swept recently. _____
Hoses, wires, etc. seem to be properly arranged. _____
Labels and signs are being used. _____

Standardize
Cleaning or 5S Plus 1 standards are visible. _____
Equipment controls are clearly marked. _____
Employees are aware of the 5S Plus 1 program. _____

Sustain
The area has been audited in the past month. _____
There is an active Audit Team to assist the area workers. _____
Management has been involved in the 5S Plus 1 program. _____

Total Score: ▆▆▆▆

Ray, the IT manager, who was part of the Audit Team created the following Sustain Audit sheet for their department, noting that it would help them more if it was customized to their electronic files and folders.

The Audit Team created the following Scoring Guidelines to assist them in having a standard approach to each area's score:

Shop floor and administrative areas (except IT):

101 - 125 - Doing Well, Keep Up the Good Work. Take photos of the area and share. Continue to ask for volunteers to assist lower-scoring areas.
81 - 100 - Doing OK, Must Make More Effort. Some good things happening, but more specific activities need to be completed.

< 80 - Not Good, Very Little Effort Shown. Meetings with individuals and groups need to be held, citing specific 5S activities for improvement as well as timeline. Request management to participate on audits. Address concerns on why the program is not being accepted. Continue coaching.

IT: (similar to previous legend except for scoring ranges)

80 - 100 - Doing Well, Keep Up the Good Work
60 - 79 - Doing OK, Must Make More Effort
> 60 - Not Good, Very Little Effort Shown

Two days before the customer audit, the Audit Team conducted their second 5S Plus 1 and IT audits. There were audits a week prior to more-or-less assist the areas in what the audits would be comprised of. Subsequently, audits would be done once per month. The following are the results of the audits as well as other measurements attributed to the re-energized 5S program:

Issue or Improvement Opportunity in Case Study			*Lean, Six Sigma or Leadership Tool Used*
Area	Previous Week Score	Current Week Score	
Assembly - Day	95	105	
Assembly - Evening	85	95	
Testing - Day	95	115	
Testing - Evening	105	115	
Quality - Day	110	110	
Quality - Evening	105	105	5S and Visual Management Board
Admin Areas	90	95	(pgs. 261 - 266)
IT	84	90	
	Pre 5S Plus 1	Post 5S Plus 1	
Time Spent Searching for Tools or Supplies:	64 minutes/ day/shift	12 minutes/ day/shift	
Supplies Inventory (daily average):	$8,754.00	$7,204.00	
FAD of the month re: project			Communications, Managing Change (pg. 262)

All in all, John was very pleased with the results and the customer audit was very successful, having achieved their highest score to date. John held an All Hands Employee Meeting the next day at lunch, provided pizza, and recognized everyone for embracing the 5S program as well as how informative the Visual Management Boards were. He thanked everyone for their efforts and stated he looked forward to discussing their upcoming improvement projects.

Sensei Tips

Note: Many of the following Sensei Tips can be used or applied in the other Kaizen Events, where and when appropriate.

❖ Be flexible in the one day (or less) meeting at the end of the Planning Phase. Since root cause is likely known, the time assigned to each of the scheduled agenda items may not take as long. Adjust the schedule accordingly.

❖ This type of Event can also be used for the implementation of a specific tool. For example, if management has determined that an area needs to be better organized, then a Today's Kaizen Event could simply be a "5S day." The Follow-Up portion would subsequently be the 5S Audit or the 5th S of Sustain.

❖ Spend the time to ensure everyone is in agreement as to the root cause and the known solution during the one day or less meeting. If there is any doubt, spend the necessary time to resolve any concerns. This "agreement" will be needed for the PDCA Implementation and Follow-Up Phases.

Wiki Kaizen Event

Overview

Note: It is suggested that the Standard 5 Day Kaizen Event section be read first to fully understand the basic structure and activities required that comprise all types of Kaizen Events (to some degree). Even though the Wiki Kaizen Event is not team-based and many of the team-based activities will not be used, it is still recommended to read the Standard 5 Day Kaizen Event in the event that the improvement for the Wiki Event may evolve into another type. This section will only *reference* the activities that are unique to this Kaizen Event type.

Wiki (or Quick) Kaizen Events *are quick, easy-to-implement improvements by the front-line worker that does not typically require any type of team collaboration or approval.* This type of Event is becoming popular due to emerging technologies that allow for sharing of information effortlessly and communicating with colleagues real-time, with those organizations that encourage employees to make improvements happen.

The following is the Wiki Kaizen Event Quick Determination Checklist to ensure this is the type of Kaizen Event required given your specific situation. Ensure the majority of Characteristics are checked as Yes or Likely in the Your Situation column. Your Situation should closely follow the Yes or Likely column.

Wiki Kaizen Event Quick Determination Checklist					
Characteristic	**YES or LIKELY**	**Your Situation**	**Characteristic**	**YES or LIKELY**	**Your Situation**
Large Scope (crosses departments)			Management Involvement		
			5S Applied		
Small Scope (within the department)	✔		Training Costs a Factor		
			Requires Detailed Planning Meetngs		
Immediate Attention Required					
Process Immediately Accessible	✔		May Require Statistical Methods to Determine Root Cause		
Root Cause May Be Known	✔				
Specific Training Required	✔		Web-based Collaboration Application Main Form of Communication		
Broad Training Required			Team Required		
Team Members Physically (Locally) Available			Value Stream or Process Map Required		
Meeting Times < 4 Hours	✔		Will Impact Balanced Scorecard or Performance Dashboard Metric		
Process Change (PDCAs) Continuously Applied Over a Few Days	✔		Team Charter Required		

Wiki

The term "wiki" comes from the Hawaiian phrase, "wiki wiki," which means "super-fast" or "quick." A wiki is also a Web site that allows users to add and update content on the site using their own Web browser. A great example of a large wiki is the Wikipedia, the free online encyclopedia that anyone can edit. If you have thousands of users adding content to a Web site on a regular basis, the site could grow "super-fast" in a very short time period. We have taken that Wiki meaning of "quick" and "super-fast" and applied it to the Kaizen concept of "continuous improvement." Businesses today must continually change and update (improve) their processes and systems faster than ever. Therefore, Wiki (or Quick) Kaizen Events are quick, easy-to-implement improvements by the front-line worker that does not typically require any type of team collaboration or approval. The subsequent documentation and sharing of this improvement knowledge would be available throughout the organization. This self-perpetuating business improvement model would allow improvements to expand at a faster rate than before. The Wiki Kaizen Event is meant to assist the front-line worker to gain a basic understanding of Lean and use this information to "quickly" improve their daily work processes by eliminating wasteful activities.

A successful Wiki Kaizen Event must have following conditions present:

- ❖ Process or area within control of person making the change.
- ❖ Improvement will improve work flow or quality of the work being done.
- ❖ Requires little, if any, management support.
- ❖ Resources are not an issue.
- ❖ Training is minimal.
- ❖ Employees are empowered to make change happen.
- ❖ All employees are treated with dignity and respect.

Employees are faced with many challenges throughout the day. The following may be some of their thoughts:

"I am drowning in emails with no end in sight."
"I constantly have to request the same information from colleagues again and again, and that creates stress for me."
"No one wants to make a decision, so we just keep making the same old mistakes."
"I spend countless hours manipulating data from our CRM system."
"I am constantly helping colleagues with their Excel reports and at times it gets me behind on my work."
"Our inventory management system is not integrated to our sales order system which causes duplication of work."
"I do not understand why someone sends me an incomplete or inaccurate report."
"Everyone has their own work-arounds and nothing is standardized which makes it frustrating when some-one is on vacation and we have to do their work."
"My boss is constantly asking me to generate reports…something that I am sure he is expected to do."
"I have no idea what type of information the next process needs, they just want everything - which takes time as it is pulled from different systems."
"We are always inundated at the end of the month with extra work. Can't this be scheduled better?"
"It seems like our priorities change daily."
"It does not seem like the workload is evenly distributed among the work group."

These statements or thoughts can be dis-heartening for the employee. If these thoughts are in employee's minds, it is likely the employee is feeling stressed. This stress can lead to a lack of focus, energy, motivation, etc. which decreases productivity at all levels of the organization. To remedy this situation, and provide employees with new opportunities, the Wiki Kaizen Event approach can have the employees take more control of their work processes; thereby, eliminating those "frustrations," be more productive, and feel less stressed.

It is the employees doing their job, working that process level detail (i.e., processing information for a product or service), day in and day out that have the best ideas on how to reduce and eliminate waste. However, they may not be aware of the impact that waste has in their process. The Wiki Kaizen is meant to engage those employees to gain additional ownership of their processes through self-initiated improvements (and waste elimination). Once Wiki Kaizens become a way of life for all employees within an organization, then a true continuous improvement culture will have emerged.

Wiki

Steps and Forms

The following steps and forms should be used as a guide to customize a Wiki Kaizen Event to fit your organization requirements. There are many variables to consider, some of which are:

❖ Number of employees with Lean and Six Sigma or problem solving experience and/or training
❖ Independence upon which employees do their daily tasks
❖ Root cause is known
❖ Changes made will have no direct impact on the next process

The Wiki Kaizen Event is comprised of three phases:

Part 1. Determination Phase (spans 1 - 2 days)

Part 2. PDCA Implementation Phase (spans 1 - 2 weeks)

Part 3. Sharing Phase (spans 1 - 2 weeks)

Each of these will be explored in detail along with the recommended forms to be used.

Part 1. Determination Phase (spans 1 - 2 days)

The phase should confirm the need for the improvement idea or initiative with an identifiable waste. Lean is all about identifying and eliminating waste, therefore for this small-focused improvement the waste should be fairly easy to identify and subsequently eliminate.

During the Determination Phase use the following steps as a guide:

1. Complete the following Wiki Kaizen Event Determination Worksheet.

Kaizen Event	**Wiki Kaizen Event Determination Worksheet**

Your Name: _____

Your Manager: _____

Date: _____

Department or Value Stream: _____

Instructions: Please ✔ the appropriate response to each statement.					

Use the follwoing five level Likert item scale for scoring: 1 = Strongly Disagree 2 = Disagree 3 = Neither Agree nor Disagree 4 = Agree 5 = Strongly Agree Statements	1 Strongly Disagree	2 Disagree	3 Neither Agree nor Disagree	4 Agree	5 Strongly Agree
1. The project will have a positive impact impact on my work performance.					
2. The project requires no additional training upstream.					
3. The project requires no additional training downstream.					
4. The project willl have no impact on others.					
5. The project can easily be shared with others.					
6. The project can be proven successful with measurements.					
7. The project can be completed with little or no resources.					
8. The project will improve a critical process of my work.					
9. The project will make my job easier.					
10. The project will be easy to implement.					
11. The project process improvement can be standardized.					
12. The project will improve my quality of work.					
13. The project will eliminate waste in my work.					
14. The project will reduce stress in my daily work.					
15. The project can be completed quickly in less than 4 hours of my time.					
16. The project is well within my scope of work.					
17. The project is customer focused.					
18. The project is process focused and not people focused.					
19. The project does not require a value stream map.					
20. The project root cause is known.					

Total: _____

Note: There typically may be some form of communication between the worker and their manager regarding the proposed improvement initiative. This will depend on the type of initiative, how currently communications occur - formally or informally, and the culture of the organization. It may be as simple as submitting this Wiki Kaizen Event Determination Worksheet to the manager.

In large organizations, a version of the Wiki Kaizen Determination Worksheet (or a Kaizen Event Proposal) may include:

❖ All proposals being viewed by managers weekly or monthly to ensure workers do not overcommit.
❖ All proposals being viewed by managers weekly or monthly to "sense" trends or trouble areas that would require a team-based Kaizen Event.
❖ Employees may sign-up or be involved in a certain number of Wiki Kaizen Events.

2. Use the following Scoring Guidelines to determine Wiki Kaizen Event feasibility.

Scoring Guidelines

Score

80 - 100 Ready for Wiki Kaizen

Your score indicates the improvement initiative you have in mind could easily be implemented with little or no assistance. Ensure any improvements are well-documented to demonstrate success as well as share with others.

60 - 79 May Need Additional Support

Your score indicates the improvement project you have in mind may require some assistance from upstream suppliers or downstream customers (i.e., IT, another colleague, or your manager). If this is the case and you are not sure, submit a Kaizen Event Proposal to your manager listing the potential benefits the improvement project may have as well as the resources required. Your initiative will be appreciated. Work within any guidelines provided. If your manager believes the project or initiative is broader in its scope, be open to leading a team to work on the improvement project as a team-based Kaizen Event.

3. Solicit assistance from a colleague, if required. If the proposed improvement or problem resolution idea requires assistance from another colleague, share with them any information that is available to solicit their assistance. Be specific to WIIFM (What's In It For Me?) and WIIFT (What's In It For Them?). Use the following Wiki Colleague Request form as a guide when soliciting assistance from a colleague for a Wiki Kaizen Event.

Kaizen Event

Wiki Colleague Request

Date: _____

Name: _____   Department: _____

Upstream Supplier: _____   Downstream Customer: _____

The Wiki Colleague Request is to be used when requesting "light" assistance from a colleague to help provide a solution to a problem or implement an improvement. This improvement or solution should also benefit the colleague directly or indirectly and not require any significant amount of their time or resources (less than an hour or two).

Step 1: Describe the Problem or Opportunity.	Include photos, charts, and graphs, if necessary. Include current measurements.

Problem Viewed by Initiator	Type of Waste

Problem Viewed by Colleague (Perceived)	Type of Waste (Perceived)

Proposed Start Date: _____

Step 2: List Potential Benefits.	Be specific in terms of how the team's success will be measured. Use Balance Scorecard measures, if possible.

Benefits for Initiator (WIIFM)	Benefits for Colleague (Perceived) (WIIFT)

Proposed End Date: _____

Step 3: List Resources Required.	Include support needed from Colleague. Be specific in terms of technical expertise, departmental cooperation as a trial, etc.

Type of Support	Estimated Hours Needed	Dates Requested

Step 4: Determine Feasibility and Next Steps.

❏ Agree As Is

❏ Need More Information Before Agreeing

❏ Currently Being Addressed

❏ Suggest To Formalize As A Team Type Kaizen Event

Sign-Off Date: _____

Once the form is submitted to the colleague, the colleague should:

Agree As Is – Colleague thanks the requestor for the suggestion on improving their work process. Colleague commits to a date and time to get started.

Need More Information Before Agreeing – Colleague thanks the requestor for the suggestion on improving their work process; however, more information is needed before the colleague can make a fact-based decision about the proposed Wiki Kaizen Event. The colleague should be specific as to what type of information they require in order to render a decision. Is it another type of measurable? Are resources not clear, or is something else necessary for the colleague to make an informed decision regarding the request.

Currently Being Addressed - Thank the requestor for their idea. Explain how a current program or project will address the issue that was identified in the request. If this is the case, better communication with the on-going project must occur.

Suggest To Formalize As A Team Type Kaizen Event – Thank the requestor for their idea. From the colleague's perspective, it seems to be a departmental or cross-departmental opportunity that will impact others. It is suggested another type of Kaizen Event proposal be submitted to the next higher level of management.

Adapt the Wiki Colleague Request form to your organization given your organizational culture of communicating to colleagues in requesting their support.

The intent of the Wiki Kaizen Event is to provide an avenue for employees to get more involved in continuous improvement and problem solving on a daily basis as well as have them experience ownership of their processes. Managers and supervisors must balance "knowing" what their employees are doing with "trusting" their employees to improve (i.e., change) on their own. This is not all-or-nothing; it is a progression of behavioral change and trust on part of the employee as well as the manager or supervisor. It is recommended to establish a team and create the appropriate guidelines that fit your organization's needs.

Note: The Determination Phase, as with the Planning Phase for the team-based Kaizen Events, includes all the activities prior to any process change. Keep in mind that these are guidelines and the various activities listed can be completed in different parts of this Phase, as well as, at times, be incorporated into another Phase.

Part 2. PDCA Implementation Phase (spans 1 - 2 weeks)

During the PDCA Implementation Phase use the following steps as a guide:

1. Use the following Wiki PDCA Activity Worksheet as a guide in listing the specific activities that need to be completed and when these activities need to be done. Even though the project is small in scope, or being done by one person, documenting the activities will accomplish the following:

   ❖ Provide others the detail process changes to learn from once it has been proven successful and allow the gains to be leveraged to other similar areas.
   ❖ If changes are not what are expected, the detail will help narrow down what may need to be "tweaked."
   ❖ Provide the documentation to update any standard work procedures.
   ❖ Provide a foundation on what specific training may be required if there is any departmental roll-out of the change.

Kaizen Event			**Wiki PDCA Activity Worksheet**		
Process Name:			**Date:**		
Department:			**Colleagues:**		
Process Name/Activity	**Problem or Waste**	**Lean Tool**	**Specific Activities (What)**	**Who**	**When**
			Plan / Do / Check / Act		
			Plan / Do / Check / Act		
			Plan / Do / Check / Act		
			Plan / Do / Check / Act		
			Plan / Do / Check / Act		
			Plan / Do / Check / Act		
			Plan / Do / Check / Act		
			Plan / Do / Check / Act		

Parking Lot Items for Wiki Kaizen Events or Other Types of Kaizen Events

2. Adapt the Wiki PDCA Activity Worksheet to your organization given your organizational culture of getting employees involved in process change and ownership.

Note: The organization must balance an individual's time to detail the improvement activities with sharing organizational knowledge. It may seem excessive for only one person to fill this worksheet out, however, consider if that person left abruptly and nothing was documented (i.e., "nada" on organizational knowledge then); things could quickly revert back to the old ways.

3. Ensure process changes had a positive impact on measurements. Document.

4. Incorporate the PDCA(s) into new work standards.

Part 3. Sharing Phase (spans 1 - 2 weeks)

Success is measured by some type of improvement referenced in the Kaizen Event Proposal and/or Wiki Colleague Request forms. Once the implementation of the activities has occurred, use the following steps as a guide:

1. Use the following Sharing Worksheet to document the improvements.

Kaizen Event

Sharing Worksheet

Name: [   ]   Department: [   ]

Colleague: [   ]   Date: [   ]

The Sharing Worksheet is a communication tool to share the results of a Wiki improvement project. The Sharing Worksheet should be distributed to colleagues that have similar-type work processes. The Sharing Worksheets should be stored in a central location for others to review. The supervisor or manager can use the Sharing Worksheets as part of the performance appraisal for their employees.

Step 1: Convey Pre and Post Measurements in Simple Form.

Pre Measurements	Post Measurements

Step 2: Identify Wastes that were Eliminated.

☐ Overproduction	☐ Overprocessing
☐ Inventory	☐ Skills and Knowledge
☐ Waiting	☐ Unevenness
☐ Motion	☐ Overburden
☐ Transport	☐ Environmental Resources
☐ Defects or Errors	☐ Social Responsibility

Step 3: Identify the Main Lean Tools Used.

☐ 5S	☐ Impact Map	☐ Pull System	☐ Voice of the Customer
☐ 5 Why Analysis	☐ Just-In-Time	☐ Run Chart	☐ Waste Audit
☐ Brainstorming	☐ Kanban	☐ Runner	☐ Work Load Balancing
☐ Continuous Flow	☐ Mistake Proofing	☐ Standard Work	☐
☐ Fishbone Diagram	☐ Pareto Chart	☐ Takt Time/Demand Analysis ☐	☐
☐ Gantt Chart	☐ Paynter Chart	☐ Training	☐
☐ Heijunka/Leveling	☐ Pitch	☐ Value Stream Mapping	

Step 4: List Recommendations.

Recommendations to Colleagues	Recommendations to Management

Other Information	Contact Information

Note: The Sharing Worksheet can also be referred to as a Yokoten Worksheet. **Yokoten** *means "best practice sharing" or "taking from one place to another."* It encompasses communicating, documenting, and distributing knowledge within an organization about what worked and what did not work from a project. It is a form of knowledge management.

2. Distribute the Sharing Worksheet to appropriate colleagues. This should also be shared with the employee's immediate supervisor or manager.

In summary, the Wiki Kaizen Event is meant to be a tool used by every employee within an organization to continually improve their work processes.

Wiki

Case Studies

The following case studies demonstrate many of the tools explained in this section as well as some of the "people-side" issues that are encountered. A sample of the tools and worksheets are demonstrated in the following case studies. As with any improvement project, you too would select only the appropriate activities (i.e., tools, worksheets, forms, etc.) to meet your specific Kaizen Event requirements for planning, implementing, and reporting.

Case Study for Lacy's, Inc. on Visual Control

Lacy's, Inc., with corporate offices in Los Angeles and New York, is one of the nation's premier retailers, with fiscal 2010 sales of $10.5 billion. The company operates over 400 Lacy's department stores and furniture galleries in 35 states, the District of Columbia, Guam, and Puerto Rico. Lacy's, Inc.'s diverse workforce includes approximately 86,000 employees.

Nearly 80 years after its founding, Lacy's, Inc. is one of the nation's most successful and respected retail institutions. The company continues to prosper by adapting to the new and ever-changing needs of their customers. Embracing the words and philosophy of one of its founders, John B. Williams Sr., Lacy's, Inc. succeeds by striving to be "a living mirror of our civilization in which we see the constant changing needs and wishes of our people."

Susan Wellman has been with Lacy's for over 10 years, starting there after obtaining her degree in Fashion Merchandising from an East Coast college. Susan had held the following positions in their Chicago department store: assistant manager for women's clothes and shoes, assistant buyer for women's clothes and shoes, and most recently was the main buyer for women's clothes and shoes for the entire Midwest chain of stores. This new promotion as the main buyer had come as a surprise to her. She had enjoyed her previous job as it allowed her to travel 1 - 2 days a week, which gave her a change of pace, but the promotion required more management-type duties.

Susan had always prided herself with a tenacious and can-do work attitude with good computer skills. She preferred to use a Windows 7 version of Sticky Notes for her daily tasks (which she each day transferred from her hardcopy pocket calendar. Also, Susan had physically placed Post-it Notes on many areas of her desk as well as around the edges of her Desktop computer screen to keep track of what needed to be done and meetings that she had to attend. She also used an app on her iPhone to sync any changes that were made when she was out of the office with using the iPhone for business. This had worked for Susan for the past 5 years given her level of responsibility.

The previous main buyer had abruptly left the position to go to a competitor; therefore, there was not the typical ramp-up training time she thought she would have in learning this new job. Susan also knew, given the amount of meetings and contracts she had to negotiate seasonally, that she had to better organize her time. Susan had attended numerous quality improvement seminars presented by the corporate office, but had not the desire, time, or belief that any of them would benefit her.

Susan googled "Lean" as it was one of the terms she had heard in operation-type meetings, as well as Six Sigma, and there was recently posted on their company web site a Lean administrative success story in their credit department. The team formed in the credit department has used the concept of Lean to reduce Days Outstanding from 45.8 days to 34.6, which given the volume of dollars, was a very significant savings for the organization. Further research had Susan purchasing a few books from Amazon's Kindle program to understand how Lean could benefit her in her new job. She came across one of *Today's Lean!* books and found it informative and to-the-point. This book, and the case studies, provided Susan was a desire to make some changes in her work given this new responsibility. As the new main buyer and process owner for Sales and Customer Service, Susan had to regularly meet with the Sales and Customer Service improvement teams regarding on-going performance improvement initiatives.

During the first two weeks on her new job, Susan felt overwhelmed. She was working nearly 70 hours a week and still having trouble scheduling her time to meet all the obligations and commitments the job required. Susan was stressed, beginning to lose sleep over this new opportunity, and was wondering if this job was worth the struggle.

Lacy's Part 1. Determination Phase (spans 1 - 2 days)

After reading about Lean and the concept of waste and Kaizen, Susan decided to quickly implement a "Wiki Kaizen" on her work priorities in scheduling her time to ensure everything is completed on time. Susan realized the best way to learn about Lean is to do it. Susan realized that she needed to get control of her tasks and priorities and stop "wasting" time in writing these "reminder" notes (motion and overprocessing wastes). Susan completed the following Wiki Kaizen Event Determination Worksheet:

Wiki

Wiki Kaizen Event Determination Worksheet

| Your Name: | Susan | Event Dates: | 6/12-6/22 |
| Your Manager: | Jody | Department or Value Stream: | All |

Instructions: Please ✔ the appropriate response to each statement.

Use the follwoing five level Likert item scale for scoring:
1 = Strongly Disagree
2 = Disagree
3 = Neither Agree nor Disagree
4 = Agree
5 = Strongly Agree

Statements	1 Strongly Disagree	2 Disagree	3 Neither Agree nor Disagree	4 Agree	5 Strongly Agree
1. The project will have a positive impact impact on my work performance.					✔
2. The project requires no additional training upstream.					✔
3. The project requires no additional training downstream.					✔
4. The project willl have no impact on others.					✔
5. The project can easily be shared with others.				✔	
6. The project can be proven successful with measurements.					✔
7. The project can be completed with little or no resources.					✔
8. The project will improve a critical process of my work.				✔	
9. The project will make my job easier.					✔
10. The project will be easy to implement.					
11. The project process improvement can be standardized.		✔			
12. The project will improve my quality of work.				✔	
13. The project will eliminate waste in my work.					✔
14. The project will reduce stress in my daily work.					
15. The project can be completed quickly in less than 4 hours of my time.				✔	
16. The project is well within my scope of work.					✔
17. The project is customer focused.		✔			
18. The project is process focused and not people focused.					✔
19. The project does not require a value stream map.					✔
20. The project root cause is known.					✔

Total: 80

Susan's score of 80 indicated that this type of project would be worth the time and effort.

Susan reviewed her daily planner and documented the following:

Pre-Wiki Kaizen Event Metrics (first two weeks)

❖ Having information requested by her manager (which means it was late): 5 times
❖ Being late for a meeting: 4 times (as defined by not being there at exactly the start time)
❖ Having vendors calling and requiring a new contract (missing commitment when contract was due): 4 times

Susan wanted to understand her "wastes" to further relate to the current continuous improvement teams. She identified the following:

Overprocessing – creating and then discarding the physical Post-It Notes as they were just "reminders"
Excessive queue times – not having information to her manager when it was needed
Rework (defects) – arriving to a meeting late and having to be brought up-to-speed
Excessive motion - having to stop in the middle of something, save the file, and then find a new contract to get to the vendor

Lacy's Part 2. PDCA Implementation Phase (spans 1 - 2 weeks)

Susan decided to learn the Desktop application version of Post-It Notes, as she referred to as a visual control. She needed to sync her iPhone app with her Desktop so she would have one comprehensive time management tool to keep her on schedule. The following benefits of using an app such as this were:

- ❖ Increased productivity by using a smart note taking software that helps you organize and control your daily tasks and events
- ❖ Increased efficiency by having all information at your fingertips (documents, links, etc.) customized to set quick reminders to ensure what gets scheduled gets done.
- ❖ Increased communications by allowing you to automatically send notes to colleagues as well as share ideas via the Internet.

After the first two weeks on the job, putting out fires, and getting an understanding of what was required in the position, Susan decided to stay late one evening. Typically she worked until about 7:00 pm, but that night she had committed to going paperless in her scheduling of work and priorities. Susan had acquired a Post-It Note application on a 30-day free trial. The following are the PDCA activities that comprised her mini or "Wiki" Kaizen Event:

- ❖ All Sales and Customer Service meetings were created as two groups, each color-coded
- ❖ Alarms were set for all meetings, to notify her 5 minutes prior to any meeting.
- ❖ All appropriate spreadsheets and files were noted in the note portion of the new Post-It Note
- ❖ No more than 10 Post-It Notes would be visible at one time to ensure her Desktop computer screen would not be over-crowded with icons.
- ❖ All Notes were considered critical activities which included meetings, report deadlines, manager's requesting a due date for information, etc.

The following screen shot is an example of Susan's Post-It Note application:

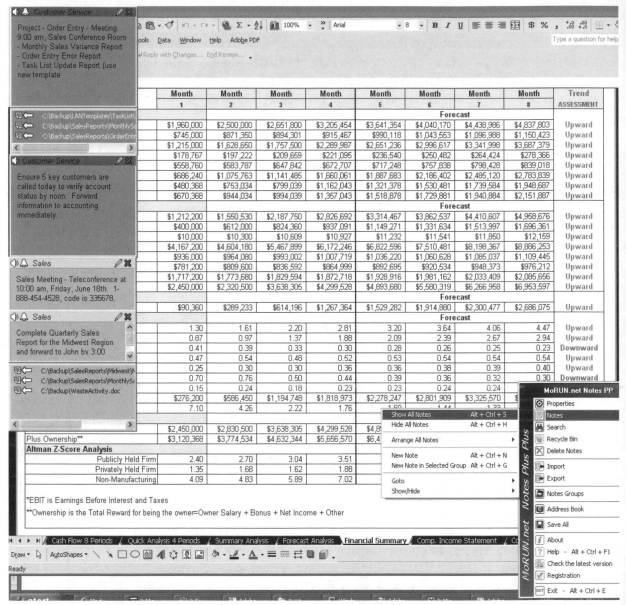

After two weeks of using the new app, Susan kept track of these improvements:

Post-Wiki Kaizen Event Metrics (second two weeks)

- ❖ Having information requested by her manager: 1 time (80% improvement)
- ❖ Being late for a meeting: 0 times (as defined by not being there at exactly the start time) (400% improvement)
- ❖ Having vendors calling and requiring a new contract: 1 time (75% improvement)

Additionally, Susan knew that creating standards were part of any Lean initiative; Susan's standards for this app were:

- ❖ Spend 5 minutes at the end of the morning and 5-10 minutes at the end of the day and update Notes accordingly
- ❖ Update Addresses for the email option once a week

Lacy's Part 3. Sharing Phase (spans 1 - 2 weeks)

Susan contacted the marketing department who was responsible for publishing inter-company information on their web site. She provided them with this Lean case study with the focus on how visual controls can be used in a Lean project. She summarized the following benefits of visual controls:

- ❖ Enhances employee attentiveness to what is the process requirement
- ❖ Provides guidance on what "to" do, and what "not" to do, as well as "how" to self-detect errors and self-correct them
- ❖ Builds process capability that "embeds" critical knowledge and information into processes that reduce business risk
- ❖ Reduces the reliance on a small number of resident experts who retain a disproportionate amount of knowledge about critical business processes and work flows
- ❖ Reduces rework
- ❖ Reduces data entry errors
- ❖ Improves quality
- ❖ Improves work throughput

Susan, after using this new app, found her job much more rewarding and subsequently was getting out of the office by 6:00 pm each day. The new application, along with her willingness to change, allowed her to have control of this new job as well as begin to enjoy her work again. Once her success story was published, she had over 20 emails from her colleagues commenting on how they too now have taken up initiatives to improve their work flow.

Note: The example in this case study used the MoRun.net application. Other ones can be found at:
http://www.sticky-notes.net/
http://www.veign.com/application.php?appid=102
http://notes.aklabs.com/
http://msdn.microsoft.com/en-us/library/aa480731.aspx
http://www.zhornsoftware.co.uk/stickies/
http://www.conceptworld.com/qnp/
http://windows.microsoft.com/en-us/windows7/products/features/sticky-notes

Many of the applications have similar functions and offer a 30 day FREE trial. Determine your business needs and select one of the many types that are in the market. Any of them will most likely improve your work productivity!

Wiki

Case Study for the San Francisco Bay Liners on Work Load Balancing

The business of sports is a multi-billion dollar global industry propelled by enormous consumer demand. The San Francisco Bay Liners is a professional hockey team that has an excellent loyal and active fan base. This team has been around for over 56 years. The Bay Liners, being a very popular team and having a solid financial foundation, and not having any need to change processes for the past 10 years, has a lot of waste going unnoticed.

The employees in the accounting department have been working together for many years. They have their systems and particular way of working to get things done and are not very receptive to new ideas. You could say they were stuck in their ways – nothing seemed broken, so why fix it (was the prevailing attitude). Their attitude was, as long as the organization was profitable, they must be doing things right. However, there was an ongoing issue within the Accounting department. Throughout the day some employees were waiting on others to get work turned into them before they could get their work done for the day (or week). This had forced many employees to work overtime on a regular basis.

Lindsey is a new employee and the youngest account representative in the accounting department. She had just replaced another employee, Greg, who was recently promoted due to his hard work (noted by his overtime commitment throughout the past few years). Lindsey had just graduated from college and was very excited to be in the work force. She had many new ideas, was eager to please, and had a lot of energy to make things happen. She had one of her senior level classes on business performance and had a conceptual knowledge of Lean and Six Sigma.

San Francisco Bay Liners Part 1. Determination Phase (spans 1 - 2 days)

Feeling very overwhelmed on this being her first job, she found herself constantly having to work overtime, well past 5:00 pm many days. Wanting to make a good impression she did not complain, but also was thinking of ways to eliminate this overtime since there are times throughout the day that there was not enough to do. Lindsey was not the only one doing this particular job, and knowing she did not want to offend anyone, struggled with how to work to eliminate or better balance her work load throughout the day to reduce or eliminate the overtime. She was not sure how others in the department would accept these ideas.

Lindsey reviewed one of her college textbooks, *The Lean Six Sigma Pocket Guide XL* and focused on the Employee Balance Chart. Even though that particular example dealt with multiple people balancing work within a group, Lindsey found no reason it could not be applied to her. And, it was a good visual to show the processes that comprise her day relative to the amount of time in a day.

The main problem that Lindsey has was there were certain days that projects had to get finished. Scanning was a job that could only be done on Tuesdays and Thursdays. This also happened to be the same day that Bank Reconciliations were completed. This forced Lindsey to work at least two hours overtime that day. The only good part was that Fridays she had less work to complete. Working overtime every Tuesday and Thursday left Mondays, Wednesdays, and Fridays with two hours of waiting around for other employee's work. This was a very large waste since she still had to be in the office during this time. Lindsey was able to take a lot of breaks during the day and felt her time was being wasted. She spoke to the person whose job she had taken over and he said that she should be happy with the free time and just work the overtime because the money was good. Lindsey knew that the overtime Greg had worked was probably not necessary.

Another important concept about Lean and Six Sigma was data collection and measurements. Lindsey knew that whatever changes she would propose required solid data. Therefore, Lindsey collected data on the following:

Pre-Wiki Kaizen Event Metrics (first two weeks)

* On average, time spent updating daily cash roll forward: 55 minutes
* On average time spent updating credit card deposits: 55 minutes
* On average time spent updating sponsorship folder and Excel spreadsheet: 75 minutes
* On average time spent updating suite folder and Excel spreadsheet: 75 minutes
* On average time spent scanning: 240 minutes
* On average time spent filing: 30 minutes
* On average time spent doing cash deposits: 75 minutes
* On average time spent checking others work: 150 minutes
* On average time spent completing bank reconciliations: 660 minutes
* On average time spent in meeting: 120 minutes
* On average time spent waiting around doing nothing: 360 minutes

The following spreadsheet is a representation of this data:

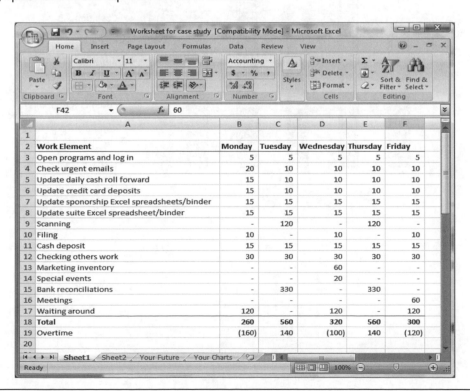

Work Element	Monday	Tuesday	Wednesday	Thursday	Friday
Open programs and log in	5	5	5	5	5
Check urgent emails	20	10	10	10	10
Update daily cash roll forward	15	10	10	10	10
Update credit card deposits	15	10	10	10	10
Update sponorship Excel spreadsheets/binder	15	15	15	15	15
Update suite Excel spreadsheet/binder	15	15	15	15	15
Scanning	-	120	-	120	-
Filing	10	-	10	-	10
Cash deposit	15	15	15	15	15
Checking others work	30	30	30	30	30
Marketing inventory	-	-	60	-	-
Special events	-	-	20	-	-
Bank reconciliations	-	330	-	330	-
Meetings	-	-	-	-	60
Waiting around	120	-	120	-	120
Total	260	560	320	560	300
Overtime	(160)	140	(100)	140	(120)

Lindsey wanted to relate the "wastes" she identified to her work processes. She identified the following:

❖ Excessive motion and Waiting - having to stop in the middle of an Excel spreadsheet, save the file, and contact the employee to get the needed information
❖ Unevenness – appearing that some employees get comparable work done throughout the day while others have to work overtime
❖ Overprocessing – entering the same data in multiple spreadsheets (i.e., documents that were scanned, daily cash roll forward, credit card deposits, etc.)

The typical workday for Lindsey was 8 hours or 480 minutes. But, subtracting meetings, breaks, etc. she decided that 400 minutes was reasonable. Lindsey created the following current state Employee Balance Chart with 400 minutes being her performance goal for each day throughout the week. She did not consider this a takt time, which was how the Chart was explained in the book, but adapted the concept to her situation.

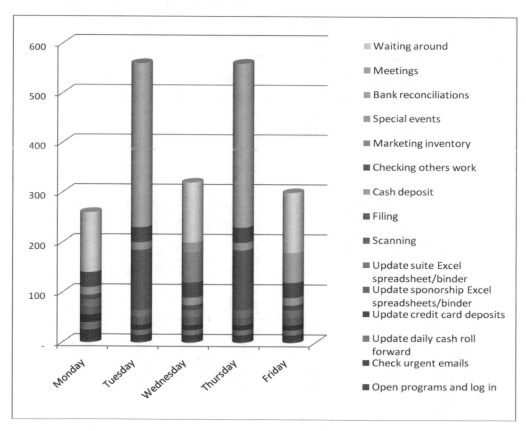

San Francisco Bay Liners Part 2. PDCA Implementation Phase (spans 1 - 2 weeks)

To save time, Lindsey combined the Excel files for daily cash roll forward, credit card deposits, sponsorship, and suites into one workbook. Prior to this, each of these files had three or four different Excel files all representing the same information which was updated individually.

She also condensed the Excel spreadsheet for credit card deposits to just one spreadsheet instead of four different ones as well as combining the spreadsheets for daily case roll forward to just one. She no longer had to click between different spreadsheets to input the data. Using four different Excel spreadsheets just for credit card deposits and two different Excel spreadsheets for daily cash roll forward was a big waste of time!

Lindsey was also responsible to check or verify other's work. This was part of her job because each Excel spreadsheet had two employees assigned to ensure accuracy. Lindsey had specific times that she would check other's work. This allowed others to know exactly when she was available to check their work and allowed her to get out of the office on-time on those busy Tuesdays and Thursdays. This also cut out some of her waiting time when she would be waiting on others to get her files. Previously, Lindsey would spend 150 minutes a week and now she only has to spend 110 minutes a week. The 40 minutes that she eliminated came from not having to wait on co-workers along with less non-related work conversations when employees would come to her desk.

Lindsey also started taking two days to complete the bank reconciliations. She "pulled" forward some of the work to eliminate overtime on Tuesdays and Thursdays. This work included printing off all necessary Excel spreadsheets, finding all the checks, tickets, and lunch money on the bank reconciliation. Bank Reconciliations only needed to be turned in once a week by Friday at five. Since it was the previous week's reconciliations, and as long as Lindsey had everything else completed on time, it did not matter what she "pulled" forward.

At the weekly Friday meeting each employee would discuss where they were with closing their books. The meetings last at least an hour. It was more of a social event and not a lot was discussed. Now with the help of the creating a Meeting Agenda with designated times for each person, the meetings now only run 45 minutes on Friday, if that!

Post-Wiki Kaizen Event Metrics (second two weeks)

- ❖ On average, time spent updating daily cash roll forward: 30 minutes
- ❖ On average time spent updating credit card deposits: 30 minutes
- ❖ On average time spent updating sponsorship folder and Excel spreadsheet: 45 minutes
- ❖ On average time spent updating suite folder and Excel spreadsheet: 45 minutes
- ❖ On average time spent scanning: 240 minutes
- ❖ On average time spent filing: 30 minutes
- ❖ On average time spent doing cash deposits: 75 minutes
- ❖ On average time spent checking others work: 110 minutes
- ❖ On average time spent completing bank reconciliations: 660 minutes
- ❖ On average time spent in meeting: 120 minutes
- ❖ On average time spent waiting on others turned into time for other projects: 390 minutes

The following spreadsheet is a representation of this data:

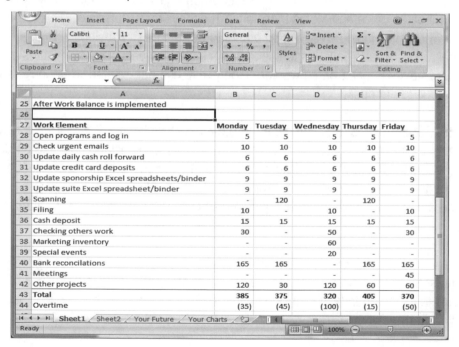

Work Element	Monday	Tuesday	Wednesday	Thursday	Friday
Open programs and log in	5	5	5	5	5
Check urgent emails	10	10	10	10	10
Update daily cash roll forward	6	6	6	6	6
Update credit card deposits	6	6	6	6	6
Update sponorship Excel spreadsheets/binder	9	9	9	9	9
Update suite Excel spreadsheet/binder	9	9	9	9	9
Scanning	-	120	-	120	-
Filing	10	-	10	-	10
Cash deposit	15	15	15	15	15
Checking others work	30	-	50	-	30
Marketing inventory	-	-	60	-	-
Special events	-	-	20	-	-
Bank reconcilations	165	165	-	165	165
Meetings	-	-	-	-	45
Other projects	120	30	120	60	60
Total	385	375	320	405	370
Overtime	(35)	(45)	(100)	(15)	(50)

The following future state Employee Balance Chart represents the times relative to the goal of 400 minutes.

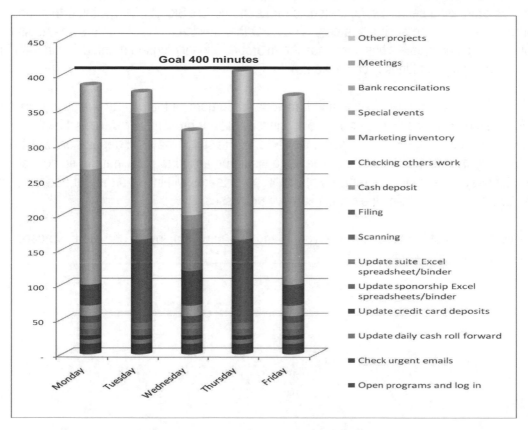

San Francisco Bay Liners Part 3. Sharing Phase (spans 1 - 2 weeks)

Lindsey now had to decide how to explain Greg's unnecessary overtime to the CFO, to whom Lindsey reported. After using the Lean tool for two weeks and seeing the improvements, Lindsey decided to set up a meeting with the CFO to explain her improvements. She was worried about this meeting since she was new and did not want to create any hard feelings with Greg. However, Lindsey knew the company hired her for the new ideas and knowledge that she could bring to the table.

At the meeting with the CFO Lindsey showed the pre- and post-Lean spreadsheets. The CFO probably realized that Greg did not need to put in the overtime he had and may not have known any better. (Appropriately, there was no discussion about Greg at the meeting). The CFO realized that even though they were a profitable organization, waste should always be eliminated. The CFO commended Lindsey on her initiative and stated that this is the way everyone must think throughout the organization. Even though times are good now, they will more likely stay that way if these types of improvements can be made. The CFO asked Lindsey to prepare a 10 minute presentation for the monthly departmental meeting.

Wiki

The organization did not have a continuous improvement or training department, however, on the functional order chart, it fell under Human Resources. The CFO contacted the Human Resources department to find out if they had any resources or useful materials on Lean and Six Sigma. They stated that there was no current program and had no such resources. The CFO then decided to implement some additional Lean and Six Sigma tools and create a business case for an organizational program (hoping that in 6 – 12 months that may be something that Lindsey can head up).

The CFO had their next monthly meeting and had Today's Burgers as the caterer, which was recently featured on Man versus Food cable television show. Lindsey did her presentation, followed by the CFO passing out *The Lean Six Sigma Pocket Guide XL* for everyone. He stated that their department was to establish a Continuous Improvement Team and that everyone would be asked to participate in some fashion in the near-term. Lindsey also provided examples of other sports teams within the area that had success using Lean and Six Sigma to streamline their administrative processes.

Lindsey realized that just because she was young and the "new" employee, she did have good ideas for making the company run Leaner!

Case Study for Tri-Star Cablevision on Process Mapping, Error Proofing, and Histograms

Tri-Star Cablevision was founded in November 1997 in Chicago, Illinois. After completing a network build in June 1999, Tri-Star initially served about 22,000 people in the Chicago area. In August 2000, CableOne, an overbuilt system in the Midwest built and operated by West Channel Media, Inc., was purchased by Tri-Star for an undisclosed amount per subscriber, estimated to have been at a cost of $1,000 per subscriber. This purchase opened Tri-Star to over 310,000 new customers in areas surrounding the cities of Chicago, Detroit, Denver, Cleveland, and Columbus. Tri-Star currently provides service in the metropolitan areas of Detroit, Chicago, Columbus, Cleveland, and Indianapolis.

Beside subscriber fees, Tri-Star relies heavily on advertising from both local and national advertisers wishing to reach the lucrative markets it serves. Tri-Star has a local sales team in each market it serves as well as a national sales force.

Advertising is a perishable commodity. If a commercial is supposed to air at 8 pm on Monday night and due to a scheduling error it does not, the sale is lost. Sometimes an advertiser will allow a make-good commercial to be scheduled to make up for the missed commercial. However, because most commercials are used to support a sale or special event, action has to be taken quickly to make sure the sale is not lost for good.

Bob Dale, the sales manager of Tri-Star Cablevision has always joked that selling cable advertising was a little like selling air. It was intangible. You couldn't touch it or feel it and once the time passed it was gone forever and you could not get it back. He had to coordinate the sales people who sold the commercials, the production people who produced the commercials or got them ready to air, and the scheduling people who were responsible for scheduling each commercial in the right time slot to meet the advertiser's requirements.

Tri-Star Cablevision Part 1. Determination Phase (spans 1 - 2 days)

Bob had just received the Exception Report (next page) for the month of April. It listed all the commercials that for some reason or another did not run in their proper time slots and the advertiser refused to pay for them. There are four categories in the Exception Report where an error could prevent a commercial from running as it was ordered. The first category was "Wrong Commercial." This is where the commercial that was played was not the commercial that was intended to be played. In most cases, this was due to the fact that the commercial was mislabeled with the wrong number. The Second category was "No Commercial." This is where there was no commercial available for the control room to run. This could be due to the Production Department not getting the commercial into the control room by the time it was supposed to run. It could also happen if there was a communication breakdown between the Sales and Production Departments in getting the information correctly distributed. The next category was "Mis-scheduling." This can happen when the Production Department, which is responsible for scheduling the commercial at the time the advertiser ordered it, does not schedule it properly. The final category is "Technical Malfunction." This happens when there is an equipment breakdown and the commercial does not play properly.

		Exception Report For April		
Week of	Technical Malfunction	Mis-scheduling	No Commercial	Wrong Commercial
4-Apr	4	37	2	20
11-Apr	6	29	3	18
18-Apr	3	31	1	25
25-Apr	5	36	4	19
Total	18	133	10	82

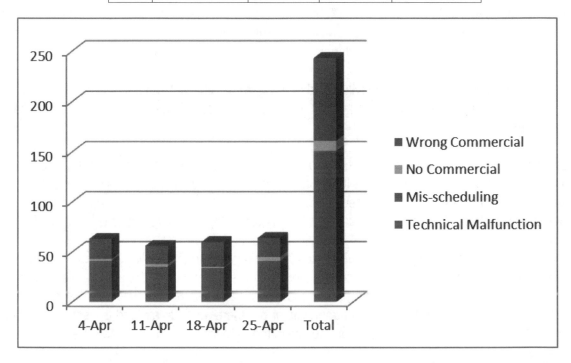

This problem had become an increasingly larger problem over the last several months. The company was losing large amounts of money on commercials that were sold but never ran due to internal errors (i.e., communications) within and between the Sales and Production Departments. He had to find out why these errors were happening and quickly correct the problem. Bob believed that the fixes were fairly simple and did not require a cross-functional team. He submitted a Wiki Colleague Request to solicit assistance from one person in Sales and one person in Production. The following is his Wiki Colleague Request form.

Kaizen Event	Wiki Colleague Request

Sales

Name:	Bob	Department:	Sales
Upstream Supplier:	Sales	Downstream Customer:	Production/Scheduling

The Wiki Colleague Request is to be used when requesting "light" assistance from a colleague to help provide a solution to a problem or implement an improvement. This improvement or solution should also benefit the colleague directly or indirectly and not require any significant amount of their time or resources (less than an hour or two).

Step 1: Describe the Problem or Opportunity. Include photos, charts, and graphs, if necessary. Include current measurements.

Problem Viewed by Initiator	Type of Waste
Commercials that for some reason or another did not run in their proper time slots and the advertiser refused to pay for them.	Defects, Delays, Overprocessing

Problem Viewed by Colleague (Perceived)	Type of Waste (Perceived)
Scheduling - traffic orders incomplete	Defects
Production - incomplete information from Sales and duplicate info	Defects

Proposed Start Date: 6/2

Step 2: List Potential Benefits. Be specific in terms of how the team's success will be measured. Use Balance Scorecard measures, if possible.

Benefits for Initiator (WIIFM)	Benefits for Colleague (Perceived) (WIIFT)
Sales - Improved revenue from sales	Production - Higher %correct commercials run
Sales - Less make-good runs	Scheduling - Less errors in running commericals

Proposed End Date: 6/9

Step 3: List Resources Required. Include support needed from Colleague. Be specific in terms of technical expertise, departmental cooperation as a trial, etc.

Type of Support	Estimated Hours Needed	Dates Requested
Production Assistant	4 hours - 1 hour increments	6/3,6/4,6/5,6/9
Scheduler (days)	4 hours - 1 hour increments	6/3,6/4,6/5,6/9

Step 4: Determine Feasibility and Next Steps.

☐ Agree As Is

☐ Need More Information Before Agreeing

☐ Currently Being Addressed

☐ Suggest To Formalize As A Team Type Kaizen Event

Sign-Off Date: _____

Once submitted by Bob, the V.P. of Sales immediately signed-off by calling Bob and said that he liked the aggressive schedule. He also stated to let him know if there is anything he could do.

Wiki

Bob and the two colleagues reviewed their current process map.

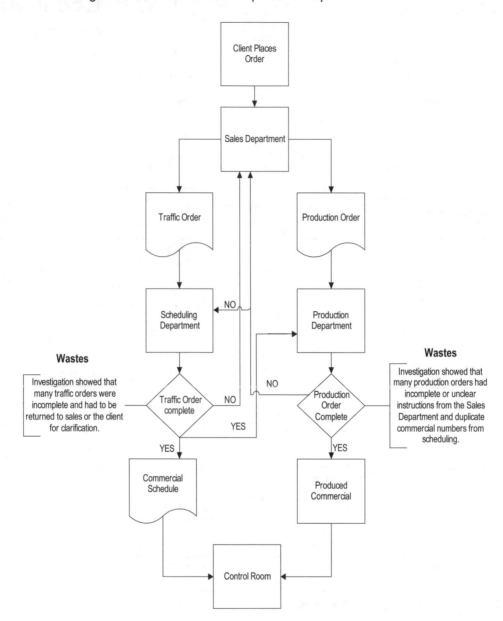

The overall process for getting a commercial on the air is as follows:

The process for the Sales Department is:

- ❖ Sales representatives call upon local and regional advertisers to get advertising dollars.
- ❖ Once an order is placed, the sales representative must enter the information about the number of commercials, time of day, start date and end date and into the traffic order part of the system. This provides information to the Scheduling Department.
- ❖ The sales representative takes information from the client/advertiser on what they would like to be in the commercial and fill-out a production order for the production department to produce the commercial. In some cases the advertiser may have a commercial already produced by an advertising agency or another production source. The Sales Department will turn in this commercial with the production order.

The process for the Scheduling Department is:

- ❖ A scheduler will take the information off the traffic order generated by the Sales Department and schedule the commercials in the proper time-slots and days to meet the advertiser's request. If there are inconsistencies or missing information in the traffic order, they will send it back to the Sales Department for correction.
- ❖ The Sales Department will then generate a number that represents the commercial to be run for that advertiser and send it to the Production Department to put on the advertiser's commercial so the right commercial will run at the right time.
- ❖ The Production Department will then generate a traffic log with all the programs and commercials listed in the proper time slots that will be used in the control room that day to run the day's programming.

The process for the Production Department is:

- ❖ A production assistant will take the production order from the Sales Department and produce the commercial to air for specified advertiser.
- ❖ Once the production assistant receives the advertiser number from the Scheduling Department they will place it on the commercial so the control room runs the right commercial at the right time. If there is a conflict in a number they receive from the Scheduling Department and a number they already have they will contact Scheduling.

As Bob looked at the process, he determined that there was a lot of waste. There was wasted time in chasing down information that was left off traffic and production orders. Also, the Production Department spent a lot of time insuring proper numbers got on the right commercials. There was also the waste of duplicating information from one department to another.

The following "wastes" were identified:

- ❖ Overprocessing - the constant entering of customer information into the various fields of the Production and Sales Department programs
- ❖ Defects - numbers were different from the Scheduling to the Production Departments (lack of standards, data entry errors, double-entry, etc.)
- ❖ Transport - constantly email or walking over to the department to get information that was not on the traffic order
- ❖ Lost revenue (not traditionally defined as a waste as it is a financial result of all the wastes) - $64,500

The biggest waste, of course, was the lost revenue for missed commercials. For the month of April a total of 243 commercials did not run as scheduled. At an average cost of $325 per commercial that was a potential loss of $78,975. As Bob checked further, he found out that $14,325 of the total was re-scheduled for the advertisers in make-goods. That left $64,500 of lost revenue for the month of April due to this problem.

Tri-Star Cablevision Part 2. PDCA Implementation Phase (spans 1 - 2 weeks)

The vast majority of errors in the process were due to errors in communicating information. Most were in entering data into the various Sales and Production Department systems, including leaving critical information blank.

They decided to error-proof the process of transferring information in the scheduling and production of commercials by implementing the following PDCAs.

1. The sales representatives were to use specially designed software and tablet application to fill-out their traffic orders. The software prevented them from submitting the traffic order until all fields in the form were filled-out. This prevented them from forgetting to include important information.
2. Instead of having the Scheduling Department assign a random number to identify the advertiser for the traffic log and Production Department, the software automatically generated an ID number that included both letters and numbers to uniquely identify the advertiser.
3. The production order is now generated in the same manner as the traffic order. The software prevented the form from being submitted without completing each field in the form.
4. Both the traffic order and the production order were submitted electronically with all the information being automatically distributed to the proper department and automatically inserted into corresponding software that they use to schedule and produce the commercials.

The team had met for their four hours during the week, however, additional time was required due to the extensive software changes that needed to be coordinated with IT. No one had a problem with the extra time as it proved to be a worthy project for the departments.

Tri-Star Cablevision Part 3. Sharing Phase (spans 1 - 2 weeks)

It took Bob a month to implement the changes he wanted in the scheduling and production processes. However, when the June exception report came out all his work was justified. The errors due to the miscommunication of information had been reduced dramatically. The following is the data table and Histogram for the month of June:

	Exception Report - June			
	Technical Malfunction	Mis-scheduling	No Commercial	Wrong Commercial
5-Jun	3	3	2	2
12-Jun	5	2	2	1
19-Jun	2	3	3	2
26-Jun	3	3	1	2
Total	13	11	8	7

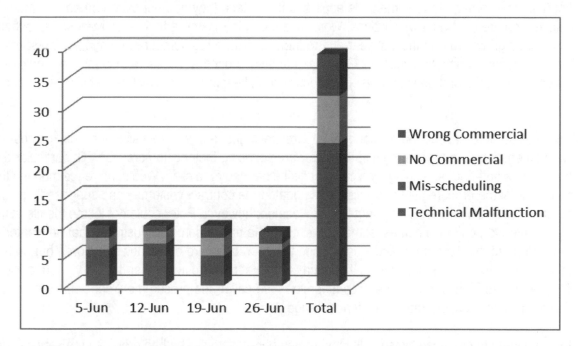

Bob conveyed to the V.P. the Histogram above as well as lost revenue for the month of June was less than $5,000. The V.P. rewarded Bob, as well as the two other members working on this project, with an extra day off anytime in July.

Case Study for Greybeck, Inc. on 5S

Greybeck, Inc. specializes in the procurement of products and services for companies where these services and products are outside their area of expertise and normal channel of procurement responsibility. The business is complex, with a diverse client base and a vast network of suppliers and contacts. Their success is solely due to their ability to find the exact products and services their customers need and deliver it quickly to them. This meant that they needed a vast network of suppliers all around the world in almost every type of industry. The products and services ranged from supplying latex products to distributors in the U.S. to providing accounting solutions to customers in Asia.

Greybeck, Inc. has a large number of procurement specialists to negotiate the best contract for their clients in providing these goods and services. There was nothing fancy or proprietary about their software. They used Windows 7 and Microsoft Office for most of their communication and organization informational needs, expecting this year to migrate to some table applications. In fact, they had not even tapped into many of the advanced features of Windows, Outlook, Word, and Excel to maximize their effectiveness. Greybeck, Inc. has recently grown 10% in the last year due to the increase in the number of companies outsourcing their specialty needs, which was good for Greybeck but also caused additional stress for the employees. This was especially true for those that worked in procurement, keeping track of all Greybeck's customer and client files.

Peter Straub is the International Sales Manager for Greybeck, Inc. and is responsible for their key customers as well as ensuring the procurement specialists were servicing their customers. On this particular day, Peter had spent a half-hour searching for a contract file he needed for a client Web conference meeting that afternoon. One of the procurement specialists had updated the contract yesterday and supposedly placed it in the shared directory where all the client files are located; however, Peter could not locate the file at this time, given the hundreds of file names, some very similar. He had become so frustrated that he wanted to throw his laptop out the third story window. He used the search feature of Windows Explorer, but he now was not sure what drive it was on, thinking that it may have been saved in another directory. And, once he found it, he wondered if it was the most recent version. He called the procurement specialist but he was away at a training session, so Peter just left a message.

Peter took a minute to compose himself. He had remembered last year he had procured the services of a Lean consultant for one of his clients. This client wanted to eliminate the waste in their processes from their front office through the shop floor and out the back door through shipping. The client had called and was very frustrated about all the mistakes and inefficiencies that were causing significant problems with their quality and on-time-delivery metrics. Greybeck, Inc. provided this client with a Lean business consultant with a manufacturing and accounting background. This client was pleased with the results with a 12% increase in productivity and a 18% savings in costs (reduced scrap, improved quality, and less paperwork being generated). Peter wondered if the same principles could be applied to improve the efficiency of a business like Greybeck, which was so dependent on the flow of electronic information. Peter had called his client to touch base with him and further gain information on how their company was doing. After a ten minute discussion Peter had explained his immediate problem to this client and the client was first to suggest that the Lean tool of 5S be diligently applied to Greybeck's files and folders.

With this advice and a returned call from the procurement specialist, Peter found that the file had been renamed to reflect this particular specialist's file naming convention. Upon questioning the procurement specialist about the name change, Peter learned that this was how all of the files were named. This file had originally been worked on by Peter, so the procurement specialist knew no better. Peter knew that with the increase in business and the procurement specialists working more as a work-group, this could pose a significant problem in the near future. Peter obtained the file and had it for his meeting with the client. The deal with the client was sealed, but it also allowed Peter to "see" an opportunity for improvement.

Greybeck, Inc. Part 1. Determination Phase (spans 1 - 2 days)

Peter purchased *The 5S Desktop (PC) Pocket Handbook* which gave him additional insights into organizing his Desktop files and folders. Even though many files were on the shared directory Peter decided to apply these principles to his Desktop and C: drive files. This would be used as the example that he could then share with the group. At that time he would establish a team and go through the same five steps.

Peter decided to track the amount of time he had to search for files. If a change throughout the department was to occur, he wanted the "What's In It For Me?" question answered, with data. For two weeks, Peter collected the following measurements from only the files he had on his Desktop (these were files that eventually were placed on the shared J: drive, but were work-in-progress):

Pre-Wiki Kaizen Event Metrics (first two weeks)

- ❖ Number of times using Windows Explorer searching for files: 18
- ❖ Number of minutes spent searching for files: 112 minutes

The following "wastes" were identified:

- ❖ Defects – file and folder names not known causing file version problems
- ❖ Excessive queue times – not having information when it was needed
- ❖ Excessive motion – calling someone to obtain the file name or file location to ensure it was the most recent one

Greybeck, Inc. Part 2. PDCA Implementation Phase (spans 1 - 2 weeks)

Peter diligent spent each day incorporating each step of the 5S process.

Sort

Peter used Windows Explorer to Sort for just Billing files from these folders.

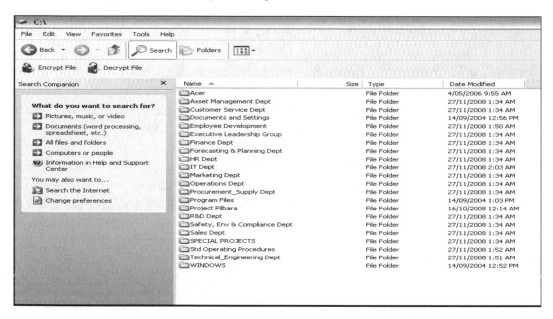

Peter had become efficient in using Windows Explorer to search for files using the available options. He proceeded to create a folder just for Billing. He also did this for other main topics.

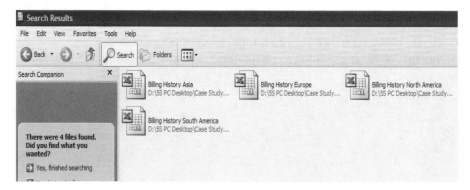

Peter also had access and rights to the J: drive that was used for old reports, presentations, etc. Peter decided also to apply the Sort phase to that drive. The following is the before file structure.

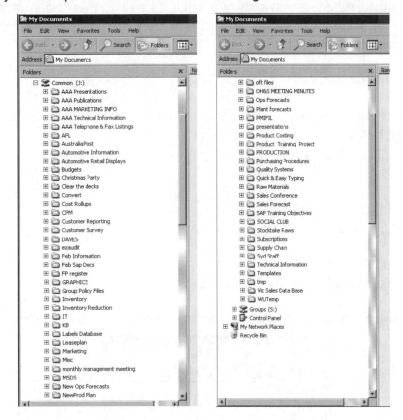

Note the following issues with the J: drive.

- ❖ In excess of 60 individual file names
- ❖ Many folder names are meaningless to anyone but the creator/user, such as "KB", "oft files", and many more
- ❖ Users have typed the letters "AAA" in front of the folder name to ensure it appears at the top of the Explorer screen
- ❖ Both business and personal folders in the shared directory
- ❖ Folders named after specific user names
- ❖ Different folder names for different revision levels (e.g., "Ops Forecast" and "New Ops Forecast")
- ❖ Different folder names for the same activity (e.g., "Inventory" and "Inventory Reduction")
- ❖ Files over 12 months old that have never been archived or deleted
- ❖ Files/folders created and accessed only once
- ❖ Lack of standardized naming conventions for files
- ❖ Lack of any organizational standards or naming convention for folders by department/division/activity

Set-In-Order

Peter developed a standardized naming system/convention for all his files, folders, and directories in Outlook and Explorer. He would later use this as a basis for gaining a consensus with the work group for a similar-type file naming convention.

The following were the standards:

Client: - First four characters of the customer name – "BedR" (as used in the ERP system)
Project Name – "MillerAcq"
Document Name – "FixedAssetChicago"
Document Type – "val"
Revision - "1.1"
Date Created – "010312"
Author's Name (initials) - "jwc"

Which translated into the following file name.
BedR_MillerAcq_FixedAssetChicago_val1.1_010312_jwc.doc

Peter, using the above Set-In-Order conventions, applied them to the J: drive as shown below.

Note the following:

❖ Key departments by name
❖ Over 60 folders have either been deleted, archived, or stored as sub folders
❖ The ability to create folder names has been restricted to the IT Dept only, with formal written requests required to create new folders
❖ Visibility of folders is now limited or restricted

Shine (or Scrub)

As Peter worked through the first 2 S's the first couple of days, he started to understand how easy it was for your computer Desktop to get cluttered and steal productive time from your daily tasks. It was just like a virus; you did not notice it until it was too late. Peter thought that waste was like a computer virus; it was more deadly than many other computer viruses and yet people did not even realize they were infected.

Standardize

Peter realized that he was reasonably sure he could get his department to buy into the Lean concept of 5S. It made too much sense just to be dismissed. But, getting people to buy into an idea intellectually was much different than actually getting behavioral change. He knew people did not like to change the way they do things. They get comfortable and change makes them feel vulnerable. He knew he was going to have to make them see that being a little vulnerable for the short-term was worth it for the long-term benefits they would get. Things like reduced stress, more time, less pressure, and increased productivity with less effort. In order to accomplish that he had to standardize everything and make sure everybody knew the standards. This would also help him evaluate what was working and what was not so they could make improvements and change the parts of the process that were not working that well.

Sustain

Peter knew from experience, even if he implemented the first four S's successfully it would ultimately fail if he could not implement the last phase of Sustain effectively.

Peter also knew that he would have to develop a system for employees to make suggestions on ways to improve the process once he got everyone involved. They most likely would not follow the standards if they believed they were written in stone. There had to be a quick and flexible way to change the standards if a better way was found.

Greybeck, Inc. Part 3. Sharing Phase (spans 1 - 2 weeks)

All in all, this had been a very productive week for Peter. He could envision massive improvements in productivity just through the principles of 5S with his work group (and organization). Hopefully, this would lead to the implementation of other Lean tools in his business. After all, 5S was just one of many Lean tools! After implementing 5S for his Desktop and the J: drive, Peter collected the following data for an additional two week period:

Post-Wiki Kaizen Event Metrics (second two weeks)

- ❖ Number of times using Windows Explorer searching for files: 2 (90% reduction)
- ❖ Number of minutes spent searching for files: 8 minutes (86% reduction

Peter created a 5S team for his sales team, shared his results, and took his department through the 5 steps as he just had done.

Sensei Tips

Note: Many of the following Sensei Tips can be used or applied in the other Kaizen Events, where and when appropriate.

- ❖ As a supervisor or manager, work with your group and create guidelines and/or standards allowing employees to attain ownership of their processes.
- ❖ If a large number employees are working on similar processes, begin to assign ownership to those processes. Create appropriate flowcharts, standard cycle times, review dates, etc. for each process.
- ❖ Ensure employees are trained on the various wastes.
- ❖ Allow employees to benchmark other departments or organizations that have similar issues or problems.
- ❖ Support employees to assist Wiki or other Kaizen Event types.
- ❖ Publish/post successes of Wiki Kaizen Events to let everyone know how simple and easy they can be (as well as any recognition or reward given). Success breeds success!
- ❖ Ensure all types of Kaizen Events eliminate some type of waste as well as there is a before and after metric.
- ❖ Work with employees to connect Wiki Kaizens to departmental measures or Balance Scorecard metrics (if at all possible). Many times these improvements may not have this type of impact.

Chapter 3. Lean Six Sigma Tools

The following are brief descriptions listed alphabetically of the common Lean and Six Sigma tools.

5 Why analysis allows organized brainstorming to methodically determine the causes of a problem (i.e., effect). Most often teams observe a symptom of the problem rather than the problem itself. Always ask "Why?" while arriving at the answer with data.

5S ensures physical areas and paper-based or electronic documents are systematically kept clean and organized. This assures employee safety in meeting customer expectations while providing the foundation to build a Lean Sigma organization. 5S provides an opportunity to involve all employees in the Lean Sigma process. 5S is a simple and common-sense approach to improving a process or work area. The five steps for 5S are:
Step 1 - Sort
Step 2 - Set-In-Order
Step 3 - Shine (or Scrub)
Step 4 – Standardize
Step 5 - Sustain

A3 Report is designed to help you "tell the story" in a logical and visual way with reference to a particular subject matter. The A3 refers to size 11" X 17" paper, however, in today's applications it can be any type of medium that is easily viewed. The main types of A3 Reports are: Continuous Improvement and Problem Solving (or Project), Status, Proposal, and Strategic (or Hoshin) Planning. The A3 Project Report was originally developed by Toyota to represent a problem or improvement initiative in the field with paper.

Brainstorming is used to generate a high volume of ideas with team members' full participation that is free of criticism and judgment within a 5 - 15 minute time period. In brainstorming, there is one cardinal rule: No idea is criticized!

Cause and Effect (or Fishbone) Diagram allows a team to graphically display and explore, in increasing detail, all the possible causes of a problem or issue. This assists the team in determining the true root cause(s). The problem or effect is identified on the head of the diagram, and brainstorming and/or other data collection techniques are used to identify and prioritize all possible causes. If done properly and completely, the cause(s) of the problem should be somewhere on the diagram. (A Fishbone Diagram can be used once the problem (i.e., effect) has been clearly defined.)

Charting is the process of making the most sense of the data. It is turning the "data" into useful information. Common charts are Pareto, Paynter, Pie, Run, Histogram, Bar, Control, Radar, and Scatter and Concentration.

Constraint or Bottleneck Analysis is the identification of the slowest process step(s) in the product or service being provided. It can be done in a number of ways and is commonly called the constraint or bottleneck for a process. If a VA versus NVA Analysis has been completed, the constraint is simply the slowest process step in the sequence. Consider additional reading on Theory of Constraints. A constraint or bottleneck will usually lead to a backup, delay, or added wait time. Applying a thorough analysis with subsequent improvements can help alleviate many of these constraints.

Continuous flow is when customer orders or demands are initiated and the process continues uninterrupted until the orders or demands are satisfied. Continuous flow is most successful when the following conditions exist:
* Order Urgency = High
* Order Pattern = Irregular or unpredictable
* Order Fulfillment Process = Predictable or standardized

Cross-training is used when one employee if required to do another employee's work. Cross-training applies to nearly every area of Lean Sigma implementations. The simplest way to manage cross-training is to complete a training matrix for the organization. The four levels of training that must be implemented for every member of the organization are:
1. Job description responsibility level
2. Improvement and problem solving tools training level
3. Next level job growth preparation level
4. Cross-training

Demand Analysis Plots identify customer demand in terms of transactions or needs over a given time period for non-repetitive goods or services. The historical or proposed current demand is plotted relative to a time period (i.e., one day, to one year, or season) or another variable depending on the type of good or service provided.

Effective meeting is an efficient use of people's time when they are gathered together working to obtain a desired result. Meetings, like any process, can be studied and improved upon. Meetings can be one of the most powerful business tools. While many decisions can be made by phone, email, or in hallway discussions, there will be other times that people will need to meet (in person or through Web conferencing) to gain a consensus on an issue or problem. It is when physical meetings occur that people need to be most efficient and effective.

Employee Balance Chart is a visual display, in the form of a bar chart, that represents work elements and cycle times relative to the total value stream cycle time and takt time (or pitch). Create a current and future Employee Balance Chart.

FIFO system is a work-controlled method which ensure the oldest work (i.e., electronic documents, supply items, etc.) upstream (first-in) is the first to be processed downstream (first-out). The team can be creative in establishing the signal method which is typically referred to as a Kanban within the FIFO system to ensure the work is processed as first-in is first-out (or serviced) to the next process.

Force Field Analysis is an extremely useful tool for understanding and illustrating the forces for and against an idea, direction, decision, or strategy. The logic behind this technique is that when change occurs there are always two sides to change: one side is proactive and is driving the change while the other side is resistant to change and preventing change from occurring.

Heijunka Leveling works to level or smooth flow by delivering goods and/or services in an alternating or patterned manner rather than large chunks of time.

Histogram utilizes data and displays the spread and shape of the distribution. Histograms are simple bar chart representations of the range, amount, and pattern of variation for data (i.e., the population).

Impact Map is a method by which a team can identify the solutions that will most likely have the greatest impact on the problem with the least effort. Opportunities and action ideas that have a high impact on the organization and are easily completed should take top implementation priority. Opportunities that have a high impact, but will take more time and effort to accomplish should be targeted next. Ideas that have little impact, but are easily completed should be done as time permits. Finally, projects or ideas that have a low potential impact on the organization and are difficult or expensive to implement could be considered at a later date. In summary, teams should reach a consensus on the EASE of implementation, as well as the IMPACT that it will have on the result.

Interrelationship Diagram is an analysis tool that allows a team to understand and identify the cause-and-effect relationships among critical issues. Interrelationship Diagrams are used to understand and illustrate the inputs, outputs, and relationships of key processes or data. They make it easy to identify the factors in a situation that drive the observed outcomes.

Kaizen Events, sometimes called "Rapid Improvement Events" or "Kaizen Blitzes" are targeted events conducted by improvement teams to implement improvements quickly in a specific area. Kaizen Events are comprised of the Planning, PDCA, and Follow-Up Phases.

Kanbans (pronounced Con – Bons) or "pull signals" are visual (or auditory, electronic, etc.) signals used to control flow and trigger action between processes. Pull signals can be used to identify a demand. Things such as a bar code, text message, service bell or alarm, containers, etc. can be used as this "signal." These "pull signals" help organizations deliver goods and services with minimal waste.

Layered Process Audits (LPA) is a system of process audits performed by multiple levels of workers, supervisors, and managers to monitor key process characteristics and verify process conformance on an ongoing basis. LPAs ensure that standard work methods are used and that processes are performing as expected to desired outcomes.

Lean Sigma Assessment and Gap Analysis creates an understanding of what may be some potential improvement opportunities as well as provides a baseline to compare with future improvement initiatives (and subsequent assessments). The Lean Sigma Assessment and Gap Analysis will align management objectives with employee needs, desires and attitudes towards change, open communications regarding issues and problems, and provide a perspective on where the organization needs to focus resources.

Managing change is the process of how to manage the way changes in the working environment are implemented and how to lessen its effect on the workforce. It is a key topic for leaders to understand. In today's fast paced world, change and improvement are required for an organization to survive. Improper management of change and/or natural resistance to change can cripple an organization.

Mass customization combines the low costs of mass production processes with the variable output required to meet individual customer needs. Some best examples of mass customization are fast food restaurants. Fast food restaurants combine a variety of products with standard processes and order combinations to allow their customers to determine choices on the spot with quick and efficient order/service request fulfillment.

Measurement System Analysis (MSA) is a specially designed experiment that seeks to identify the components of variation in the measurement system. Often measurements are made with little regard for the quality (accuracy) of such measurements. All too often, the measurements are not representative of the true value of the characteristic being measured. This might be because the measurement system is not accurate or precise enough which introduces bias into the measurement, or is not being used properly by the staff. Measurement System Analysis evaluates the test method, measuring instruments, and the entire process of obtaining measurements to ensure the integrity of data used for analysis and to understand the implications of measurement error for decisions made about a product or process. MSA is an important element of Six Sigma methodology and of other quality management systems.

Mistake proofing is a system designed to ensure that it is impossible to make a mistake or produce a defect. Mistake proofing is also known as error proofing. The Japanese name, poka-yoke, is derived from "poka" - inadvertent mistake and "yoke" - avoid. A poka-yoke device is any physical or electronic mechanism that prevents a mistake from being made or ensures that if a mistake is made it is obvious at a glance. Poka-yoke ensures subsequent actions from becoming defects. Defects are caused by process errors, equipment and material errors, and worker errors; defects are the results of those errors. Mistakes will not turn into defects if they are discovered and eliminated beforehand. Defects occur because of errors; the two have a cause-and-effect relationship. However, errors will not turn into defects if feedback and action takes place prior to the error stage. Visual controls can play a large role in reducing the opportunity for error occurrence, thereby ensuring that no defects result from the process.

Paced flow processing is used where customer order fulfillment tasks are done with regular frequency on timed schedule. Paced flow can be leveled by volume or process type. Paced flow is most successful when the following conditions exist:
- ❖ Order Urgency = Medium
- ❖ Order Pattern = Regular and predictable
- ❖ Order Fulfillment Process = Predicable or standardized

Pareto Chart uses a bar chart format and represents the Pareto principle which states that 20% of the sources cause 80% of the problems.

Paynter Chart is a visual representation over time relative to the subgroups based on Pareto Chart information. It is a further analysis of the bars of the Pareto Chart.

PDCA or Plan-Do-Check-Act is an interactive four-step problem solving and improvement process typically used to implement business process improvements. PDCA is also known as the Deming or Shewhart cycle. Numerous mini-improvements may need to be implemented to meet the deliverables as defined in the Team Charter. Mini-improvements should be defined or proposed in by using the tools of VA versus NVA Analysis, Histograms, 5 Why Analysis, Force Field Analysis, Impact Maps, etc. For these improvements to be implemented and verified as to their effectiveness, the use of the PDCA process may be used.

Pie Chart is a circular chart divided into sectors; each sector shows the relative size of each value. Pie Charts and Pareto Charts basically illustrate the same data. Pie Charts are typically used to compare multiple sets of data, where comparing the size of one Pie Chart to another can illustrate a difference in size or magnitude of the situations.

Pitch is the adjusted takt time that establishes an optimal and smooth workflow throughout the value stream. Pitch can be used to regulate workflow using any of these three flow methods.

Process Capability analysis is used to determine if a process, given its natural process variation in a stable state, is capable of meeting customer specifications or requirements. Determining process stability is done by monitoring a process output over time, using Run Charts and/or Statistical Process Control. True improvement in a process is achieved by balancing stability with the capability of meeting the customer's requirements, otherwise known as process capability.

Process map (or flowchart) is a visual representation of a series of operations (tasks, activities) consisting of people, work duties, and transactions that occur in the delivery of a product or service. (In this book, process maps and flowcharts are used interchangeably.) When creating a process map, the project team should tackle the activity as if it were doing an investigation (find out exactly what is and is not happening in the process). Process maps use standard symbols to represent a type of operation, process, and/or set of tasks to be performed which provides a common language for the project team to visualize problems and also allows for the process to be easier to read and understand, thus making it a visual tool to see areas of waste, process variation, and/or redundancy.

Process or Work Area Layout is the process of reducing the distance between or collocation of resources or people to ensure that service is delivered to the customer with minimal or no waste. The goal for optimum process or work area layout/collocation is to minimize wastes of delay, motion, and transportation (total distance traveled by materials or people to complete a process), and to improve flow. To minimize delay, motion, and transportation waste, it is common for work areas and processes to be arranged in U or L-shapes which allows key workers and materials to be collocated.

Project Charter is a high level document used to launch or initiate multiple improvement teams. It is usually initiated by leadership and targeted at a major improvement need of the organization.

Project Identification is the process of determining areas that are not meeting performance or operational goals. Determining the project requires data from Balanced Scorecards, Performance Dashboards, Voice of the Customer surveys, competitor's product or service, market demands, customer surveys, etc. It is helpful to create a Project Prioritization Worksheet and/or Distribution Report. The Project Prioritization Worksheet is a listing of the main areas of concern relative to the significant factors important to the organization. The Distribution Report is a historical listing on the volume of work or service completed within a specific time period for a department or work group.

Project management is the process of establishing, prioritizing, and carrying out tasks to complete specific objectives. This involves identifying and prioritizing tasks, identifying and assigning resources, in-process performance management of progress-to-outcomes, and taking actions to ensure success.

Pull System is a process to ensure nothing is produced upstream (i.e., supplier process) until the downstream (i.e., customer) process "signals" the need for it. This allows the product or service to be provided without detailed schedules.

Quality Function Deployment (QFD) is a tool that takes the VOC information and turns it into specific and measurable quality requirements that can be used to design improved processes. QFD methods provide a systematic approach to the design of a quality process. QFD uses a comprehensive matrix system to relate VOC priorities to specific measurable characteristics and to a quality measurement and improvement plan.

Quick Changeover is the ability to quickly change from delivering one product or service to delivering a completely different product or service. During delivery, providers are often required to quickly switch from delivering one product or service to delivering a completely different product or service to satisfy customer needs. The goal of QCO is to improve the customer experience by reducing waiting or delay due to change-over and adjustments. The speed in which a provider can change their delivery or service process is critical to the customer experience and overall satisfaction.

Radar Chart, also known as a Spider Chart or a Star Chart, because of its appearance, plots the values of each category along a separate axis that starts in the center of the chart and ends on the outer ring.

Run Chart is a method to display several data points over time. Because our minds are not good at remembering patterns in data, a visual display allows us to see the measurement(s) of an entire process.

Scatter (and Concentration) Plots are used to study the possible relationship between one variable and another. Through visual examination and additional mathematical analysis, problem solvers can determine relationships between variables.

Scheduled flow is most successful when the following conditions exist:
- ❖ Order Urgency = Low
- ❖ Order Pattern = Irregular or unpredictable
- ❖ Order Fulfillment Process = Unpredictable or non-standard

Scheduled flow is where customer orders or demands are identified and then scheduled or reserved for fulfillment at a specific time.

SIPOC Diagram is a tool used by a team to identify all relevant elements of a process improvement project or identified value stream to help ensure all aspects of the process are taken into consideration and that no key components are missing. SIPOC is an acronym for the Suppliers (the 'S' in SIPOC) of the process, the Inputs (I) to the process, the Process (P) that is under review, the Outputs (O) of the process, and the Customers (C) that receive the process outputs.

Stakeholder Analysis is the technique used to identify the key people who have to be influenced for a project implementation or change initiative. After analysis, stakeholder planning builds the necessary support for project success. A stakeholder is any person or organization, who can be positively or negatively impacted by, or cause an impact on the actions of a company, government, or organization. Stakeholder Analysis is critical to the success of every project in every organization. By engaging the right people in the right way before, during, and after the completion of a major initiative (i.e., Lean Sigma or business improvement project) or change within an organization, you can make a big difference in its success.

Standard work establishes and controls the best method to complete a task without variation from original intent. Tasks are then executed consistently performed, without variation, ideally to an established takt time or performance goal. Standard work provides consistent levels of productivity, quality, and safety, and promotes a positive work attitude based on well-documented standards. Standard work, done properly, reduces process variation. It is the basis for all continuous improvement activities.

Standard Work for Leaders prescribes specific tasks, actions, and time frames for completion of work for a manager or supervisor. Standard Work for Leaders is a concept derived from general standard work practices. Every position in every organization should have standard work processes to follow. This can also be referred to as leadership behaviors and methods.

Statistical Process Control is used to monitor and control process outputs. SPC monitors processes to determine if they are in control, are developing trends, and know when they go out of control. Processes are said to be in control if only natural or common cause variation is present. SPC Charts also referred to as Control or Shewhart Charts, identify when special cause variation has entered into the process. They are used to predict the future performance of a process. If special cause variation has entered into the process, additional actions are required to contain the process output and regain control.

Structured Brainstorming is where each team member contributes his/her ideas in order until all ideas are exhausted.

Supermarket describes a specific inventory management process using Kanbans and specified or standard storage locations and package quantities. A Supermarket inventory tool can be used to control flow where make-to-order is not possible. Supermarket is a term taken directly from the inventory management and replenishment system of today's supermarkets. In a modern supermarket, items are provided a specific location, and as items are pulled and purchased by the customers, replenishment is completed to a specified quantity or location. This system ensures that the supermarket rarely runs out of an item and customers never have to wait for replenishment.

Takt time defines the pace of repetitive customer demand. Takt time is presented in units of time and is calculated with the following equation: Takt Time = Time available to work / Average daily demand

Team building is the process of leading a group of people on a team in a way that strengthens bonds and cohesiveness in order to achieve harmony and success. Teaming can be done in-person (i.e., face-to-face) or through the use of remote communications via Web-collaboration applications or tools. The principles of teaming are the same regardless of the industry, type of project, or communication platform.

Team Charter documents the team structure, membership, and overall objectives, measures, and resources required for an improvement project to be successful. It is developed by the project team and is used to fully explore the scope and resources required to complete an improvement project. Multiple Team Charters may be derived from the Project Charter, or simply, a Project Charter can be modified to be the Team Charter.

Team selection is the process of selecting people to work together on a team.

Total Productive Maintenance (TPM) refers to the tools, methods, and activities used to improve machine or equipment availability and reliability times. Organizations employ a variety of machines and equipment to deliver products and services to their customers (external and internal). Organizations can reduce waste and improve their equipment effectiveness by implementing TPM practices. The overall goal of a TPM program is to reduce and eliminate equipment-related productivity losses and improve overall customer satisfaction. TPM practices involve all the people in an organization that plan, design, use, and maintain equipment and provide a system of comprehensive maintenance for the life-time of equipment.

Unstructured Brainstorming is where team members contribute their ideas as they occur (or come to mind) until all ideas are exhausted.

VA versus NVA Analysis is used to illuminate the waste in a process. Once the process steps are documented by a value stream or process map, VA and NVA times can be measured and placed into a simple data table to compare the Value-Added (VA) to Non Value-Added (NVA) time content for a portion (one process) of the value stream or for all the processes at the system level. The VA versus NVA Analysis is a form of a time study. When conducting time studies, do not be overly concerned with whether the time is from the fastest or slowest person. Take accurate measurements and document them. If there is concern regarding the relative speed (or lack thereof) for an individual process, simply document the concern to be later addressed. The fact that there is this concern over the possible variation in times will lead to discussions and will very well lead to key process improvements.

Value stream map is a visual representation of the material, work, and information flow, as well as the queue times between processes for a specific customer demand. The value stream map is a very powerful tool and does an excellent job highlighting wastes (i.e., delays, excess transport, etc.) for processes. A current state value stream map provides a representation of how the process is currently running. A future state value stream map represents the process with the proposed improvements that are to be implemented. The future state value stream map is a road map for improvement.

Visual control is a technique employed whereby control of an activity or process is made easier or more effective by deliberate use of visual signals (signs, information displays, maps, layouts, instructions, alarms, and poka-yoke or mistake proofing devices). These signals can be of many forms, from simple signs in a lobby area and different function keys on the keyboard, to various types of measurements about a problem or departmental goal, to kanbans and heijunka boxes; these signals can also be audio. A visual control effectively communicates the information needed for decision-making. The four levels of visual controls are:

> Level 1 - Indicators - provide information about the immediate environment
> Level 2 - Signals - cause a visual or auditory alarm that grabs your attention and warns that a mistake or error may occur
> Level 3 - Controls - physical or electronic limit prevents something from occurring due to the negative impact it will have on the process (or area)
> Level 4 - Guarantees - ensure correct decisions are made (mistake proofing)

Visual Management is the use of visual techniques that graphically display relevant business performance data. The relevant business performance data can be Key Performance Indicators (KPIs), customer mandates, governmental compliances, etc. Visual management techniques can include visual displays such as Performance Dashboards, Storyboards, Hoshin Planning, A3s, or other means by which performance is closely monitored and displayed.

Voice of the Customer (VOC) is a term used in business and Information Technology to describe the in-depth process of capturing a customer's expectations, preferences, and aversions. The VOC tool is a process that will deliver a greater understanding of a customer's expressed and unexpressed needs. The VOC is done by conducting market research through a variety of potential methods. Customer needs then can be ranked and prioritized to create an improved process. A common tool to do this is the customer feedback survey. Other tools intended to create a better understanding of customer desires are: focus group studies, complaint analysis, internet monitoring, and customer interviews. In each case, customer needs and priorities are documented and used for further analysis.

Waste is any activity that does not add value to the product or service. The following are the 12 wastes and are also referred to as The Dirty Dozen:

1. Overproduction
2. Waiting (or Delay)
3. Motion
4. Transport
5. Overprocessing
6. Inventory
7. Defects or Errors
8. People's Skills and Knowledge
9. Unevenness
10. Overburden
11. Environmental Resources
12. Social Responsibility

Waste Walk is an activity when project team members visit a process area that is being considered for improvement, ask questions, and then identify the wastes on the current state value stream or process map. Many of the team members will be very familiar with the project area as it is their actual work area. Conducting this Waste Walk, the team members, along with their Lean Sigma training, will be viewing their areas with a fresh perspective as they look at the processes and work flows.

Chapter 4. Worksheets

The following pages are the full size version of the worksheets, forms, and checklists referenced in each of the Kaizen Event types:

Introduction

Waste Audit
Waste Walk
A3 Report (Key Questions)

A3 Report (Lean Six Sigma Tools)
Kaizen Event Summary Matrix
Kaizen Event Proposal

Standard 5 Day Kaizen Event

Team Charter
Meeting Information Form
Effective Meeting Evaluation
SIPOC Diagram
Cycle Time Table
Document Tagging Worksheet
PDCA Kaizen Activity Worksheet
Project Prep Status
Kick-Off
Daily Recap

Summary
Standard Kaizen Event Planning Phase Checklist
Action Item Log
Standard Kaizen Event PDCA Phase Checklist
Weekly Project Dashboard
Monthly Project Dashboard
Going to the Gemba Checklist
Kaizen Event Participation Evaluation
Standard Kaizen Event Follow-Up Phase Checklist

Rolling Kaizen Event

Rolling Kaizen Event Planning Phase Summary
Rolling Kaizen Event Planning Phase Checklist
Rolling Kaizen Event PDCA Phase Time Bucket Matrix

Rolling Kaizen Event PDCA Phase Checklist
Rolling Kaizen Event Follow-Up Phase Time Bucket Matrix
Rolling Kaizen Event Follow-Up Phase Checklist

Web Based Kaizen Event

Web Based Kaizen Event Collaboration Matrix
Web Based Kaizen Event Planning Phase Checklist

Web Based Kaizen Event PDCA Phase Checklist
Web Based Kaizen Event Follow-Up Phase Checklist

Today's Kaizen Event

Today's Kaizen Event Planning Phase Checklist
Today's Kaizen Event PDCA Phase Checklist

Project Scorecard
Today's Kaizen Event Follow-Up Phase Checklist

Today's Kaizen Event

Wiki Kaizen Event Determination Worksheet
Wiki Colleague Request

Wiki PDCA Activity Worksheet
Sharing Worksheet

Note: The worksheets specifically titled for a Kaizen Event type can also be used in one of the other types as determined by the needs of the team.

Kaizen Event

Waste Audit

Your Name (optional): [ ]   **Event Dates:** [ ]

Black Belt or Lean Sensei: [ ]   **Department or Value Stream:** [ ]

Instructions: Please ✔ the appropriate response to each statement.

Use the follwoing five level Likert item scale for scoring: 1 = Strongly Disagree 2 = Disagree 3 = Neither Agree nor Disagree 4 = Agree 5 = Strongly Agree **Statements**	1 ☹☹☹ Strongly Disagree	2 ☹☹ Disagree	3 ☺ Neither Agree nor Disagree	4 ☺ Agree	5 ☺☺☺ Strongly Agree
1. We have no problems with mistakes or errors.					
2. We always have the right information when work needs to be done.					
3. We never struggle with getting the right data from our system.					
4. We only handle paperwork or an electronic document once, with no rework.					
5. We use the standard shortcuts and keystrokes to get to the data.					
6. We have a standard file naming convention.					
7. We have all our emails organized in appropriate folders for easy access.					
8. We never have to search for a tool, part, email, etc.					
9. We have our areas well organized using 5S principles.					
10. We are well cross-trained in each other's work.					
11. We continually improve our workflow through real-time communications.					
12. We know our performance standard for the day.					
13. We never have to recheck or reenter data.					
14. We have minimum paper copies around.					
15. We have established cycle times for our processes and they are monitored.					
16. We always know when work or information needs to be processed.					
17. We know the capability of our processes.					
18. We have a standard way to respond to emails.					
19. We have established email rules or filters to identify critical emails in real-time.					
20. We have a process to share information within and across departments.					
21. We have a robust continuous improvement program.					
22. We have all our employees trained in waste identification.					
23. We have a robust recycling program in place.					
24. We use visual management principles for processes and measurements.					
25. We have a process to share best practices with other organizations.					

Scoring Guidelines   **Total:** [ ]

A score of 90+ – Doing Very Well
A score of 80 - 89 – Good Foundation
A score of 70 - 79 – Some Good Things Happening, but More Needs to be Done
A score of 60 - 69 – Not Much Happening to Keep Pace with Competition

Kaizen Event

Waste Walk

Value Stream:

Date:

Department:

Team Members:

Type of Waste	Waste Observations
Overproduction Producing more material, information, or a service than is needed or used.	
Skills and Knowledge Not using people's minds and getting them involved.	
Transport Moving supplies, materials, documents, people, etc. excessively.	
Inventory Any unnecessary material, information, documents, etc. that resides between two processes.	
Motion Any unnecessary movement that does not add value.	
Defects or Errors Redoing work that has been done previously.	
Overprocessing Providing work or service that is not part of the customer requirement.	
Waiting or Delays The time spent waiting for material, information, people, etc.	
Overburden Work that is added with no additional support or resources.	
Unevenness Work that arrives without being scheduled and in varying amounts.	
Environmental Products, processes, activities, etc. that are not good for the planet.	
Social Communicating and networking via social networks that does not add value.	

Process Attributes

Process Name	Attributes	Process Name	Attributes

A3 Report

Kaizen Event

Value Stream Impacted:

Executive Champion:

Process Owner:

Timeframe:

Lean Sensei/Black Belt:

Date of Report:

1. Problem Statement

What data do we have to support the significance of the problem?
What percent of the time are we meeting customer expectations?
What is the impact of the problem on the customers of the process?
What is the "Business Line of Sight" between our strategic goals and dashboards, to this particular issue?

2. Current State

What is the value stream or process map, with data, for this process?
What does the map tell us about the complexity of our process?
What is the detailed process flow?
What is the feedback from employees/stakeholders on how the process is working for them?
What other data do we need to collect to understand the process?
Can we create a current state with a value stream map (with data)?

3. Improvement Opportunity

How will we know when we have achieved success?
Are there benchmarks or comparative data that we should review?
What should we measure in order to (a) compare "before" and "after" and (b) know how we have made a difference in the process?
Have we identified the wastes?
Can we show goals using a balanced scorecard?
What will the future state look like?

4. Problem Analysis

Who will be impacted by changes in this process?
What is the demand for the process – how many requests by hour of the day and/or day of the week?
What is the detailed process flow?
Can we use a Fishbone Diagram to find and show any likely problem areas?
How much waste is there in the process?
Have we asked the "5 Whys" for each step?
Can we show that we have identified the major problems using a Pareto Chart?
Have we used an Impact Map or other tool to prioritize the wastes/problems?
Do we understand the root causes of the problem?

Methods/Processess

Problem Statement

Materials

Man (People)   **Machines/Equipment**

5. Future State

What gaps are there between the current and future state and what are the specific PDCAs?
What stakeholders will be involved in the action plan?
What is the communication plan?
Can we show a high-level summary of process steps that need to be changed?

6. Implementation Plan

What improvement tools and resources will we need?
What steps need to be taken to accomplish the improvement plan?
Who will take the lead for each step?
What time frame will be required?
What is the training/education plan?
How will the data be collected and reported?
Can we show a high-level 4 W's of Who (does) What (by) When, and Why for this project?

7. Verify Results

Can we show a chart to display the process "before and after" to show success?
Is the new process meeting the target?

8. Follow-Up

Has SPC or a Visual Management system been considered to ensure for monitoring improvements?
What have we learned from this project?
How will the results continue to be shared with stakeholders and customers?
How will we share the learnings with others across the system?

A3 Report

Kaizen Event

Value Stream Impacted:

Executive Champion:

Process Owner:

Timeframe:

Lean Sensei/Black Belt:

Date of Report:

1. Problem Statement

**Charters
Team Selection and Buidling
Effective Meetings
Project Management**

2. Current State

**Value Stream and Process Maps
(w/ SIPOC Diagrams)**

3. Improvement Opportunity

**Waste Walk
VA versus NVA Analysis
Constraint Analysis
Demand Analysis Plots and Takt Time
VOC/QFD
MSA
Process Capability**

4. Problem Analysis

**Charting
Brainstorming
Cause and Effect (or Fishbone) Diagram
5 Whys
Interrelationship Diagram
Employee Balance Chart
Force Field Analysis
Impact Map**

Problem Statement

Materials

Methods/Processes

Man (People)

Machines/Equipment

5. Future State

(Value Stream and Process Maps)
Kaizen Events
PDCAs

6. Implementation Plan

**5S   Mass Customization
Visual Controls   Flow
Mistake Proofing   Quick Changeovers
Standard Work   Total Productive
Process or Work   Maintenance
Area Layout   Cross-Training**

7. Verify Results

(Charting)

8. Follow-Up

**Statistical Process Control
Visual Management
Standard Work for Leaders
Layered Process Audits**

Kaizen Event Summary Matrix

Characteristic	Standard 5 Day	Rolling	Web Based	Today's	Wiki (or Quick)
Length of Project	3 - 4 Months	3 - 4 Months	3 - 4 Months	1 - 4 Weeks	1 - 2 Weeks
Large Scope (crosses departments)	YES	YES	YES	NO	NO
Small Scope (within the department)	YES	YES	YES	YES	YES
Immediate Attention Required	YES	NO	YES	YES	NO
Process Immediately Accessible	YES	NO	YES	YES	YES
Root Cause May Be Known	NO	NO	NO	YES	YES
Specific Training Required	YES	YES	YES	YES	YES
Broad Training Required	YES	YES	NO	NO	NO
Team Members Physically (Locally) Available	YES	YES	NO	YES	NO
Meeting Times < 4 Hours	NO	YES	YES	NO	YES
Process Change (PDCAs) Continuously Applied Over a Few Days	YES	NO	NO	YES	YES
Management Involvement	YES	YES	YES	YES	NO
5S Applied	YES	YES	YES	NO	NO
Training Costs a Factor	YES	YES	YES	NO	NO
Requires Detailed Planning Meetngs	YES	YES	YES	NO	NO
May Require Statistical Methods to Determine Root Cause	YES	YES	YES	NO	NO
Web-based Collaboration Application Main Form of Communication	NO	NO	YES	NO	NO
Team Required	YES	YES	YES	YES	NO
Value Stream or Process Map Required	YES	YES	YES	NO	NO
Will Impact Balanced Scorecard or Performance Dashboard Metric	YES	YES	YES	YES	NO
Team Charter Required	YES	YES	YES	NO	NO

Kaizen Event

Kaizen Event Proposal

Name: [ ]   Department: [ ]

Upstream Supplier: [ ]   Downstream Customer: [ ]

*The Kaizen Event Proposal is a communication tool between the supervisor or manager of a department and the next level to determine the feasibiliy of an improvement project. The proposal may be initiated due to a problem or issue facing the employees in the department. The proposal will provide an overview of the issue or problem as well as the resources required. **It may also be used to verify or align improvement activities with departmental performance goals.***

Step 1: Describe the Problem or Opportunity.	Include photos, charts, and graphs, if necessary. Include current measurements.

Proposed Start Date: _____

Step 2: List Potential Benefits.	Be specific in terms of how the team's success will be measured. Use Balance Scorecard measures, if possible.

Proposed End Date: _____

Step 3: List Resources Required.	Include support needed from IT, HR, etc. Also, estimate the time commitment for each, if appropriate.

Type of Support	Estimated Hours Needed	Department/Colleague	Dates Requested

Step 4: Determine Feasibility and Next Steps.

❑ Approved As A Standard 5 Day Kaizen Event
❑ Approved As A Rolling Kaizen Event
❑ Approved As A Today's Kaizen Event

❑ Approved As A Web Based Kaizen Event
❑ Approved As A Wiki Kaizen Event
❑ Need More Information
❑ Currently Being Addressed

Sign-Off Date: _____

Team Charter

	Name	
Process Owner:		

Black Belt or Lean Sensei:

Start Date:

End Date:

Value Stream:

Objective:

Team Members:

	Name	Dept/Site
Facilitator:		
Scribe:		
Team Leader:		
Team Members:		

Meeting Fequency:

| Dates: |
| Times: |

Lean Objectives:

Deliverables:

What are the specific metrics that will be improved?

What are the specific opportunities for:

Growth?		Customer Satisfaction?	
Current:	Target:	Current:	Target:

Efficiency?		Quality (Defects or DPPMs, Errors, etc.)?	
Current:	Target:	Current:	Target:

Operational Excellence?		Dashboard or Performance Measure?	
Current:	Target:	Current:	Target:

What are any issues or concerns that may impact this team's objective?

Concerns:

Sign-Off: Executive Sponsor:_____   Date:_____

Champion/Value Stream Manager/VP:_____   Date:_____
(maybe the same as Executive Sponsor)

Process Owner: _____   Date:_____

Deliverables to be included with this Charter: ❑ Value Stream or Process Map for the project
❑ Supporting High Level Data

Kaizen Event

Meeting Information Form

Meeting Title: [   ]   **Date:** [   ]

Time: [   ]

Place: [   ]

Distribution: **FYI Copies:**

Participants	Roles	Stakeholders	Roles

Agenda:

Time	Item	Who	Duration

Action Items: (to be completed by the next meeting or sooner)

No.	Action Item	Who	Start Date	End Date	Status

Worksheets

Effective Meeting Evaluation

Meeting Title: ⬚⬚⬚⬚⬚⬚⬚⬚⬚⬚⬚⬚⬚⬚⬚⬚⬚ **Date:** ⬚⬚⬚⬚⬚

Time: ⬚⬚⬚⬚

Place: ⬚⬚⬚⬚⬚⬚⬚⬚⬚⬚⬚⬚⬚⬚⬚⬚⬚⬚⬚⬚

Use the following 5 level Likert item scale for each statement:
1- Strongly Disagree 2- Disagree 3- Neither Agree nor Disagree 4- Agree 5- Strongly Agree

		Score
1	We stayed on the agenda.	
2	We focused on the right issues during the meeting.	
3	We focused on the issues and did not place blame.	
4	Time was used wisely.	
5	Information was presented accurately and clearly.	
6	Everyone participated.	
7	Action Items were assigned properly.	
8	The pace of the meeting was appropriate.	
9	Questions and concerns were addressed appropriately.	
10	All ideas were explored given the time element.	
	Total Score	

Scoring Guidelines
45-50 Doing Well - Keep up the good work. 40-44 Doing OK - Must make more effort during meeting. 35-39 Not So Good - Must improve dramatically.

Kaizen Event

SIPOC Diagram

Value Stream: [   ]   **Date:** [   ]

Objective: [   ]

Team Members: [   ]

Suppliers (5)	**I**nputs (4)	**P**rocesses (1)	**O**utputs (3)	**C**ustomers (2)

Worksheets

Kaizen Event

Cycle Time Table

Department: [ ]

Data Collection Dates: [ ]

Type:
- ☐ Historical (database)
- ☐ Direct Observation (real-time)
- ☐ Voice of the Customer (survey)

Totals: [ ]

Process Name			Process Name			Process Name		
Step	Description	Cycle Time	Step	Description	Cycle Time	Step	Description	Cycle Time
	Total			Total			Total	

Process Name			Process Name			Process Name		
Step	Description	Cycle Time	Step	Description	Cycle Time	Step	Description	Cycle Time
	Total			Total			Total	

Process Name			Process Name			Process Name		
Step	Description	Cycle Time	Step	Description	Cycle Time	Step	Description	Cycle Time
	Total			Total			Total	

Process Name			Process Name			Process Name		
Step	Description	Cycle Time	Step	Description	Cycle Time	Step	Description	Cycle Time
	Total			Total			Total	

Process Name			Process Name			Process Name		
Step	Description	Cycle Time	Step	Description	Cycle Time	Step	Description	Cycle Time
	Total			Total			Total	

Document Tagging Worksheet

Value Stream:

Department:

Start Date In:

Start Date Out:

Step	Process/ Dept.	In		Out		Task Activity	Delay/Wait Time from Previous Step	Cycle Time	Elapsed Time	Value-Added Time	Non Value-Added Time
		Date	Time	Date	Time						

Kaizen Event

PDCA Kaizen Activity Worksheet

Value Stream: _____   **Date:** _____

Department: _____   **Team Members:** _____

Process Name/Activity (as identified on the value stream, process map, etc.)	Problem or Waste	Lean Tool	Specific Activities	Who	When

Parking Lot Items or Wiki Kaizen Event Ideas

Kaizen Event

Project Prep Status

Process Owner:		**Black Belt or Lean Sensei:**	

Start Date:

End Date:

Objective:

Communication Plan:

Measurement:

Initial Data:

Current Data:

Percent Improvement:

What (PDCA Activity)	Additional Info	Measurement Impacted	Course of Action

Sign-Off: Process Owner: _____ Date:_____

Kaizen Event

By: [ ]   Date: [ ]

Team Name: [ ]

Measurements	Target % Change

Objective: [ ]

Team Members	Job Function	Team Role

Kaizen Event

Daily Recap

By: _____   Date: _____

Team Name: _____

Measurement	# Day 1	# Day 2	# Day 3	# Day 4	# Day 5	# Target

Accomplishments:

Issues/Plans:

Issue:
Plan:
Issue:
Plan:
Issue:
Plan:
Issue:
Plan:
Issue:
Plan:
Issue:
Plan:
Issue:
Plan:
Issue:
Plan:
Issue:
Plan:
Issue:
Plan:
Issue:
Plan:
Issue:
Plan:

Kaizen Event

Summary

By: [   ]   Date: [   ]

Team Name: [   ]

Measurement	# At Start	# Target	Target % Chg.	# At End	Actual % Chg.

Objective: [   ]

Team Members:

Standard Kaizen Event
Planning Phase Checklist

Kaizen Event

| Process Owner: | | Black Belt or Lean Sensei: | | Start Date: End Date: |

Objective:

Weeks Denote Prior to Next Phase

3 Weeks (4 hour meeting time)

1. **Determine project scope.**
   - Negative trends for Balance Scorecard or Performance Dashboard
   - Addressing customer mandates or audits that require immediate action
   - Reducing costs to remain competitive
   - Launching a new product line
   - Addressing employee turnover issues

2. **Gather initial data set.**
   - Adjustment times, batch sizes, changeover times, cycle times, delay times, delivery schedules, down times, efficiency percentages, failure rates, quality yields, number of shifts, sigma value, value-added times, etc.

3. **Create high level value stream or process map.**
   - It is the 30,000-foot view

4. **Determine initial team members.**
   - Team Champion or Executive Sponsor, Team Leader, Facilitator, Timekeeper, Scribe, Technical Representative, Informaticist, Team Members

5. **Create the initial Team Charter.**
   - Use Team Charter form
   - Aligns team to management
   - Allows team to stay on track and not have scope creep
   - Encourages communication at all levels
   - Reduces stress
   - Allows for project standardization

6. **Assemble the team and conduct first meeting.**
   - Keep meeting to no more than 3 hours
   - Clarify roles and responsibilities
   - Conduct broad overview of Lean Sigma (simulation)
   - Ensure everyone commits to Action Items
   - Use Meeting Information Form
   - Use Effective Meeting Evaluation worksheet

7. **Complete A3 Report - Section 1. Problem Statement.**

Other Activities:

2 Weeks (4 hour meeting time)

8. **Create a SIPOC Diagram, if needed.**
   - Supplier, Input, Process, Output, Customer identify suppliers, customers, and requirements
   - Helps ensure improvement project focus

9. **Create detailed current state value stream or process map.**
   - Provides more detail than high level map
   - Provides visual to help determine what data may need to be collected
   - Maps come in all shapes and sizes

10. **Create a Cycle Time Table (or appropriate method to obtain accurate cycle times).**
    - Ensure start and stop cycle times are understood by all
    - Be satisfied w/ 80% of data collected, but strive for more
    - Gather data process real-time
    - Consider Measurement System Analysis

11. **Conduct a Waste Walk.**
    - Ensure process area employees know in advance of the Waste Walk
    - Assign one person to take notes
    - If group greater than 5, split into smaller groups
    - Start downstream and work your way upstream
    - Do not cause any disruption to the process area
    - Ensure questions are determined before the walk

12. **Update current state value stream or process map.**
    - Use Post-it Notes to identify wastes on current state map
    - Consolidate similar wastes by reaching a consensus
    - Use data from Waste Walk, Cycle Time Table, etc.

13. **Complete A3 Report - Section 2. Current State and Section 3. Improvement Opportunity**

Other Activities:

1 Week (4 - 8 hours meeting time)

14. **Conduct a Stakeholder Analysis.**
    - Ensure all key players are considered and proper communication occurs, before, during, and after the Event

15. **Conduct specific Lean tool training.**
    - 5S, Standard Work, Mistake Proofing, Continuous Flow and Kanbans, Leveling, Visual Controls, etc.
    - Distribute *The Lean Six Sigma Pocket Guide XLs*

16. **Determine specific improvement activities and use the Plan – Do – Check – Act (PDCA) format.**
    - Consider Valued-Added versus Non Value-Added Analysis, Histograms, 5 Why Analysis, Brainstorming, Cause and Effect, etc.
    - *Plan*–define the improvement activity/experiment, what will be done, who will do it, and how it will be measured
    - *Do*–implement the improvement plan/experiment
    - *Check*–ensure that the intended improvement was successful in terms of the measurements set forth
    - *Act*–confirm that improvement experiment worked with improved performance; act to standardize the process
    - Document activities on PDCA Kaizen Activity Worksheet

17. **Create a future state value stream or process map.**
    - Use different colored Post-it Notes for Lean tool application then create a future state map

18. **Create Reporting and Communication forms.**
    - Project Prep Status, Kickoff, Daily Recap, Summary

19. **Create PDCA Implementation Phase schedule.**
    - Be somewhat flexible in the schedule, everything cannot be planned out exactly on how it will go

20. **Communicate to Executive Sponsor and other managers the schedule.**
    - Recommend face-to-face meeting
    - Keep all stakeholers informed

21. **Complete A3 Report - Section 4. Problem Analysis, Section 5. Future State, and Section 6. Implementation Plan.**

Other Activities:

Sensei Tips: Consider additional team members, use good project management skills, listen to employee's concerns, and use this Checklist.

Kaizen Event

Action Item Log

Process Owner: [ ] Black Belt or Lean Sensei: [ ] On Schedule ☐ Delayed ■

Objective: [ ] Date: [ ]

Action Item - Task Description	Who	Start Date	Expected Completion	Completion Date	On Schedule or Delayed	Comments/Notes/Why

Standard Kaizen Event
PDCA Phase Checklist

Kaizen Event

Process Owner: _____

Black Belt or Lean Sensei: _____

Start Date: _____
End Date: _____

Objective: _____

Day 1 (8 hour meeting time)

☐ 1. Review team goals.
☐ 2. Review before documentation and data.
☐ 3. Determine takt time or performance goal.
☐ 4. Review/update process or value stream map.
☐ 5. Conduct or review Waste Walk.
☐ 6. Take before photos.
☐ 7. Identify wastes.
☐ 8. Review maps and update.
☐ 9. Meet with stakeholders.
☐ 10. Plan 5S activities for Day 2.
☐ 11. Complete Daily Recap and Kick Off documents.
☐ 12. Review documents with management.

☐☐☐ Other Activities:

Day 2 (8 hour meeting time)

☐ 1. Review/discuss info from Day 1.
☐ 2. Create/review PDCA Kaizen Worksheet.
☐ 3. Create/review plan for new process or work area.
☐ 4. Meet with stakeholders.
☐ 5. Notify/confirm ancillary groups for support.
☐ 6. Draft standard work of new process.
☐ 7. Review PDCAs.
☐ 8. Develop training plan.
☐ 9. Communicate training plan to stakeholders.
☐ 10. Update Daily Recap document; present to management.
☐ 11. Initiate 5S in process area.

☐☐☐ Other Activities:

Day 3 (8 hour meeting time)

☐ 1. Review/discuss info from Day 2.
☐ 2. Create/review PDCA Kaizen Worksheet.
☐ 3. Conduct training with stakeholders.
☐ 4. Implement PDCA.
☐ 5. Correct problems as needed.
☐ 6. Create or enhance visual controls.
☐ 7. Work on 5S or safety issues.
☐ 8. Collect data on new process.
☐ 9. Update Daily Recap document; present to management.

☐☐☐ Other Activities:

Day 4 (8 hour meeting time)

☐ 1. Review/discuss info from Day 3.
☐ 2. Continue PDCA activities and training stakeholders on new work layout and/or process.
☐ 3. Fix any/all problems from Day 3.
☐ 4. Continue support and data collection.
☐ 5. Listen to stakeholders and adjust as necessary.
☐ 6. Update with standard work.
☐ 7. Take after photos of new process.
☐ 8. Conduct debriefing with stakeholders.
☐ 9. Create visual management plan.
☐ 10. Update Daily Recap document; present to management.

☐☐☐ Other Activities:

Day 5 (8 hour meeting time)

☐ 1. Review/discuss info from Day 4
☐ 2. Ensure all stakeholders are trained on new process.
☐ 3. Fix any/all problems from Day 4.
☐ 4. Determine support roles.
☐ 5. Create enterprise-wide roll out plan, if appropriate.
☐ 6. Prepare and present final presentation to management.
☐ 7. Complete To-Do List.
☐ 8. Ensure participants complete Kaizen Event Participation Evaluation form.
☐ 9. Team Leader consolidate Participant Evaluations and appropriately shares.
☐ 10. Share all documents (e.g., A3 Report).
☐ 11. Reward and recognize team members.

☐☐ Other Activities:

Complete A3 Report - Section 7. Verify Results

Sensei Tips: Keep management informed, respect the process area employees, and use this Checklist.

Kaizen Event

Weekly Project Dashboard

Type of Project: [ ]

Value Stream Impacted: [ ]

Timeframe: [ ]

Executive Champion: [ ]

Lean Sensei/Black Belt: [ ]

Process Owner: [ ]

Measurement	Project Start	Target/ Units	Dates				Project End
			7 Day Date:	14 Day Date:	21 Day Date:	28 Day Date:	
Process Yield %							
Performance compared to target %							
Key: Green - Performance Meets or Exceeds Target / Yellow - Performance is Short of but close to Target / Red - Performance is Unfavorable to Target	Project Start	Target/ Units	7 Day Date:	14 Day Date:	21 Day Date:	28 Day Date:	Project End

If the process metric is not meeting traget(s) the WWWW (below) must clearly indicate how you plan to meet or exceed target.

What	Who	When (m/d/y)	Why	Comments/Status

Additional Notes:

Kaizen Event

Monthly Project Dashboard

Type of Project: [   ]

Value Stream Impacted: [   ]   Timeframe: [   ]

Executive Champion: [   ]   Lean Sensei/Black Belt: [   ]

Process Owner: [   ]

Measurement	Project Start	Target/ Units	Month 1:	Month 2:	Month 3:	Month 4:	Project End
			Dates				
Process Yield %							
Performance compared to target %							

Key:
Green - Performance Meets or Exceeds Target
Yellow - Performance is Short of but close to Target
Red - Performance is Unfavorable to Target

Measurement	Project Start	Target/ Units	Month 1:	Month 2:	Month 3:	Month 4:	Project End

If the process metric is not meeting traget(s), the WWWWW below must clearly indicate how you plan to meet or exceed target.

What	Who	When (m/d/y)	Why	Comments/Status

Additional Notes:

Going to the Gemba Checklist

Kaizen Event

Your Name (optional):

Manager's/Director's Name:

Event Date(s):

INSTURCTIONS: Use the following checklist to evaluate the area or process. Space is for comments.

	Questions to Consider	Yes	No	Comments
1.	Are the measures/metrics/scorecard updated, color-coded to standards, and have assignable causes been identified for unacceptable variations in any key areas?			
2.	Are there any positive performing areas to complement and/or thank the workers? (Go thank people, say you noticed, and tell them to keep up the good work!)			
3.	Are there poorly performing areas that need countermeasures and corrective actions? (Look for the beginning of trends as well. Use an A3 format to track improvement and countermeasure initiatives. Use the 5 Whys process and Pareto charts to drill down to root causes. Ask the workers for PDCA improvement ideas to try.)			
4.	Are the countermeasures and corrective action plans, with dates, names and status, clearly identified on the scorecard or A3?			
5.	Is there evidence that the workers are getting involved and continuing to learn and use Lean methods and tools?			

Additional Notes and Comments

Kaizen Event
Participation Evaluation

Kaizen Event

Your Name (optional): _____

Event Date(s): _____

INSTURCTIONS: Please 'X' the appropriate response to each question.

How satisfied were you...	Strongly Disagree ☹☹☹	Disagree ☹	Neither Agree nor Disagree 😐	Agree 🙂	Strongly Agree 🙂🙂🙂	Comments
1. ...that the pre-event team meetings provided adequate instruction and planning to ensure a successful event?						
2. ...that the current state value stream or process map and baseline data provided the team enough information to begin assessing the areas for improvement?						
3. ...that the majority of process wastes were identified?						
4. ...that the quality of the recommendations developed by the team were good?						
5. ...that the action planning process resulted in specific, measurable PDCA plans?						
6. ...That the facilitation supported achievement of objectives?						
7. ...that the Kaizen Event overall was successful?						

8. Which part of the Kaizen Event added most value? Why?

9. Which part of the Kaizen Event could be improved? How?

10. Would you like to participate in another Kaizen Event? Why or Why not?

☐ Yes
☐ No

Standard Kaizen Event
Follow-Up Phase Checklist

Kaizen Event		
Process Owner:	Black Belt or Lean Sensei:	Start Date:
		End Date:
Objective:		

Follow-Up Activities

☐ **1. Continue communications.**
Consider the following charts:
Pareto Chart
Paynter Chart
Pie Chart
Scatter (Concentration) Plots
Radar Chart
Run Chart
Histogram
Statistical Process Ctrl. Charts

☐ **2. Complete all PDCA activities.**

☐ **3. Provide support after the Follow-Up Phase.**
Lean Sensei/Black Belt

☐ **4. Create and distribute the Kaizen Event Dashboards.**
Weekly Kaizen Dashboard
Monthly Kaizen Dashboard
Maintained by process owner

☐ **5. Establish an avenue for stakeholders to provide feedback.**
Kaizen Suggestion Box
Emails
Walk and talk
Google Drive

Other Activities:
☐ ☐ ☐ ☐

☐ **6. Practice Gemba.**
Observe the process
Informally ask questions
Show concern
Arrive with a purpose
Comment on visuals
Notify the area
Include different mgmt levels
Build upon each Gemba
Thank employees for their efforts

☐ **7. Apply Kaizen to the Kaizen Event.**
Kaizen Event Participation
Evaluation form

☐ **8. Reward and recognize the team.**
Verbal recognition
Gift cards
Lunches, dinners, etc.
Recognition letters, awards, etc.
Corporate gifts
Time off
Green fees

☐ **9. Compete A3 Report - Section 8. Follow-Up**
Share appropriately

Other Activities:
☐ ☐ ☐ ☐

Comments/Notes

Sensei Tips: Ensure all PDCAs are completed, share results throughout the organization, and reward and recognize team members and any other employees that contributed.

Kaizen Event

Rolling Kaizen Event Planning Phase Summary

Process Owner:		Black Belt or Lean Sensei:		Start Date:	
				End Date:	

Objective:

Team Representation:
TL - Team Leader
PO - Process Owner
ES - Executive Sponsor

BB - Black Belt/Lean Sensei, or Continuous Improvement Specialist
ATM - All Team Members (highlighted)
STM - Sub Team Members

	Steps	# of 1 Hour Time Buckets	*Team Representation	Additional Representation	Lean, Six Sigma or Project Management Tool	Comments/Notes
☐	1. Determine project scope.	1	TL, PO, ES, BB	Customer or supplier, if applicable	Balanced Scrorecard, Performance Dashboard, Customer Survey results, Pareto Chart, etc.	
☐	2. Gather initial data set.	2	TL, PO, BB		Take time, cycle times, quality yields, value-added times, etc.	
☐	3. Create high level value stream or process map.	1	TL, PO, BB		Value stream or process map; use appropriate mapping software	Microsoft Excel, Visio, or PowerPoint can be used.
☐	3. Determine initial team members.	.25	TL, PO, BB			
☐	5. Create the initial Team Charter.	.5	TL, PO, BB		Team Charter	
☐	6. Assemble the team and conduct effective meeting.	2	ATM	Trainer, consultant	Lean and/or Six Sigma overview (include waste), Effective Meeting Evaluation Worksheet	Conducting a Lean simulation would be helpful.
☐	7. Complete A3 Report - Section 1 Problem Statement	.25	TL, PO, BB		A3 Report	To be posted and shared with team.
☐	8. Create a SIPOC Diagram.	.5	STM		SIPOC Diagram, value stream or process map, Post-it Notes	
☐	9. Create initial detailed current state value stream or process map.	2	STM			
☐	10. Create Cycle Time Table.	2	STM	Informaticist	Document Tagging Worksheet, Cycle Time Table, Database Reports, Pareto Chart, Run Chart, etc.	Consider MSA if multiple sources are collecting data.
☐	11. Conduct a Waste Walk.	1	ATM		Waste Walk Audit, Elevator Speech	Do not disrupt the process!
☐	12. Update current state value stream or process map.	0.5	ATM		Post-It Notes, good facilitation, value stream or process map	Make the mapping process visual so everyone is involved.
☐	13. Complete A3 Report - Section 2. Current State and Section 3. Improvement Opportunity	0.25	TL, PO, BB		A3 Report	To be posted and shared with team.
☐	14. Conduct a Stakeholder Analysis.	0.5	STM		Stakeholder Analysis	Ensure all types of stakeholders are included.
☐	15. Continue with specific Lean tool training.	1	ATM	Trainer, consultant		Directed to potential solutions to guide the team.
☐	16. Determine specific improvement activities and use PDCA format.	2	ATM	Trainer, consultant	5 Why Analysis, Impact Map, Fishbone Diagram, Brainstorming, PDCA Kaizen Activity Worksheet.	Do not rush this step!
☐	17. Create a future state value stream or process map.	1	STM		Value stream or process map; use appropriate mapping software; Post-It Notes (various colors)	Microsoft Excel, Visio, or PowerPoint can be used.
☐	18. Create Reporting and Communication forms.	1	TL, PO, BB		Project Prep Status, Kick Off, Weekly Recap, Summary, etc.	Use current forms and update with Lean focus.
☐	19. Create PDCA Implementation Phase schedule.	2	ATM		Project timeline, PDCA Kaizen Activity Worksheet or Action Item Log	Be flexible and work with team.
☐	20. Communicate to Executive Sponsor and other managers the schedule.	0.25	TL, PO, BB		Reporting and Communication forms	Meet face-to-face if at all possible.
☐	21. Communicate A3 Report. Problem Analysis, Section 5. Future State, and Section 6. Implementation Plan	0.25	TL, PO, BB		A3 Report	To be posted and shared with team.

* If multiple representation is listed, it can be one or all, depending on the experience of the individuals.

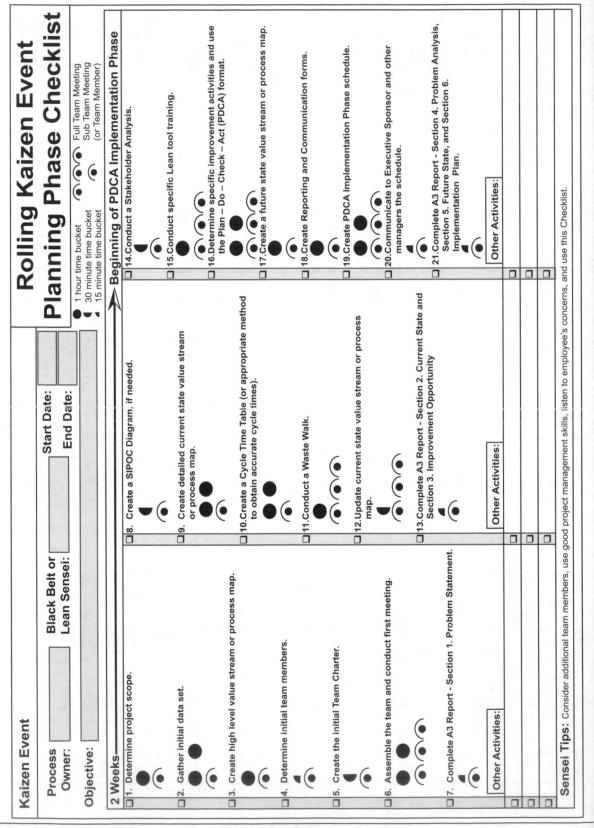

Rolling Kaizen Event
Planning Phase Checklist

Kaizen Event

Process Owner:

Objective:

Black Belt or Lean Sensei:

Start Date:

End Date:

● 1 hour time bucket
◗ 30 minute time bucket
▪ 15 minute time bucket

●◗▪ Full Team Meeting
◗ Sub Team Meeting
▪ (or Team Member)

2 Weeks

1. Determine project scope.
2. Gather initial data set.
3. Create high level value stream or process map.
4. Determine initial team members.
5. Create the initial Team Charter.
6. Assemble the team and conduct first meeting.
7. Complete A3 Report - Section 1. Problem Statement.

Other Activities:

8. Create a SIPOC Diagram, if needed.
9. Create detailed current state value stream or process map.
10. Create a Cycle Time Table (or appropriate method to obtain accurate cycle times).
11. Conduct a Waste Walk.
12. Update current state value stream or process map.
13. Complete A3 Report - Section 2. Current State and Section 3. Improvement Opportunity

Other Activities:

Beginning of PDCA Implementation Phase

14. Conduct a Stakeholder Analysis.
15. Conduct specific Lean tool training.
16. Determine specific improvement activities and use the Plan – Do – Check – Act (PDCA) format.
17. Create a future state value stream or process map.
18. Create Reporting and Communication forms.
19. Create PDCA Implementation Phase schedule.
20. Communicate to Executive Sponsor and other managers the schedule.
21. Complete A3 Report - Section 4. Problem Analysis, Section 5. Future State, and Section 6. Implementation Plan.

Other Activities:

Sensei Tips: Consider additional team members, use good project management skills, listen to employee's concerns, and use this Checklist.

Kaizen Event

Rolling Kaizen Event PDCA
Phase Time Bucket Matrix

Process Owner:		Black Belt or Lean Sensei:		Start Date:	
				End Date:	

Objective:

	Tools	1 Hour Time Bucket Expectations	Limitations	Minimum Number of Team Members	Additional Lean and/or Six Sigma Tool Support	Comments/Notes
☐	5S	4	None.	3 - 4, or entire team	Creates awareness of waste as well as allows everyone in the department or process area to be involved.	Sort - establish sort guidelines (30 minutes); Set-In-Order - create labels, markings, etc. (60 minutes); Shine - clean area (30 minutes); Standardize - create and train everyone to standards (60 minutes); Sustain - create audit and establish audit team (30 minutes)
☐	Visual Controls	2	May require assistance from Facilities or IT.	1 - 2, or entire team	Nearly all Lean tools have some form of visual control.	Ensure the team understands the four levels of visual controls.
☐	Mistake Proofing	1	May require assistance from Facilities or IT.	1 - 2, or entire team	Tied closely with Visual Controls Level 4.	Can eliminate and/or reduce errors significantly.
☐	Standard Work	2	Must have access to SOPs.	1 - 2, or entire team	Standard Work Combination Table and Chart can be used to document procedures and times.	All process should be standardized; it is the basis for continuous improvement.
☐	Process or Work Area Layout	4	May require assistance from Facilities.	3 - 4, or entire team	Spaghetti Diagram can be used to map before and after work flows.	Remove barriers of all kinds for improved work flow. Think in terms of continuous flow.
☐	Mass Customization	1	Familiar characteristics are required.	3 - 4, or entire team	Brainstorming, Data/Demand Analysis can be used to determine if this is practical.	May be difficult to apply at times, but can provide significant cost savings.
☐	Flow	2	Other departments may need to be involved.	1 - 2, or entire team	Consider continuous flow, paced, or scheduled flow to improve processes. Use pitch if appropriate.	Focus on removing bottlenecks and delays.
☐	Pull Systems	2	Requires use of signals.	1 - 2, or entire team	Consider kanbans, supermarkets, and FIFO Lanes. Use pitch and visual controls as needed.	Requires good communications with upstream and downstream processes.
☐	Quick Changeovers	1	Requires variety of products and/or services.	1 - 2, or entire team	Allows organization to provide Just-In-Time products and/or services.	Allows for smaller batches of products and/or services.
☐	Total Productive Maintenance	2	Requires critical equipment to the process.	1 - 2, or entire team	Requires reliability studies and standard work.	Equipment must be critical to the value stream or process.
☐	Cross-Training	1	Should include everyone.	1 - 2, or entire team	Training on problem solving skills and additional Lean Six Sigma may be of value.	This importance of this is usually underestimated.

Notes:

Rolling Kaizen Event
PDCA Phase Checklist

Kaizen Event

Legend:
- ● 1 hour time bucket
- ◗ 30 minute time bucket
- ◖ 15 minute time bucket
- (◗◗◗) Full Team Meeting
- (◖) Sub-Team Meeting (or Team Member)

Process Owner:

Black Belt or Lean Sensei:

Objective:

Start Date:

End Date:

Week 1 (2 hours)

☐ 1. Understand specific Lean tools and continue to apply as needed:
- 5S
- Visual Controls
- Mistake Proofing
- Standard Work
- Process or Work Area Layout
- Mass Customization
- Flow
- Quick Changeovers (QCO)
- Total Productive Maintenance (TPM)
- Cross-Training

● (◗◗◗)

☐ 2. Update Kaizen Activity PDCA Worksheet.
- Rolling Kaizen Event
- Time Bucket Matrix
- PDCA Kaizen Activity Worksheet

● (◗◗◗)

Other Activities:

☐ ☐ ☐

Week 2 (2 hours)

☐ 1. Review/discuss PDCA implementations (Action Items).
◗ (◗◗◗)

☐ 2. Update PDCA schedule.
◗ (◗◗◗)

☐ 3. Evaluate sub-teams implementation with appropriate metrics.
● (◗◗◗)

☐ 4. Create Action Items.
● (◗◗◗)

☐ 5. Update timeline for sub-teams implementation of PDCAs.
● (◗◗◗)

Other Activities:

☐ ☐ ☐

Week 3 (2 hours)

☐ 1. Review/discuss PDCA implementations (Action Items).
◗ (◗◗◗)

☐ 2. Update PDCA schedule.
● (◗◗◗)

☐ 3. Evaluate sub-teams implementation with appropriate metrics.
● (◗◗◗)

☐ 4. Create Action Items.
● (◗◗◗)

☐ 5. Update timeline for sub-teams implementation of PDCAs.
● (◗◗◗)

Other Activities:

☐ ☐ ☐

Week 4 (2 hours)

☐ 1. Review/discuss PDCA implementations (Action Items).
◗ (◗◗◗)

☐ 2. Update PDCA schedule.
● (◗◗◗)

☐ 3. Evaluate sub-teams implementation with appropriate metrics.
● (◗◗◗)

☐ 4. Create Action Items.
● (◗◗◗)

☐ 5. Update timeline for sub-teams implementation of PDCAs.
● (◗◗◗)

Other Activities:

☐ ☐ ☐

Weeks 5+ (2 hours)

☐ 1. Review/discuss PDCA implementations (Action Items).
◗ (◗◗◗)

☐ 2. Update PDCA schedule.
● (◗◗◗)

☐ 3. Evaluate sub-teams implementation with appropriate metrics.
● (◗◗◗)

☐ 4. Create Action Items.
● (◗◗◗)

☐ 5. Update timeline for sub-teams implementation of PDCAs.
● (◗◗◗)

Other Activities:

☐ ☐ ☐

Sensei Tips: Keep management informed, respect the process area employees, and use this Checklist.

Rolling Kaizen Event Follow-Up Phase Time Bucket Matrix

Kaizen Event

Process Owner:		Black Belt or Lean Sensei:		Start Date:	
				End Date:	

Objective:

Tools	1 Hour Time Bucket Expectations	Limitations	Team Representation	Additional Lean and/or Six Sigma Tool Support	Comments/Notes
Project Management	1	May require assistance from IT for appropriate software use.	Team Leader, Process Owner	The A3 Report can be used to relay project completion as well as be a guide for the overall project. Gantt Charts can be used to detail the activities or the CRM program may have options available.	Additonal detailed listing throughout the scope of the project will need to be done to ensure action items are completed on time. This is critical for the success of this type of Kaizen Event.
Statistical Process Control	1	May require assistance from the Quality.	Black Belt or equiv., Process Owner	Allows for monitoring processes to determine if they are in control or if trends are developing.	Helps to determine when special cause variation has crept into the process.
Visual Management	3	Must have access to data.	Process Owner, Sub-Team Member	Storyboards can be used to convey project success. Department performance charts should be up-to-date.	Can improve productivity and quality immensely.
Standard Work for Leaders	2	Must have access to job requirements of leaders.	Team Leader, Process Owner	Need leaders to agree to a schedule to meet with employees and share information regularly.	Regularly scheduled short morning or afternoon meetings can help sustain improvements.
Performance Management	2	May require assistance from Human Resources.	Team Leader, Process Owner, Sub-Team Member	Individual, group, and department measurements should all tie together. This is essential to sustain process changes for the long term.	Use SMART Goals of: Specific Measureable Assigned Realistic Time-Bounded
Layered Process Audits	2	Need to have system in place that everyone has bought into.	Team Leader, Process Owner, Sub-Team Member	Need to define standard work and expectations from all levels of the department. Audit recommended.	May seem redundant with Visual Management and Performance Measurements, but can provide value if done with buy-in by all employees..

Notes:

Rolling Kaizen Event
Follow-Up Phase Checklist

Kaizen Event

Process Owner:

Black Belt or Lean Sensei:

Start Date:

End Date:

Objective:

● Full Team Meeting
◐ Sub-Team Meeting
◑ (or Team Member)

● 1 hour time bucket
◐ 30 minute time bucket
◑ 15 minute time bucket

Week 1 (30 minutes)

☐ 1. **Continue communications.**
Consider the following charts:
Pareto Chart
Paynter Chart
Pie Chart
Scatter (Concentration) Plots
Radar Chart
Run Chart
Histogram
Statistical Process Ctrl. Charts
◑ ◐

☐ 2. **Discuss outstanding issues.**
◑ ◐

Other Activities:

☐ ☐ ☐ ☐

Week 2 (30 minutes)

☐ 3. **Provide support after the PDCA Phase.**
Lean Representative
◑ ◐

☐ 4. **Create and distribute the Event Dashboards.**
Weekly Kaizen Dashboard
Monthly Kaizen Dashboard
Maintained by process owner
◑ ◐

Other Activities:

☐ ☐ ☐ ☐

Week 3 (30 minutes)

☐ 5. **Establish avenue for primary stakeholders to provide feedback.**
Kaizen Suggestion Box
Emails
Walk and talk
Google Drive
◑ ◐

☐ 6. **Work with management to practice Gemba.**
Observe the process
Informally ask questions
Show concern
Arrive with a purpose
Comment on visuals
Notify the area
Include different mgmt levels
Build upon each Gemba
Thank employees for their efforts
◑ ◐

Other Activities:

☐ ☐ ☐ ☐

Week 4 (30 minutes)

☐ 7. **Apply Kaizen to the Kaizen.**
Kaizen Event Participation
Evaluation form
◑ ◐◐◐

☐ 8. **Reward and recognize the team.**
Verbal recognition
Gift cards
Lunches, dinners, etc.
Recognition letters, awards, etc.
Corporate gifts
Time off
Green fees
◑ ◐◐◐

Other Activities:

☐ ☐ ☐ ☐

Sensei Tips: Ensure all PDCAs are completed, share results throughout the organization, and reward and recognize team members and any other employees that contributed.

Web Based Collaboration Matrix

Characteristic	Vendor				
	TeamLab	Infinite Conferencing	ProjectSpaces	WebOffice (WebEx)	Huddle
Cost	Free	Price not listed Must call for quote	7 Membership options available	Price depends on # of users	Price not listed Must call for quote
Can you create calendars?	Yes - user can create/share calendar	No	Yes - user can create/share calendar	Yes - user can create/share calendar	Yes - user can create/share calendar
How do you manage tasks?	Create/Share to-do lists	Cannot create/share to-do lists	Create/Share to-do lists	Create/Share to-do lists	Create/Share to-do lists
Are there reminders for tasks that have been assigned?	Yes - notifications sent via email	N/A	Yes - notifications sent via email	Yes - notifications sent via email	Yes - notifications sent via email
Can you share files with others? (MS Office?)	Yes	Yes	Yes	Yes	Yes
How does communication occur?	Open blogs and forums or IM	Private or open chat room/discussion	Onsite email	Open blogs and forums or IM	Onsite email or discussion forums
Is video conferencing available?	No	Yes - extra fee applied	No	Yes - extra fee applied	Yes
Other useful features	Time Tracker, Report Creater	Polling, Audio Conferencing	Ability to assign tasks to people	Whiteboard feature, assign tasks	Whiteboard feature, assign tasks
Can site be customize for your business?	Yes - change color scheme/layout	No	Yes - change color scheme/layout	Yes - change color scheme	Yes - custom URL, add logos
Can you make certain documents private?	Yes	Yes	Yes	Yes	Yes
Can you share your Desktop?	No	Yes	No	Yes	No
Is there a free trial?	N/A	Yes - 10 day free trial	Yes - 30 day free trial	Yes - 30 day free trial	Yes - 14 day free trial
Access to secured storage and data retrieval database system (cloud)?	Yes - allows cloud storage	Yes - allows Cloud storage	Yes - allows Cloud storage	Yes - allows Cloud storage	Yes - allows Cloud storage
Access to secured chat room environments	Yes	Yes	Site offers onsite e-mail-not chat rooms	Yes	Yes
Does the site offer collaborative file sharing in real-time?	Yes	Yes	No - cannot edit in real-time	Yes	No - cannot edit in real-time
Does the site support mobile devices?	Yes - supports Droid and iOS phones	No	No	Yes - supports Droid and iOS phones	Yes - supports Droid and iOS phones

Kaizen Event

Web Based Kaizen Event
Planning Phase Checklist

Process
Owner:
Black Belt or
Lean Sensei:

Start Date:
End Date:

Objective:

@ Email
Web Conferencing

Posted/Published
• Text

● 1 hour time bucket
● 30 minute time bucket
▪ 15 minute time bucket

●●● Full Team Meeting
●●● Sub-Team Meeting
● (or Team Member)

Beginning of PDCA Implementation Phase

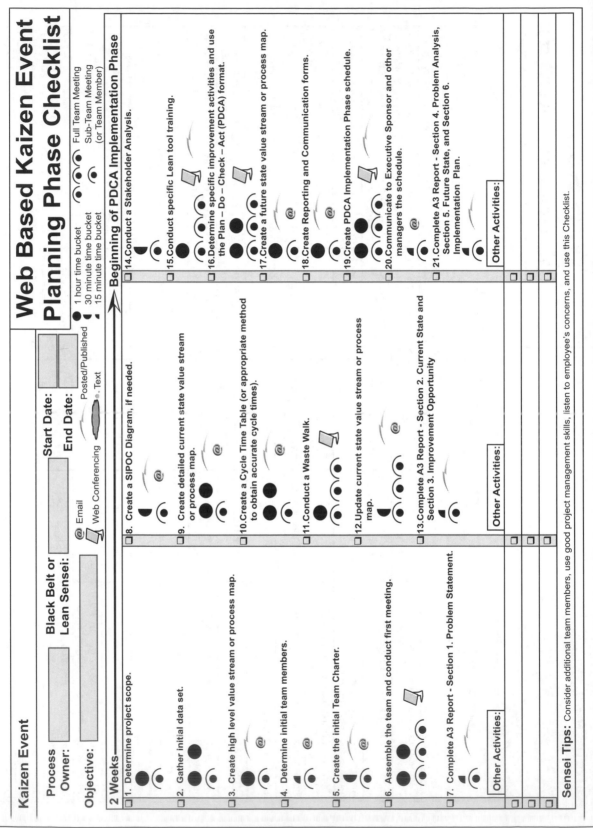

2 Weeks

1. Determine project scope.

2. Gather initial data set.

3. Create high level value stream or process map.

4. Determine initial team members.

5. Create the initial Team Charter.

6. Assemble the team and conduct first meeting.

7. Complete A3 Report - Section 1. Problem Statement.

Other Activities:

8. Create a SIPOC Diagram, if needed.

9. Create detailed current state value stream or process map.

10. Create a Cycle Time Table (or appropriate method to obtain accurate cycle times).

11. Conduct a Waste Walk.

12. Update current state value stream or process map.

13. Complete A3 Report - Section 2. Current State and Section 3. Improvement Opportunity

Other Activities:

14. Conduct a Stakeholder Analysis.

15. Conduct specific Lean tool training.

16. Determine specific improvement activities and use the Plan – Do – Check – Act (PDCA) format.

17. Create a future state value stream or process map.

18. Create Reporting and Communication forms.

19. Create PDCA Implementation Phase schedule.

20. Communicate to Executive Sponsor and other managers the schedule.

21. Complete A3 Report - Section 4. Problem Analysis, Section 5. Future State, and Section 6. Implementation Plan.

Other Activities:

Sensei Tips: Consider additional team members, use good project management skills, listen to employee's concerns, and use this Checklist.

Web Based Kaizen Event
PDCA Phase Checklist

Kaizen Event

Process Owner:

Black Belt or Lean Sensei:

Start Date:

End Date:

Objective:

Legend:
- @ Email
- Web Conferencing
- Posted/Published
- Text
- ● Full Team Meeting
- ● Sub-Team Meeting (or Team Member)
- ● 1 hour time bucket
- ▪ 30 minute time bucket
- ◂ 15 minute time bucket

Week 1 (2 hours)

1. Understand specific Lean tools and continue to apply as needed:
   - 5S
   - Visual Controls
   - Mistake Proofing
   - Standard Work
   - Process or Work Area Layout
   - Mass Customization
   - Flow
   - Quick Changeovers (QCO)
   - Total Productive Maintenance (TPM)
   - Cross-Training

2. Update Kaizen Activity PDCA Worksheet.
   - Rolling Kaizen Event
   - Time Bucket Matrix
   - PDCA Kaizen Activity Worksheet

Other Activities:

Week 2 (2 hours)

1. Review/discuss PDCA implementations (Action Items).
2. Update PDCA schedule.
3. Evaluate sub-teams implementation with appropriate metrics.
4. Create Action Items.
5. Update timeline for sub-teams implementation of PDCAs.

Other Activities:

Week 3 (2 hours)

1. Review/discuss PDCA implementations (Action Items).
2. Update PDCA schedule.
3. Evaluate sub-teams implementation with appropriate metrics.
4. Create Action Items.
5. Update timeline for sub-teams implementation of PDCAs.

Other Activities:

Week 4 (2 hours)

1. Review/discuss PDCA implementations (Action Items).
2. Update PDCA schedule.
3. Evaluate sub-teams implementation with appropriate metrics.
4. Create Action Items.
5. Update timeline for sub-teams implementation of PDCAs.

Other Activities:

Weeks 5+ (2 hours)

1. Review/discuss PDCA implementations (Action Items).
2. Update PDCA schedule.
3. Evaluate sub-teams implementation with appropriate metrics.
4. Create Action Items.
5. Update timeline for sub-teams implementation of PDCAs.

Other Activities:

Sensei Tips: Keep management informed, respect the process area employees, and use this Checklist.

Web Based Kaizen Event
Follow-Up Phase Checklist

Kaizen Event

Process Owner:	Black Belt or Lean Sensei:
Objective:	Start Date:
	End Date:

Legend:
- @ Email
- Web Conferencing
- Posted/Published
- Text

- ● 1 hour time bucket
- ▌ 30 minute time bucket
- ▌ 15 minute time bucket

- ●●● Full Team Meeting
- ● Sub-Team Meeting (or Team Member)

Week 1 (30 minutes)

1. **Continue communications.**
Consider the following charts:
Pareto Chart
Paynter Chart
Pie Chart
Scatter (Concentration) Plots
Radar Chart
Run Chart
Histogram
Statistical Process Ctrl. Charts

2. **Discuss outstanding issues.**

Other Activities:

Week 2 (30 minutes)

3. **Provide support after the PDCA Phase.**
Lean Representative

4. **Create and distribute the Event Dashboards.**
Weekly Kaizen Dashboard
Monthly Kaizen Dashboard
Maintained by process owner

Other Activities:

Week 3 (30 minutes)

5. **Establish avenue for primary stakeholders to provide feedback.**
Kaizen Suggestion Box
Emails
Walk and talk
Google Drive

6. **Work with management to practice Gemba.**
Observe the process
Informally ask questions
Show concern
Arrive with a purpose
Comment on visuals
Notify the area
Include different mgmt levels
Build upon each Gemba
Thank employees for their efforts

Other Activities:

Week 4 (30 minutes)

7. **Apply Kaizen to the Kaizen.**
Kaizen Event Participation
Evaluation form

8. **Reward and recognize the team.**
Verbal recognition
Gift cards
Lunches, dinners, etc.
Recognition letters, awards, etc.
Corporate gifts
Time off
Green fees

Other Activities:

Sensei Tips: Ensure all PDCAs are completed, share results throughout the organization, and reward and recognize team members and any other employees that contributed.

Today's Kaizen Event
Planning Phase Checklist

Kaizen Event

Process Owner:		Black Belt or Lean Sensei:		Start Date:	
				End Date:	

Objective:

Legend:
- ● 1 hour time bucket — ◐◐◐ Full Team Meeting
- ◗ 30 minute time bucket — ● Sub-Team Meeting (or Team Member)
- ◗ 15 minute time bucket

Days 1 - 4

- ☐ 1. Determine project scope.
- ☐ 2. Review data set.
- ☐ 3. Determine team members.
- ☐ 4. Communicate to team members date for full team meeting.
- ☐ 5. Conduct a Stakeholder Analysis.
- ☐ 6. Conduct specific Lean tool training.
- ☐ 7. Create Reporting and Communication forms.
- ☐ 8. Communicate to Executive Sponsor and other managers the schedule.
- ☐ 9. Prepare for full day meeting.

Other Activities:

Other Activities:

Day 5 Agenda (8 hour meeting time)

- ☐ Review the problem.
- ☐ List issues and barriers.
- ☐ Create second and third level Pareto Analysis.
- ☐ Determine potential solutions.
- ☐ Assess specific solutions.
- ☐ Select solutions.
- ☐ Create implementation plans.

Other Activities:

Sensei Tips: Consider additional team members, use good project management skills, listen to employee's concerns, and use this Checklist.

Today's Kaizen Event
PDCA Phase Checklist

Kaizen Event

Process Owner:

Black Belt or Lean Sensei:

Objective:

Start Date:

End Date:

● Full Team Meeting
◖ Sub-Team Meeting (or Team Member)

● 1 hour time bucket
◖ 30 minute time bucket
◗ 15 minute time bucket

Week 1

1. Continue communications.
2. Perform PDCAs.
3. Provide support after the PDCA.
4. Update Project Dashboard or Scorecard.

Other Activities:

Week 2

1. Continue communications.
2. Perform PDCAs.
3. Provide support after the PDCA.
4. Create Project Dashboard or Scorecard.

Other Activities:

Other Activities:

Other Activities:

Other Activities:

Sensei Tips: Keep management informed, respect the process area employees, and use this Checklist.

Kaizen Event

Project Scorecard

Type of Project: [____]

Start Date: [____]
End Date: [____]

Value Stream Impacted: [____]

Executive Champion: [____]

Lean Sensei/Black Belt: [____]

Process Owner: [____]

Specific Improvement Activity (PDCA)	Who	Current Measurement			Implementation Date/ Target	Post Measurements			
		Name	% or #	Date		% or #	Date	% or #	Date

If the measurement is not meeting traget(s) the WWWWW (below) must clearly indicate how you plan to meet or exceed target.

What	Who	When (m/d/y)	Why	Comments/Status

Additional Notes:

Today's Kaizen Event
Follow-Up Phase Checklist

Kaizen Event

Process Owner:	**Black Belt or Lean Sensei:**	**Start Date:**
		End Date:

Objective:

● 1 hour time bucket
🍴 30 minute time bucket
◢ 15 minute time bucket

◖◗●◖ Full Team Meeting
◖● Sub-Team Meeting (or Team Member)

Week 1

☐ **1. Continue communications.**
Consider the following charts:
Pareto Chart
Paynter Chart
Pie Chart
Scatter (Concentration) Plots
Radar Chart
Run Chart
Histogram
Statistical Process Ctrl. Charts
◢ ◖●

☐ **2. Update Project Scorecard.**
◢ ◖●

Other Activities:

☐ **3. Work with management to practice Gemba.**
Observe the process
Informally ask questions
Show concern
Arrive with a purpose
Comment on visuals
Notify the area
Include different mgmt levels
Build upon each Gemba
Thank employees for their efforts
◢

☐ **4. Establish avenue for primary stakeholders to provide feedback.**
Kaizen Suggestion Box
Emails
Walk and talk
Google Drive
◢ ◖●

Other Activities:

☐ **5. Apply Kaizen to the Kaizen.**
Kaizen Event Participation
Evaluation form
◢ ◖◗●◖

☐ **6. Reward and recognize the team.**
Verbal recognition
Gift cards
Lunches, dinners, etc.
Recognition letters, awards, etc.
Corporate gifts
Time off
Green fees
◢ ◖◗●◖

Other Activities:

Other Activities:

Other Activities:

Other Activities:

Sensei Tips: Ensure all PDCAs are completed, share results throughout the organization, and reward and recognize team members and any other employees that contributed.

Kaizen Event

Wiki Kaizen Event Determination Worksheet

Your Name:

Your Manager:

Date:

Department or Value Stream:

Instructions: Please ✔ the appropriate response to each statement.

Use the follwoing five level Likert item scale for scoring: 1 = Strongly Disagree 2 = Disagree 3 = Neither Agree nor Disagree 4 = Agree 5 = Strongly Agree **Statements**	1 Strongly Disagree	2 Disagree	3 Neither Agree nor Disagree	4 Agree	5 Strongly Agree
1. The project will have a positive impact impact on my work performance.					
2. The project requires no additional training upstream.					
3. The project requires no additional training downstream.					
4. The project willl have no impact on others.					
5. The project can easily be shared with others.					
6. The project can be proven successful with measurements.					
7. The project can be completed with little or no resources.					
8. The project will improve a critical process of my work.					
9. The project will make my job easier.					
10. The project will be easy to implement.					
11. The project process improvement can be standardized.					
12. The project will improve my quality of work.					
13. The project will eliminate waste in my work.					
14. The project will reduce stress in my daily work.					
15. The project can be completed quickly in less than 4 hours of my time.					
16. The project is well within my scope of work.					
17. The project is customer focused.					
18. The project is process focused and not people focused.					
19. The project does not require a value stream map.					
20. The project root cause is known.					

Total:

Kaizen Event	Wiki Colleague Request

Date: ☐

Name: ☐   **Department:** ☐

Upstream Supplier: ☐   **Downstream Customer:** ☐

The Wiki Colleague Request is to be used when requesting "light" assistance from a colleague to help provide a solution to a problem or implement an improvement. This improvement or solution should also benefit the colleague directly or indirectly and not require any significant amount of their time or resources (less than an hour or two).

Step 1: Describe the Problem or Opportunity.	Include photos, charts, and graphs, if necessary. Include current measurements.

Problem Viewed by Initiator	Type of Waste

Problem Viewed by Colleague (Perceived)	Type of Waste (Perceived)

Proposed Start Date: _____

Step 2: List Potential Benefits.	Be specific in terms of how the team's success will be measured. Use Balance Scorecard measures, if possible.

Benefits for Initiator (WIIFM)	Benefits for Colleague (Perceived) (WIIFT)

Proposed End Date: _____

Step 3: List Resources Required.	Include support needed from Colleague. Be specific in terms of technical expertise, departmental cooperation as a trial, etc.

Type of Support	Estimated Hours Needed	Dates Requested

Step 4: Determine Feasibility and Next Steps.

☐ Agree As Is   ☐ Suggest To Formalize As A Team Type Kaizen Event

☐ Need More Information Before Agreeing

☐ Currently Being Addressed

Sign-Off Date: _____

Kaizen Event

Wiki PDCA Activity Worksheet

Process Name: _____   **Date:** _____

Department: _____   **Colleagues:** _____

Process Name/Activity	Problem or Waste	Lean Tool	Specific Activities (What)		Who	When
			Plan			
			Do			
			Check			
			Act			
			Plan			
			Do			
			Check			
			Act			
			Plan			
			Do			
			Check			
			Act			
			Plan			
			Do			
			Check			
			Act			
			Plan			
			Do			
			Check			
			Act			
			Plan			
			Do			
			Check			
			Act			
			Plan			
			Do			
			Check			
			Act			
			Plan			
			Do			
			Check			
			Act			

Parking Lot Items for Wiki Kaizen Events or Other Types of Kaizen Events

Kaizen Event	Sharing Worksheet

Name: [ ]　　　　Department: [ ]

Colleague: [ ]　　　　Date: [ ]

The Sharing Worksheet is a communication tool to share the results of a Wiki improvement project. The Sharing Worksheet should be distributed to colleagues that have similar-type work processes. The Sharing Worksheets should be stored in a central location for others to review. The supervisor or manager can use the Sharing Worksheets as part of the performance appraisal for their employees.

Step 1: Convey Pre and Post Measurements in Simple Form.

Pre Measurements	Post Measurements

Step 2: Identify Wastes that were Eliminated.

- ❏ Overproduction
- ❏ Inventory
- ❏ Waiting
- ❏ Motion
- ❏ Transport
- ❏ Defects or Errors

- ❏ Overprocessing
- ❏ Skills and Knowledge
- ❏ Unevenness
- ❏ Overburden
- ❏ Environmental Resources
- ❏ Social Responsibility

Step 3: Identify the Main Lean Tools Used.

- ❏ 5S
- ❏ 5 Why Analysis
- ❏ Brainstorming
- ❏ Continuous Flow
- ❏ Fishbone Diagram
- ❏ Gantt Chart
- ❏ Heijunka/Leveling

- ❏ Impact Map
- ❏ Just-In-Time
- ❏ Kanban
- ❏ Mistake Proofing
- ❏ Pareto Chart
- ❏ Paynter Chart
- ❏ Pitch

- ❏ Pull System
- ❏ Run Chart
- ❏ Runner
- ❏ Standard Work
- ❏ Takt Time/Demand Analysis
- ❏ Training
- ❏ Value Stream Mapping

- ❏ Voice of the Customer
- ❏ Waste Audit
- ❏ Work Load Balancing
- ❏ [ ]
- ❏ [ ]
- ❏ [ ]

Step 4: List Recommendations.

Recommendations to Colleagues	Recommendations to Management
Other Information	**Contact Information**

Chapter 5. Kaizen Event Leadership

Overview

Leading or facilitating a Kaizen Event requires effective communication and leadership skills as explained in this chapter. The following is a guide to direct you to an appropriate section of this chapter given your particular Kaizen Event situation or issue:

Kaizen Event Leadership Tools Matrix

Issue	Communications	Conflict Management	Decision Making	Discipline	Innovation and Creativity	Layered Process Audits	Leadership and Coaching	Managing Change	Meeting Leading	Motivation	Performance Management and Goal Setting	Reward and Recognition	Stakeholder Analysis	Standard Work for Leaders	Stress Management	Team Selection and Building	Time Management	Trust Building	Valuing Diversity
Not completing Action Items	◆									◆	◆	◆				◆	◆		
Managers not sending right people to meetings	◆							◆					◆			◆			
Arriving late	◆			◆						◆	◆	◆				◆	◆		
Lack of participation/ not engaged	◆				◆			◆		◆	◆	◆			◆	◆		◆	◆
Completing Action Items late	◆									◆	◆	◆				◆	◆		
Poor/disruptive behavior		◆		◆											◆				
FAD of the month attitude re: project	◆							◆										◆	
Meeting objectives never met							◆	◆	◆										
Effective meetings not established							◆		◆										
Lack of making data-based decisions			◆																
Lack of support from other departments	◆	◆											◆			◆			◆
1-2 people dominating meetings									◆										◆
Lack of confidence in sustaining changes						◆	◆		◆					◆				◆	
Constant disagreements about process changes		◆					◆						◆					◆	
Trouble reaching consensus			◆		◆													◆	
Priorities constantly changing	◆							◆			◆		◆					◆	

Leadership

Kaizen Events are focused quality improvement tools, but continuous improvement (CI) (i.e., a Lean Sigma transformation) is more than just tools or facilitation by a Kaizen leader. The cultural change required for continuous improvement as a way of doing business on a daily basis, requires each person to see themselves as a vested participant in the process. A Kaizen leader or specially selected team leader acting as a lone ranger leading and achieving improvement success (or failure) does not bring CI success by itself. If employees refuse to buy-in or look to someone else to do the CI work in their area, sustainment is doomed because there is no ownership. The concept and practice of Kaizen and Kaizen Events has to be internalized by everyone, individually and collectively. And, it all starts with good, effective leadership.

Skeptical supervisors, managers, and leaders must overcome their gut reaction to scare people into doing better or providing a solution, instead of asking themselves why? - Why are there feelings that CI or this Lean Sigma program is someone else's job? Scare tactics and doing someone's thinking are not what continuous improvement is all about. Skeptics in leadership must get comfortable asking themselves: *What can I do differently to reinforce in using Kaizen to encourage folks to gain confidence and to work through their challenges and opportunities for improvement?* If using scare tactics or providing their solutions, employees are robbed of gaining ownership and control of their processes thus relieving them of personal responsibility for improvement.

Employees generally want to do a good job and contribute positively. Kaizen Events when done properly teaches people the Plan-Do-Check-Act (PDCA) cycle so they can use the thought process to continue working at improving their enterprise, every day and everywhere, not just when a Black Belt, Lean Sensei, etc. is brought in to work with them. Getting employees to take ownership and be empowered is what will make the continuous improvement culture spread. In that endeavor, the following tools can be used to sincerely engage the employees in planning, implementing, and sustaining process improvements.

Note: The following sections are from the book, *Today's Lean Leader (MCS Media, 2012)* and have been adapted for this publication.

Communication

This section will be helpful if the following issues are occurring in your Kaizen Event:

- ❖ Not completing Action Items on time
- ❖ Managers not sending right people to meetings
- ❖ Arriving late
- ❖ Lack of participation/not engaged

- ❖ Completing Action Items late
- ❖ FAD of the month attitude re: project
- ❖ Lack of support from other departments
- ❖ Priorities constantly changing

Communication is a formal process where information is transferred from a sender to a receiver. A large part of improving communications is recognizing and reducing the "noise" in the system. The diagram below illustrates how this "noise" in the process can impede effective communications. In any type of Kaizen Event there will be multiple layers and methods of communication.

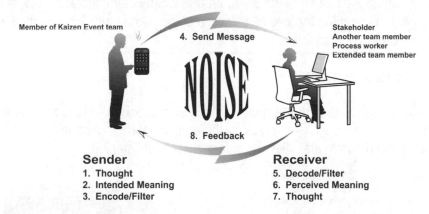

There are many sources of noise that can impede communication, some of which are:

- ❖ Absence of or poor feedback
- ❖ Improper message delivery method
- ❖ Physical distractions - phone ringing, reading emails or text messages, etc.
- ❖ Status effects or the personal relationships
- ❖ Cultural and gender differences

- ❖ Tone or emotions
- ❖ Terminology problems
- ❖ Inconsistent body language
- ❖ Communication styles
- ❖ Lack of trust
- ❖ Unintended, mixed signals
- ❖ Technology voids

There are few things as important for a leader as the ability to communicate well. For the leader, achieving a common understanding for the vision can only be achieved through effective communication. It is important for a leader to communicate effectively with the Kaizen Event team members as well as with management, as this is the way leaders inspire others to succeed.

Communication Channels

When trying to communicate, be careful when selecting the appropriate communication channel. The wrong communication channel leads to confusion and can actually offend people. Use the concept of communication richness as illustrated in the following diagram to select the most appropriate communication channel.

Postings	Memos	Emails/Text Messages	Telephone	Face-to-Face
				(Skype, FaceTime, etc.)

Low Richness
Inpersonal
One-way
Fast

High Richness
Personal
Two-way
Slow

Team members may require different communications channels that would depend on the situation. For example, the Team Charter and Meeting Minutes will be posted on the company's Web page, but the Action Item Log will be mailed to the team members. Be precise when communicating to team members throughout the Kaizen Event. Determine the overall objective of the communication and then work with the team to provide the most effective channels.

Verbal Communications

Better listening skills help us reduce the "noise" in communications. This is the key to improving verbal communications. To improve your listening skills, there must be an understanding of the different levels of listening. The following diagram identifies the different levels of listening:

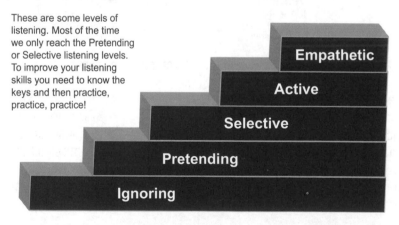

These are some levels of listening. Most of the time we only reach the Pretending or Selective listening levels. To improve your listening skills you need to know the keys and then practice, practice, practice!

Empathetic
Active
Selective
Pretending
Ignoring

Listed below are seven ways to improve your listening skills when communicating one-on-one and well as in small groups:

1. Stop talking! *Listen for the message content.*

2. Ask clarifying questions. *Listen for feelings.*

3. Respond to feelings. *Don't defend or criticize.*

4. Note all clues. *Body language, emotions, etc.*

Kaizen Demystified

5. Paraphrase and Restate. *"I hear you say…is that right?"*

6. Reflect the feeling. *"That must make you feel outraged!"*

7. Rephrase content and Reflect feeling. *"So, you're saying… and that makes you feel…"*

You will find people really open up if you use some of these seven listening skills. These can also diffuse team members' frustrations and stress.

The following are the key points for Verbal Communications and Better Listening:

- ❖ Stop talking.
- ❖ Put the other person at ease.
- ❖ Show that you want to listen.
- ❖ Remove any potential distractions.
- ❖ Empathize with the other person.
- ❖ Be patient, don't respond too quickly.
- ❖ Hold your temper. Don't get mad.
- ❖ Go easy on arguments and criticisms.
- ❖ Ask non-threatening questions to help you understand the person.
- ❖ Seek to understand the other person as a first priority.

Communication Inhibitors

Have you ever noticed that occasionally the ability to communicate comes to a complete and abrupt stop? This happens when a listener becomes unintentionally offended. You know it when it happens, but may not be sure why. The following "communications inhibitors" checklist is a listing of some phrases that can offend people. How many times have you heard or used them?

The following are twelve 'Communication Inhibitors' that would cause communication to stop.

Don't Do These…

1. Tell the other person what to do. Instead of: "You must…" or "You cannot…" Try this: Ask…"Could you please…" or "I would recommend..."

2. Threatening with "or else" implied. Instead of: "You had better…" or "If you don't..." Try linking a consequence to an action, for example, "If you do that, this may happen."

3. Tell the other person what they "ought" to do. Instead of: "You should…" or "It's your responsibility to…" Try this: Ask, "What if we tried it this way?" or say "If I were you, I'd do it differently."

4. Make un-asked for suggestions. Instead of "Let me suggest…" or "It would be best if you…" Try this: Ask "Do you want my opinion?" or "Can I make a suggestion?"

5. Attempt to educate the other person. Instead of: "Let me give you the facts…" or "Experience tells us that…" Try this: explain, "Here's how I see it…" or "When that happened to me I…"

6. Judge the other person negatively. Instead of: "You're not thinking straight." or "Your dead wrong…" Try this: Ask "What if you looked at it another way?" or "This is how I understand it, is that correct?"

7. Give insincere praise. Instead of: "You are an intelligent person…" or "You have such potential…" Try this: Compliment a specific behavior… "I like the way you…"

8. Put labels on people. Instead of: "You're a sloppy worker." or "You really goofed on this one…again!" Try this: Tell them what they do well.

9. Analyze the other person. Instead of: "You're jealous!" or "You're having problems with my authority." Try this: Asking about feelings. "Do you feel jealous?"

10. Make light of a person's problems or generalize. Instead of: "Things will get better." or "Behind every cloud there's a silver lining." Try this: Ask, "How can I help make this a positive?"

11. Give the third degree. Instead of: "Why did you do that?" or "Who told you to…" Try this: Expressing your feelings, "I am concerned for you…"

12. Make light of their problem by inappropriate joking. Instead of "Think about the positive…" or "You think you've got problems…" Try this: "I understand how this must make you feel, is there anything I can do to help?" or "That sounds terrible, how can I help?" Only use humor when it is appropriate.

In general…use more "I" or "We" statements and less "You" statements! "You" statements tend to raise the emotional level in other people, which can create excessive noise in the communications process. By keeping to "I" or "We" statements you can reduce the tension and noise in the communication process.

- ❖ Say "I (or We) need your help." instead of "Why won't you do what was assigned?"
- ❖ Say "I need you to improve." instead of "You must get these things done."
- ❖ Say "I don't see things that way." instead of "You're wrong!"
- ❖ Say "I don't feel right about this, instead of "You have no idea how I feel!"
- ❖ Say "I'm optimistic about our improvements." instead of "You're so negative about any change."

Written Communications

Written communication (i.e., emails, letters, text messages, postings on Facebook, etc.) is as critical as verbal communication. Leaders must create written communications with the same level of clarity and effort that is given to verbal communication. Written communication is often done with no feedback and for this reason can sometimes lead to more confusion.

The following are the key points for better Written Communications:

- ❖ Consider your audience.
- ❖ Make sure the communication needs to be in writing.
- ❖ Outline what you want to communicate.
- ❖ Be clear. In the first sentence of the communications describe what it is for. (Eg. The attached document reflects the latest data for the upcoming Kaizen Event. Please...)
- ❖ Be comprehensive and complete.
- ❖ Use readable language targeted to the recipient.
- ❖ Use spell-check to ensure professionalism.
- ❖ Always read over a document before sending.
- ❖ Consider emerging technologies to communicate the message.

Presentations

Kaizen Events may involve presentations being given by the team leader, facilitator, etc. Presentations may also be required throughout the event by various team members to other stakeholders and management. Presentations are a way to verbally, in writing and graphically, communicate information to groups of people. The key to group presentations if everyone is in the same conference or training room or via Web conferencing is to know your audience and focus on the desired outcomes. Whenever communicating, recognize who your audience is and address their interests.

Usually, the most difficult part with presentations is the fear of presenting itself. More people claim to be afraid of public speaking than are afraid of death! The key to reducing your fears and nervousness is preparation and practice (or experience).

The following are the key points for Presentations:

- ❖ Be prepared - know what to say and how to say it.
- ❖ Set the right tone - act audience centered, make eye contact, be pleasant and confident.
- ❖ Sequence points - state your purpose, make important points, follow with details, then summarize.
- ❖ Support your points - provide specific reasons to help them understand.
- ❖ Use good visual aids and provide appropriate handouts.
- ❖ Have the room and equipment working before everyone arrives.

Leadership

Emerging Technology

Leaders must recognize that the key to emerging technologies and social networking communications is that, as people mature, they will progress through dependence to independence to interdependence. Leaders must recognize this progression for themselves as well as for others. Communications within the social network is done by a computer, smart phone, or iPad-type device. Text messaging and video communications has rapidly become popular new ways to communicate among people due to the addition of the smart phone. Smart phones, as well as the iPad-tablet devices, allow communications within the social network, and organizations are increasingly becoming more active in their use.

As the trend of employees working remotely increases, Web Based Kaizen Event types will become more common, and, as more of the younger generation enters the workforce with advanced smart phones and iPad-type devices, communications through networks such as these will be a main avenue for communications for continuous improvement and problem solving initiatives.

Many people prefer text messaging because it is fast, easy, and efficient. Many organizations are no longer providing email addresses; they are expecting all communications to be through their smart phone or iPad-type device. As many people realize in the business world, it is not easy to find time to talk or to have a conversation. Text messaging allows you to easily have a conversation with multiple people using many convenient features.

The following are the key points for Business Communications via Social Networks:

- ❖ Think before you post!
- ❖ Be respectful. Don't post anything you would be uncomfortable saying.
- ❖ Be transparent.
- ❖ Maintain confidentiality.
- ❖ Use good ethical judgment; follow federal and company guidelines.

Kaizen Events will require some type of communications on the various channels discussed in this section. Continue to address the teams' needs and concerns by using the most effective communication channel. (Eg., No point in texting a team member information on their Action Item if they do not have a smart phone.)

Most problems occurring for Kaizen Event teams when dealing with process changes and issues within the team will stem from some sort of miscommunication.

Conflict Management

This section will be helpful if the following issues are occurring in your Kaizen Event:

- ❖ Poor/disruptive behavior
- ❖ Lack of support from other departments
- ❖ Constant disagreements about process changes

Conflict management *is the process of working with people to resolve issues in a constructive and positive environment.* Some of the benefits of properly managed conflict are:

- ❖ Increases awareness of an issue or problem confronting the team or individual
- ❖ Builds team commitment and loyalty
- ❖ Promotes change and improvement
- ❖ Strengthens relationships and morale
- ❖ Promotes awareness of self and others
- ❖ Enhances personal development

Conflict is perfectly normal between individuals, teams, within a team, or inside your own mind. Conflict comes from:

- ❖ Different group or individual needs
- ❖ Misunderstandings
- ❖ Other intangible dilemmas

The cost of improperly managed conflict can be extreme and cause tremendous loss of productivity within the Kaizen Event. It can affect quality, safety, team harmony, and/or product or service image. The nature of conflict can be complex and confusing. The most difficult conflicts are characterized by the following symptoms:

- ❖ Competitive or conflicting processes or needs
- ❖ Misperceptions and biases
- ❖ Emotionally charged individuals
- ❖ Communication breakdowns
- ❖ Ambiguous issues
- ❖ Rigid commitments
- ❖ Escalation of issues

To properly manage conflict, understanding all sides of the issues is important. All sides must work to identify ways for constructive interests to be satisfied. The following steps or guidelines can be used to manage
conflict and create the Win-Win situation:

Note: This can also be considered a way to negotiate in a positive manner.

1. Get over personalities.

2. Work to understand opposing parties' interests and develop an objective statement regarding the issue
   or problem.

3. Understand and use the following diagram to convey to people that the best solution is where there is a
   high concern for the interests of everyone and problem solving being the common goal.

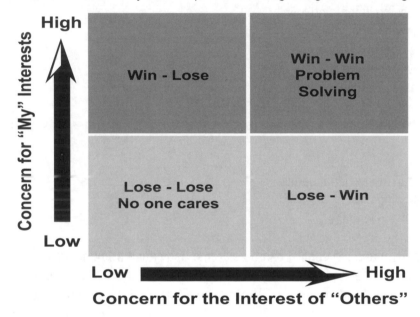

Conflict resolution can be difficult because people are usually more concerned about their own interests,
than the interests of the other party or parties. When this occurs, participants adapt a "contending"
strategy and battle it out.

4. Invent and discover new solutions to issues where everyone's interests can be satisfied. This is a true
   "Problem Solving" or "Win - Win" strategy.

5. Openly document the interests of each party on a Conflict Resolution Worksheet or something similar.

Conflict Resolution Worksheet

Issue or Dilemma:
(What is the conflict about? What do you want to accomplish?)

Interests of each party involved:
(If there are more parties involved, use additional sheets. What does each party want? Use this section to get all parties to understand all the different perspectives. Focus people on interests, not on each other.)

Party #1	Party #2	Party #3
1.	1.	1.
2.	2.	2.
3.	3.	3.
4.	4.	4.
5.	5.	5.
6.	6.	6.

Alternatives?
(Brainstorm creative solutions that can satisfy as many interests as possible. The more creative, the better. Focus people on options and not each other. Use this to build teamwork.)

How will we determine a "fair" settlement?
(Jointly determine how a settlement will be achieved. Ask what is "fair" for all. Focus on objective criteria.)

---

6. Jointly establish criteria for each agreement.

7. Invent or create alternatives that each side can live with.

8. Jointly select the alternatives that provide the greatest mutual gain by using the over-riding themes of problem-solving to ensure a Win-Win resolution for the matter or issue. The following points should be considered:

   ❖ Separate the people from the problem.
   ❖ Focus on interests, not positions.
   ❖ Invent options for mutual gain.
   ❖ Develop objective criteria for moving forward.

The following are the key points for Conflict Management:

- ❖ Deal with the conflict immediately.
- ❖ Identify the source of the problem.
- ❖ Handle it face-to-face (not by email or texting).
- ❖ Consider the personality traits involved.
- ❖ Ask for input, interests, and proposed solutions.
- ❖ Seek to understand all sides of the issue, then express your side.
- ❖ Avoid emotions - use logic and concept of "fairness."
- ❖ Schedule a follow-up method to ensure conflict stays resolved upon mutually agreed upon items.

Kaizen Events may have various levels of conflict between team members as well as process area employees that may not have been part of the change process (mistakenly). It is imperative as the leader, as well as those informal leaders within the team, to quickly address conflict in its early stages so it does not disrupt the Kaizen Event PDCA Implementation and Follow-Up Phases. This should be done privately. If there exists a larger conflict with the team, in that, as a leader you sense a number of team members resisting the proposed change or a major reluctance to participate, then consider allocating time to address these issues or schedule a separate meeting with those specific team members.

Decision Making

This section will be helpful if the following issues are occurring in your Kaizen Event:

- ❖ Lack of making data-based decisions
- ❖ Trouble reaching consensus

Decision making *is a mental process resulting in the selection of a course of action among several alternative scenarios.* Every decision making process produces a final choice which can be an action or an opinion of choice.

Decision making is a critical function of Kaizen Event teams. Decision making methods and tools make it easier to process information faster for more effective, more accurate, and better communicated decisions. Using decision making tools and methods is a means to improve the speed in which decisions can be processed.

There are several different models to assist in making decisions. Some teams will procrastinate over a decision, while others will make quick decision. The use of a decision making model and tools will help teams make better decisions.

Decision making methods follow the basic five step process:

1. Identify the decision to be made.

2. Collect and analyze data and information regarding the decision, and develop alternatives.

3. Determine the best Decision Making Method.

Decision Making Methods				
Decision Method	**Leader Time**	**When to use**	**Risk**	**Example**
Delegation	Low	Delegate decisions to other people or teams if they have the information needed to make a quality decision, there is no one more correct solution, and their commitment to implementation is critical to success.	Low	How to arrange the work cell, or who will work the weekend shift.
Multi-Voting	Low – Medium	Everyone gets a "vote." Use when a "fair" and participative process is needed and everyone has a good understanding of the situation.	Low	When to schedule a training session or group lunch.
Team Consensus	Medium	Talk things out and periodically "poll" for consensus on direction. Ask, "Do we have a consensus?" Use this when a less formal process is needed and the success depends on the group's support.	Medium	How to develop a standard process or what represents a "quality" product.
Decision Matrix	High	A formal decision making process where a matrix of decision options and criteria are established, ranked, and scored. Use this method when there are many potential correct options/opinions, and the "stakes" are high, and a "fair" and participative process is needed to gain everyone's support.	High Potential	Which new machine to purchase or where to locate a new facility.

4. Use the following Decision Matrix and steps for working through complex decisions where the risk is high or uncertain.
   - a. State the decision to be made.
   - b. Identify the decision alternatives.
   - c. Determine decision criteria and weight or rank them.
   - d. Rank the features of each decision alternative to the criteria.
   - e. Multiply the rating by the criteria weight and total up the scores for each alternative.
   - f. Use the total score as discussion points and make the final decision.

Decision Making Matrix

Decision Statement:

Decision Team:	Date:	Alternative 1		Alternative 2		Alternative 3		Alternative 4		Alternative 5	
Decision Criteria	**Criteria Weight** (1Low – 10 high)	Rank	Score (Rank ×Weight)	Rank	Score (Rank ×Weight)	Rank	Score (Rank ×Weight)	Rank	Score (Rank ×Weight)	Rank	Score (Rank ×Weight)
Features											
Totals											
Decision Made and Reason:											

5. Implement the decision.

Continue work to gain consensus on all decision making. If a consensus cannot be achieved, consider reevaluating the Features and Alternatives. At times Kaizen Events may need additional expertise to assist in complex decisions...consider this as an option.

Discipline

This section will be helpful if the following issues are occurring in your Kaizen Event:

- ❖ Arriving late
- ❖ Poor/disruptive behavior

Discipline is the act of influencing behavior through reprimand or negative reward. It is delivered based on the belief that the employee will correct their behavior in order to avoid negative rewards.

Disciplinary processes are a necessary function in organizations and may be needed a times during a Kaizen Event. Disciplinary processes are used to correct undesirable behaviors like, absenteeism, tardiness, poor quality work, harassment, discrimination, falsifying records, fighting, not using work time appropriately, as well as many others. Many of these will not be encountered during a Kaizen Event, however, unfortunately some may be. Specifically, during a Kaizen Event discipline may need to be imposed for tardiness or a team member always arriving late for meetings or not arriving at all, poor work quality that impacts the initiative, insubordination on proposed changes, etc. Prior to any discipline, other methods/tools (i.e., Motivation, Performance Management and Goal Setting, Handling Conflict, etc.) should be considered if at all possible. If none of those other tools work, then a formal disciplinary action may be required.

The goal of disciplinary systems is to bring conformance to an organization's goals, standards, and/or expectations. It is important to follow the organizations' rules for delivering discipline. For best results, discipline should be consistently applied, in a "firm but fair" manner. The approach is no different for a Kaizen Event - team members must conform to the purpose and scope of the activity due to its importance to the organization.

The following steps or guidelines can be used for giving various forms of discipline:

1. Ensure all the facts are known. A leader who truly gives the team member that seems to warrant some discipline an opportunity to explain first, will often find that there is no need for discipline. The worker never has to know, indeed, some of the possibly unkind or judgmental thoughts and concerns passing through the leaders' mind. Permitting employees to explain their perspective first is the most important principle in employee discipline, and more than any other, one that will save the leader from destroying employee trust. Another benefit of permitting the employee to speak up first, is that it helps to reduce high tensions and emotions. Consider mitigating circumstances which could reduce, but not necessarily eliminate, any disciplinary action. Could the employee's action have some justification?

Note: Kaizen Events rarely would encounter this level of employee interaction.

2. If discipline is required, use a simple Plan - Do - Check - Act (PDCA) process.

PLAN the discipline.

  ❖ Be specific in the behavior that needs to be corrected.
  ❖ Identify why the type of behavior is unacceptable.
  ❖ Have the employee acknowledge in some form or fashion what is now expected of them.

DO deliver the discipline in a firm but fair manner.

  ❖ Be immediate when other methods have not worked or was not appropriate.

CHECK for understanding and commitment to improve.

  ❖ Identify a time frame for evidence of correct behavior.

ACT to follow up to ensure permanent improvement.

  ❖ Establish how the performance will be monitored.
  ❖ Document the new performance.

With any type of discipline, use a consistent or standard format to document actions. Request assistance from Human Resources to follow company policy if this has an impact on the individual's performance appraisal. It would be unfortunate (and unlikely) to have someone in a Kaizen Event requiring formal discipline. If an employee is exhibiting traits that require "improvement behavior" and you as the team leader or facilitator is not in their chain of command, privately discuss the questionable behavior with his or her manager (or process owner). Many times that will be all that is needed.

Innovation and Creativity

This section will be helpful if the following issues are occurring in your Kaizen Event:

- ❖ Lack of participation/not engaged
- ❖ Trouble reaching consensus

Creativity is the creating of a new idea. *Innovation is the translation of the idea into use.* Innovation and creativity was once believed to be only the responsibility of the leadership of an organization. Today, innovation and creativity is expected of everyone in every position so that they can improve safety, quality and productivity of their work. Innovation and creativity can be learned and facilitated by using appropriate tools and techniques. When brainstorming is used throughout the Kaizen Event, it will be up to the leader to bring out the creative and innovator ideas from the team members.

Much of the confusion about creativity and innovation comes from the generation of new ideas and the transition from divergent thinking to convergent thinking. *Divergent thinking or "out-of-the-box" thinking is a thought process or method used to generate creative ideas by exploring many possible solutions.* Divergent thinking typically occurs in a spontaneous, free-flowing manner with many possible solutions explored in a short amount of time, and unexpected connections are drawn. After the process of divergent thinking has been completed, ideas and information are organized and structured using convergent thinking. *Convergent thinking is deductive reasoning, thinking in which ideas are examined for their logical validity or in which a set of rules is followed.* It is the opposite of divergent thinking.

The following steps or guidelines can be used to help team members improve their creative and innovative abilities:

1. Determine problem or opportunity by using one of the following five "triggers" to stimulate creativity and generate ideas (divergent thinking):

---

1. **Forced Association** - Force association between two unlike things. Go explore! Examples; compare a factory to a car. What are the inputs? What are the outputs? What is the fuel? The purpose?

2. **Reversing Hidden Assumptions** - What if what we think we know is completely wrong? Examples; What if there was no gravity? What if we could provide same-day delivery of parts? What would our operation look like?

3. **Metaphorical Thinking** - How is our organization (i.e., plant, office or work area, etc.) like a tree? How do ants know what to do? How do we know what to do?

4. **The Outrageous Ideas** - What would it take to have a fully automatic work environment? No people do the work. What if our competitor found a way?

5. **Extreme "What if's"** - What if cost were no object? What if we had no computers? How would we work?

---

2. Generate and analyze ideas by reviewing and practicing some of the following ideas to improve divergent thinking:

   ❖ Read and study a text book, familiar or not.
   ❖ Write and keep a log or journal or do a Strengths - Weaknesses - Opportunities - Threats (SWOT) Analysis.
   ❖ Draw or paint a picture to "picture a solution."
   ❖ Exercise, eat right, and get proper rest.
   ❖ Build or create something.
   ❖ Cook a new or familiar food dish.
   ❖ Learn something new.
   ❖ Listen to music, familiar and not.
   ❖ Travel and observe how others do things.
   ❖ Visit a museum, store, new work site/company, or magazine stand - see new trends.
   ❖ Work a new job in your organization for a day or week.
   ❖ Meet new people.
   ❖ Act out a role; be a kid, the boss, a guru, a CIA operative, anything to gain a new perspective.

Though many of these activities will not be utilized in a Kaizen Event, consider how some of them can be adapted. For example:

❖ Conduct a SWOT Analysis: This can be done fairly easily and will open team members' minds to those external events or issues.
❖ Draw or paint a picture to "picture a solution:" The A3 Report or Storyboard format will allow this to occur.
❖ Exercise, eat right, and get proper rest: Provide a healthy lunch, snacks, and have the team take a walk for five minutes (or just the Waste Walk) will help.
❖ Learn something new: Present other industry solutions to a similar problem.

3. Prioritize ideas using an Implementation Grid to help individuals and teams prioritize ideas for implementation.

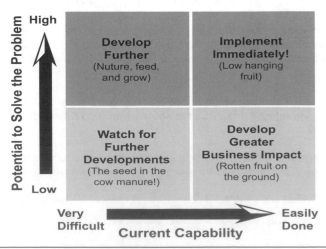

Kaizen Demystified

The following are the key points for Innovation and Creativity:

❖ Ensure the issue or problem requiring creativity and innovation is clear.
❖ Do not judge or criticize ideas.
❖ Do not jump to conclusions when ideas are expressed.
❖ Do not create artificial standards or rules (i.e., just because it has been done in a certain way does not mean it is the best or correct).
❖ Ensure everyone contributes.
❖ Allow for acceptable risks.
❖ Never ignore the majority opinion.
❖ Include different perspectives.
❖ If stuck, step back from the problem and attack from a different angle or time.
❖ Review competitor's products and services.

Kaizen Events are meant to improve current processes while at the same time team members may be "stuck" in thinking their processes cannot be improved or that some IT solution will fix everything. To get team members to start thinking outside-the-box, consider allowing a person from another department or area of the organization that has previous Lean and Six Sigma experience to contribute. They will be looking at the problem or issue from a different perspective as well as can relate to issues some of the team members may be experiencing.

Layered Process Audits

This section will be helpful if the following issue is occurring in your Kaizen Event:

❖ Lack of confidence in sustaining changes

Layered Process Audits (LPA) are a system of process audits performed by multiple levels of workers, supervisors, and managers to monitor key process characteristics and verify process conformance on an ongoing basis. LPAs ensure that standard work methods are being used and that processes are performing as expected. These will ensure the Follow-Up portion of the Kaizen Event is successful. Nothing is more frustrating for a team member than to contribute to improvements just to see the process revert back to the old ways within a short period of time after the Event.

Typically a Layered Process Auditing system is comprised of a series of process audits on critical or high risk processes, multiple layers of audits by workers, supervisors and managers from different areas, and a system of reporting and follow-up that ensures conformance and corrective actions are implemented. Layered Process Audits provide an excellent tool for minimizing variation and sustaining improvements in processes. LPAs also help organizations error-proof their processes/systems and make significant progress toward achieving perfection.

To get the most out of a LPA system, it is best to perform audits as close to real- time as possible. An audit performed on last week's work may be revealing, but will not provide the opportunity for avoiding problems, only fixing them in hindsight. An audit performed as a task is being completed affords the worker the opportunity to correct undesirable behaviors as they go.

The following steps or guidelines can be used to help team members improve their creative and innovative abilities:

1. Understand the following four elements that comprise an effective Layered Process Audit system:

   a. A Collection or Series of Audits - Audits are simply an organized group of questions designed to examine equipment, supplies, or a process. LPA audits should focus on areas where errors represent a high-risk for customers and organizations.
   b. Layers of Auditors - In an LPA system, your collection of audits is performed on a scheduled basis, at a predetermined frequency, by multiple layers of management from across the organization.
   c. Prevention and Containment - For a Layered Process Audit system to be truly effective, it must integrate analysis, action, and improvements. If an auditor finds a non-conformance while performing an audit, that auditor should not only record their finding, but also take immediate initial corrective action to ensure customers are not affected by the potential error.
   d. Reporting and Follow-up - Information about the finding should be recorded and readily available to management for later analysis. A regular system of LPA reviews should be put in place to ensure the effectiveness of the entire LPA system.

2. Understand the following audit types of LPAs. Each type of audit can be performed to a set and published schedule, or conducted by surprise.

   a. Simple audit - This is a simple yes or no question and answer format to determine if the process is working properly and may be performed concurrent or after the process is delivered.
   b. Concurrent audit – This LPA is completed as the process is being delivered to ensure completeness, accuracy, customer satisfaction, and/or perfection.
   c. Layered audit - This is an audit by a different level of leadership to ensure the LPAs are being performed to plan.
   d. Self-audit - This is an audit completed by the worker making the part or delivering the service. This audit is basically a checklist to ensure the process is complete and accurate, and that the customer is satisfied.
   e. Co-worker audit - This is similar to a Self-audit, but it is completed by a co-worker or peer.
   f. Internal audit - This is to verify that current policies and procedures are in keeping with the current operating environment or conditions.

3. Develop a layered audit process form and specify the items, who will perform the audit, and the frequency of audit.

4. Perform audits to the plan, post visually, and monitor audit system outputs and results. The bottom line is that audits have to be about processes and standards and the compliance to each.

5. Take corrective and preventative actions as necessary.

The following are the key points for Layered Process Audits

- ❖ Ensure a schedule is created for the audits and most importantly, followed.
- ❖ Continually review the audit and update as necessary.
- ❖ Gain a consensus of those being audited on the audit-type questions.
- ❖ Follow-up on corrective measures as audit reveals non-compliance issues.
- ❖ Take this process seriously, as others will be watching if these audits are for real.

The overall success of a Kaizen Event will be determined in how the process changes are sustained (or managed in the Follow-Up Phase). Implementing a version of a Layered Process Audit system will allow process area employees to be part of the improvement and audit process. This will ensure accountability at all levels.

Leadership and Coaching

This section will be helpful if the following issues are occurring in your Kaizen Event:

- ❖ Meeting objectives never met
- ❖ Effective meetings not established
- ❖ Lack of confidence in sustaining changes
- ❖ Constant disagreements about process changes
- ❖ Priorities constantly changing

Leadership is creating and communicating the "vision" for the organization and inspiring or influencing others to be motivated to work hard to accomplish tasks consistent with achieving the vision. The vision defines what the organization will be in the future or the direction to head. Research shows that a positive vision of the future precedes success.

Supervision or management is broader than leadership. Supervision consists of planning, directing, organizing, coaching, and monitoring activities and tasks to achieve specific goals. It involves getting work or goals accomplished through others. The tools to do this are defined throughout this book. In general, people prefer to be led rather than managed, but both may be required.

Note: Leadership and trust go hand-in-hand. Please see the section on Trust Building later in this Chapter to further enhance your leadership and coaching abilities.

The following steps or guidelines can be used to help formal and informal leaders improve their leadership and coaching abilities:

1. Accurately assess the situation at hand and then use the most effective leadership approach (or style). A key to this is to understand leadership styles, or approaches, and develop the ability to assess situations. An effective leader knows when to apply the different styles and to whom. The key is that the leader must know the situation and his or her people well enough to know what style to use. Use the following to assist this process:

Situation Question	Approach
How urgent is the situation?	Urgent issues require command and control leader style, while non-urgent issues can be dealt with more participatively.
How willing and able are the followers?	Willing and able followers usually need only goals and expectations to be successful. Unwilling or unable followers need a more directive approach and/or additional training.
Who has the critical information or expertise in the situation?	If the followers have the critical information or expertise, leaders need to be more participative. If the leader has the critical information or expertise, direction can be set by the leader. *Be careful here and not assume the leader knows everything.*
How critical is acceptance of the directions?	If acceptance of the directions is critical for success, it is best to develop the direction participatively. If not, set the plan and go!

2. Use the following Leadership Preference Grid for a "quick" determination of your preferred leadership style. Capitalize on specific strengths and compensate for specific weaknesses when dealing with leading a Kaizen Event. Consider working with someone who is strong in your weakness to improve your overall job effectiveness. An element that is important to consider is whether the situation presents a chance for the leader to teach versus just getting the job done. It is also the leader's responsibility to teach others about leadership at every opportunity. When a leader directs in order to just get the job done, very few of the participants will mature in their leadership. The style used needs to be a thoughtful decision on the part of the leader.

Note: It is possible to be split between two or three, but usually one style is dominant.

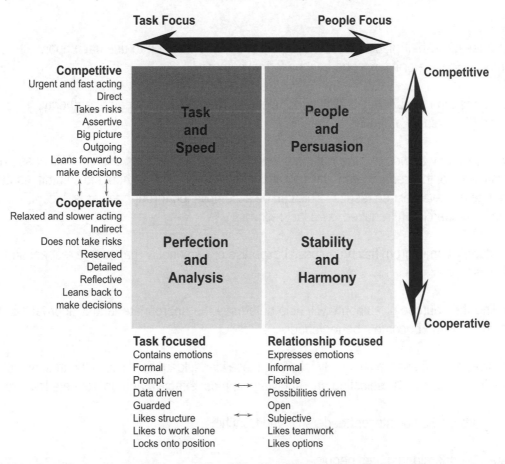

The fact is, that there is no one best leadership style. All styles can be effective; however, some styles are more effective in certain situations than others. Individuals will have a preferred or natural style, but should be able to "flex" to other styles when needed. It is best to learn to adapt your leadership style to the situation at hand.

Communication problems can often be traced to these style differences as well. To improve communications, try to communicate in a manner that best suits the other person's style preference.

3. Determine if a situation calls for a "push" or "pull" approach. Leadership styles and leader power must co-exist to get people to do what you want them to do. Supervisors and leaders can either "push" people or "pull" people to get things done.

Pushing *people means making them do something through force, coercion, power, and/or fear. This is often referred to as "the stick" or Theory X leadership style. Leaders with the authority to punish are said to have coercive power and can push.*

Pulling *people means inspiring them to accomplish the desired action. This is often referred to as "the carrot" or Theory Y leadership style. Leading without legitimate or position authority must use the pulling style.*

Both techniques have their place. A good leader knows how and when to use each approach. Pushing or pulling can be made easier if someone has the formal authority.

4. Determine the type of authority that may be needed. There are two types of authority: (1) *position authority* and (2) *personal authority*.

Position or legitimacy authority is the authority that comes from being the boss, in this case, the process owner or manager of the department. This usually includes having the authority to commit resources of the organization to achieve desired results. This can be accomplished through rewards, incentives, directives, co-optation, and coercion (if required, as a last resort).

Personal authority comes from having a special expertise or personality that people respect and/or need to achieve results.

Understanding the sources of authority will help determine the appropriate leader approach to use to improve performance and become a better leader.

5. Address the situation appropriately. By following these ideas, leaders will build the trust and commitment within their organization by selecting and applying the most effective and appropriate leadership style.

The following are the key points for Leadership and Coaching:

- ❖ Listen to understand others people.
- ❖ Mission or objective first, people always.
- ❖ Have everyone's best interest in mind.
- ❖ Give credit to others as often as possible.
- ❖ Be optimistic and encouraging.
- ❖ Give responsibility and expect accountability.
- ❖ Keep commitments and promises.
- ❖ Be open to new ideas.
- ❖ Help others be successful!

Managing Change

This section will be helpful if the following issues are occurring in your Kaizen Event:

- ❖ Managers not sending right people to meeting
- ❖ FAD of the month re: project
- ❖ Meeting objectives never met

Please see Chapter 1. Introduction pages 44 - 52 for the information on Managing Change.

Meeting Leading

This section will be helpful if the following issues are occurring in your Kaizen Event:

- ❖ Lack of participation, not engaged
- ❖ Meeting objectives never met
- ❖ Effective meetings not established
- ❖ 1 - 2 people dominating meetings
- ❖ Lack of confidence in sustaining changes

Please see Chapter 2. Standard 5 Day Kaizen Event pages 81 - 86 for the information on Meeting Leading.

Motivation

This section will be helpful if the following issues are occurring in your Kaizen Event:

- ❖ Not completing Action Items
- ❖ Arriving late
- ❖ Lack of participation/not engaged
- ❖ Completing Action Items late

Motivation is the desire of a person to complete tasks. In general, motivation comes from the desire to fill needs or avoid consequences. Motivation is directly proportional to leadership. Improve employee motivation can be a positive force in a Kaizen Event.

Which approach would motivate you more?

> *"How did you mess this up?"* or
> *"Here are the work instructions. Let me know if you need any help."*

How leaders treat and communicate with people are critical success factors to a highly motivated organization. Good leadership is the key to a motivated workforce. It has been stated that leaders cannot "motivate" other people; they can only create an environment where people can motivate themselves. Good leadership is creating an environment where people can motivate themselves to achievement and success.

The following steps or guidelines can be used to more effectively lead and motivate the workforce:

1. Understand how important it is to know what people want from work. Research shows that people rank what they want from work in the following order:

   1. Full appreciation of work done
   2. Feeling of being in on things
   3. Sympathetic help on personal issues
   4. Job security
   5. Good wages
   6. Interesting work
   7. Promotion and growth opportunities
   8. Management loyalty to employees
   9. Good working conditions
   10. Tactful discipline

Items 1, 2, 3, 6, 8, and 9 easily apply to Kaizen Events.

Many "managers" think that job satisfaction is a product of money. The "leader" should understand and know how to appreciate others for their contributions. People want to be appreciated and know that they are making a difference. The leader should continually be demonstrating appreciation.

2. Understand the two key motivational theories. Motivation theories can be split into two types, content and process theories. Maslow's and Hertzberg's theories are considered content theories, as they concern factors that drive (needs being met) motivating behaviors. Process theories drive direction (this way or that way and what are the outcomes) of behaviors, and a few examples are House's Path Goal, Vroom's expectancy, and Skinner's reinforcement theories. The scopes of content theories are broad and not covered specifically in this book. By following many of the lessons in this book, leaders will be employing process theory motivation techniques.

Maslow's Hierarchy of Needs states that people fill needs from lower level needs: Survival, to higher level needs: Self-actualization. What motivates a person depends on what level they have already satisfied. Herzberg's Two Factor Theory state that there are basic needs that if not satisfied, cause de-motivation (Hygiene Factors), and additional needs that act to motivate (Satisfier Factors).

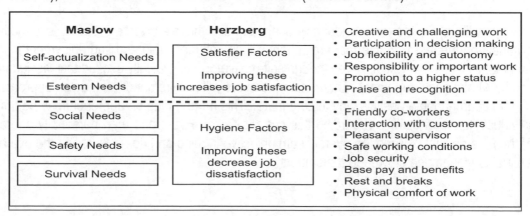

3. Understand and use the "Hawthorne Effect." *The **Hawthorne Effect** is the effect or motivation that people get from having leaders pay attention to them.* By pleasantly greeting employees each morning as they arrive at work (or at the beginning of the meeting) and taking interest in them as people, leaders can have an impact on their motivation.

4. Understand and use House's Path - Goal theory. *The **Path - Goal theory** states that people motivate themselves for their own reasons, and that leaders should adapt their style, rewards, and consequences to capitalize on the needs of the worker(s).* Path-goal theory assumes that leaders are flexible and that they can change their style, as situations require. This theory basically states that people do things or "follow a path" to achieve a goal. The goal may be a reward or to avoid reprimand. People consider positive (+) rewards to follow this path:

Do well => Receive Reward => Do Well Again => Get Reward Again

Leaders should reward the behaviors they want to continue.
People consider negative (-) rewards to follow this path:

Do Poorly => Get Reprimand => Do Well to Avoid Reprimand.

Leaders should punish or reprimand the behaviors they wish to stop.

5. Understand that people ask the question "What's in it for me?" before they become motivated to do tasks. People ask...

- ❖ Is the vision, goal, or objective possible?
- ❖ What's in it for me if I do, or do not act?
- ❖ Is this reward fair or can I accept the consequence?
- ❖ How bad do I want the reward or need to avoid the consequence?

6. Address these issues and create a motivating environment.

The following are the key points for Motivation:

- ❖ Determine what are others' interests.
- ❖ Show appreciate early and often in a project.
- ❖ Ensure management is involved.
- ❖ Be a positive role model and set the example.

Kaizen Events will require the team leader or process owner to have a diverse set of skills to motivate various individuals on the team. Some team members will be self-motivated and find enjoyment in just being part of the team. These individuals, even though self-motivated, will typically exceed task assignments with little or no individual encouragement. Other team members will require a more hands-on approach and will have to be encouraged in a positive way to contribute. This more hands-on approach may be determining their individual likes and dislikes regarding this current Kaizen Event and then personally addressing as many of them as possible. Keep the overall team objective in mind and do not sacrifice the overall project objective just to please one or two team members.

Performance Management and Goal Setting

This section will be helpful if the following issues are occurring in your Kaizen Event:

- ❖ Not completing Action Items
- ❖ Arriving late
- ❖ Lack of participation/not engaged
- ❖ Completing Action Items late
- ❖ Priorities constantly changing

Performance Management *is the process of establishing desired performance outcomes or goals, monitoring progress to goals through measurements, and then taking action to ensure success.* The performance management process provides a vehicle through which employees and their supervisors collaborate to enhance work results and satisfaction. This process is most effective when both the employee and the supervisor take an active role and work together. Organizations should consider participation in Kaizen Events as a component in performance management.

The following steps or guidelines can be used to enhance a performance management and/or goal setting process:

1. Understand that the key to managing human performance is to follow a consistent system or approach. The following diagram illustrates the repeating process or steps to the performance management and goal setting process which follows the classic Plan–Do–Check–Act (PDCA) cycle, the same one used to implement improvements in all types of Kaizen Events. (The Act portion of the cycle can be used to "tweek" or modify goals and objectives if required, as well as provide performance improvement adjustments.)

The Steps to Performance Management

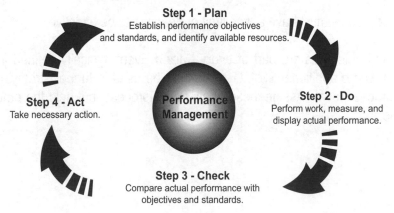

Step 1 - Plan
Establish performance objectives and standards, and identify available resources.

Step 2 - Do
Perform work, measure, and display actual performance.

Step 3 - Check
Compare actual performance with objectives and standards.

Step 4 - Act
Take necessary action.

Performance Management

2. Establish performance objectives and standards, and identify available resources by using the following SMART Goals Worksheet (SMART stands for Specific, Measurable, Assigned, Realistic, and Time-bounded) for the team. It can also be used for individual developmental needs.

SMART Goals Worksheet

Use this for quarterly reviews on individual or team performances as well as for yearly performance reviews.

Name: _____
Department: _____

Initial Date: _____
Review Date (+3 months) _____

Review Date (+6 months) _____
Review Date (+ 9 months) _____

Specific Task	Measurement of Success (How will we know the goal is achieved?)	Who is Responsible (Assigned)	Comments (Realistic)	Time Frame for Completion (Time-bounded)

3. Update appropriate forms and worksheets with SMART Goals Worksheet data, if and when appropriate. This can be used in lieu of the Action Item Log or PDCA Kaizen Activity Worksheet, again, depending on the team's requirements.

The following are the key points for Performance Management and Goal Setting:

❖ Specific - goals and objectives should always be specific, leaving room for misunderstanding or interpretation.
❖ Measurable - goals must be able to be measured. What gets measured gets done.
❖ Assigned - goals must define who is responsible to achieve the goal or objective.
❖ Realistic - goals must be challenging, but achievable. If not, team members cannot motivate themselves.
❖ Time-bounded - goals must have a time limit or deadline to be effective.

Establishing goals and objectives are part of every Kaizen Event, typically defined in the Team Charter. There may be times where additional SMART goals may be used in further stratifying the measurement system down to a process level. Assign these goals to the process, but hold the employees working the process accountable.

Reward and Recognition

This section will be helpful if the following issues are occurring in your Kaizen Event:

- ❖ Not completing Action Items
- ❖ Arriving late
- ❖ Lack of participation/not engaged
- ❖ Completing Action Items late

Rewards are a way for leaders to influence individual and group behaviors within organizations. Everyone wants to be appreciated and have his or her esteem grow. Recognition is a form of a reward where the leader acknowledges to an individual or team that their work is appreciated and valuable to the organization.

The topic of rewards is closely linked to individual and group motivation or behavior. Simply put, positively rewarding the behavior you want to have, should encourage more of that behavior in the future.

The following are the two common types of rewards:

Extrinsic - a reward a person gets from someone else. Common examples are: pay, bonuses, promotions, time off, special assignments, offices, plaques, certificates, and/or verbal praise.

Intrinsic - a self-satisfying reward a person gets from the work or accomplishment itself. These are self-administered and motivating. They can be even more powerful than extrinsic rewards.

Rewards need not be elaborate (i.e., costly items). Rather they can be low cost or no cost, items such as a simple "Thank you" to an employee at the right time noting the specific behavior. These reflect rewards of recognition for a job well done.

It is critical to connect rewards and recognition with productivity or performance for maximum effectiveness. It is important that the reward or recognition is balanced. If you do it too often, it loses its effectiveness. The reward or recognition must also be specific, visible to others, and timely.

The following steps or guidelines can be used to provide effective reward and recognition:

1. Determine the criteria for rewards and recognition.

2. Determine which type of reward to deliver from the following types:

To Positively (+) Reward Someone:
- ❖ Be specific regarding the behavior or work being rewarded.
- ❖ Fit the reward to the accomplishment.
- ❖ Customize the delivery of the reward to gain maximum affect for the employee.
- ❖ Be timely.

To Negatively (-) Reward Someone:
- ❖ Be specific regarding the behavior or work being punished.
- ❖ Fit the punishment to the infraction.
- ❖ Discuss the issue with the person privately.
- ❖ Be timely.

To constructively criticize someone, use a "Criticism Sandwich." A "Criticism Sandwich" is a simple, quick and effective way to let people know that they need to change their behavior.
- ❖ Give a compliment to get their attention (e.g., "You really worked hard today.").
- ❖ Deliver the criticism or behavior to correct and let them know why it is important (e.g., "You need to put the bolts in tighter. Loose bolts can cause problems down the line.").
- ❖ Give them some encouragement (e.g., "I know you can do it, you've done well so far today.").

This does not take the place of legitimate disciplinary action, but may be enough to get the behavior corrected. Reference the Discipline section for additional details regarding formal disciplinary actions.

3. Consider using the servant leader question; "I want you to be successful in achieving your goals, what can I do to help you meet the objectives?"

This question does the following three things.
(1) It puts the leader on the employee's side by saying they want them to succeed.
(2) It puts the leader in a supportive role.
(3) It puts the responsibility for achievement squarely with the employee.

4. Plan a reward and recognition process that will inspire the Kaizen Event team with its positive outcomes. Review previous Kaizen Event documentation to review the types of rewards and recognition that were previously used.

The following are the key points for Reward and Recognition:

- ❖ Be specific when giving rewards and recognition.
- ❖ Reward employees how they want to be rewarded, if at all possible.
- ❖ Rewards need not be monetary.
- ❖ Always, always, always, praise in public, criticize in private.

Team members of a Kaizen Event may not expect much in terms of reward and recognition. They probably feel somewhat "honored" to be selected. However, everyone likes to be recognized and it will help in soliciting their input on future Kaizen Events. They too will speak highly of the Event. At the end of the Kaizen Event, it is recommended that some type of reward be issued, whether it is comp time, especially if additional hours were worked, or a gift card. If throughout the Kaizen Event something personal about that team member has been learned, then consider personalizing the reward appropriately.

Stakeholder Analysis

This section will be helpful if the following issues are occurring in your Kaizen Event:

- ❖ Managers not sending right people to meeting
- ❖ Lack of support from other departments
- ❖ Constant disagreements about process changes
- ❖ Priorities constantly changing

Please see Chapter 2. Standard 5 Day Kaizen Event pages 102 - 105 for the information on Stakeholder Analysis.

Standard Work for Leaders

This section will be helpful if the following issue is occurring in your Kaizen Event:

❖ Lack of confidence in sustaining changes

Standard Work for Leaders *prescribes specific tasks, actions, and time frames for completion of work for a manager or supervisor.* Standard Work for Leaders is a concept derived from general standard work practices. Every position in every organization should have standard work processes to follow. These should be updated or created after the process changes that comprise the Kaizen Event, as appropriate.

Standard Work for Leaders is critical on several levels. First, standard work is the basic building block for continuous improvement. Without standard work for everyone, there is no baseline for improvement efforts, and improvements cannot be properly documented and measured. Leaders need to be responsible and accountable to continually improve their personal effectiveness. Standard Work for Leaders, a basic predictable approach to leading, is an essential first step.

Secondly, Standard Work for Leaders, assists leaders to understand how the organization, teams, and individuals are performing and to address areas of abnormalities and waste with countermeasures (or PDCA improvements), or to say "Thank you" where appropriate. Much of the Standard Work for Leaders involves monitoring the Key Performance Indicators (KPIs) of the organization or department and taking corrective and preventative action as required. This is critical to an organization's sustained success that is the focus of the Kaizen Event's Follow-Up Phase.

Additionally, as Kaizen Event teams see leaders performing standard work they will better understand that standard work for their positions must occur. The best way to show people that the organization is serious about implementing Lean Sigma methods and tools is for the leaders to practice the methods and tools themselves. By "walking the talk," leaders will build trust with workers, and trust is another key ingredient for sustained Lean Sigma success.

The following steps or guidelines can be used to create or enhance Standard Work for Leaders:

1. Create a table listing the main functional levels within the organization.

2. Ensure all job descriptions are up-to-date.

3. Create and ensure each functional level of the organization understands and has available relevant measurements.

4. Create a list for frequency of review for the measurements of each functional level (i.e., daily, monthly, quarterly, etc.).

5. Determine frequency of meetings to review measurements for each functional level.

6. Create and communicate action plans to address areas of concern or problems.

7. Use the following Standard Work for Leaders' example (next two pages) when establishing standard work for the leaders within your organization.

Activity and Frequency

Level	Daily	Weekly
Corporate Leader (Executive Sponsor)	Follow appropriate work instructions, procedures, and complete Job Description activities. Lead by example!	Establish rolling weekly agendas and conduct weekly meetings with each departmental manager. Use the DMAIC, process and project management format. Meeting should focus on KPIs and on-going improvement initiatives
	Complete and analyze required corporate productivity reports. Meet with appropriate departmental managers to review reports. Acknowledge success.	Track requirements from what was discussed and expected at weekly meetings.
	Focus on reports that show a negative trend. Gather data and conduct appropriate meetings. Communicate once per day to all direct reports demonstrating engagement and involvement.	Continue to monitor KPIs that show a negative trend. Continue to work to support improvement efforts.
Departmental Manager or Supervisor (Process Owner)	Follow appropriate work instructions, procedures, and complete Job Description activities. Lead by example!	Establish and conduct weekly meetings with supervisors and team leaders.
	Complete and analyze departmental productivity reports. Meet with appropriate leaders to review reports. Acknowledge success.	Be available for direct reports for contact.
	Establish pro-active actions to address any and all negative trends. Initiate Lean Sigma teams for appropriate issues. Look for other continuous improvement activities.	Monitor all performance measurements and follow-up with teams or individuals that have responsibility to address negative trends.
Work Team Leader	Follow appropriate work instructions, procedures, and complete Job Description activities. Lead by example!	Establish and conduct weekly meetings for continuous improvement efforts.
	Complete daily tasks, encourage improvement initiatives, support departmental initiatives, and acknowledge workers that contribute ideas for improvement.	Be attentive to employee's concerns (and ideas for improvement).

Kaizen Demystified

Activity and Frequency

Monthly	Semi-Annually	Annually
Complete and submit monthly highlights to owners, stockholders, board of directors, etc.	Review all organizational level KPIs, goals, and individual subordinate performance measurements. Check for alignment with organizational strategy. Modify as needed.	Review all organizational level KPIs, goals, and individual subordinate performance measurements. Check for alignment with organizational strategy. Modify as needed.
Establish rolling monthly agenda and conduct monthly meetings with departmental managers.	Provide mini-performance feedback sessions for each direct report. Assign appropriate improvement plans to ensure employee development and KPIs are met, as applicable.	Conduct performance appraisals for each direct report. Assign appropriate improvement plans to ensure employee development and KPIs are met, as applicable.
		Review strategic direction, adjust to market conditions, and develop alignment with new or revised KPIs.
Review monthly departmental goals or KPIs with team leaders and employees, if appropriate.	Communicate the organizations priorities including customer satisfaction.	Create and implement an innovative communication plan to clearly define to organization members the vision and mission that includes customer satisfaction.
Continue to support continuous improvement and problem solving teams.	Communicate progress to date to all employees. Continue to support continuous improvement efforts.	Continue to address departmental areas of concern and allocate appropriate resources to ensure success.
		Learn and communicate any and all new or revised improvement methodologies to leads and employees.
Review monthly goals with employees, if appropriate.	Communicate the organizations priorities including customer satisfaction to all employees.	Implement an innovative communication plan to clearly define to organization members the vision and mission.
Continue to demonstrate support and enthusiasm for continuous improvement efforts.	Provide employees with specific improvement initiatives that have contributed to improving departmental measures and/or KPIs.	Continue to work to develop employees.

The following are the key points for Standard Work for Leaders:

- ❖ Identify the tasks, frequency, etc. in a checklist a leader is responsible for - PLAN.
- ❖ Complete checklist on scheduled dates and times - DO.
- ❖ Ensure level above and level below to audit - CHECK.
- ❖ Take appropriate corrective action - ACT.

Kaizen Events can be an impetus to either create Standard Work for Leaders or update current management or supervisory practices to connect daily work activities with departmental measures as well as assuring continuous improvement ideas are heard and subsequently acted upon. Standard Work for Leaders will improve information sharing and communication, ensure better decision making, and will build trust among the work group. Post the appropriate standard work items or schedule so the team can see that their leader also practices standard work. Consider laminating standard work items and cross items off with a grease pencil as tasks are accomplished. This provides a powerful demonstration to the team that the leader is serious about their role and responsibility.

Stress Management

This section will be helpful if the following issues are occurring in your Kaizen Event:

❖ Lack of participation/not engaged
❖ Poor/disruptive behavior

Stress Management is the process of identifying stressors and developing effective strategies to reduce and cope with stress. Excessive stress in the workplace can cause anger, illnesses, accidents, productivity losses, poor quality, and turnover. This stress can cause personality shifts, lack of sleep, depression, lack of concentration, and burnout. Burnout is the effect of poorly managed stress. Burnout symptoms are; weight shifts, tardiness, quick loss of temper, emotional outbursts, and poor judgment. All of these can affect performance, relationships, and communication with others.

It is important to note that there are positive stressors, the kind that in the right amount stimulate achievement, and negative stressors, which lead to problems.

The "quantity" of stress, whether it is positive or negative, also has an impact on performance of how well team members are engaged in a Kaizen Event. Even too much positive stress can be counter-productive, and lead to burn-out. Stress overload situations can turn what would normally be positive stress into a productivity problem. The figure below illustrates how stress affects productivity.

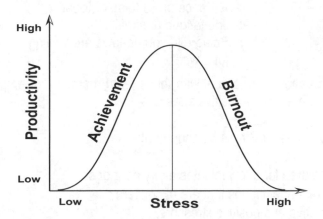

As stress such as deadlines and goals are added, a person's performance, output, and productivity increase. As additional stress is added, additional improvement is realized until the inflection point is reached at the top of the bell-shaped curve. The Kaizen Event leader must provide realistic goals and objectives as positive stressors and keep as many negative stressors as possible to a minimum.

The following steps or guidelines can be used for better stress management:

1. Examine the work environment for the following types of positive and negative stressors.

Positive stressors are:
*   Predictable
*   Necessary for higher achievement
*   Positive outcomes

Some examples of positive stressors are:
*   Personal goals
*   Schedules
*   Project deadlines for Action Items

Negative stressors are:
*   Unpredictable
*   Not necessary for higher achievement
*   Negative outcomes

Some examples of negative stressors are:
*   Crisis
*   Last minute requests or schedule changes
*   Unrealistic Kaizen Event objectives

2. Recognize the following:

*   Positive stressors are needed for high levels of achievement.
*   People will avoid working with someone with a negative or stress personality.

3. Understand that stresses are made worse by the following:

*   Long working hours
*   Lack of sleep
*   Lack of exercise
*   Poor diet
*   Poor self-image or self-esteem
*   Reliance on caffeine or tobacco
*   Job fatigue or strain
*   Being told your in-laws are visiting for a week

4. Create an appropriate action plan to deal with those team members or employees exhibiting negative stress attributes. Provide as many positive stressors.

The following are the key points for Stress Management:

*   Get away from the area for a few minutes every hour or so.
*   Communicate to manager issues that are of concern.
*   Keep a log of negative and positive stressors.
*   Seek professional assistance, if needed.

Kaizen Events will produce stress. The leader must recognize the negative stressors early on in the Kaizen Event so they do not disrupt the team. The Kaizen Event leader must understand that team members may also be experiencing personal issues that they may not be comfortable discussing. If that is the case, privately demonstrate your concern, explaining how their behavior or lack of participation is impacting the team, and ask is there is anything that you can do at this time. Showing this concern for the team member should help the situation.

Team Selection and Building

This section will be helpful if the following issues are occurring in your Kaizen Event:

- ❖ Not completing Action Items
- ❖ Managers not sending right people to meetings
- ❖ Arriving late
- ❖ Lack of participation/not engaged
- ❖ Completing Action Items later
- ❖ Lack of support from other departments

Team selection is the process of selecting people to work together on a team. Team building is the process of leading a group of people on a team in a way to strengthen bonds and cohesiveness in order to achieve harmony and success. Teaming can be done in-person (i.e., face-to-face) or through the use of remote communications via Web-collaboration applications or tools. The principles of teaming are the same regardless of the platform in which teaming is conducted.

Team building is the process of leading a group of people on a team in a way to achieve harmony and success. Teams can outperform individuals in almost every instance. This is because teams capitalize on their diversity and variety of skills, knowledge and abilities. The leader must know the team members to the point that he or she understands their individual and collective strengths and weaknesses. Only with this knowledge will the leader be able to leverage strengths to accomplish the objectives of any Kaizen Event type. Kaizen Event leaders must strive for a diversified, yet functionally balanced, team make up.

The following steps or guidelines can be used to select and build a team:

1. Form the team. The *Forming Stage* (or step) of teaming involves reviewing the project and team mission, establishing team roles, determining meeting times, and ensuring the right members are on the team. (See pages 77 - 79.) There is excitement, anticipation, and optimism. There is also the pride a member feels since he or she has been chosen to be part of the team. The "flip-side" are feelings of suspicion, fear, and anxiety about what is to come. It is critical at this stage to establish a clear leader. It may or may not be the supervisor. Only with this identification do you get true responsibility and accountability. Additionally, one of the best ways to develop a clear and understandable team mission is to use the 5 W's of Who, What, Where, When, and Why. Or a condensed version of identifying "task" (what needs to be accomplished), "purpose" (intent…why does this need to be accomplished), and end-state (what will it look like when it is accomplished).

2. Facilitate the team through their **Storming Stage**. At this stage, the team members begin to realize the task is different and/or more difficult than they first imagined. This is the stage where team members experience difficulties from working as individuals to contributing as a team member. Impatience about the lack of progress and inexperience on group dynamics has some team members wondering about the entire project. Team members may delay or not complete Action Items, act disengaged from the project, etc. This stage can be difficult for any team. Teams that do not understand and acknowledge the five stages - especially this stage - most likely

3. Monitor and reward as progress is being made. This stage is referred to as the **Norming Stage**. Team members accept the team concept. The team ground rules are being adhered to, communication is occurring without disruptions, and progress is being made toward the objective. At this stage, everyone feels that the team concept is working. Everyone is contributing in a positive way - Action Items are being completed on time, everyone arriving on time for the meetings, etc. Continued communications and acknowledgement of the team members' efforts should be done often, allowing progression to Stage 4 and preventing the team from falling back to Stage 2.

4. Effectively solve problems and involve everyone on the team. This **Performing Stage** has the team diagnosing and solving problems with relative ease. Every member is contributing to their fullest. Many may be expressing ideas of future type Kaizen Events.

5. Learn and share results. Closure of the project team is the final stage of teaming. In this **Closing Stage**, the team has accomplished their goals, shared their results, and has disbanded. Closure brings mixed feelings to team members. By this time, the team members have been through a lot together and the thought of not working as a team anymore can be disappointing. Kaizen Event teams are not usually designed to be together forever. The Follow-Up Phase ensures team recognition and closure.

The following are the key points for Team Selection and Building:

- ❖ Establish clear and common goals and objectives.
- ❖ Establish good communication standards from the beginning.
- ❖ Continually evaluate team meetings, look for opportunities to improve.
- ❖ Create team meeting standards.
- ❖ Constructively resolve conflicts.
- ❖ Ensure team members show respect for one another.

Selecting the right team members for a Kaizen Event is half the battle. The other half will be to keep the team members engaged in the project. Strengthen team unity by setting clear goals and expectations for team members' personal responsibility as well as their team duties. Recognize that the strongest teams have fun together accomplishing tasks. Kaizen Events do not all have to be work. Consider arranging "fun" breaks or activities throughout the Event.

Time Management

This section will be helpful if the following issues are occurring in your Kaizen Event:

- ❖ Not completing Action Items
- ❖ Arriving late
- ❖ Completing Action Items late

Time management *is the process of organizing, prioritizing and executing tasks to achieve objectives.* There are many different techniques for managing one's time: personal planners, calendars, computer/ smart phone apps, or simple writing a list of activities on a pad of paper are ways people list their "things to do." Most successful people have some regular way of managing their "To Do" list.

There is a lot of advice on how to manage time, cope with a big workload, while at the same time trying to minimize stress. But… what does all this mean in today's work environment? In practical terms, some initial goals may be:

- ❖ Stop misplacing or losing important emails or documents.
- ❖ Stop forgetting what you have committed to for your boss and co-workers.
- ❖ Stop missing deadlines for Action Items or any other work tasks.
- ❖ Stop feeling stressed all the time.
- ❖ Coach employees more.
- ❖ Dedicate more time to the Kaizen Event Action Items assigned.
- ❖ Work on professional development.

The amount of stress reduced once time management is practiced is often huge. Also, productivity for most workers who actively practice "time management" during the workday will improve (as much as one full hour per day has been reported). That is one hour more per day that can be used for a number of things, one of which could be going home earlier if overtime has been an issue. Good time management is also an investment into a higher quality of work. Time management will allow Kaizen Event activities to go more smoothly by having employees better balancing regular work assignments and any additional team duties.

The following steps or guidelines can be used to better manage time:

1. Identify "time wasters." Start a tracking sheet for one week (or during the first day of a Standard 5 Day Kaizen Event if processes are being monitored at this time) to better understand activities, especially include those interruptions. Consider the following questions for the process area employee:

   Is there someone else that can or should do any of these tasks identified even though it may take longer or may not be done quite as well?
   Is there someone who can do any of these tasks better than I can? Am I taking advantage of the abilities and experience of my work group or team?
   Is there someone who can do any of these tasks in less time and/or more efficiently?
   Would this task contribute to the development of another employee's professional development?

2. Eliminate or reduce the time wasters identified in step 1. This may include delegating, redirecting the work, or training someone else.

3. Manage the interruptions and/or time wasters that were identified in step 1. This may include training some employees on new aspects of the business, communicating to another department that they should be handling some of these interruptions or time wasters, and/or saying No as it is not really part of your job function but "somehow" has been incorporated into your job. If all interruptions and/or time wasters are within your job function, consider handling them in the following ways:

   ❖ All at once
   ❖ During a low-priority time
   ❖ With an email, text message, etc.
   ❖ As delegated tasks
   ❖ In a group meeting

4. Every day, identify a personal "To Do" (or Action Item) list. Organize the list in what needs to be done each day. If something needs to be done at a certain time, ensure the time is included and an alert email or text message is sent as a reminder.

5. Prioritize the "To-Do's" (Hi, Med, Lo... 1, 2, 3 etc.). For example, 1 - Must be done today, 2 - Can be done today, if time warrants, and 3 - Has to be done sometime this week. Color-coding or some other type visual aid may be used to identify the various priorities. Also, time "buckets" can be used, for example, 1's handled between 8 - 10 am, 2's 10 - 11 am, and 3's anytime during the day. Assign similar priority levels for any Action Items assigned during a Kaizen Event.

6. Take action to complete the "To Do" list tasks. If something that must be done on a scheduled day cannot be completed, ensure that the appropriate person is contacted and the reason explained, as well as when it is expected to be completed.

7. Cross off completed tasks from the "To Do" list. This will provide a sense of accomplishment.

8. Carry-over tasks not completed to the next day's "To Do" list. (If a "To Do" list task is carried over for more than a week, ask "Does it really need to be done?" If the answer is yes; do it!

9. Eliminate procrastination - if this is a problem. If you tend to procrastinate use the following as a guide:
   a. Analyze what you procrastinate about. Keep a log and write down tasks that you are putting off. Is there a common pattern? Do you tend to put off tasks that involve certain work? Or conflicts?
   b. Note your common "delay tactics." What kind of excuses do you look for and find to put off doing that tough and unpleasant task? Recognizing those traps will help you avoid them.
   c. Experiment with some of the following solutions that may work:
      ❖ Subdivide that big, tough task into small pieces that can be done one at a time.
      ❖ Start with an easy or enjoyable piece to get going.

- ❖ Get someone to work with you: It will be less difficult and painful.
- ❖ Get prepared for the tough task by having all the information available and make sure you pick a time when you are rested and energetic.
- ❖ Block out distractions: close the door, place cell phone/smart devices on mute or turn-off completely, and deal with the task if it can be done via phone or it requires full concentration and no distractions.
- ❖ If it is a creative project you may want to "retreat" to an off-site location to minimize distractions.
- ❖ Reward yourself along the way.

The following are the key points for Time Management:

- ❖ Learn to set priorities.
- ❖ Do it now if it is deemed important - keep that attitude all day, every day.
- ❖ Divide large tasks into smaller tasks, list, and check each one off as it is accomplished.
- ❖ Learn delegate and say "no."
- ❖ For detailed and time consuming project tasks, work backwards to develop a time line.
- ❖ Minimize wastes in your routine tasks, which will free up more time for continuous improvement activities.

Kaizen Events requires effective time management for all team members. It is suggested each team member adopt the following when it pertains to Action Items and any other activities comprised of a Kaizen Event:

PLAN - and prioritize Action Items to do when.
DO - the Action Items.
CHECK - progress of Action Items.
ACT - to address Action Items each day.

Work to eliminate, delegate, and/or avoid time wasters and interruptions from daily work duties to allow for better time management.

Trust Building

This section will be helpful if the following issues are occurring in your Kaizen Event:

- ❖ Lack of participation/not engaged
- ❖ FAD of the month attitude re: project
- ❖ Lack of confidence in sustaining changes
- ❖ Constant disagreements about process changes
- ❖ Trouble reaching consensus
- ❖ Priorities constantly changing

Trust Building *is creating the reliance on the integrity, strength, ability, surety, etc. of a person.* It is having the ability to provide confidence in another person in that something will be done. Trust is fundamental to leadership and really deserves focused study. Kaizen Event team members must trust in the focus and direction of the team.

To truly be a leader you must have people who are willing to follow. That is where the trust issue comes in. Trust is personal. Trust is the product of time spent between individuals or between the leader and his or her team. Trust is the product of a relationship between people and an essential component of effective leadership.

The critical issue surrounding trust is the understandings that trust must be earned. Additionally, the reality of trust is that it is something that may take a great deal of time to achieve and yet take only a matter of seconds to lose. This reality is what makes being a leader so difficult, as the leader must always be "on," to a degree, in the face of the follower.

The following steps or guidelines can be used to build trust:

1. Understand the various approaches leaders have when building trust. In that, it requires the leader to be an influencer from the front of the effort, from inside the effort, and from the rear of the effort. (Repeat from pages 53 - 54.)

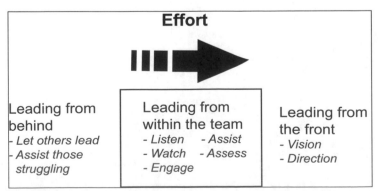

The Kaizen Event leader may initially start leading from the front, then, by the end of the improvement project, will be leading from behind.

2. Conduct the Trust Building Self-Assessment. This will provide you with an honest "snapshot" of your current trusting abilities. Be honest. (Typically, the leader will score themselves higher.)

Note: Example shown.

Trust Building Self-Assessment

Use the five-level Likert item scale for each of the statements.   **Date:**

1 - Strongly Disagree
2 - Disagree
3 - Neither Agree nor Disagree
4 - Agree
5 - Strongly Agree

To develop a trusting environment, leaders should address the following statements.	Score (1 - 5)
1. My team knows what is expected of them.	4
2. My team has the resources available to do their job properly.	4
3. My team has the opportunity to do their best everyday.	3
4. I provide recognition or praise for doing good work on a consistent and fair basis.	4
5. I genuinely care about my people, team's, and co-worker's success.	5
6. I provide the opportunity for individuals and teams to share their opinions, and I act on many of them.	4
7. I share the mission or purpose of my organization, and my teams feel that they are of value.	4
8. I develop a work environment that is friendly and supportive.	5
9. I talk with my teams and individuals periodically about their overall performance and development.	2
10. I criticize fairly and constructively with the person or team's best interest in mind, without prejudice.	5

It is recommended this survey be conducted, as well as the Trust Building Colleague Assessment, every 6 months as long as you are making sincere efforts to improve your leadership and trust building skills.

Leadership

3. Conduct the Trust Building Colleague Assessment to attain the "perceived" trust level that your employees or team members have in your current trusting abilities. It is suggested to select colleagues from your organization to include peers, previous team members or co-workers, and a manager. Inform them that this is an individual continuous improvement effort by you to better manage your resources that the organization has placed their trust in you and that their input would be greatly appreciated.

Trust Building Colleague Assessment

Use the five-level Likert item scale for each of the statements.   **Date:**

1 - Strongly Disagree
2 - Disagree
3 - Neither Agree nor Disagree
4 - Agree
5 - Strongly Agree

You have been asked for input on your team leader or supervisor to improve his or her leadership and trust building skills. Use team leader and supervisor interchangeable.	Score (1 - 5)
1. My team knows what is expected of them.	2
2. My team has the resources available to do their job properly.	4
3. My team leader provides us the opportunity to do our best everyday.	4
4. My team leader provides recognition or praise for doing good work on a consistent and fair basis.	2
5. My team leader genuinely cares about worker's success.	4
6. My team leader provides the opportunity for individuals and teams to share their opinions, and many of them are acted upon.	3
7. My team leader shares the mission or purpose of the organization, and teams feel that they are of value.	1
8. My team leader develops a work environment that is friendly and supportive.	3
9. My team leader talks with the teams and individuals periodically about their overall performance and development.	2
10. My team leader criticizes fairly and constructively with the person or team's best interest in mind, without prejudice.	4

Thank you for your honest input in this survey.

The information gathered from colleagues need not be part of the Kaizen Event team. The leader will typically have those same leadership attributes in the daily work environment as well as when leading an improvement team.

4. Plot (1) and (2) on a matrix.

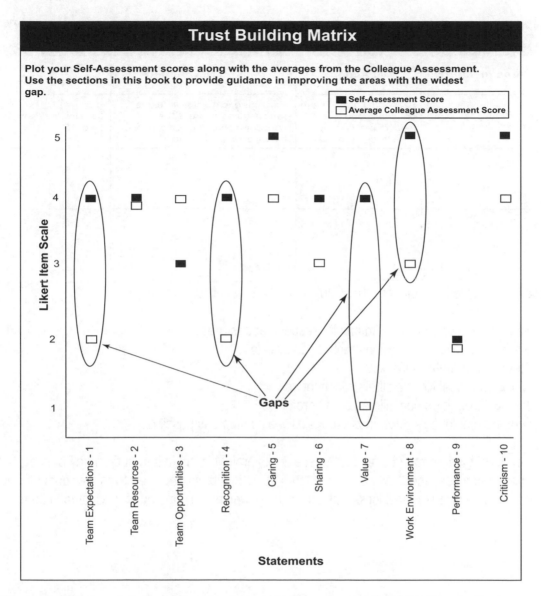

5. Identify the 3 - 4 areas that show the widest gap. In this example, there are four areas that warrant a possible change in how the leader communicates and interacts with his or her team.

Note: Many organizations have 360 degree appraisal systems to assist in this type of analysis.

6. Use following Trust Building Work Plan to improve the trust with team members:

Trust Building Work Plan

Area to Improve	Old Action	Desired New Action	Dates of Accomplishment
Ex. Team expectations	Ex. Would often ignore or not respond to a team requesting my assistance - too busy.	Ex. Agree to meet with teams regularly and address their concerns regarding projects and their work assignments.	Ex. Nov. 12, Nov. 19 Dec. 15

The following are the key points for Trust Building:

- ❖ Always treat employees with dignity, respect, and fairness.
- ❖ Praise in public, criticize constructively in private.
- ❖ Reward the "right" behavior.
- ❖ Make your goal to help others reach theirs.
- ❖ Follow through on commitments and promises.
- ❖ Expand employee's roles and responsibilities as much as possible.

The Kaizen Event leader may be "tested" to see if this project is any different than any previous ones that may not have been sustained. As a leader, ensure all Action Items and objectives are "doable" and can be sustained. Openly discuss roadblocks with the team as well as any approaches to remove them.

Valuing Diversity

This section will be helpful if the following issues are occurring in your Kaizen Event:

- ❖ Lack of participation/not engaged
- ❖ Lack of support from other departments
- ❖ 1 - 2 people dominating meeting

Valuing Diversity is capitalizing on the fact that no two individuals have the exact same knowledge, experiences, skills, and abilities. By harnessing this diversity, a team can become more effective and creative, and enjoy great success and accomplishment.

Team Diversity leads to the following:

- ❖ More resources for problem solving and continuous improvement projects
- ❖ Improved creativity and motivation
- ❖ Improved quality of decision-making
- ❖ Greater commitments to Action Items assigned
- ❖ Higher motivation through collective actions
- ❖ Better control and work discipline
- ❖ More individual need satisfaction
- ❖ Better overall results and performance

The phenomenon where a team's performance is greater than the sum of its parts is called synergy. Diversity adds synergy.

Smart organizations are taking steps today to prepare for the diverse work force and customers they will be serving tomorrow. These smart organizations believe that by embracing diversity today, it will pay off tomorrow.

The following steps or guidelines can be used to capitalize on building diversity:

1. Understand your organization's current state of diversity. Develop a Diversity Map to show voids and opportunities. Leaders can use the Leadership Preference Grid to map the diversity of the team or organization. (See page 379.) The mapping process of the organization or team allows leaders to identify diversity imbalances, voids, and areas for improvement. This can be done by mapping each of the team member's individual scores on the same map, and then a team map can be created. The team map shows all the team members scores on one map so teams can spot areas of imbalance, and act to make improvements and to capitalize on diversity. Kaizen teams can use this process to examine their collective strengths and weaknesses, and work to improve balance. This should be done in the Planning Phase by the team leader, facilitator, and/or process owner.

2. Manage diversity through hiring and promotions. If organizations exist to unite diverse perspectives, capabilities, and talents in pursuit of common purposes and mutually beneficial results, why do they stifle diversity, seek sameness, discourage individuality, promote conformance, reward uniformity, and punish nonconformity? Because managing diversity is harder than managing uniformity - managing diversity is more challenging, expensive, time consuming, demanding, stressful, and prone to fail. For Kaizen Event teams, this can be done by having additional or extended team members.

3. Develop an environment of acceptance, tolerance and valuing of others. This can be accomplished through the development of the company's culture; the collective acceptable behaviors and "chemistry" between people and among groups of people. Strive and work to develop a culture where diversity is not just accepted but is welcomed, then you will stop having issues evolving from diversity. Focus on those things that detract from the chemistry and note that many of the problems will originate from people who just cannot get on board with the culture. The Kaizen Event team leader must work to engaged all team members throughout the three phases.

4. Treat everyone with respect and fairness. This must be demonstrated by the leader. Leaders must also hold people and teams accountable when this is not occurring. Once people understand what is and is not acceptable behaviors, they will either respond positively, or leave the organization - at their or your choice.

5. Use leadership techniques to ensure everyone has a voice and is heard. Diversity is also all about leadership. It is incumbent on the leader to go into every situation with the understanding that EVERYONE has something to offer. The leader's challenge is to know his or her people well enough to know what that something is.

The following are the key points for Valuing Diversity:

- ❖ Spend the necessary time and create a Diversity Map of your team members.
- ❖ Determine possibilities to improve the diversity of the team by adding additional team members or recognizing and addressing any gaps.
- ❖ Brainstorm with the team if diversity gaps exist and develop a plan.
- ❖ Consider additional training and education, diversity workshops, team building exercises, and forced association to fill in gaps of an unbalanced team.

Kaizen Event leaders should continually recognize and address the importance of diversity. It is incumbent upon the team leader to ensure that diversity is embraced by the team with all ideas respectfully considered and discussed. Private meetings may need to be held one-on-one with any individuals that do not show a mutual respect for valuing diversity.

Appendix

Glossary

5 Why - Allows organized brainstorming to methodically determine the causes of a problem (i.e., effect).
5S - Ensures physical areas and paper-based or electronic documents are systematically kept clean and organized.

A3 Report - Designed to help you "tell the story" in a logical and visual way relative to a particular subject matter.
Act (of PDCA) - Confirms that the improvement experiment worked with improved performance; acts to standardize the new process.
Action Item (AI) Log - Used by the team to assign and follow-up on specific Actions Items agreed to throughout all three phases of the Kaizen Event.
Analyze Phase (of D-M-A-I-C) - The detailed examination of the processes with corresponding ideas on how to improve the processes.
Arete (uh-REE-tay) - means "habitual excellence" and is also synonymous with Lean.

Baby Boomer Generation - The second oldest generation in the workforce, and these people were born between 1946 and 1964.
Brainstorming - Used to generate a high volume of ideas with team members' full participation that is free of criticism and judgment within a 5 - 15 minute time period.

Cause and Effect (or Fishbone) Diagram - Allows a team to graphically display and explore, in increasing detail, all the possible causes of a problem or issue.
Change - A disruption; an intense human experience that requires individuals to experience loss or at least a letting go of the old way to make way for the new.
Charting - The process of making the most sense of the data.
Check (of PDCA) - Ensures that the intended improvement was successful in terms of the measurements set forth in the Team Charter.
Constraint or Bottleneck Analysis - The identification of the slowest process step(s) in the product or service being provided.
Continuous flow - When customer orders or demands are initiated and the process continues uninterrupted until the orders or demands are satisfied.
Control Phase (of D-M-A-I-C) - The use of visual management and control charts to ensure the process changes are maintained over time.
Cross-training - Used when one employee if required to do another employee's work.
Cyber Generation - The emerging workforce born after 1999.

Defects or Errors - Defect waste refers to all processing required in creating a defect and the additional work required to correct a defect or error.
Define Phase (of D-M-A-I-C) - The initial determination of purpose of the improvement, resources required, and a plan.

Demand Analysis Plots - Identifies customer demand in terms of transactions or needs over a given time period for non-repetitive goods or services.

Do (of PDCA) - Implements the improvement plan or experiment.

Effective meeting - An efficient use of people's time when they are gathered together working to obtain a desired result.

Elevator speech - A brief, comprehensive verbal overview on the purpose and related activities regarding the product, process, or service being examined.

Employee Balance Chart - A visual display, in the form of a bar chart, that represents work elements and cycle times relative to the total value stream cycle time and takt time (or pitch).

Environmental Resources - As organizations become more sustainable or "Green," they have to make extra efforts to protect environmental resources.

Facilitator - Ensures that everyone at the meetings stays on task and everyone contributes.

FIFO system - A work-controlled method which ensure the oldest work (i.e., electronic documents, supply items, etc.) upstream (first-in) is the first to be processed downstream (first-out).

Force Field Analysis - An extremely useful tool for understanding and illustrating the forces for and against an idea, direction, decision, or strategy.

Gemba (Japanese origin of genba) - A term meaning "the real place" or where the work is done.

Generation Xers - The people born between 1965 and 1980.

Generation Y (Millenials) - The youngest working generation in the workforce and these people are born between 1981 and 1999.

Heijunka Leveling - Levels flow by delivering goods and/or services in an alternating or patterned manner rather than large chunks of time.

Histogram - Utilizes data and displays the spread and shape of the distribution.

Impact Map - A method by which a team can identify the solutions that will most likely have the greatest impact on the problem with the least effort.

Improve Phase (of D-M-A-I-C) - The implementation of the tools and techniques as defined in the Analyze Phase using the Plan-Do-Check-Act (PDCA) model (or some other similar model).

Informaticist - Applies the tools of information theory to a specific discipline. This person will be responsible for organizing data and making it presentable.

Interrelationship Diagram - An analysis tool that allows a team to understand and identify the cause-and-effect relationships among critical issues.

Inventory - Excessive piles of materials, parts, paperwork, computer files, and supplies are the waste of inventory, and cause extra time spent searching or other wastes.

Kaizen Events - Called "Rapid Improvement Events" or "Kaizen Blitzes" are targeted events conducted by improvement teams to implement improvements quickly in a specific area.

Kaizen Mindset - Also known as Lean Thinking, is for employees to be continually making incremental improvements in their work processes (i.e., eliminating waste) as well as be a contributor to larger, organizational change type projects.

Kanbans (pronounced Con – Bons) - Or "pull signals" are visual (or auditory, electronic, etc.) signals used to control flow and trigger action between processes.

Key management stakeholders - Those who control critical resources, who can block the change initiative by direct or indirect means, who must approve certain aspects of the change strategy, who shapes the thinking of other critical constituents, or who owns a key work process impacted by the change initiative.

Layered Process Audits (LPA) - A system of process audits performed by multiple levels of workers, supervisors, and managers to monitor key process characteristics and verify process conformance on an ongoing basis.

Lean - A never-ending, systematic approach for identifying and eliminating waste and improving flow of a process while engaging employees.

Lean representative (Lean rep) - Has a theoretical and practical knowledge of Lean and Six Sigma and is often referred to as a Black Belt, Lean Sensei, or Continuous Improvement Specialist.

Lean Sigma Assessment and Gap Analysis - Creates an understanding of what may be some potential improvement opportunities as well as provides a baseline to compare with future improvement initiatives (and subsequent assessments).

Lean Six Sigma - The combination of customer-focused and waste elimination efforts of Lean with the quantitative analysis and structured D-M-A-I-C methodology of Six Sigma.

Managing change - The process of how to manage the way changes in the working environment are implemented and how to lessen its effect on the workforce.

Mass customization - Combines the low costs of mass production processes with the variable output required to meet individual customer needs.

Matures (Traditionalist, Veterans, and Silent) Generation - The oldest generation in the workforce and these people were born between 1925 and 1945.

Measure Phase (of D-M-A-I-C) - A full and thorough documentation of the customer needs or market demand for the process being improved as a continuation of the Define Phase.

Measurement System Analysis (MSA) - A specially designed experiment that seeks to identify the components of variation in the measurement.

Mistake proofing - A system designed to ensure that it is impossible to make a mistake or produce a defect.

Motion - Any movement of people, material, products, and/or electronic exchanges that does not add value is waste.

Overburden - Overburdening or overloading occurs when the capacity of the process is not known and/or is not adequately scheduled.

Overprocessing - Putting more effort into the work than what is required by internal or external customers is waste.

Overproduction - Producing some type of work prior to it being required is waste of overproduction.

Paced flow - Used where customer order fulfillment tasks are done with regular frequency on timed schedule.

Pareto Chart - A bar chart format that represents the Pareto principle which states that 20% of the sources cause 80% of the problems.

Paynter Chart - A visual representation over time relative to the subgroups based on Pareto Chart information.

PDCA (Plan-Do-Check-Act) - An interactive four-step problem solving and improvement process used to implement (or pilot/test) and validate business process improvements.

People's Skills or Knowledge - The underutilization of people is a result of not placing people where they can (and will) use their knowledge, skills, and abilities to their fullest potential in providing value-added work and services.

Pie Chart - A circular chart divided into sectors, each sector shows the relative size of each value.

Pitch - The adjusted takt time that establishes an optimal and smooth workflow throughout the value stream.

Plan (of PDCA) – Defines the specific improvement activity or experiment, what will be done, who will do it, and how it will be measured; this information should be well documented.

Primary stakeholders - Those ultimately affected (i.e., process area employees), either positively or negatively by an organization's actions.

Process Capability - Used to determine if a process, given its natural process variation in a stable state, is capable of meeting customer specifications or requirements.

Process map (or flowchart) - A visual representation of a series of operations (tasks, activities) consisting of people, work duties, and transactions that occur in the delivery of a product or service.

Process or Work Area Layout - The process of reducing the distance between or collocation of resources or people to ensure that service is delivered to the customer with minimal or no waste.

Project Charter - A high level document used to launch or initiate multiple improvement teams.

Project Identification - The process of determining areas that are not meeting performance or operational goals.

Project management - The process of establishing, prioritizing, and carrying out tasks to complete specific objectives.

Pull System - A process to ensure nothing is produced upstream (i.e., supplier process) until the downstream (i.e., customer) process "signals" the need for it.

Quality Function Deployment (QFD) - A tool that takes the VOC information and turns it into specific and measurable quality requirements that can be used to design improved processes.

Quick Changeover - The ability to quickly change from delivering one product or service to delivering a completely different product or service.

Radar Chart - Also known as a Spider Chart or a Star Chart, because of its appearance, plots the values of each category along a separate axis that starts in the center of the chart and ends on the outer ring.

Rolling Kaizen Events - Are targeted improvement activities (PDCAs) used by teams to implement improvements or solve a problem in a specific area that can only be accessed in-frequently and/or the resources are not available for immediate use; therefore, resources and improvements must be allocated over time.

Run Chart - A method to display several data points over time.

Scatter (and Concentration) Plots - Used to study the possible relationship between one variable and another.

Scheduled flow - Where customer orders or demands are identified and then scheduled or reserved for fulfillment at a specific time.

Scribe - Records the notes of the meeting and distributes the information within a certain period, ideally within 24 hours of the meeting.

Secondary stakeholders - The intermediaries, that is, persons or organizations who are indirectly affected by an organization's actions.

SIPOC Diagram - A tool used by a team to identify all relevant elements of a process improvement project or high level value stream or process map to ensure all aspects of the process are taken into consideration and that no key components are missing.

Six Sigma - A business tool or project methodology, is a structured, quantitative, five phase approach to continuous improvement and problem solving.

Social Responsibility - Social Responsibility waste is broad and includes poverty, discrimination, malpractices, health and injuries, nutrition, literacy and education, office politics, and social media networking.

Stakeholder – The person, group, or organization with an interest in a project.

Stakeholder Analysis - The technique used to identify the key people who have to be won over for a project implementation or change initiative.

Standard 5 Day Kaizen Events - Also referred to as Kaizen Blitzs or Rapid Improvement Events (RIE), are targeted improvement activities (PDCAs) used by teams to implement improvements quickly in a specific area.

Standard work - Establishes and controls the best method to complete a task without variation from original intent.

Standard Work for Leaders - Prescribes specific tasks, actions, and time frames for completion of work for a manager or supervisor.

Statistical Process Control - A group of tools used to monitor and control process outputs.

Structured Brainstorming - Each team member contributes his/her ideas in order until all ideas are exhausted.

Supermarket - A specific inventory management process using Kanbans and specified or standard storage locations and package quantities.

Takt time - The pace of repetitive customer demand.

Team building - Leading a group of people on a team in a way that strengthens bonds and cohesiveness in order to achieve harmony and success.

Team champion (or executive sponsor) - Has the authority to commit the necessary resources for the team.

Team Charter - Details and documents the team structure, membership, and overall objectives, measures, and resources required for an improvement project to be successful.

Team leader - Responsible for the day-to-day or week-to-week running of the team.

Team member - The most important member of the team - is responsible for keeping an open mind, being receptive to change, and contributing ideas in a respectful manner.

Team selection - Selecting people to work together on a team.

Technical representative (tech rep) - Someone with advanced computer application skills or from IT who provides insights into the technology tools available.

Timekeeper - Responsible for ensuring the scheduled times (start, stop, breaks, topics, etc.) are followed.

Today's Kaizen Events - Are used by teams to find and implement solutions to a known problem or continuous improvement initiative within a short time period (less than four weeks).

Total Productive Maintenance (TPM) - The tools, methods, and activities used to improve machine or equipment availability and reliability times.

Transport - Transport waste is the excess movement of materials, documents, information, etc. within an organization.

Unevenness - Lack of a consistent flow of inputs/information/scheduled work from upstream processes causes many types of waste previously mentioned.

Unstructured Brainstorming - Team members contribute their ideas as they occur (or come to mind) until all ideas are exhausted.

VA versus NVA Analysis - Illuminates the waste in a process.

Value stream map - A visual representation of the material, work, and information flow, as well as the queue times (and inventory levels, if appropriate) between processes for a specific customer demand.

Visual control - A technique employed whereby control of an activity or process is made easier or more effective by deliberate use of visual signals (signs, information displays, maps, layouts, instructions, alarms, and poka-yoke or mistake proofing devices).

Visual Management - The use of visual techniques that graphically display relevant business performance data.

Voice of the Customer (VOC) - The in-depth process of capturing a customer's expectations, preferences, and aversions.

Waiting (or Delay) - Waiting for anything (people, signatures, information, etc.) is waste.

Waste - Any activity that does not add value to the product or service.

Web Based Kaizen Events - Are targeted improvement activities (PDCAs) used by team members using emerging technologies to plan, implement, and sustain improvements or solve a problem over time.

Wiki (or Quick) Kaizen Events - Are quick, easy-to-implement improvements by the front-line worker that does not typically require any type of team collaboration or approval.

Index

Notes

Notes

Best Selling Books from The Lean Store

Visit **www.TheLeanStore.com** to see these and other best selling books to assist you in your continuous improvement activities:

Lean Office Demystified II - Using the Power of the Toyota Production System in Your Administrative, Desktop and Networking Environments

Lean Six Sigma for Service - Pursuing Perfect Service - Using a Practical Approach to Lean Six Sigma to Improve the Customer Experience and Reduce Costs in Service Industries!

The 5S Desktop (PC) Pocket Handbook - Using the Power of the Toyota Production System (Lean) to Organize and Control Your Electronic Files and Folders

The A3 Pocket Handbook for Kaizen Events - Any Industry - Any Time

The New Lean Healthcare Pocket Guide - Tools for the Elimination of Waste in Hospitals, Clinics, and Other Healthcare Facilities

The New Lean Office Pocket Guide - Tools for the Elimination of Waste in Paper-Based and Electronic Workflow Environments

The New Lean Pocket Guide - Tools for the Elimination of Waste

The Simply Lean Pocket Guide - Making Great Organizations Better Through PLAN-DO-CHECK-ACT (PDCA) Kaizen Activities

Today's Lean Leader - A Practical Guide to Applying Lean Six Sigma and Emerging Technologies to Leadership and Supervision

Value Stream Management for Lean Healthcare - Four Steps to Planning, Mapping, Implementing, and Controlling Improvements in All Types of Healthcare Environments

The Practical Lean Six Sigma Pocket Guide for Healthcare - Tools for the Elimination of Waste in Hospitals, Clinics, and Physician Group Practices

The Practical Lean Six Sigma Pocket Guide - Using the A3 and Lean Thinking to Improve Operational Performance in ANY Industry, ANY Time

TODAY'S LEAN! SERIES OF BOOKS

Today's Lean! - Learning About and Identifying Waste
Today's Lean! - Using 5S to Organize and Standardize Areas and Files
Today's Lean! - It's All About Workflow
Today's Lean! - Value Stream Mapping for Healthcare

PRACTICAL LEAN SIX SIGMA APPS

Practical Lean Sigma for Healthcare - Overview
Practical Lean Sigma for Healthcare - 5S
Practical Lean Sigma for Healthcare - A3 Report
Waste Walk and Audit

...plus many types of Lean training sets, games, eforms, and books in Spanish and Chinese!